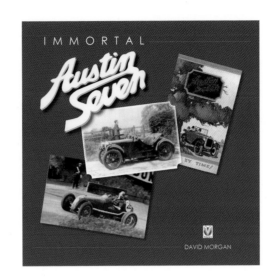

IMMORTAL

Austin Seven

DAVID MORGAN

THOSE WERE THE DAYS ... SERIES
Alpine Trials & Rallies 1910-1973 (Pfundner)
American 'Independent' Automakers – AMC to Willys 1945 to 1960 (Mort)
American Station Wagons – The Golden Era 1950-1975 (Mort)
American Trucks of the 1950s (Mort)
American Trucks of the 1960s (Mort)
American Woodies 1928-1953 (Mort)
Anglo-American Cars from the 1930s to the 1970s (Mort)
Austerity Motoring (Bobbitt)
Austins, The last real (Peck)
Brighton National Speed Trials (Gardiner)
British and European Trucks of the 1970s (Peck)
British Drag Racing – The early years (Pettitt)
British Lorries of the 1950s (Bobbitt)
British Lorries of the 1960s (Bobbitt)
British Touring Car Racing (Collins)
British Police Cars (Walker)
British Woodies (Peck)
Café Racer Phenomenon, The (Walker)
Don Hayter's MGB Story – The birth of the MGB in MG's Abingdon Design & Development Office (Hayter)
Drag Bike Racing in Britain – From the mid '60s to the mid '80s (Lee)
Dune Buggy Phenomenon, The (Hale)
Dune Buggy Phenomenon Volume 2, The (Hale)
Endurance Racing at Silverstone in the 1970s & 1980s (Parker)
Hot Rod & Stock Car Racing in Britain in the 1980s (Neil)
Last Real Austins 1946-1959, The (Peck)
Mercedes-Benz Trucks (Peck)
MG's Abingdon Factory (Moylan)
Motor Racing at Brands Hatch in the Seventies (Parker)
Motor Racing at Brands Hatch in the Eighties (Parker)
Motor Racing at Crystal Palace (Collins)
Motor Racing at Goodwood in the Sixties (Gardiner)
Motor Racing at Nassau in the 1950s & 1960s (O'Neil)
Motor Racing at Oulton Park in the 1960s (McFadyen)
Motor Racing at Oulton Park in the 1970s (McFadyen)
Motor Racing at Thruxton in the 1970s (Grant-Braham)
Motor Racing at Thruxton in the 1980s (Grant-Braham)
Superprix – The Story of Birmingham Motor Race (Page & Collins)
Three Wheelers (Bobbitt)

GREAT CARS
Austin-Healey – A celebration of the fabulous 'Big' Healey (Piggott)
Jaguar E-type (Thorley)
Jaguar Mark 1 & 2 (Thorley)
Triumph TR – TR2 to 6: The last of the traditional sports cars (Piggott)
Rally Giants Series
Audi Quattro (Robson)
Austin Healey 100-6 & 3000 (Robson)
Fiat 131 Abarth (Robson)
Ford Escort MkI (Robson)
Ford Escort RS Cosworth & World Rally Car (Robson)
Ford Escort RS1800 (Robson)
Lancia Delta 4WD/Integrale (Robson)
Lancia Stratos (Robson)
Mini Cooper/Mini Cooper S (Robson)
Peugeot 205 T16 (Robson)
Saab 96 & V4 (Robson)
Subaru Impreza (Robson)
Toyota Celica GT4 (Robson)

GENERAL
1½-litre GP Racing 1961-1965 (Whitelock)
AC Two-litre Saloons & Buckland Sportscars (Archibald)
Alfa Romeo 155/156/147 Competition Touring Cars (Collins)
Alfa Romeo Giulia Coupé GT & GTA (Tipler)
Alfa Romeo Montreal – The dream car that came true (Taylor)
Alfa Romeo Montreal – The Essential Companion (Classic Reprint of 500 copies) (Taylor)
Alfa Tipo 33 (McDonough & Collins)
Alpine & Renault – The Development of the Revolutionary Turbo F1 Car 1968 to 1979 (Smith)
Alpine & Renault – The Sports Prototypes 1963 to 1969 (Smith)
Alpine & Renault – The Sports Prototypes 1973 to 1978 (Smith)
An Incredible Journey (Falls & Reisch)
Anatomy of the Classic Mini (Huthert & Ely)
Anatomy of the Works Minis (Moylan)
Armstrong-Siddeley (Smith)
Art Deco and British Car Design (Down)
Autodrome (Collins & Ireland)
Automotive A-Z, Lane's Dictionary of Automotive Terms (Lane)
Automotive Mascots (Kay & Springate)
Bahamas Speed Weeks, The (O'Neil)
Bentley Continental, Corniche and Azure (Bennett)
Bentley MkVI, Rolls-Royce Silver Wraith, Dawn & Cloud/Bentley R & S-Series (Nutland)
Bluebird CN7 (Stevens)
BMC Competitions Department Secrets (Turner, Chambers & Browning)
BMW 5-Series (Cranswick)
BMW Z-Cars (Taylor)
BMW Boxer Twins 1970-1995 Bible, The (Falloon)
BMW Cafe Racers (Cloesen)
BMW Classic 5 Series 1972 to 2003 (Cranswick)
BMW Custom Motorcycles – Choppers, Cruisers, Bobbers, Trikes & Quads (Cloesen)
BMW – The Power of M (Vivian)
Bonjour – Is this Italy? (Turner)
British 250cc Racing Motorcycles (Pereira)
British at Indianapolis, The (Wagstaff)
British Café Racers (Cloesen)
British Cars, The Complete Catalogue of, 1895-1975 (Culshaw & Horrobin)
British Custom Motorcycles – The Brit Chop – choppers, cruisers, bobbers & trikes (Cloesen)
BRM – A Mechanic's Tale (Salmon)
BRM V16 (Ludvigsen)
BSA Bantam Bible, The (Henshaw)
BSA Motorcycles – the final evolution (Jones)
Bugatti – The 8-cylinder Touring Cars 1920-34 (Price & Arbey)
Bugatti Type 40 (Price)
Bugatti 46/50 Updated Edition (Price & Arbey)
Bugatti T44 & T49 (Price & Arbey)
Bugatti 57 2nd Edition (Price)
Bugatti Type 57 Grand Prix – A Celebration (Tomlinson)
Caravan, Improve & Modify Your (Porter)
Caravans, The Illustrated History 1919-1959 (Jenkinson)
Caravans, The Illustrated History From 1960 (Jenkinson)
Carrera Panamericana, La (Tipler)
Car-tastrophes – 80 automotive atrocities from the past 20 years (Honest John, Fowler)
Chrysler 300 – America's Most Powerful Car 2nd Edition (Ackerson)
Chrysler PT Cruiser (Ackerson)
Citroën DS (Bobbitt)
Classic British Car Electrical Systems (Astley)
Cobra – The Real Thing! (Legate)
Competition Car Aerodynamics 3rd Edition (McBeath)
Competition Car Composites A Practical Handbook (Revised 2nd Edition) (McBeath)
Concept Cars, How to illustrate and design – New 2nd Edition (Dewey)
Cortina – Ford's Bestseller (Robson)
Cosworth – The Search for Power (6th edition) (Robson)
Coventry Climax Racing Engines (Hammill)
Daily Mirror 1970 World Cup Rally 40, The (Robson)
Daimler SP250 New Edition (Long)
Datsun Fairlady Roadster to 280ZX – The Z-Car Story (Long)
Dino – The V6 Ferrari (Long)
Dodge Challenger & Plymouth Barracuda (Grist)
Dodge Charger – Enduring Thunder (Ackerson)
Dodge Dynamite! (Grist)
Dorset from the Sea – The Jurassic Coast from Lyme Regis to Old Harry Rocks photographed from its best viewpoint (also Souvenir Edition) (Belasco)
Draw & Paint Cars – How to (Gardiner)
Drive on the Wild Side, A – 20 Extreme Driving Adventures From Around the World (Weaver)
Ducati 750 Bible, The (Falloon)
Ducati 750 SS 'round-case' 1974, The Book of the (Falloon)
Ducati 860, 900 and Mille Bible, The (Falloon)
Ducati Monster Bible (New Updated & Revised Edition), The (Falloon)
Ducati Story, The - 6th Edition (Falloon)
Ducati 916 (updated edition) (Falloon)
Dune Buggy, Building A – The Essential Manual (Shakespeare)
Dune Buggy Files (Hale)
Dune Buggy Handbook (Hale)
East German Motor Vehicles in Pictures (Suhr/Weinreich)
Fast Ladies – Female Racing Drivers 1888 to 1970 (Bouzanquet)
Fate of the Sleeping Beauties, The (op de Weegh/Hottendorff/op de Weegh)
Ferrari 288 GTO, The Book of the (Sackey)
Ferrari 333 SP (O'Neil)
Fiat & Abarth 124 Spider & Coupé (Tipler)
Fiat & Abarth 500 & 600 – 2nd Edition (Bobbitt)
Fiats, Great Small (Ward)
Fine Art of the Motorcycle Engine, The (Peirce)
Ford Cleveland 335-Series V8 engine 1970 to 1982 – The Essential Source Book (Hammill)
Ford F100/F150 Pick-up 1948-1996 (Ackerson)
Ford F150 Pick-up 1997-2005 (Ackerson)
Ford Focus WRC (Robson)
Ford GT – Then, and Now (Streather)
Ford GT40 (Legate)
Ford Midsize Muscle – Fairlane, Torino & Ranchero (Cranswick)
Ford Model Y (Roberts)
Ford Small Block V8 Racing Engines 1962-1970 – The Essential Source Book (Hammill)
Ford Thunderbird From 1954, The Book of the (Long)
Formula One - The Real Score? (Harvey)
Formula 5000 Motor Racing, Back then ... and back now (Lawson)
Forza Minardi! (Vigar)
France: the essential guide for car enthusiasts – 200 things for the car enthusiast to see and do (Parish)
From Crystal Palace to Red Square – A Hapless Biker's Road to Russia (Turner)
Funky Mopeds (Skelton)
Grand Prix Ferrari – The Years of Enzo Ferrari's Power, 1948-1980 (Pritchard)
Grand Prix Ford – DFV-powered Formula 1 Cars (Robson)
GT – The World's Best GT Cars 1953-73 (Dawson)
Hillclimbing & Sprinting – The Essential Manual (Short & Wilkinson)
Honda NSX (Long)
How to Restore & Improve Classic Car Suspension, Steering & Wheels (Parish, translator)
Immortal Austin Seven (Morgan)
Inside the Rolls-Royce & Bentley Styling Department – 1971 to 2001 (Hull)
Intermeccanica – The Story of the Prancing Bull (McCredie & Reisner)
Italian Cafe Racers (Cloesen)
Italian Custom Motorcycles (Cloesen)
Jaguar, The Rise of (Price)
Jaguar XJ 220 – The Inside Story (Moreton)
Jaguar XJ-S, The Book of the (Long)
Japanese Custom Motorcycles – The Nippon Chop – Chopper, Cruiser, Bobber, Trikes and Quads (Cloesen)
Jeep CJ (Ackerson)
Jeep Wrangler (Ackerson)
The Jowett Jupiter – The car that leaped to fame (Nankivell)
Karmann-Ghia Coupé & Convertible (Bobbitt)
Kawasaki Triples Bible, The (Walker)
Kawasaki Z1 Story, The (Sheehan)
Kris Meeke – Intercontinental Rally Challenge Champion (McBride)
Lamborghini Miura Bible, The (Sackey)
Lamborghini Urraco, The Book of the (Landsem)
Lambretta Bible, The (Davies)
Lancia 037 (Collins)
Lancia Delta HF Integrale (Blaettel & Wagner)
Lancia Delta Integrale (Collins)
Land Rover Series III Reborn (Porter)
Land Rover, The Half-ton Military (Cook)
Laverda Twins & Triples Bible 1968-1986 (Falloon)
Lea-Francis Story, The (Price)
Le Mans Panoramic (Ireland)
Lexus Story, The (Long)
Little book of microcars, the (Quellin)
Little book of smart, the – New Edition (Jackson)
Little book of trikes, the (Quellin)
Lola – The Illustrated History (1957-1977) (Starkey)
Lola – All the Sports Racing & Single-seater Racing Cars 1978-1997 (Starkey)
Lola T70 – The Racing History & Individual Chassis Record – 4th Edition (Starkey)
Lotus 18 Colin Chapman's U-turn (Whitelock)
Lotus 49 (Oliver)
Marketingmobiles, The Wonderful Wacky World of (Hale)
Maserati 250F In Focus (Pritchard)
Mazda MX-5/Miata 1.6 Enthusiast's Workshop Manual (Grainger & Shoemark)
Mazda MX-5/Miata 1.8 Enthusiast's Workshop Manual (Grainger & Shoemark)
Mazda MX-5 Miata, The book of the – The 'Mk1' NA-series 1988 to 1997 (Long)
Mazda MX-5 Miata Roadster (Long)
Mazda Rotary-engined Cars (Cranswick)
Maximum Mini (Booij)
Meet the English (Bowie)
Mercedes-Benz SL – R230 series 2001 to 2011 (Long)
Mercedes-Benz SL – W113-series 1963-1971 (Long)
Mercedes-Benz SL & SLC – 107-series 1971-1989 (Long)
Mercedes-Benz SLK – R170 series 1996-2004 (Long)
Mercedes-Benz SLK – R171 series 2004-2011 (Long)
Mercedes-Benz W123-series – All models 1976 to 1986 (Long)
Mercedes G-Wagen (Long)
MGA (Price Williams)
MGB & MGB GT– Expert Guide (Auto-doc Series) (Williams)
MGB Electrical Systems Updated & Revised Edition (Astley)
Micro Caravans (Jenkinson)
Micro Trucks (Mort)
Microcars at Large! (Quellin)
Mini Cooper – The Real Thing! (Tipler)
Mini Minor to Asia Minor (West)
Mitsubishi Lancer Evo, The Road Car & WRC Story (Long)
Montlhéry, The Story of the Paris Autodrome (Boddy)
Morgan Maverick (Lawrence)
Morgan 3 Wheeler – back to the future!, The (Dron)
Morris Minor, 60 Years on the Road (Newell)
Moto Guzzi Sport & Le Mans Bible, The (Falloon)
The Moto Guzzi Story - 3rd Edition (Falloon)
Motor Movies – The Posters! (Veysey)
Motor Racing – Reflections of a Lost Era (Carter)
Motor Racing – The Pursuit of Victory 1930-1962 (Carter)
Motor Racing – The Pursuit of Victory 1963-1972 (Wyatt/Sears)
Motor Racing Heroes – The Stories of 100 Greats (Newman)
Motorcycle Apprentice (Cakebread)
Motorcycle GP Racing in the 1960s (Pereira)
Motorcycle Road & Racing Chassis Designs (Noakes)
Motorcycling in the '50s (Clew)
Motorhomes, The Illustrated History (Jenkinson)
Motorsport In colour, 1950s (Wainwright)
MV Agusta Fours, The book of the classic (Falloon)
N.A.R.T. – A concise history of the North American Racing Team 1957 to 1983 (O'Neil)
Nissan 300ZX & 350Z – The Z-Car Story (Long)
Nissan GT-R Supercar: Born to race (Gorodji)
Northeast American Sports Car Races 1950-1959 (O'Neil)
Norton Commando Bible – All models 1968 to 1978 (Henshaw)
Nothing Runs – Misadventures in the Classic, Collectable & Exotic Car Biz (Slutsky)
Off-Road Giants! (Volume 1) – Heroes of 1960s Motorcycle Sport (Westlake)
Off-Road Giants! (Volume 2) – Heroes of 1960s Motorcycle Sport (Westlake)
Off-Road Giants! (volume 3) – Heroes of 1960s Motorcycle Sport (Westlake)
Pass the Theory and Practical Driving Tests (Gibson & Hoole)
Peking to Paris 2007 (Young)
Pontiac Firebird – New 3rd Edition (Cranswick)
Porsche 356 (2nd Edition) (Long)
Porsche 908 (Födisch, Neßhöver, Roßbach, Schwarz & Roßbach)
Porsche 911 Carrera – The Last of the Evolution (Corlett)
Porsche 911R, RS & RSR, 4th Edition (Starkey)
Porsche 911, The Book of the (Long)
Porsche 911 – The Definitive History 2004-2012 (Long)
Porsche – The Racing 914s (Smith)
Porsche 911SC 'Super Carrera' – The Essential Companion (Streather)
Porsche 914 & 914-6: The Definitive History of the Road & Competition Cars (Long)
Porsche 924 (Long)
The Porsche 924 Carreras – evolution to excellence (Smith)
Porsche 928 (Long)
Porsche 944 (Long)
Porsche 964, 993 & 996 Data Plate Code Breaker (Streather)
Porsche 993 'King Of Porsche' – The Essential Companion (Streather)
Porsche 996 'Supreme Porsche' – The Essential Companion (Streather)
Porsche 997 2004-2012 – Porsche Excellence (Streather)
Porsche Boxster – The 986 series 1996-2004 (Long)
Porsche Boxster & Cayman – The 987 series (2004-2013) (Long)
Porsche Racing Cars – 1953 to 1975 (Long)
Porsche Racing Cars – 1976 to 2005 (Long)
Porsche – The Rally Story (Meredith)
Porsche: Three Generations of Genius (Meredith)
Powered by Porsche (Smith)
Preston Tucker & Others (Linde)
RAC Rally Action! (Gardiner)
Racing Colours – Motor Racing Compositions 1908-2009 (Newman)
Racing Line – British motorcycle racing in the golden age of the big single (Guntrip)
Rallye Sport Fords: The Inside Story (Moreton)
Renewable Energy Home Handbook, The (Porter)
Roads with a View – England's greatest views and how to find them by road (Corfield)
Rolls-Royce Silver Shadow/Bentley T Series Corniche & Camargue – Revised & Enlarged Edition (Bobbitt)
Rolls-Royce Silver Spirit, Silver Spur & Bentley Mulsanne 2nd Edition (Bobbitt)
Rootes Cars of the 50s, 60s & 70s – Hillman, Humber, Singer, Sunbeam & Talbot (Rowe)
Rover P4 (Bobbitt)
Runways & Racers (O'Neil)
Russian Motor Vehicles – Soviet Limousines 1930-2003 (Kelly)
Russian Motor Vehicles – The Czarist Period 1784 to 1917 (Kelly)
RX-7 – Mazda's Rotary Engine Sportscar (Updated & Revised New Edition) (Long)
Scooters & Microcars, The A-Z of Popular (Dan)
Scooter Lifestyle (Grainger)
Scooter Mania! – Recollections of the Isle of Man International Scooter Rally (Jackson)
Singer Story: Cars, Commercial Vehicles, Bicycles & Motorcycle (Atkinson)
Sleeping Beauties USA – abandoned classic cars & trucks (Marek)
SM – Citroën's Maserati-engined Supercar (Long & Claverol)
Speedway – Auto racing's ghost tracks (Collins & Ireland)
Sprite Caravans, The Story of (Jenkinson)
Standard Motor Company, The Book of the (Robson)
Steve Hole's Kit Car Cornucopia – Cars, Companies, Stories, Facts & Figures: the UK's kit car scene since 1949 (Hole)
Subaru Impreza: The Road Car And WRC Story (Long)
Supercar, How to Build your own (Thompson)
Tales from the Toolbox (Oliver)
Tatra – The Legacy of Hans Ledwinka, Updated & Enlarged Collector's Edition of 1500 copies (Margolius & Henry)
Taxi! The Story of the 'London' Taxicab (Bobbitt)
This Day in Automotive History (Corey)
To Boldly Go – twenty six vehicle designs that dared to be different (Hull)
Toleman Story, The (Hilton)
Toyota Celica & Supra, The Book of Toyota's Sports Coupés (Long)
Toyota MR2 Coupés & Spyders (Long)
Triumph & Standard Cars 1945 to 1984 (Warrington)
Triumph Bonneville Bible (59-83) (Henshaw)
Triumph Bonneville!, Save the – The inside story of the Meriden Workers' Co-op (Rosamond)
Triumph Motorcycles & the Meriden Factory (Hancox)
Triumph Speed Twin & Thunderbird Bible (Woolridge)
Triumph Tiger Cub Bible (Estall)
Triumph Trophy Bible (Woolridge)
Triumph TR6 (Kimberley)
TT Talking – The TT's most exciting era – As seen by Manx Radio TT's lead commentator 2004-2012 (Lambert)
Two Summers – The Mercedes-Benz W196R Racing Car (Ackerson)
TWR Story, The – Group A (Hughes & Scott)
Unraced (Collins)
Velocette Motorcycles – MSS to Thruxton – New Third Edition (Burris)
Vespa – The Story of a Cult Classic in Pictures (Uhlig)
Vincent Motorcycles: The Untold Story since 1946 (Guyony & Parker)
Volkswagen Bus Book, The (Bobbitt)
Volkswagen Bus or Van to Camper, How to Convert (Porter)
Volkswagens of the World (Glen)
VW Beetle Cabriolet – The full story of the convertible Beetle (Bobbitt)
VW Beetle – The Car of the 20th Century (Copping)
VW Bus – 40 Years of Splitties, Bays & Wedges (Copping)
VW Bus Book, The (Bobbitt)
VW Golf: Five Generations of Fun (Copping & Cservenka)
VW – The Air-cooled Era (Copping)
VW T5 Camper Conversion Manual (Porter)
VW Campers (Copping)
Volkswagen Type 3, The book of the – Concept, Design, International Production Models & Development (Glen)
Volvo Estate, The (Hollebone)
You & Your Jaguar XK8/XKR – Buying, Enjoying, Maintaining, Modifying – New Edition (Thorley)
Which Oil? – Choosing the right oils & greases for your antique, vintage, veteran, classic or collector car (Michell)
Wolseley Cars 1948 to 1975 (Rowe)
Works Minis, The Last (Purves & Brenchley)
Works Rally Mechanic (Moylan)

WWW.VELOCE.CO.UK
First published in October 2017 by Veloce Publishing Limited, Veloce House, Parkway Farm Business Park, Middle Farm Way, Poundbury, Dorchester DT1 3AR, England.
Fax 01305 250479 / e-mail info@veloce.co.uk / web www.veloce.co.uk or www.velocebooks.com. ISBN: 978-1-845849-79-5 UPC: 6-36847-04979-9.

British Library Cataloguing in Publication Data – A catalogue record for this book is available from the British Library. Typesetting, design and page make-up all by Veloce Publishing Ltd on Apple Mac. Printed in India by Parksons Graphics.

IMMORTAL

Austin Seven

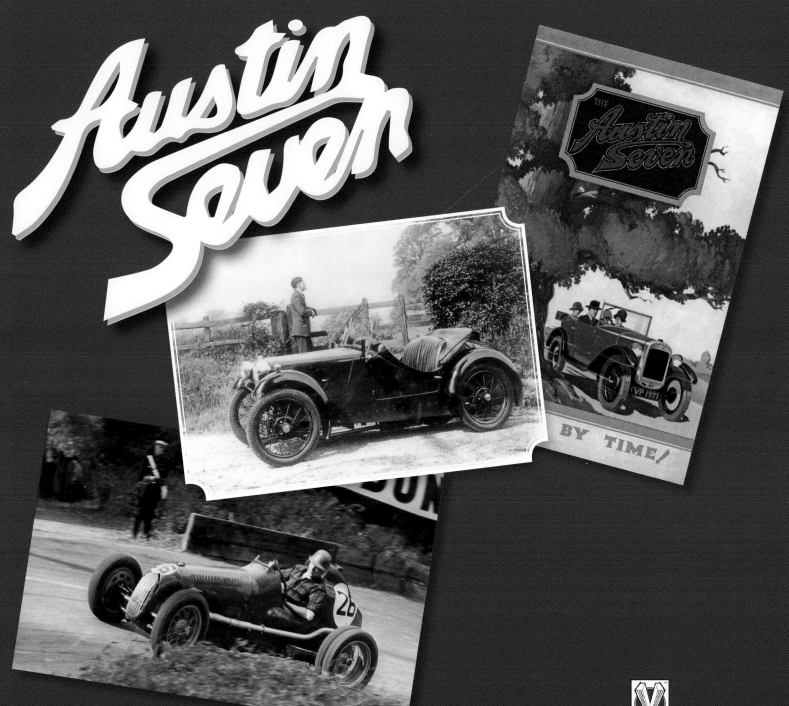

DAVID MORGAN

CONTENTS

ACKNOWLEDGEMENTS

A BOOK about the most celebrated, loved, and influential small motor car that the world has even known could not be written without the personal input – conscious or not – of a great number of people over a great number of years. The author has been privileged to have owned, rebuilt, and driven a succession of Austin Sevens, of many types and over the course of 60 years, and to have met many fellow travellers on the way. The author, however, makes no claim to be expert on the subject, and has sought the knowledge of other enthusiasts, historians, and specialists in compiling this appreciation of Sir Herbert Austin's favourite baby.

In particular my warm thanks go out to Mike Ware for his original encouragement in completing this title, and to the late Bill Boddy for decades of dedicated promotion of the significance, history, and use of the Austin Seven.

I would also like to express enormous thanks to Phil Baildon, Chris Garner, and David Cochrane for proof-reading, corrections, and additions; the Board of 750 Motor Club and archivist Bryan Norfolk for use of the club's published material; and Ken Cooke for his friendship, knowledge, recall, and photographic archive.

I sincerely thank my many contributors; in no particular order: Ed Waugh and Hugh Barnes, Andy Owen, Peter Richards, David Charles, Ruairidh Dunford, Stuart Ulph, Geoff Roe, Graham Fullalove, Luc Wynen, Cliff Bradshaw, Mike Peck, Martin Eyre, Ted Walker of Ferret Fotographics, Tony Southgate, Michael Fitzmaurice, John Way, Mike and Giles Martin, Peter Butler, Andy Storer, Graham Beckett, Ian Bancroft, David Fletcher, Chris Gould, Rod Spollon of Château Impney, Frank Fletcher, Helmut Kazimirowicz, Alex Myall, Jean-François Bouzanquet, Iain Mansell, Steve Bradford-Best, Richard Mallock, Ken Rush, Janet Edroff, and Nick Salmon.

I am hugely in debt to Gayle Cannon for transcribing my many drafts into useable text, and for editing and putting the document together. I also thank David Bowman of Deadline Reprographics for his help with the images.

The foreword generously written by John Miles is much appreciated, and I am very grateful to Rod Grainger and his team at Veloce Publishing for the design and production of this book.

To all others who contributed but who remain unnamed, my apologies, and any omissions and errors are of course down to me alone.

Finally, my undying thanks to Christine for putting up with a dining table covered in photographs and paper for the best part of a year.

David Morgan

FOREWORD

BY JOHN MILES

SIR Herbert Austin and Stanley Edge created one of the very few vintage British cars that exemplified proper production design and manufacturing principles. It was a car that satisfied demand, stood the test of time, and – like all good concepts – had the potential for continuous development and locally-adapted production in Germany, France, Japan, and the US. It also had major competition successes, and set world records at well over 100mph. However, with the Austin Motor Company in financial trouble following WW1, Austin found himself initially unable to convince co-management that there would soon be a market crying out for a new type of car. This was to be a small car, but with all the technical features of a much larger machine; a complete package so much better than the wonky cyclecars of old.

The car was designed almost solely by Edge and Austin, and built in secret at a factory 'skunkworks,' and, when the prototypes appeared – complete with four wheel brakes, four-cylinder engines and rear seats – Austin Motor Company management soon changed its mind … well, sort of! This book makes strong reference to the chemistry between Herbert Austin and the just 18-year-old Stanley Edge; the former was an engineer, as well as a car and boat racer, while the latter was a precocious designer and extremely talented drawing board operator, who had already worked in many fields including aircraft design. Perhaps this was the key to Edge's lightweight approach to design, and his talent for designing chassis components able to perform several functions at once, in a style akin to Colin Chapman. The obvious example of this mentality was the A7's cast-steel nose piece, conjoining its A-plan chassis rails, but also mounting the front spring, damper, 'cow horns,' valances, and wing stays.

Clearly, Austin was deeply affected by his visit to the US, where he saw the Ford factory that was producing Model Ts. He realised that the only way quality cars could be built for an affordable and profitable price was through good design, quality materials, and making virtually everything in-house. The book details how Austin and Edge minimised reliability and warranty issues by applying modern day 'selective assembly techniques,' especially on the engine, gearbox, and rear axle parts. Where possible, Ford-like production line techniques were employed – although this was not so easy where ash-framed bodies were concerned. The book also deals extensively with most of the important independent body builders, who took rolling chassis and engines. The most important of these were Mulliner, Jensen, and, of course, Swallow – the genesis of Jaguar, under Sir William Lyons. Military versions of the Seven are described, along with the Flying Flea, marine applications, and even a railway Austin Seven! Of course, the Austin Seven engine also led to the postwar Reliant power unit, which in turn went on to power 750 Formula racing cars for many years.

Austin truly believed that 'racing improves the breed,' having built and raced the delightful-handling (from the writer's experience) 1908 GP car – a worthy 20hp model that morphed into 'Pobble,' the famous super-aerodynamic Brooklands racer. Colonel Arthur Waite and Gordon England were early works drivers in Sevens, the latter's tuning and build shop producing the Brooklands 75mph model. All the important racing and record-breaking achievements are dealt with, including the incredibly brave Parker/Bland/Chase Montlhéry run that took the 1000km, 1000mile, and 2000km records, as well as

John Miles – the 1970 Team Lotus Formula One driver, development design engineer, writer, and Austin Seven enthusiast – in his Lotus 72. (Courtesy Lotus)

the 24hr class record, at an average speed of just under 66mph. The ruggedness of the Austin Seven platform, even when highly tuned, was becoming legendary; even more so when supercharged and running in the 1929 Ards TT, where all four Austin Sevens finished behind Caracciola's Mercedes and Campari's Alfa. Frazer-Nash placed 3rd and Holbrook 4th, the latter having led the 300-mile handicap road race in the early stages. Caracciola was impressed, observing that the Austins were "wonderful; I take my hat off to those little midget cars and their brave drivers." Thus was born the legend of the Austin Ulster. After a period of engine failures, the next year's works cars were to stage perhaps their greatest triumph, winning the BRDC 500 Mile Race at Brooklands when Sydney Charles Houghton ("Sammy") Davis and the Earl of March's car just held on to the lead, crossing the line six minutes in front, having averaged no less than 83.4mph (134km/h).

All the developments that followed are covered, leading to the not-so-successful highly-supercharged 25-stud quasi-single seat Rubber Ducks that did battle with MG Midget-based machines, with their more powerful 750cc overhead camshaft engines. Gwenda Stewart was then sent to Montlhéry with a streamlined Austin and broke four records; the fastest at 109.129mph (175km/h) for five kilometres. Later on, this very quick and brave lady driver carried out testing on lightened versions of the side-valve record breaker, to be used for sprints and track racing. This led seamlessly to the development of the Murray Jamieson/Amherst Villiers-developed dry sump 32-stud big crankshaft magnesium crankcase 85bhp side-valve single-seater, and ultimately on to jewels like the Murray Jamieson-designed 1936-39 Twin-Cam Austin monopostos, as driven by Bert Hadley, Charles Goodacre, Pat Driscoll, and Charles Dodson. The famous privately-built Maclachlan single seat sprint car, known as the 'Tiddler' is also assiduously dealt with. Jamieson's fascinating proposal for a monocoque 750cc 250bhp supercharged mid-engined aero racer proved a step too far for Herbert Austin …

Production car developments and improvements arrived year by year, weathering the depression after the Wall Street Crash. All this was set against a background of rapidly-changing politics and fashion, including the emancipation of women as WW2 loomed on the horizon. The Austin Seven became heavier and more luxurious, but still fulfilled small family car role required of it. Even after the war, it was to provide the basis of amateur-designed road cars and 750 Formula race cars, where the likes of Colin Chapman, Gordon Murray, Eric Broadley, Les Ballamy, Maurice Philippe, Tony Southgate, Len Terry, et al, were to hone their design talents. Jack French, Arthur Mallock, and Bill Williams were also there at the beginning, along with, of course, Holly Birkett and Bill Boddy, who were deeply involved in forming the 750 Motor Club in the first place, encouraging all the impecunious enthusiasts in their special building activities. Meanwhile, the supreme abilities of an Austin Seven-based trials car still irritated some competitors, with the cars also surviving the traversal of rugged terrain over long distances – as Coleman's Drive was to prove.

Herbert Austin had anticipated the demand for his tiny – yet practical and economical – Seven after WW1. Perhaps his competitors at the time were unable to see any other direction for small family motoring, as it would be more than half a decade until Morris took up the challenge. By this time, however, the Austin Seven was a cheaper and, in many ways, more attractive proposition. This was doubly so once the depression really started to bite, at which point Herbert Austin introduced the Ruby and Pearl models, costing just over £100. It is possible that the enthusiastic public reaction to the Austin Seven actually suppressed the ability of competitors to design anything better.

No other single book I know of so concisely captures the extraordinary history, versatility, and development of the Austin Seven as well as this one.

INTRODUCTION

WHEN Sir Herbert Austin announced his new baby car was to be 'motoring for the millions,' a leap of imagination was required by the buying public to grasp the idea.

The early motoring 'owner driver' was seen as an eccentric, and in possession of a mysterious expertise required to keep his mechanical device in good order and under control.

The cyclecars, which had been popular immediately before and after the First World War, were for the most part strange and flimsy things – one might get wet, burned, or thrown about while driving. 'Real' motor cars, meanwhile, were expected to be large, expensive devices, almost always driven by a expert hired chauffeur.

The contemporary middle road between these two was the combination of a motorcycle and sidecar. This was a prospect that might have been fine for the father of a family, but meant the wife was consigned to the pillion seat, or to a cramped, noisy, and odorous journey with the children in the outrigger sidecar.

Sir Herbert's concept for the Austin Seven was to be a miniaturised version of those larger cars, rather than a cyclecar with extra bells and whistles. He described it directly in the first handbook of the model:

"The Austin Seven was introduced to supersede the sidecar combination. It seats two adults and three small children, or, if children are not carried, a large space is available for luggage. Everyone is brought within the hood, while the car is fitted with a double-windscreen, and side curtains opening with the doors …

"This little car, which can be run for about a penny a mile, is an ideal car for a woman to use herself, enabling her to do the shopping without fatigue, to visit her friends more frequently and attend social and recreative functions.

"Another appeal is to the businessman, as it enables the executive to make the utmost use of his time, while his expenditure is no more than it would be on tram or bus fares; and there is no need to point out the value of such a car for the commercial traveller, who can penetrate into districts that poor train services would make it hardly worth his while to cover otherwise.

"The Austin Seven also serves as a tender for the country house, enabling a servant to go down to the village or post, or to the doctor at any time of the day or night, without the expense and trouble of getting out the big car.

"The speed, economy and road-holding qualities of this small car place it beyond all comparison with the sidecar combination, and it is, in addition, a thoroughly good job, planned and made with the car instead of the motorcycle aspect in mind."

The public bought in to this concept, and the Seven was an immediate success. Sir Herbert's creation entirely vindicated his judgement and clarity of thought over that of his fellow directors, bringing with it immense wealth for Austin during the last two decades of his life.

The Austin Seven would already have earned its place in history if that was all there was to its story. Nobody, however, could have foreseen the influence that the car would have after WW2 on both production and racing car design – particularly in the United Kingdom, where the Seven contributed directly to the growth of the UK motorsport industry.

Even now, the Austin Seven is the best known, best loved, most versatile, and most numerous of all prewar motor cars, enjoyed for recreation and sport by thousands of enthusiastic owners. The Austin Seven is also welcomed at hundreds of motoring events every year, throughout the UK and on every continent.

This book traces the fascinating history, extraordinary success, and unmistakable influence of the Austin Seven over a period of almost a century.

David Morgan
Mill Green, Hertfordshire

CHAPTER ONE

THE
CONCEPT

AN unlikely pairing of two men was behind the original concept of the Austin Seven: Herbert Austin, a intuitive and highly successful – though conservative and largely self-taught – industrial entrepreneur in his mid-50s, and Stanley Howard Edge, a 17-year-old talented and innovative draughtsman. The melding of Herbert Austin's need for his concept to succeed, and Stanley Edge's enthusiastic response to the task of detail design, gave their project – a practical 'baby' car for the masses – an impetus that may never have existed in different circumstances.

Stanley Edge was born in 1903, at Old Hill, Staffordshire – in the Black Country. The area was so named for its rich deposits of coal and iron ore, and marked the birthplace of the Industrial Revolution, giving rise to British supremacy in many fields of development, and leading directly to the creation and expansion of the British Empire under Queen Victoria. Being immersed in this mix of industrial heartland and beautiful surrounding countryside would provide great stimulus to the young Stanley.

Sir Herbert Austin poses happily in the 1922 prototype, at that stage fitted with oil lamps, a hand plunger Klaxon horn, and a shallow fold-flat windscreen. (Austin publicity)

Stanley was born to a mother who was a teacher, and a father who worked as a clerk in a lawyer's office, and later as a secretary at a large Birmingham furniture shop. He was privately educated at Halesowen Primary, where he would go on lone exploring 'expeditions,' seeking to satisfy a healthy curiosity. This curiosity was frequently piqued by such marvels as the regular thumping of steam hammers, the local destination of the many coal and goods wagons, the pit-head gear of winding engines, and the canal and river workings that fed the local industries. To an inquisitive boy, the pleasure of roaming the local natural countryside – interspersed with surveying man's innovations in harnessing nature for his own use – was an unwitting but profound education on the means of exploiting creative forces. Stanley gained a sense of understanding on how problems might be solved, and a view of an industry that was all about making things.

Stanley's first sight of a motor car was when John Burton, a friend of his father, arrived at their home driving a Standard, with its Union Jack radiator badge. Stanley was delighted to be taken for a spirited drive to Burton's works, which had a stamping machine and produced plain washers for industrial use.

A graduation to Halesowen Grammar School in 1913 was almost immediately affected by the start of World War One, while Stanley became more interested in drawing and making things than some of his more academic studies. He was strong in both History and English, and, with his inquisitive nature, had a keen and broad sense of interest in many subjects.

Stanley's father wished to contribute more to the war effort, and decided in 1916 that he would join the Austin works cashiers' department. By that time, the company was expanding fast, deeply involved in producing artillery shells, in addition to trucks and other vehicles for the Army, and even military-type aircraft.

Stanley urged his father to see what opportunities there might be at Austin for him, that he might get involved with motor cars. He did so with such conviction – and aided by a friend, who had

80-year-old Stanley Edge takes the wheel of the much-travelled and researched ex-John Moon Nippy, owned by his neighbour and friend Peter Richards. (Courtesy Peter Richards)

ambitions to be an engineering draughtsman – that Edge Senior wrote to ask if his school could make some provisions for instructions in draughtsmanship. Stanley had produced a folio of largely self-taught engineering drawings over the course of a year or so, which his father showed to the head of the Austin works drawing office. As a result, Stanley started with the company immediately after his 14th birthday, in August 1917, working initially on aircraft parts.

His journey to work was on the joint line for Midland Railway and Great Western Railway, from Old Hill to Longbridge. As the war continued, Stanley found that the train was often overcrowded, usually travelling in the guard's compartment. This train line, and the timetable of its trains, would by chance prove to be a crucial ingredient in Stanley's subsequent career.

His first work in the aircraft department was on the Austin-Ball AFB1 – a 200bhp Hispano-Suiza-powered scout biplane – and subsequently, in the summer of 1918, the Austin AFT3 Osprey triplane. Stanley attended the first flight of the latter, at Castle Bromwich aerodrome.

The talented youngster spent some time on practical tasks in the aero metalworking shop, learning to weld, testing aero engines, and working on the novel twin-turret Austin armoured cars that had been ordered by Russia.

Stanley had made his own personal ambitions clear to his fellow staff in the works, and was judged sufficiently proficient to move on to the car drawing office. This was a role that was considered at the time to be amongst the highest junior positions available, and Stanley's appointment was likely based on the personal approval of (by then, *Sir*) Herbert Austin himself.

Herbert Austin had been knighted in 1917 for services to the war effort, but had lost his only son, Vernon, in 1915. Killed by a single sniper's bullet on the Western Front, Vernon's death was a tragedy that Herbert never got over; Herbert had intended to retire early, and hand the control of the Austin company over to Vernon when that time came. It seems very likely that Herbert had taken a personal shine to the enthusiastic and youthful Stanley very early in his career. This was an element that was reflected in their subsequent discussions; the middle-aged successful and practical entrepreneur, honoured by his country, and the talented Stanley with the priceless gift of youth on his side.

After the Great War, Austin changed its car type policy. It went from offering a variety of model types to instead producing just one main type of car; a course of action that stemmed from Herbert being heavily persuaded by the American approach, and in particular by Henry Ford – a signed photograph of whom was on the wall of Herbert's Longbridge office. The continued international success of

the Model T Ford had struck a profound chord with Herbert Austin, who conceived his 20hp Austin in 1919, in the expectation that he had the British 'Tin Lizzie' on his hands.

Stanley Edge worked on the designs for this car under AJW Hancock, who ran the chassis department and design office, and AV Davidge, who ran the engine department (later to be merged, with Hancock overseeing both). The design office was on the ground floor, and close to Sir Herbert's own office, and Herbert Austin would move between the two at a swift pace, any loose papers which had been left lying around flying about in his wake.

Herbert Austin would frequently visit the design office, and kept a very personal eye on everything that was being done in his name, often staying late into the evenings and at weekends. He had the complete respect of his staff – partly on account of the number of hours that he put in exceeding the normal working week by a considerable margin.

Stanley Edge worked directly under Austin's engine designer, Jack Clarke, and discussions between Sir Herbert Austin, Jack Clarke, and Stanley would often take place around Stanley's drawing board. Herbert got to know Stanley quite well during this time, although he was always sparing with direct praise to employees; much went unsaid, but was silently acknowledged.

As Stanley used to catch the convenient works train, he always arrived at the factory by 8:00am, even though the drawing office staff didn't start work until 9:00am, and so he was at his desk an hour early. The only other person in that part of the building at that time of day was Sir Herbert Austin himself, and so conversations between the two became something of a habit. These began on the topic of stationary engines, which were being designed for a time by CB Dicksee, who had the drawing board next to young Stanley.

Stanley attended the Austin Technical College, and read everything he could on the topic of motoring, and indeed any forms of wheeled transport. His particular focus, however, was on engine design, and at weekends he sometimes worked at a Birmingham garage, just for the experience. Several of his teenage friends were also immersed in the national centre of cycle, motorbike, car, and truck manufacturers that proliferated in the Coventry and Birmingham area at the time, with Stanley learning to drive an Alldays truck and a Connaught motorcycle.

Herbert Austin was respected by the skilled workers at Longbridge, as a man who could perform most of the operations that they were themselves called upon to carry out with his own hands. Herbert, therefore, cut a benign figure amongst the employees – willing to listen, but entirely at ease, and with confidence in his own opinions. The affection workers felt towards Austin was expressed in his

Sir Herbert Austin, at his desk in the famous oak-panelled office. (750 Motor Club archive)

Sir Herbert Austin, at his desk in the famous oak-panelled office. (750 Motor Club archive)

nicknames; being referred to as 'Pa Austin' and 'The Old Man' by different sections of the workforce.

After the hectic years of war and almost exponential expansion, there came the choice of which car type should take advantage of the huge manufacturing facilities that Government funding had provided. Fluctuating sales of the Twenty, for which Austin had such high hopes, influenced this decision. Despite confidence in his own judgement, Herbert had mistaken the demand for such a relatively large car – the design of which was partly based on American experience – and by 1921 a scaled-down Twenty, in the form of the 1.6-litre Austin 12, was well received by the press and public. Financially, however, it was too little, too late – the Austin company was placed into receivership.

Austin was not alone in its financial troubles at this time, but crucially, it was allowed by the receivers to continue trading while other car-producing companies around it collapsed. As Herbert wrestled to find a solution that would allow his factory to carry on – and eventually prosper – he was again reminded that in America, Ford's Model T had been aimed squarely at the common man. In a continent the size of the United States, that meant anybody from a Missouri farmer to a Harvard student. It was at this point that Sir Herbert decided to produce an even further scaled down small car, to be built on simple lines. Not dissimilar examples of such vehicles were already being produced by Rover, amongst others, but without going to the extremes displayed by the cyclecars of the war period. Herbert wanted to produce a quality small car that could be sold in considerable numbers.

With this in mind, he put his proposal to the Austin board of directors, but, in the somewhat fraught atmosphere then prevailing in the factory, he failed to get substantial support. Convinced of the basic good sense of his idea, he decided that the only way forward was to fund the design and development of a prototype himself; it was at this point that the lives of Herbert Austin and Stanley Edge truly meshed together. With receivers breathing down his neck, Herbert decided to carry out the design work away from the bustle of his factory, and

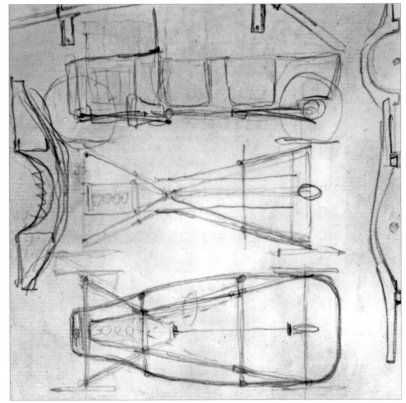

Herbert Austin's earliest design sketches, exploring triple triangulation of chassis, suspension, and four wheel brakes, with superimposed bodyshell outer boundaries and frame members. (750 Motor Club archive)

away from any interference with his plans. He needed freedom to form his conceptual ideas, and the detailed design needed to be done at a real pace. He therefore required someone who could grasp a new challenge in both hands, and could translate on to the drawing board exactly what he had in mind without outside influences slowing down the process.

For this private and important task, he chose Stanley Edge, the now-17-year-old draughtsman with whom he had, by this time, an extremely good working relationship. An excited, but somewhat apprehensive, Stanley was duly installed at a board in the billiards room at Austin's family home, Lickey Grange, a few weeks after his 18th birthday.

Once there, Stanley found Herbert Austin a much softer character, and he quickly took to the kindly and ordered atmosphere at Lickey Grange, with Lady Austin supervising the cooking. Meals were provided, with Stanley sleeping at the house lodge on weekdays, and returning home at weekends or Sundays on a brand new Connaught motorcycle, provided for Stanley as an encouragement by his now very proud father. From September 1921, Stanley worked every day except Sundays. This continued for the next seven months, frequently from 8:30am through to ten o'clock in the evening, with just a couple of breaks for meals. He became entirely immersed in the detailed design process, enjoying the relationship with his mentor and committing to paper all that was discussed between them once a conclusion or

direction had been reached. He usually took his meals either without leaving the billiards room, or in the library next door.

Herbert Austin spent some time considering the merits of limiting the number of cylinders in what would be a very small engine for his 'baby' car concept. However, even the best and most favoured of these, such as the Rover Eight air-cooled twin, ran poorly at idle and felt rough at speed. A Rover Eight was obtained and examined, and some design work done with a basically similar version. It was at this time that Stanley Edge was surprised to realise that Herbert Austin's thinking was mainly empirical and intuitive, and based on his own long experience of solving design problems, rather than on any calculated design.

Herbert also naturally and instinctively included the probable costs of making a design in the factory and out into the market place into his approach, treating costs as an inbuilt and essential element. His overall grasp of a multitude of factors deeply impressed the young Stanley. Stanley, meanwhile, felt he himself could contribute most with his knowledge of alternative engine layouts and systems, having avidly read everything published on the topic that he could lay his hands on.

Herbert had prepared some full-size layout schematics, in part drawn free-hand. Included in these were various parts worked up in greater detail, and some of which were committed to paper by Stanley. Stanley took occasional breaks while working on his own, to attend to a flickering electric lighting system, driven by an elderly Crossley gas engine. He also spent some time in the adjacent library, with its bound volumes of fictional literature – he was surprised to note that there were few, if any, technical works.

The debate on the engine design slowly moved away from Sir Herbert's preference for a flat-twin – which, even with all its shortcomings in rough running, had been very popular amongst many British light car designs – and towards a small vertical water-cooled four-cylinder engine. This thinking was already an established trait on the continent, but had been resisted somewhat by Herbert Austin. Stanley Edge, meanwhile, accepted it as an entirely rational and practical approach, and said in later life that if he had contributed anything to

Lickey Grange, Lickey Hills; the 'arts and crafts'-style home of Sir Herbert and Lady Austin, with the turreted billiard room on the right. (Austin publicity)

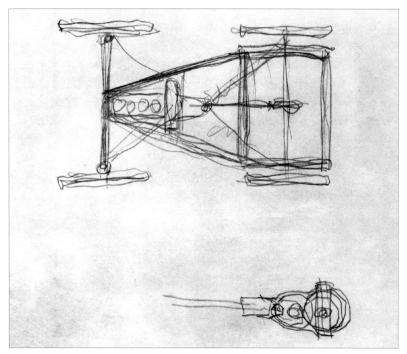

Herbert Austin's later developed design sketch; from its wobbly line-work, it was clearly executed whilst in motion in a train or car. As with earlier sketches, it shows a four-cylinder engine, but previous central chassis channel elements have been dispensed with. (750 Motor Club archive)

A note from Sir Herbert Austin to Stanley Edge about the scuttle section of body, showing his confidence in leaving young Stanley to work-up detail from concept. (Stanley Edge archive)

the design of the Austin Seven, the small vertical water-cooled engine was at the heart of it. It was the smallness of the proposed engine that highly concerned Herbert, and before accepting the principle of a front-mounted four-cylinder engine, myriad other cylinder and placement alternatives were examined and discarded, including a three-cylinder radial rear-mounted engine, a diamond-pattern road wheel layout, and rear-wheel steering.

Viewed from almost a century on, this casting about for alternative design solutions must be viewed in the light of contemporary knowledge; there was no particular orthodoxy, if one wished to move forward and progress, and many motor cars were still being designed and built at that time that barely worked at all. The Austin Seven, when finally designed, included what we now know as 'conventional' controls, in the arrangement and function of the clutch, brakes, accelerator pedals, and hand controls. In this sense, it can also be considered to be something of a pioneering design. The Seven was the first mass-produced British car with what we now accept as universally conventional controls, allowing the vehicle to be driven in a safe and controllable manner.

The initial design debate was not decided until the start of the new year, when the in-line vertical water-cooled four-cylinder engine was adopted as the preferred motive power; albeit aptly expanded, and worked up as a concept for a small version of a larger car, rather than simply a better quality cyclecar. This main decision also allowed the overall design to be developed along similar lines, ultimately sharing many design elements with Austin's larger car range, taking design clues from its bigger brothers, and maintaining a family design identity.

Unwittingly, perhaps, the design ethos of the 'small, large car' also had the embedded potential for development and future-proofing subsequent models – something that would have been denied in a more quirky lightweight design, and a factor that would be unlikely to have been apparent in 1922, but which was to serve the Austin company well for the next 17 tumultuous years. The key was to enable Austin to build a civilised, small, four-cylinder water-cooled engine, for no more cost than a similarly-sized engine with fewer cylinders. This required very careful and efficient engineering design.

Stanley Edge had carried out research in pursuit of this principle. He presented his findings to Herbert Austin in the form of a list, featuring as many continental and British manufacturers of small four-cylinder engines as he could find – numbering 26 companies in total. Many of these were French, and of particular note was the fairly recently introduced Peugeot Quadrilette. With a bore of 50mm and stroke of 85mm, the engine gave a swept volume of 668cc, and was a direct successor to the power unit of the 1914 Peugeot Bebé, of which 3000 had been sold in its first year of production – an astonishing figure for the period. Whilst it appears that neither Stanley Edge nor Herbert Austin had seen a Quadrilette at that time, the Peugeot engine had a complicated crankcase, block, and cylinder head in one single cast iron casting, the design of which was not difficult to improve upon. The Peugeot chassis layout did, however, include a transverse front spring and quarter-elliptic springs at the rear.

The engine that Stanley Edge laid out for Herbert's expert comments featured a bore of 50mm and a stroke of 77mm, giving a capacity of 696cc. An early design decision had been made to include aluminium pistons; a considerable advance at a time when many engines still used cast iron. While using aluminium pistons reduced the engine's reciprocating mass – an important factor in reducing stress in a relatively long stroke engine – they also required a larger amount of clearance when used with a cast iron block, to take into account the aluminium's increased thermal expansion.

The list prepared for Herbert Austin by Stanley Edge, comparing the vital statistics of French and British (as well as one Italian) light cars in 1922. (Stanley Edge archive)

The 1921 Peugeot Quadrilette small four-cylinder side-valve engine that first attracted the attention of Stanley Edge. Note the design of the valve chest, log manifold, and top water outlet.

THE PEUGEOT QUADRILETTE

Founded in 1890, SA Automobiles Peugeot is the oldest car manufacturing company still engaged in producing cars today. Its early speciality was to create the smallest practical motorised vehicle that could sell in large numbers, and which they affectionately named 'Bebé,' or 'baby.' The first version of the Peugeot Bebé was built in 1904; a primitive, four-wheeled, 5hp, single-cylinder, rear-engined chassis, with an open-to-the-elements bench seat for two passengers in front, and the driver sitting on a central saddle behind.

Meanwhile, no less a figure than Etorre Bugatti had, in 1912, designed a much more advanced small car from first principles for the German company Wanderer. The most notable features of this vehicle

The early tandem seat Peugeot Quadrilette of 1921. Later versions had a wider body, with conventional seating for four persons. (Author collection)

were its small in-line, four-cylinder 855cc water-cooled engine, mounted under a bonnet in front, with the driver and passengers in a separate body behind; a full size glass windscreen; and an effective hood to keep the weather out. The instantly recognisable shape of a scaled-down larger car. Wanderer were in no position to commence production of this Bugatti design, so Etorre offered his concept to Emil Peugeot, who immediately agreed terms for a licence to manufacture the car. 3000 were built, at the time a considerable production number for a single model.

After the Great War, Peugeot developed the design in the form of the new Quadrilette, or 'small four' – the name alluded not to the number of people it could carry, but to the design of the engine. The Quadrilette of 1920 was initially a two-seater car with the driver seated in front of the single passenger, and as a result the car was unusually narrow. It had an even smaller version of the in-line four-cylinder engine, displacing only 667cc, sat in a triangular-plan chassis with a transverse leaf spring front suspension – like a Ford Model T – and quarter-elliptic rear leaf springs that took care of the rear axle location. It remained in production for ten years.

Prior to designing the Austin Seven, apparently neither Herbert Austin nor Stanley Edge had seen a Quadrilette in the flesh. Nevertheless, the model was well publicised, and Stanley had been so taken with the engine statistics (which he had researched) that he had no doubt that the small in-line four-cylinder engine, now so favoured by those in mainland Europe, was the future. For Herbert Austin, the practicality of the small 'big' car was the key feature, doing away with the limitations of the cruder cyclecar.

There is thus a distinct and direct line from Etorre Bugatti, through Emile Peugeot, Herbert Austin with his Austin Seven, and – post WW2 – to Colin Chapman of Lotus. Chapman was just one of many engineers that followed whose early design experiences were shaped by the Austin Seven.

Stanley came to realise that, as long as he could give a rational engineering reason, Herbert Austin was content to let him get on with the engine design, with a daily report on progress and a list of items requiring discussion and approval. Austin favoured an aluminium crankcase with a cast iron block and detachable cylinder head, and the company already had access to the foundry and manufacturing facilities required to construct such an engine.

Costs were a principal concern in the design. The simple two-bearing crankshaft in roller bearings kept the engine length down. The whole lubrication system could be jet fed, with no additional

pipes, all the oil running down drilled galleries in the easily-machined aluminium crankcase. The crankshaft received oil from two jets for the narrow white metal big end bearings. The side-valve layout relied on oil mist entering the valve chest on the nearside of the cylinder block, the camshaft receiving splash from the rotating crankshaft for the cam lobe faces, and a drilling in the camshaft bush mating with an oil gallery discretely served by the oil pump.

There was some debate about optimum compression ratios, partly in view of the inconsistent octane equality of available petrol or 'motor spirit' (still available from larger chemist shops at the time).

Stanley Edge proposed keeping the compression ratio towards 5:1, by eliminating most of the combustion chamber space above the pistons. The compromise design consisted of a cylinder head that had enough spare metal that it could be readily machined to raise compression if needed or desirable, without compromising other aspects. Putting some of this to the test in 1923, Edge recorded that, when tuned experimentally, an Austin Seven engine was capable of giving almost 30bhp.

It would appear that internal combustion expert Harry Ricardo may have had some input into the earliest combustion chamber shapes: his published papers had been read by Stanley Edge, and his company was to play an important part in detail revisions much later in the life of the Seven.

In the design of the layout of the Seven head, Edge kept a flowing line moving inwards between the valve heads and the individual cylinders, thereby gaining space for the water cooling cavities, and at the same time eliminating wasted combustion chamber volume. The compression ratio was thus kept fairly high, and the critical surface

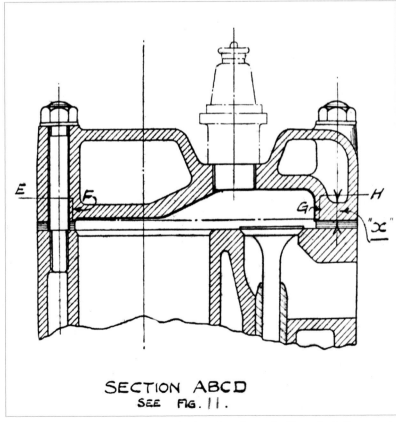

SECTION ABCD
SEE FIG. 11.

Original Stanley Edge sectional plan drawing of a Ricardo-influenced cylinder head design, showing casting cores for water jacket.
(Stanley Edge archive)

ORIGINAL DESIGN – THE CHASSIS NOSE PIECE

A good test of design quality is an apparently simple design solution; if a single component can be made to perform more than one job, there is an economy of materials, labour, and cost, as well as an improvement in performance and service.

The Austin Seven incorporates many examples of good engineering design; perhaps one of the best of which is the cast-steel chassis nose piece. The steel casting is of constant thickness, with a hollowed-out underside to save weight, material, and money, and to give good flow characteristics for the casting process. This carefully thought-out component performs many functions, each of which required a design decision, and for every shared function there is the saving, not only of an additional component, but also the space that would otherwise somehow have to be provided to accommodate that second component.

The original Austin Seven nose piece, as installed in the 1930s, does at least ten jobs. Firstly, it joins together the chassis frame rails as a front cross-member. Being a casting, rather than a pressing like the rest of the chassis, it also considerably stiffens the front of the frame. The nose piece also forms the mounting for several components, including: the front spring; the front shock-absorber; the front engine mounts; the bodywork 'cow horns;' the front wing stays, incorporating the mountings for the front headlights; the radiator and front of bonnet support; the number plate mounting, and, on some military Sevens, the front towing eye. Quite a design achievement!

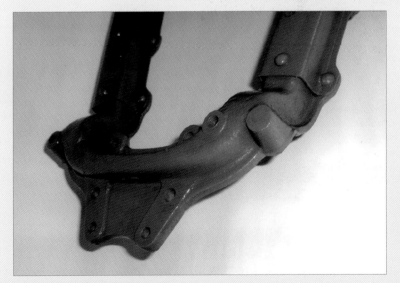

The familiar and deceptively simple cast steel chassis nose piece is an element of very well-thought-out and masterly design, typical of its original creators.

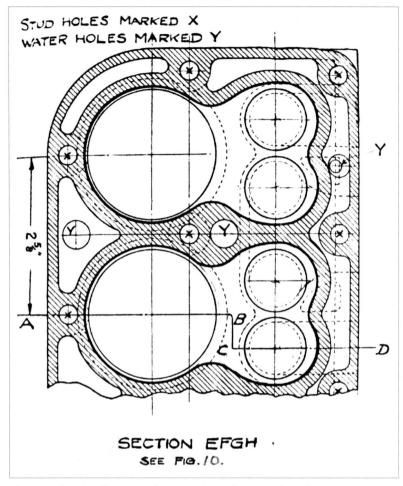

Original Stanley Edge section drawing of a Ricardo-influenced cylinder head and top face of cylinder block. (Stanley Edge archive)

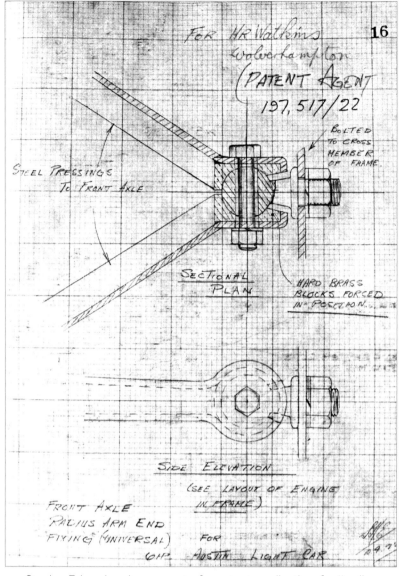

Stanley Edge drawing as part of a patent application for "radius arm end fixing," dated 1922. (Stanley Edge archive)

area of the chamber reasonably low, guaranteeing what, at the time, was considered to be a good level of efficiency.

The general layout of a triangular plan form for the frame – possibly influenced by an American Gray light truck used at the factory, tapering in from the rear axle to a point at the front – was established in Herbert's sketches very early on, with quarter-elliptical springs at the rear, and a transverse front spring (the latter had, by then, become well established for more than a decade by the Model T Ford).

Simple direct cable-operated brakes were light, allowed a flexible arrangement and were cheap. It was the norm at this time for small cars to have rear brakes only. From discussion, however, it became evident that cable front brakes were feasible, if the cable operation was kept in line with the triangulating radius arms. This still allowed good steering lock, and a 'big car' approach led to the adoption of four wheel brakes, with the front set operated by a hand brake quite separately from the rear. The inclusion of four wheel brakes was very advanced for a light car, at a time when fast and heavy contemporary Rolls-Royce vehicles only had braking on the rear wheels. Again, this advanced thinking gave scope for future-proofing the design of the Seven.

Herbert Austin had taken to sketching out his ideas at odd moments, and also when travelling by train. Many hand drawings with very wobbly pencil lines are evidence of this habit, and show a man bursting with design ideas, seizing the moment, intent on recording them as quickly as possible. By Easter of 1922, much of the detailed drawing work had been completed at Lickey Grange, and it was time to translate the drawings into metal.

The Seal; a diabolical device, where the driver was seated in the 'car,' and the steering wheel connected to the single front wheel of the 'motorcycle.' Sir Herbert did rather better. (Courtesy Ken Cooke)

COLONEL ACR WAITE, MC

Arthur Waite was born in Adelaide, Australia, in 1894. At the outbreak of the Great War, Waite signed up for the Australian Field Artillery, rising quickly to the rank of Second Lieutenant, before setting sail for Egypt in October 1914. His service took him to Gallipoli, in North Africa, and France, where – in 1916 – he was awarded the Military Cross.

Col Arthur Waite in the very first works racing Seven. In 1923, he drove the car from Bromsgrove to Brooklands, won his race, turned round, and drove back again – his mission accomplished, and all within a few hours. (Austin publicity)

The dynamic young Arthur married Irene Austin – Sir Herbert's vivacious elder daughter – in 1918, and joined the Austin Company after the war had ended. He quickly became involved with the competition and racing side of the business, and was especially motivated by the announcement of the Austin Seven. By this time, Herbert Austin had spent considerable time in Australia, where he had married Helen, who was also Australian-born. Waite must have felt very much at home as a part of the Austin family. Herbert had named his earlier powerful 280bhp racing boats 'Irene I' and 'Irene II,' after his daughter – these twice held the Water Speed Record, once when piloted by Herbert himself.

Discussion between Sir Herbert, Arthur Waite, and Alf Depper had won Sir Herbert over to the idea that the Seven that he had created could easily perform sufficiently well to be competitive in its class. So, very early in 1923, a super-lightweight fabric body (built by the aircraft workshop) was fitted to a chassis with a 4.5:1 rear-axle ratio, painted black with a white radiator cowl, and registered OK 7095. Waite took the car for a few test drives and, on 23rd March (Easter Monday), drove it to Brooklands for a small car handicap race. Starting as the limit man – or, the competitor with the maximum handicap – Waite averaged almost 60mph (96km/h) in the competition. He overtook all the cyclecars – mostly running with 1100cc engines – and won at

A replica 1923 Waite Racer engine, with an early choke-less Zenith carburettor, cylinder head priming taps for starting, no inlet manifold vacuum connection, and Magneto ignition, but no dynamo. (Author collection)

Geoff Wright, in the Tony Hutchings-built 1923 Replica Waite Racer, moves off at Kop Hill Climb. The car is assembled from original and correct 1923 components. (Author collection)

distance and would avoid too much bad publicity. On 29th April 1923, Waite won the 750cc class at Monza. The car covered the 250km (160mi) at almost 57mph (90km/h); an astonishing performance for the tiny and simple new side-valved car, and one that created enormous publicity and goodwill. It was, after all, the first British car to win a continental speed event for more than a decade. Two similar cars were made ready for competition and, together with OK 7095, dubbed the 'Boulogne' racers. These were driven as a team in August 1923, with Arthur Waite piloting OK 7095. In 1924, Waite drove an Austin Seven Sports at Le Mans, earning 3rd place in the 750cc class – an early Sports success.

Sir Herbert's high regard for his energetic son-in-law allowed Waite to set up a larger racing shop, converted from stables that were previously occupied by the works' internal transport Shire horses (there still being three horses in 1926). There, he built an experimental Roots lobe-type supercharger for the Seven, mounted on the engine timing cover. The three lobe impellers were profiled on a gear-hobbing machine, used previously for the cutting of clutch centre splines. This blown car was built on an extended wheelbase chassis, with the usual aircraft-type fabric on light body framing with staggered seating. The resulting vehicle averaged the two-way flying kilometre at more than 86mph (138km/h), and reached a top speed of 92mph (147km/h). By 1929, it held all the International Class H (750cc) records.

An experimental 1.5-litre straight-eight engine, using two Seven blocks, was also built. However, the crankshafts proved troublesome and the engine was ultimately never raced, with Waite putting it to one side.

Waite returned to Australia, and, in the meantime, his car was re-engined with a normally-aspirated unit by Johnny Pares, George Coldicott, and Frankie Woods. This was done in order to comply with Gordon England specification, and named 'Slippery Anne;' this car was destined to be one of the most famous of all racing Sevens. In Australia, Waite telegraphed Longbridge to ask for his car to be shipped out, so that he might take part in the inaugural 100 Miles Road Race on Phillip Island, in 1928. When the shipping crate arrived, Waite was aghast to find a pair of high-chassied prototype production sports cars, with bodywork similar to later Super Sports, in place of his super-lightweight super-low blown racer. Nevertheless, Waite carried out a few bodywork alterations and prepared the cars after their long voyage. The works engines had a pressure feed; a solid billet crankshaft with a vertical Cozette No 4 supercharger, blowing at 5lb (2.2kg); and a special four-speed gearbox in a three-speed case, with no reverse fitted.

The rules of the – rather exclusive – Victorian Light Car Club stipulated that the race cars had to carry a mechanic in addition to the

record speed. He then drove the car back to Bromsgrove, all within about six hours, and with no problems.

Considerably encouraged, Sir Herbert authorised the enthusiastic Waite and Depper to take this car to Monza for the Italian Cyclecar Grand Prix, reasoning that if the car failed, at least it would be at a

Jockey George Duller grins at the camera in the early Austin works special at Brooklands. Duller greatly influenced Alec Issigonis, a regular at his Hampstead premises. (Austin publicity)

driver, and that only tyres of Australian manufacture could be used, with a single spare permitted. 30 cars were entered, including no less than five Austin Sevens, with cars starting at fixed intervals from the largest class down to the smallest.

Later becoming known as the first Australian Grand Prix, Arthur Waite won the race at an average speed of 56.25mph (90.5km/h) in the works Austin Seven built especially for the event and shipped from England. Of the five Austin Sevens entered, only one – driven by Albert Edwards – failed to finish the event. What's more, Cyril Dickason claimed third in his 2-litre Austin Twelve, and the Sevens cleaned up the 750cc Class; a great day for the Austin Seven 'Down Under.' The little Austin was represented in model form on the Lex Davison Trophy, which was subsequently awarded to the winner of the annual Australian Grand Prix each year until the event became a round in the F1 World Championship.

Waite returned to England in 1929, where he continued to race Sevens, with success, and was made a director of the Austin Motor Company Ltd – later to become the British Motor Corporation Ltd. In 1930, Waite was a part of the team for the JCC Double Twelve at Brooklands, winning the *Autocar* award alongside his team-mate, the Earl of March. Disaster struck later in the year, however, when Waite crashed heavily at Ballystockart in the 1930 Ards TT, overturning on a bank. He was thrown into the road, and straight into the path of oncoming cars. Waite suffered a concussion and broken jaw, while his co-driver, Alf Depper, was lucky not to be more badly injured. Waite retired from competitive driving immediately after the event, to concentrate on his London office work.

At this time, Waite, as director, controlled all of Austin's motor racing and competition activities. In 1931, he directed the preparation of the special side-valve single-seater, in which Cushman recaptured a number of records back from MG. Freddie Henry joined Waite –

affectionately known by his staff as 'Skipper' – in the London office. There, he witnessed first-hand Waite's efforts at ensuring Sir Herbert's support for the works Austin racers; this was particularly true of the Twin-Cam model, which would not have been born without Waite's persuasion.

When the young Murray Jamieson, who worked with Amherst Villiers, appeared in a white production Austin Seven Ulster – supplied by Austin, but fitted with a supercharger of Jamieson's own design that proved much faster than the works version – Austin, via Arthur Waite, was impelled to offer Jamieson the job of designing the new single-seater Austin Seven Side Valve. Once developed, this produced 70bhp when blown at 24lb (10.8kg) boost. Jamieson himself took this car to Montlhéry, setting records at over 120mph (192km/h), prior to starting the sparkling design of that most beautiful of single-seater race cars – the Austin Seven Twin-Cam.

Waite's early enthusiasm for using the Austin Seven in competition had given the company, and the public, enormous confidence in the little car, and had set the scene for the huge successes that were to follow. Having contributed more to the success of the Seven than anybody else – apart from Sir Herbert and Stanley Edge – the debonair Waite retired his directorship of BMC in 1964 (the heyday of the works Monte Carlo Rally-winning Minis). He would later be a regular guest of honour at the annual 750 Motor Club National Austin Seven Rally at Beaulieu. Waite passed away in 1991, aged 97.

Captain ACR Waite at the wheel with Lord March, in the car with which they secured the *Autocar* 'Most for Money' trophy in the 1930 Brooklands Double Twelve, and the Mobiloil victory trophy in Class H at a speed of 65mph (104km/h). (Austin publicity)

THE MOTOR FOR THE MILLIONS

The Motor for the Millions is Sir Herbert Austin's 1923 manifesto, detailing his intention for his revolutionary baby car to be available to all, offering economic personal mobility. The brochure firmly and confidently states:

"A real car is now within the means of the majority in the Austin Seven, bringing health, recreation, convenience and cheap business travel in its train.

"It proffers all these benefits at the price of a good sidecar combination, and costs no more to run, yet provides far more comfortable travel.

"It protects all its occupants from exposure, and can be run at the cost of tram fares.

"… the vastly widened interest in life assured by running an Austin Seven cannot be measured in money… in health alone – fresh air, new scenes and an interest … the Austin Seven will extend one's field of interest and pleasure."

It is notable that, on the cover of the brochure, an assertively dressed young woman (probably one of Herbert's daughters), is shown loading her golf clubs into a Seven, while inside the brochure as many women as men are shown at the wheel. The brochure continues, "It is an ideal car for women's use, and there is no need to wait till the menfolk return from business … saves the time of the housewife in shopping, enabling her to visit the best markets … makes it possible for a family to live outside the city in the fresh air by providing cheap and reliable transport … it is ideal for the business man … he is able to keep perfectly clean, warm and presentable when visiting clients, and he can carry quite a large sample case in the space behind the main seats…" Sir Herbert also describes his new car as having "two main seats, both adjustable, of very roomy size, and at the back … a seat covering a tool box, which will accommodate three children, or at a pinch a third adult."

The undoubted virtues of comfort, handling, power, stability, reliability, and convenience are extolled throughout. Also included are Captain Arthur Waite's early victory in the Brooklands Easter Small Car Handicap, won at 65mph (95km/h), and victory at the Royal Monza circuit in Italy at a similar speed, as well as good results in Classic Trials – the first of the Austin Seven's considerable sporting successes.

Features listed include the brakes used on all four wheels having interchangeable parts, side curtains that open with the doors, a chassis that provides great strength without undue weight, and a grease gun system ahead of many contemporary larger vehicles. The specification points to a product design that is confident, very well thought out, and a completely integrated concept.

This was a period of rapid technological progress, which saw aircraft designs advance from canvas and string biplanes, at the time of the introduction of the Seven, through to the running of Frank Whittle's first practical jet engine towards the end of the Seven's production. It is therefore creditable and notable that Herbert Austin's original Seven was able to constantly evolve and maintain healthy sales figures with the buying public.

The Motor for the Millions,
Sir Herbert Austin's manifesto.
(Austin publicity)

CHAPTER TWO

PRODUCTION

IN order to construct a prototype Austin Seven in secret from Sir Herbert's fellow directors (who were still unaware of the project), as well as keeping away from unwanted prying eyes, it was arranged for part of one of the workshops at Longbridge to be sealed off. It was here that Stanley Edge was installed, along with a small six-man team, led by Alf Depper. Guided by their previous experiences, it was decided to make three prototype cars, allowing a degree of simultaneous development.

The works superintendent, McLellan, was under instruction to assist in the hurried supply of parts, as well as whatever else might be needed. This assistance also included farming out the first machining of the prototype internal engine components, the first crankcase, block, and cylinder head to subcontractors. A great deal of time and care was taken by Stanley Edge and the others to record and re-record precise measurements of all finished parts, to establish the tolerances of measurement variance that would be allowed in each component committed to assembly. This process of measurement spilled over into later production, where it was termed 'selective assembly;' a rigidly-controlled process, particularly in the assembly of engines,

The earliest 26in (660mm) wheels, 6in (152mm) brakes production chassis, and layout of conventional controls. (Austin publicity)

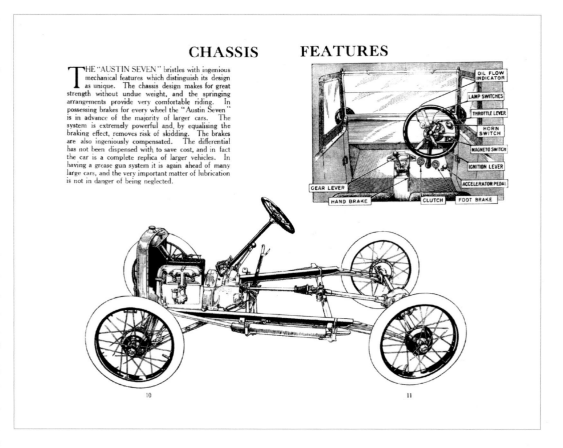

CHASSIS FEATURES

THE "AUSTIN SEVEN" bristles with ingenious mechanical features which distinguish its design as unique. The chassis design makes for great strength without undue weight, and the springing arrangements provide very comfortable riding. In possessing brakes for every wheel the "Austin Seven" is in advance of the majority of larger cars. The system is extremely powerful and, by equalising the braking effect, removes risk of skidding. The brakes are also ingeniously compensated. The differential has not been dispensed with to save cost, and in fact the car is a complete replica of larger vehicles. In having a grease gun system it is again ahead of many large cars, and the very important matter of lubrication is not in danger of being neglected.

OIL FLOW INDICATOR

LAMP SWITCHES

THROTTLE LEVER

HORN SWITCH

MAGNETO SWITCH

IGNITION LEVER

ACCELERATOR PEDAL

GEAR LEVER

HAND BRAKE

CLUTCH

FOOT BRAKE

10

11

that maintains the final build quality and running characteristics of the car on offer to the public.

From day one, it had been the intention to use lightweight wire wheels rather than heavier disc or spoked artillery wheels. The Coventry and Birmingham area was the centre for British bicycle and motorcycle manufacture, and the required wire wheels were quickly produced. In fact, several small fixings on the Seven, such as the cotter pins for retaining brake levers, are – perhaps unsurprisingly – ordinary off-the-shelf Victorian bicycle items. Local specialist subcontractors supplied road springs, the slim-cored radiator was by Peter Serck, a proprietary carburettor came from Zenith, and Watford supplied a large magneto. The overall body design displayed Austin family heritage, particularly in the shape of the radiator shell, which lent itself to miniaturisation. It was a perfect shape for the little car, and – importantly – one that placed the Seven visually within a well-established product range.

Within six weeks two cars were running under their own power, albeit using different drive trains. In addition, they used the familiar part-open, part-enclosed propeller shaft that was ultimately adopted. An entirely open propeller shaft was tried personally by Sir Herbert, but caused an amusing hopping motion (with considerable loss of dignity to the driver). An entirely enclosed shaft, on the other hand, caused geometric difficulties with the rear quarter-elliptic springs, which of course doubled as axle locators, and therefore lacked shackles.

A large Whitsun carnival crowd witnessed the first public viewing of the little cars on the works sports ground, and the general consensus amongst the employees and their families was very enthusiastic. The other Austin directors were persuaded, after some debate, and agreed that Herbert Austin's baby car might have some merit to it after all. Plans were therefore put in place to enter the Seven into limited production. This required the drawings for the prototype – produced to date by Stanley Edge – to be revised as production drawings

under Joey Hancock. It seems that Sir Herbert was instrumental in treating the production of the Seven as a special case, as the older and more experienced chassis man, Jack Rix, was tasked with working on this with Stanley. This in turn allowed Stanley to concentrate his efforts on the tiny engine, which he considered to be his own special contribution, and was of great personal interest.

The car's detailed design was refined to tailor it to production methods; orders were placed, instructions given to the works foundry, and a small number of subcontractors alerted and fed the relevant information. In this respect, Austin at this time was regarded as almost self-sufficient; it constructed complex products, all within the mighty Longbridge factory buildings that had been expanded enormously by the Great War's demands for munitions, trucks, and aircraft. A great deal more of the whole car was built by Austin itself than was the case for its big rival, Morris. By those at 'The Austin,' Morris was considered more of an assembler of components than a full blown car manufacturer, at least compared to the company governed by Sir Herbert.

The 1922 Motor Show was to be held in November, a mere four months after the first three prototypes had been completed. The excitement that the car had created, however, meant that more publicity was gained by a press release in July. *The Autocar* enthusiastically

Postcard of the semi-prototypical 'scoop-scuttle' car, registered OK 3537. It was displayed for decades at the Science Museum in South Kensington, London. (Courtesy Science Museum)

described the Seven as "a miniature car with all the attributes of a medium-sized one," having immediately appreciated the concept. "What more could a man of moderate means want for his money?" *The Light Car & Cyclecar* asked – writing priceless advertising copy for Herbert Austin in the process.

Sir Herbert was, at this point, due to go again to America. These were trips that he always returned from full of enthusiasm and ideas, and certainly with a broader view of how he might arrange his own future plans. Stanley Edge, meanwhile, worked diligently with Jack Rix on the Seven's production drawings.

Once production was in full swing, Stanley was naturally asked to contribute to racing modifications on the Seven by Herbert Austin's son-in-law, Captain Arthur Waite, who Stanley already knew from regular meetings at Lickey Grange. Waite appreciated that the Seven could probably be competitive in its class, and Sir Herbert, having already built racing cars going back 20 years, backed the construction of an especially light fabric torpedo body on a Seven chassis, followed by a pretty, metal-bodied small sports two-seater.

As far as Stanley Edge's own career was concerned, he decided to take a short holiday in mid-1925 and, on his return (and still aged only 22), had joined Triumph by the end of the year. An illustrious and multifaceted, if not quite so breathless, career in the motor industry followed. This included a huge contribution to military vehicle and component design in World War Two – though perhaps nothing to rival his lovely little engine for the Austin Seven.

THE FIRST PRODUCTION CARS

The cars that were first exhibited at the 1922 Motor Show were, initially, simply known as the Family Tourer, and given the type designation 'B.' These became popularly known as the Austin Chummy, and had a delightfully-proportioned, pram-shaped body, with a tucked under tail; a shape that was still representative of carriages from the coaching days of a century or more earlier.

The wheelbase was 6ft 3in (1900mm), with a front track of 3ft 4in (1016mm), and a rear track of 3ft 7in (1092mm). The chassis frame was formed from 'Top Hat' pressed sections for the chassis side rails, finishing just forward of the rear tyres. These were joined by a rear crossmember, on which was mounted a swivelling ball joint anchorage for the forward end of the rear axle fixed torque tube. The rear springs were held by machined pins directly through the spring eyes, and lugs on the rear axle casing. Initially this was with no shock absorbers, although Hartfords were later added, quickly superseded by Austin's own friction dampers, mounted on the chassis side rails and rear crossmember, with shackles to the rear axle via the same machined spring pin, which now performed two tasks.

Front suspension was made up of a light drop-forged H section axle beam, sitting below a transverse spring, held by U-bolts to the front chassis nose piece. This was a cast-steel item, later called upon to perform several more functions than originally intended. The front transverse axle and spring were located fore-and-aft by channel section pressed steel radius arms, which together formed an almost perfect equilateral triangle. The rear point came together, mounted on a small ball forging fixed

A very early press photograph, demonstrating how the whole family could travel together in an Austin Seven. (Austin publicity)

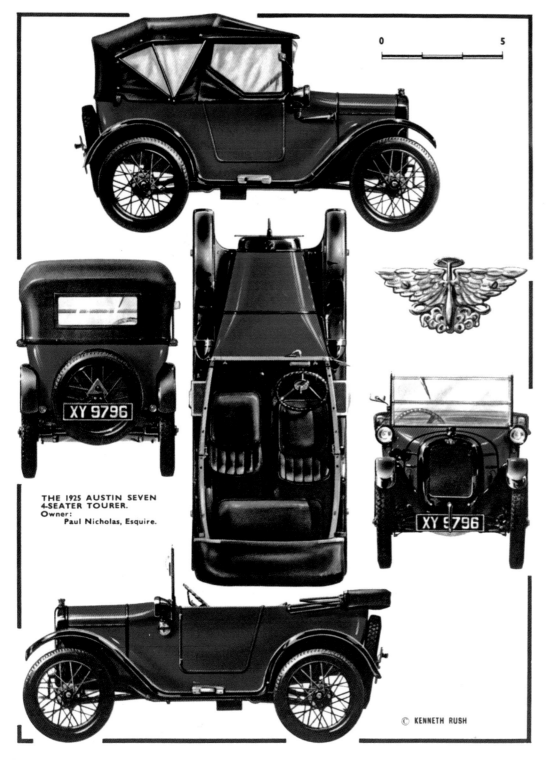

THE 1925 AUSTIN SEVEN
4-SEATER TOURER.
Owner:
Paul Nicholas, Esquire.

© KENNETH RUSH

Superb studies by Ken Rush for the popular 1960s Profile Publications booklet on the Austin Seven. (Courtesy Kenneth Rush)

The 6in (152mm) diameter brakes to all four wheels were cable operated; the foot pedal actuated the rear, as was the norm for the period, and the handbrake operated only the front brakes. Drivers were advised in operating literature to pull the handbrake on by a few clicks when descending a steep hill – a surprisingly effective and reassuring technique.

The wheels were a light wire-spoked type, and fitted with 26in x 3in (660mm x 76mm) Dunlop Magnum or – briefly – Clincher Cord tyres. A spare wheel was mounted on the back of the bodywork. The wheels featured one of Herbert's many patented ideas, with slotted holes in the wheel centre itself, allowing the wheels to be removed by only slackening off the retaining nuts, not removing the nuts completely. This avoided the possibility of losing the nuts when changing a wheel, a feature again intended to be attractive particularly to women drivers.

The large diameter of the wheels used reflected the variety of surfaces that Sevens were expected to encounter, as, although main roads had smoothly metalled surfaces, many country lanes and routes were still unsurfaced, including the lanes around Lickey Grange. The Seven was expected to be able to drive over older urban streets that were still paved with cobblestones, or laid with granite setts, as well as rough farm tracks or worse. In fact, the car later developed a genuine and deserved reputation as a practical, 'go anywhere,' off-road vehicle. Whilst the 26in (660mm) wheels appeared to be of very large

to the centre of the front face of a middle crossmember. It was again initially not considered necessary to have a front shock absorber, but again Hartfords were soon tried, and again quickly superseded by Austin units.

diameter for such a small car, their use was proportionate and based on the sound experience of Austin's larger model range (the outer diameter of the tyres of which were, of course, considerably greater than that of the Seven).

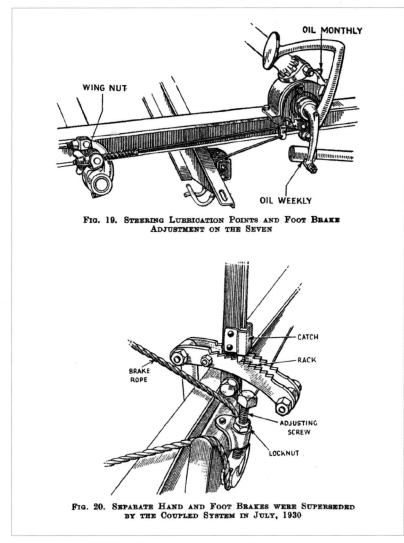

FIG. 19. STEERING LUBRICATION POINTS AND FOOT BRAKE
ADJUSTMENT ON THE SEVEN

FIG. 20. SEPARATE HAND AND FOOT BRAKES WERE SUPERSEDED
BY THE COUPLED SYSTEM IN JULY, 1930

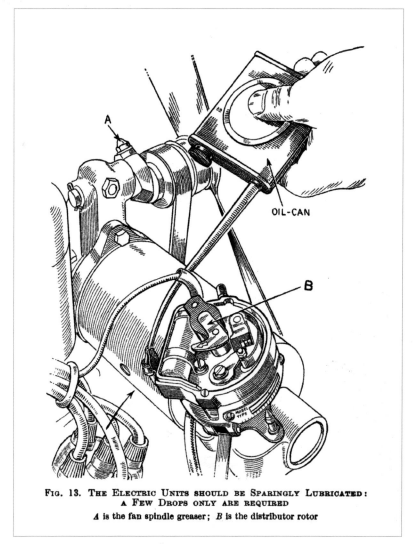

FIG. 13. THE ELECTRIC UNITS SHOULD BE SPARINGLY LUBRICATED:
A FEW DROPS ONLY ARE REQUIRED

A is the fan spindle greaser; *B* is the distributor rotor

To generations that had grown up playing with Meccano, there was no mystery in the mechanical workings of this simple motor car. (Austin publicity)

Herbert Austin expected the owners themselves to maintain their Sevens. Carefully drawn illustrations were of great assistance, and an hour each weekend was normally given to the task. (Austin publicity)

The engine was little changed from the prototype units, and the cast-aluminium alloy crankcase had integral cast-in lugs on each corner, which mounted directly on the chassis frame side rails. The cast-iron cylinder block soon had the original bore increased to 2⅛in (56mm) with a 3in (76mm) stroke, giving a swept volume of 747cc (45.6in³) and an RAC horsepower rating of 7.8hp – or 7hp for road fund licence (tax) purposes. It had been decided by Sir Herbert Austin that the capacity of the Seven engine could be increased a little from the prototypes. This would keep the car just within the well-known international 750cc class for competitive events – such as races – and keep below the next road tax bracket threshold, for marketing purposes.

The cylinder head was detachable, which greatly simplified machining for production, as well as considerably assisting assembly checking. Whist the number of components on the Seven is higher when compared to an engine with an integral cylinder head and block, the production complexity, and therefore cost, is reduced. Maintenance is also made easier; not insignificant at a time when de-coking the engine (that is, removing the build-up of carbon from incomplete combustion) was sometimes carried out by the father of the family, when out for a Sunday picnic in the country!

The engine was cooled by an integral cast-in water jacket to the cylinder block and head – the waterways between the cylinders being rather narrow – and a single water outlet to the front of the engine fed the heated water up a steeply-raked water hose to the top of the radiator. As it cooled, and became denser, the water flowed downwards from there, through the radiator matrix (or core), to a small bottom collection tank. From there, it was back to the offside of the cylinder block, where a long cast-aluminium inlet fed the cooled water to the cylinder walls of all four cylinders, to be heated up and the cycle repeated.

This 'thermosiphon' system was expected to provide adequate cooling, there being no water pump. However, it was soon found that an engine-driven fan – to pull air through the radiator – was needed when the car was stationary, when little or no cooling air was passing through the radiator. This was a simple cast-aluminium two-bladed fan, mounted in a spigot. This incorporated an eccentric belt drive adjustment above the front timing case casting, with a tiny fan belt, driven by a pulley, on the front of the camshaft.

The single gear-driven camshaft was mounted high in the crankcase on the nearside, with adjustable tappets above, directly bearing on the bases of the four inlet and four exhaust valves and springs. These were in a very neat valve chest with a pressed metal cover, which was removable via a pair of nice knurled head screws in the block. The design of this valve chest, and the ports that make it up (which are very familiar to every owner of an Austin Seven), barely changed for the whole production life of the car. This is what would now be described as a masterly piece of packaging, but back in 1922 it was simply considered basic engineering design at its best.

The inlet valve ports were twinned, or siamesed, in pairs. This meant they served cylinders one and two together, and three and four together, with an engine firing order of one, three, four, two. This provided a reasonably even flow of gas to each cylinder, whilst each of the exhaust ports were separate to avoid local hotspots.

A cast-iron 'log' exhaust manifold collected the expelled hot gases forward and downwards. A separate cast-aluminium inlet manifold served an updraught Zenith type 22 FZ carburettor, at first with no choke requiring flooding to start, then later with a choke flap operated by a wire in the radiator cowl. This was soon changed, and run to a position beneath the dashboard. The very earliest cars and racers had no choke, but had four priming taps on the cylinder head for starting, witnessed by the cylinder head castings until 1926.

Lacking an electric starter motor, early cars instead had a wooden pull handle and a starter device that needed engaging by hand with the toothed flywheel, before requiring a quick and steady pull to turn the engine. This interim measure was used until proper CAV electric starter motors were fitted.

A simple, single-plate clutch, and a relatively heavy (for smoothness of running, and to store energy for the lightweight car) flywheel fixed on a keyed taper on the crankshaft, fed a three-speed gearbox in a separate aluminium casting, including a reverse gear and an H-pattern change gate for the gearlever. The internals were readily accessible by removing the lid and change gate in one unit.

The transmission was initially via a metal claw drive, but soon changed to a cheap and reliable fabric coupling, attached to a solid propshaft (later referred to, rather rudely by Jack French, as a 'great iron stick'). Thence, it connected to a type of pot joint – of evolving design – to the front flange of the rear axle torque tube, the anchorage of which was a ball joint, very similar in design to the front suspension radius arms ball joint.

After trials were conducted, the rear axle ratio of 4.9:1 was settled upon in a banjo casing, carrying a 9/44 crown wheel and pinion, of a semi-floating type, with half shafts on ball races and keyed tapers to drive the road wheel hubs. These keyed tapers were a standard engineering solution of the day, but were also one of the design weaknesses of the Austin Seven when subjected to high mileages; the very slightest imperceptible movement between halfshaft tapers, keyway, and hub resulted in a spoiled or broken halfshaft end, and usually brought the vehicle to a standstill until repaired. Very careful lapping-in of the tapers was essential, and the hub nuts had to be kept as tight as possible, and the separate keys absolutely fitting in their keyways.

The first bodywork featured two bucket seats at the front, both adjustable and detachable, with a board covering tool storage under the driver's seat and a battery beneath the passenger's. A bench seat for two or three children at the back, with tool storage beneath, was accommodated in the production-quality stove-enamelled bodywork.

A two-piece glass windscreen allowed the top half to be opened on a pivot under certain road conditions, and a full hood with sidescreens gave excellent weather proofing. The latter was very reminiscent in shape of the elaborate large baby prams that were then in vogue, leading to the nickname of 'Pram hood' joining 'Chummy' for the early cars. Both terms implied a certain amount of affection, particularly amongst their owners, where the little car quickly became to be regarded as a member of the family – an aspect that was remarked upon and exploited in literature and magazines of the time.

The response of the public was very satisfying for Austin, with the general consensus – from enthusiastic comments from the press and public – being that the introduction of the Seven had been nothing short of a national sensation. The affection for the car was clear, but also had the effect of breeding a certain familiarity. This led some members of the press and public to make light-hearted jibes at the small size of the car, no matter how many happy owners were enjoying their motoring, some for the first time, and some making long journeys in record speed, at remarkably little cost.

On 29th July 1922, Lou Kings – Austin's chief tester – took the prototype car registered OK 2950 to the Shelsley Walsh Speed Hillclimb, where he managed a time of just under 90 seconds for his climb – faster than many cars with twice the engine capacity. That September, George Evans drove to Scotland and back in a Seven, taking in the Cairn O' Mount Hillclimb, with no car-related issues on this lengthy run.

Sir Herbert was absolutely delighted with these results, and, by 1923, produced a 20-page pamphlet famously titled *The Motor for the Millions*. A lady driver featured on the cover alongside OK 6807, one of the earliest semi-production cars, with all-over grey paint, and seen inside the pamphlet in various development guises. In a brave and bold marketing move, and one that reflected his confidence, Austin also dropped the sale price from £225 down to £165.

EC GORDON ENGLAND

One of the very earliest and most influential figures in the story of the Austin Seven is Eric Cecil Gordon England, who was already a pioneer of gliding and, in 1909, developed a sport of it, which became known as soaring.

Gordon England was born in Argentina in 1891, and, after coming to Britain, worked as an apprentice railway engineer at Doncaster – where he met WO Bentley – before working for Noel Pemberton Billing, a pioneer aviator operating at South Fambridge in Essex. It was here, in 1909, that Gordon England flew a Weiss glider to an altitude of 100ft (30.48m) above ground, and established a world record; by 1911, he was earning his Aviator's Certificate at Brooklands. Still aged only 20 years old, he established himself as a test pilot and aircraft designer with the Bristol Aeroplane Company.

Like Herbert Austin, EC Gordon England was a young man in a hurry; during World War One, he built and tested the bizarre Lee-Richards-designed annular wing monoplane, and as factory manager he built conventional Bristol Gordon England biplanes, along with other fighters and sea planes for the war effort. He clocked up an

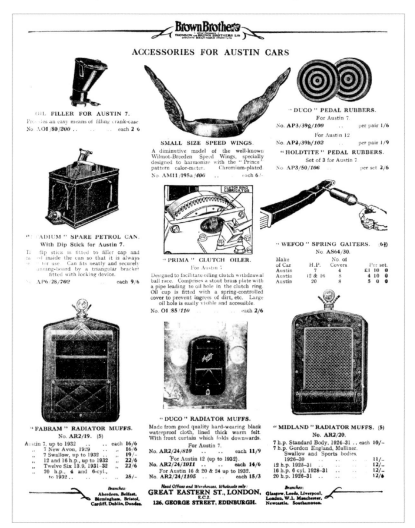

Brown Brothers was one of the main after-market accessory sellers, coming to prominence in the mid-1920s when Sevens began to sell in large numbers. (Author collection)

Gordon England's first attempt at a streamlined body shape in 1923. This car was encouragingly effective at Brooklands, setting the 750cc class 5km record at the astonishing speed of 79.2mph (127.4km/h). (Austin publicity)

astonishing 100,000mi (160,934.4km) flying in these primitive machines. Sadly, Gordon's brother Geoffrey was killed during this time, when his Henri Coandă-designed machine broke up 5000ft (1524m) in the air.

Having been exposed to a wide range of exciting and novel aircraft designs, it is therefore not surprising that Gordon saw possibilities in designing lightweight, performance versions of Austin Sevens on Austin factory chassis – a practice that was later much encouraged by Herbert Austin. Prior to this, Gordon had entered an ABC car in the Brooklands 1921 JCC 200 Mile Race, but he only became truly interested in the fast-developing small car world after a gliding accident – in which he broke an ankle – saw him turning away from flying.

In 1922, and together with his father George, Gordon England designed and patented a lightweight aircraft-style structured Seven body, with plywood box girders and panels fixed to an ash frame. The development of lightweight quality plywood had been accelerated in tandem with the demands of aircraft production during the First World War, and in the 1920s thin plywood was still regarded as something of a wonder material. New mass production applications, such as in furniture design, were still completely changing methods of manufacture. Gordon England's construction design was, in part, influenced by the limitations of the popular Weymann system for lightweight coachwork (that company being based nearby, at Putney). However, Gordon England went further, developing a structure that was less dependent on the Weymann timber frame, eventually doing away with the frame entirely, and relying merely on a plywood shell.

Gordon was so convinced about the possibilities of racing a really lightweight Austin Seven that he wrote to Sir Herbert Austin, setting out his proposals, and was invited to Longbridge as a result. The pair

February 1925 in Monserrat, Spain. Jose M Planas, in a modified GE Brooklands, ascends the hill to win the class, and a gold medal.

got on well, their first meeting lasting two hours. Sir Herbert noted, with amusement, that this eager young man was still on crutches after his latest flying accident, and yet still wished to be entrusted with a motor racing programme for Sir Herbert's new baby.

Herbert was amenable to ideas from cosmopolitan sources, and, both men having been involved with the design and production of aircraft in the First World War, they must have had much common ground for discussion and discovery between them. Again, Herbert Austin displayed his laudable and endearing trait of encouraging clearly capable younger men. This was, perhaps, in recognition that these were the survivors of a generation much depleted by the recent conflict, which had claimed Herbert's only son Vernon, and must have heavily influenced Herbert's approach to life at this time.

Gordon England greatly admired Herbert's concept of the Austin Seven and, like Austin, could see its commercial possibilities. He was, however, of the opinion that only a serious racing effort would convince the buying public that the Seven was a truly capable motoring proposition. It was this thought that mapped out Gordon England's immediate future; he gave up flying and, inspired by the possibilities of the Austin Seven, began to concentrate on his new and exciting light car project.

A racing car chassis, probably to works Boulogne specification, was despatched by train to Gordon England, who fitted it with tall – but low aerodynamic drag – single-seat bodywork. In this form, and appropriately nicknamed 'The Barrel,' Gordon England lapped Brooklands at 70.05mph (112km/h) – an astonishing speed for a brand new non-supercharged 750cc machine. This car was refitted with a much more attractive two seat fabric body, allowing much lower lines,

Garagiste J P Dingle with a modified Gordon England Brooklands. He was a regular in this car at the Surrey speed bowl in 1924. (Author collection)

and became the prototype for the Gordon England Brooklands Super Sports. Production models of this car were built from late 1923, with brushed aluminium panels affixed to the ply and ash frame.

The later Brooklands examples featured neat aluminium fairings covering the suspension elements, the passenger's seatback was staggered 9in (228mm) behind the driver's, and the spare wheel was stowed vertically in the pretty tail, concealed beneath a streamlined fairing. In 1925, Gordon England himself entered one of these cars at Le Mans, but failed to finish.

The highly desirable Brooklands had carefully-designed fixings to allow the wings, windscreen, hood, and number plates to be detached for competition use. It also boasted a variety of windscreen arrangements, as well as racing options for the engine, gearbox, and drivetrain. Some 350 of this quasi-modular type were built by the end of 1926, with Weymann partly involved in production.

The business co-operation of Gordon England and Austin was a success; the Gordon England brand was now official Austin coachwork, and Austin itself listed and advertised the Brooklands Super Sports model – 50mph (80km/h) guaranteed – at £159.00 in 1925. In December of that year, the England Fabric Saloon was launched; the very first fully-enclosed small Austin Seven family saloon car. It did, however, come with the proviso that "Messrs Gordon England take all responsibility for coachwork" (the plywood construction being prone to deterioration in the British climate, leading to an irritating number of repairs being required).

By this time, the famous Austin Seven Gordon England Cup had begun production – a sports two-seater, designed by EC Gordon England himself, and possibly the best looking and balanced design to grace an Austin Seven chassis. Each Cup body was individually made by a team of coach-builders, and there were myriad differences in the evolving detail of individual cars.

The main features were a long bonnet line and a rounded, sloping tail, covering the spare wheel that was mounted within the sloping lid. It also featured a fabric-covered body that included the engine bulkhead, leaving only the bonnet uncovered, which was finished with polished aluminium or painted.

By 1926, Gordon England had moved from Putney to Wembley Park, the site of the 1924/1925 British Empire Exhibition, where he occupied a part of the Palace of Industry building. He appropriately

A Gordon England Cup model, gently descending a slippery section with passenger assist. (Courtesy Neill Bruce)

EC Gordon England at the 750 Motor Club Beaulieu Rally in 1971. (750 Motor Club archive)

named his new updated Cup model the 'Stadium,' and his saloon the 'Wembley.' By this time, however, fabric bodies were already going out of favour, and somewhat regarded as frail and of an earlier era by younger customers.

The England Sunshine Saloon, of 1928, used Gordon England's patented 'Silent Saloon' three mounting body. This was a revelation, with the floor, dashboard, and seats mounted directly on the chassis, thus avoiding overloading the bodywork, which was cross-braced and quite rigid for the period. It even had a rudimentary heating system, venting the heat from the exhaust system through the floor, and a small boot accessed from behind the rear seat.

With the arrival of the more glamorous metal bodied Swallow Austins aimed at the same market, Gordon England had – by 1930, and still not yet 40 years old – built his last Austin Seven-based car. His subsequent career saw him managing the Vacuum Oil Company until 1935, then, until 1942, General Aircraft Ltd. He was also Chairman of the Engineering Industry Association between 1940 and 1944, and continued to head various other organisations in a truly glittering career.

THE BRITISH EMPIRE EXHIBITION AND METRO-LAND

After the trauma of the Great War, and the severe shock to the establishment of the Russian revolution, Britain sought to re-establish its position in the world. In order to reinforce the idea of Empire, and to boost trade and national morale, the immense British Empire Exhibition was announced to be taking place from April 1924, for a period of two years.

There was great national excitement. The site chosen – Wembley Park – had been the Victorian answer to the Parisian formal gardens, complete with a Wembley Tower intended to rival the

1924 British Empire Exhibition Metro-land brochure. (Author collection)

METRO-LAND

BRITISH EMPIRE EXHIBITION NUMBER

PRICE THREE-PENCE

Eiffel (but which never climbed higher than its first stage before it was demolished). By far the largest building was the strikingly-designed Wembley Stadium, which was to hold the newly introduced Football Association Cup Finals and other major athletics events. The stadium which was of Indian Mughal style – as seen with the Taj Mahal and in Lutyens' work with the recently-constructed New Delhi – combined with the Art Deco design movement, which was soon to have its apogee in the glittering Chrysler Building in New York, completed in 1930.

A Chummy involved in animal shoots in India; a somewhat shocking image now, but used back then as publicity by Austin promoting export sales. The car is fitted with a serpent bulb horn. (Austin publicity)

The Austin Chummy in its intended surroundings – a half-timbered garage saves 'the big car,' while the little one carries its cloche-hatted gamine golfers to the links. (Austin publicity)

Various pavilions, for each of the Commonwealth Countries, were constructed of reinforced concrete and given individual styling. Australia's grand colonial-style pavilion covered five and a half acres, and had a flock of 50 Merino sheep. South Africa's pavilion was styled on old Dutch gable buildings, and included a train (complete with dining car), a diamond-washing plant, and so on. There were 'Palaces' of Industry and Engineering, including a Motor Transport Section with 'representative exhibits of motor cars, motors, and accessories' – including, of course, Austin, and giving the trade delegations of the whole of the British Empire direct contact with the products of Great Britain, and vice versa.

Wembley was considered to be slightly remote from urban London, but the Metropolitan Railway line – which ran from the City of London in the east, to the newly-expanding residential areas beyond Baker Street to the west – was extended further westwards, through what were then the leafy fields of Middlesex and South Buckinghamshire. The railway company had purchased vast swathes of open countryside years before, coming before there was much thought given to creating green belts around major conurbations.

Thus was born 'Metro-land,' with the Metropolitan Railway providing the land for houses to be built upon, and the nearby railway stations to provide quick access to London and, especially, to Wembley. This, along with the publicity generated for the exhibition, meant that the visitor numbers ultimately reached the astonishing total of 20 million.

The very British garden city movement was in full swing by the 1920s, and, in contrast to the modern 'Deco' design of exhibition buildings, the new Metro-land suburbs loosely followed the principles of garden city design, and the Arts and Crafts movement inspired by John Ruskin and William Morris. Ultimately, though, the designs were watered down to become familiar 'mock Tudor' semi-detached houses. Hundreds of thousands of 'semis' were built around London and its suburbs to accommodate the newly appearing middle class – a new section of society with roots in the late Victorian period.

This expanding middle class was exactly the target customer for Herbert Austin, who was selling for the first time the idea of a planned 'lifestyle' – a proud owner of a new Austin Seven, standing in front of their new 'Tudorbethan' semi-detached in Harrow, Pinner, Uxbridge, Edgbaston, or Green Lanes, Coventry, as lovingly illustrated in the sales brochures.

In Metro-land, the emphasis was on fresh air and country living (Metro-land even gave the altitude above sea level as an incentive to purchase), but with new and fashionable facilities such as golf or tennis

The Works of the Austin Motor Company at Longbridge, 6 miles from Birmingham, cover an area of 53 acres, with 7 miles of railway sidings, and two passenger stations. Some 7,000 h.p. is generated on the spot, and runs the machines by electricity. Steel is cast in the company's own foundry. A test hill with 1 in 6 gradient adjoins the works. Employés number (1924) about 6,000

Austin

20 H.P. MODELS:	12 H.P. MODELS:
Touring Car with Spring Gaiters, Rear Wind Screen, Luggage Carrier and Clock.	**2-4 Seater Model**, with Spring Gaiters, Luggage Carrier & Clock.
Ranelagh 4-door Saloon.	**5-Seater Model**, with Spring Gaiters Rear Wind Screen, Luggage Carrier and Clock.
"**Marlborough**" three-quarter Landaulet.	"**Harley**" All-weather.
"**Mayfair**" enclosed Landaulet or Limousine.	"**Berkeley**" Single Landaulet.
	"**Windsor**" Saloon.

7 h.p. Family, Sports and Racing Models.

The AUSTIN SEVEN CAR
which has four-cylinder, water-cooled engine, three speeds, shaft drive, four-wheel brakes, electric lighting and starting. :: :: :: ::

Features common to the 12 and 20 h.p. Austin cars, respectively of 1660 and 3610 c.c. developing at 2,000 r.p.m., 20 and 25 brake horse-power, four-cylinder water-cooled engine, pump lubrication and detachable head. Magneto ignition. Single-plate clutch. Four-speed gearbox and helical bevel with road springs of exceptional length

The TOURING CAR
has a four-speed gear-box, with gate change and silent bevel drive.

SIX MONTHS FREE. For six months an Austin car bought at the Export price can be used in England, and will then be delivered, duty paid, at a chief port without extra charge. The quality of Austin cars can be judged by making use of the splendid hire services for town journeys or extended tours. Austin cars may be seen at the British Empire Exhibition, or a full range at —

479-483, OXFORD STREET, LONDON, W.1 (*Near Marble Arch*).

The
AUSTIN MOTOR CO., LTD.,
LONGBRIDGE————nr. BIRMINGHAM.

An early 1924 British Empire Exhibition Austin advertisement in the list of exhibitors, offering 7hp Family, Sports, and Racing models – Sir Herbert was a racer! (Courtesy LB Brent)

still close at hand. A small car naturally became very desirable to this style of aspirational living. With the contemporary tucked-under tail of car bodywork still resembling the bodywork of a horse-drawn coach, motor cars were visually at home in the newly built, but still quasi-historical, surroundings of half-timbered early Metro-land houses.

The Austin stand, in the Palace of Engineering of the British Empire Exhibition, displayed a commercial truck, a tractor and trailer, 20hp and 12hp motor cars, plus the great sensation of the show – the new Austin Seven.

The author's father (who, as a precision model engineer, had worked on and hand-delivered the exquisite miniature cars for the 1924 Lutyens-designed Queen Mary's Dolls House, exhibited originally in the Palace of Arts) described the crowds around the Austin stand as "simply amazing" – and the only car that they all wanted to see was the Austin Seven.

CHAPTER THREE

AUSTIN BEFORE THE SEVEN

HERBERT Austin was an extraordinary individual. A most energetic, innovative young man, Herbert demonstrated an acute sense of business acumen early on in his chosen career, which in turn gave him unshakeable confidence in his own abilities and opinions. His urge to innovate was matched by his ambitions for personal and familial wealth, but, having come from practically-minded farming stock, he had no airs or graces, and was able to relate well to his (ultimately large) workforce.

Herbert understood the potential value of his own inventions, and personally obtained the patent rights to as many as he was able, even going so far as to have little plates made, listing all the patents. These were fixed squarely in the centre of the dashboard of most factory-produced Sevens, and are very familiar to all 'Sevenists.' By the time the Seven first entered production, Herbert already had 16 patents in place, with every Seven produced – it appears – paying him one pound per patent present on the vehicle. This was at a time when the national average wage was under three pounds per week.

Herbert was born to Giles and Clara Austin on 8th November 1866, at Grange Farm, in the beautiful River Misbourne valley between

The birthplace of Herbert Austin at Little Missenden, photographed in 2017. The house was rebuilt in 1920, but Herbert would have known the barns and ancient walnut tree. (Author collection)

Little Kingshill and Little Missenden, south Buckinghamshire; to put this birthdate into context, Herbert Austin was born shortly after the end of the American Civil War. Herbert was the second of five sons, and one daughter, Albreda, who was the baby of the family. Herbert's elder brother, Ernest, died after a fall when still a teenager. His younger brothers were Walter, John, and Harry. Harry would later work with Herbert for his entire career. Herbert remembered little of his days at Grange Farm, as he was still only four years old when the family moved to Wentworth in Yorkshire.

Herbert was an extremely bright and inquisitive boy, and had an early interest in drawing, and all things mechanical. Upon leaving Rotherham Grammar School, he spent two years at Brampton Commercial College before commencing working, articled to his paternal uncle, who was an architect. He soon abandoned architecture, and instead signed up for an engineering apprenticeship with the Great Northern Railway Company. However, a chance visit by an engineer uncle – Walter Simpson, his mother's brother from Australia – fired his imagination, prompting him to go back with Walter as an engineering apprentice at a Melbourne firm. After two years, he changed employers to a nearby company that imported and installed Crossley gas engines and printing presses. At the age of 20 he moved to

work at Langlands Foundry, where he received a thorough training as a mechanic. He attended evening classes in draughtsmanship during this time, submitting an original design for a swing bridge for which he was rewarded and encouraged with a special commendation.

Christmas 1887 was a crucial celebration for Herbert, as on Boxing Day he married Helen Dron, an Australian of Scottish descent. This was just a few days after he took up what was to prove a pivotal appointment, as manager of a branch of Richard Parks & Co – precision engineer of machine components, that was currently developing machinery for Wolseley Sheep Shearing Machine Co, owned by the wealthy sheep farmer Frederick Wolseley. Herbert – a farmer's son – and Frederick struck up an immediate friendship, and improvements to the shearing equipment suggested by Herbert were soon enthusiastically taken up. Thus, the spark of entrepreneurship in Herbert was lit, which was to last him all his lifetime.

Herbert took out patents on these and other improved components in his own name. The accuracy demanded of and achieved by him enabled Herbert, by 1893, to assign all his patents that related to Wolseley's products. He undertook to sell to Wolseley all future patents that would benefit the company, in exchange for 40 fully-paid shares, with a further 40 depending on future performance.

There had been difficulties with the quality control of some sub-contractors in Australia, causing this arm of work to be transferred to England. However, this arrangement still proved unsatisfactory, so, – after six years abroad – Herbert returned to England, along with his young wife Helen, and baby daughter Irene. His initial task was a troubleshooting mission, but he was also made a manager of Wolseley's British company.

Herbert found the firm in a poor state, with thousands of defective machines having been exported. Feeling obliged, Herbert bought back the faulty machines in order to restore the company's reputation; it was a costly, but necessary, measure. In 1895, Herbert initiated the purchase of an existing factory in Birmingham, where he had complete control of operations. Here, the machines and tools required for virtually the whole manufacturing process were designed and built.

Vital lessons had been learnt during this time that Herbert was to apply to the rest of his life: that his inventive mind and practical skills could secure a good income, partly through patents; that he could organise the manufacture of complex machines; and that the more operations that were encompassed under one roof, and under his own direction, the better the product.

Once installed in his large new Wolseley factory – and in the industrial melting pot that was Birmingham – Herbert was obliged to diversify into parts for bicycles, machine tools, and, the staple activity

The 1896 Wolseley Tri-Car was the first car designed by Herbert Austin. Pictured here at Syon Park, this machine has a valid claim as the first British-built motor car. (Courtesy Ken Cooke)

since the industrial revolution, machinery for the textile industry. Herbert had, along with the rest of his generation, taken up cycling, and so was already well-versed in bicycle technology. Wisely wishing to spread risk from Wolseley's origins in the sheep and wool industry, his thoughts had turned to propelled vehicles, and he and Wolseley formed an agreement with the Northampton-based coach-builder HH Mulliner to construct innovative 'motor carriages.'

This agreement was thwarted when Mulliner went with Daimler instead (perhaps due to impatience). So, in 1895, Herbert was spurred on to begin building his own device: a three-wheeled 'Tri-Car' that may justifiably claim to be the very first British motor car. The design was influenced by a car built by the French company Léon Bollée Automobiles, based in Le Mans. Nevertheless, the Austin remained a truly original design, and was followed by an improved three-wheeler. At this point, the Wolseley directors agreed to invest in Austin's 'horseless carriage.'

Herbert Austin's valuable Birmingham connections had already contributed to parts for the Tri-Car. Frederick Simms had now set up a company in nearby Coventry to manufacture German Daimler motor cars under license, giving impetus to the exciting and burgeoning new direction for the Wolseley workforce and factory.

The Tri-Car had a flat-twin overhead camshaft, air-cooled engine with hot-tube ignition, whereas Herbert's second version – now badged as a Wolseley – had a single cylinder, water-cooled engine. In 1899, Herbert drove the new car to Rhyl and back.

His third design was a four-wheeled Wolseley Voiturette. Built in 1899, it used a channel section steel frame, and established design features for many subsequent cars. With Herbert Austin driving, the Voiturette competed in the Auto Club of Great Britain Thousand Mile Trial in 1900, winning the *Daily Mail* first prize in class, as well as a silver medal from the Club, and establishing Wolseley as a serious manufacturer, and Herbert Austin as a leading innovator.

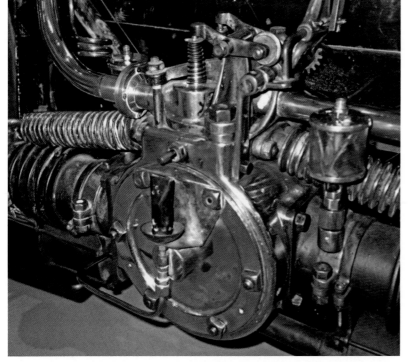

The first engine designed by Herbert Austin – a horizontal twin with overhead camshaft – for the 1895 Wolseley Tri-Car. (Courtesy Ken Cooke)

Vickers director, Sir Hiram Maxim, had already been exchanging letters with Herbert Austin on aeronautical engineering, and, impressed with Herbert's engineering skills, financed a new company. The Wolseley Tool and Motor Car Co Ltd was placed under Herbert's management, and installed into a new factory. Displaying what had now become a personality trait, Herbert quickly moved on to this new company after the original directors of Wolseley's showed reluctance to invest in this area. Austin felt that his own experimental and practical efforts with motor cars, on behalf of the original company, had not been sufficiently acknowledged and rewarded.

The Wolseley car company grew rapidly, and a factory racing team was formed to promote its products. This included an advanced five-speed mid-engined flat-four Grand Prix Beetle design, which ran in the 1904 Gordon Bennett Cup. Apart from Herbert Austin, the illustrious clique of other Wolseley Grand Prix team drivers included: Girling, later famous for braking systems; Bianchi, who later built cars in Italy; and the Hon CS Rolls, later to form Rolls-Royce. During this period, Wolseley supplied some two-cylinder cars to the British Army, which were experimentally fitted with a Maxim machine gun – an invention that was, within a decade, to take thousands of young lives, and wreck millions more.

Vickers, at this time, also acquired JD Siddeley Motor Company, with Siddeley being made sales director of Wolseley. Herbert Austin, however, had serious disagreements with Siddeley over basic engine configuration, among other matters. In a very short time, he decided that – confident that he could secure backing – now was the time to strike out as a car manufacturer on his own. By this time it was 1905, and Herbert Austin was still only 29 years old, with six of his adult years spent in fairly rugged circumstances on the other side of the globe.

Upon making his intentions known, Austin found early financial supporters in Charles Kayser and his son Frank, of the Kayser, Ellison and Co steel company, and the Du Cros family, who had extensive business in tyres, bicycles, and engineering. Herbert quickly found an empty, but recently constructed, factory building previously housing a print company. The building was close to the village of Longbridge near Birmingham, in open countryside, but with superb transport facilities, with a railway and main road running alongside the site.

The ever-ambitious Herbert noted that there was considerable scope for future expansion. By the time that he resigned from Wolseley, he had already designed his first new car, assisted by two other ex-Wolseley men – AJW Hancock and AV Davidge – and the Austin Motor Co. Ltd was officially founded in December 1905.

It had been Herbert's original intention to produce three cars every two weeks, at a net selling price of £200, giving a total of just over £300

In 1906, Herbert Austin – in bowler hat and waistcoat – drives the very first Austin car from the original converted print works. The car is a four-cylinder model, rated at 25/30 horsepower. (Austin publicity)

per week. This would cover the expenses of employing 32 mechanics, 42 assistants, and perhaps 15 men in management, design, store keeping and administration, plus of course materials.

The first car produced was the Austin 25/30 Endcliffe, which ran in 1905 and had four separate vertical cylinders and twin camshafts of a clever modular design, allowing Herbert to build engines with one, two, three, four and six cylinders, using common shared parts. Drawings of the car were displayed at the 1905 Crystal Palace Motor Car Show, where orders were taken.

The car range prophetically included a 7hp model, as well as 18/24hp, 40hp, and 60hp versions with various bodies. A Longbridge Limousine chassis was displayed at Olympia, and Gladiator cars were built for Du Cros. Austin engines were produced for marine, industrial, and even submarine purposes. Difficulties with carriage builders – particularly with respect to accuracy of dimensions – reinforced Herbert's view that he should bring as many operations as possible under one roof.

Oscar Thompson entered one of these new cars in the very first race on Locke King's new banked wonder track at Brooklands, in early 1908. This car, named 'Pobble,' ultimately lapped the course at some 90mph (145km/h). The same car and driver went on to take the fastest time of the day at Shelsley Walsh in 1910. A team of four 100hp racing Austins competed at the 1908 French Grand Prix, and the trophies it won were displayed back at the works for all to enjoy.

Herbert believed that racing improved the 'breed,' and assisted in publicity and sales, in addition to the many motor trade exhibitions that blossomed during this Edwardian era. He was careful, however, to keep a firm hold on the expenses of both activities. Nevertheless, in 1908, he shipped a power boat (named *Irene*, after his eldest daughter) all the way to Melbourne, Australia, where it duly won the Brook Trophy. The boat was re-engined in 1910, with an overhead camshaft, all-aluminium 200hp four, which – amazingly – featured positively-closing desmodromic valve gear. Herbert Austin piloted this boat himself, becoming the World Water Speed Record holder on Southampton Water.

Another example of Austin's quite remarkable early design ability was a high-speed engine, for use where corrosion damage from salt water was a potential problem. This problem was largely solved by the use of a special alloy, easily recognised by its pale green colour. This alloy was used in a 1910 V12 engine, with twin overhead camshafts, of 380bhp, and with iron cylinder liners, twin carburettors, and twin magneto ignition. It was installed in a newly-designed boat named *Irene II*, with which Herbert once again raised the World Water Speed Record in 1911. Tragically, this pioneering, and very special, engine was scrapped shortly after Herbert Austin passed away, some 30 years later.

The 100hp Austin Grand Prix car of 1908. John Miles tried this car on a test track in recent times, and found its handling very good. (Courtesy Ken Cooke)

The Austin Team at the 1908 French Grand Prix, with its 10-litre, 6-cylinder giants. Drivers were Moore-Brabazon (later Lord Brabazon), Warwick-Wright, and Resta. (Austin publicity)

One of Herbert Austin's World Record-breaking boats – *Irene* was named after his vivacious daughter, and won the 1908 Brook Trophy in Australia. (Courtesy Ken Cooke)

Another record boat, owned by the Canadian Sir Edgar McKay and aptly named *Maple Leaf III*, was built largely by Austin. This, however, had two 10.5-litre engines of similar design, but by different manufacturers; this was not a successful venture. However, the following year – 1912 – saw SE Saunders of Cowes (later to become Saunders-Roe, of flying boat fame) commissioned by McKay to build *Maple Leaf IV*. This was to be powered by two newly-designed Austin 12-litre engines, each 400hp, and 12 cylinders. After testing on the Solent by Sir Thomas Sopwith, the new vessel took the British International Boat Trophy in both 1912 and 1913.

By 1913, Herbert Austin had designed a radical commercial truck that would allow low-loading by way of a semi-space frame structure, and two separate propeller shafts – each powering a rear wheel, and so eliminating the imposition of a rear axle across the rear of the low floor. Also in 1913, Austin designed a novel twin-turret armoured car that was supplied directly to Russia, along with some armoured car chassis to be bodied by the Putilov Company in St Petersburg, Russia. Some 60 of these were modified to fit Kégresse half-tracks, with diagonally placed twin machine gun turrets. Powered by a 50hp engine, these first Austin armoured cars had a top speed of 37mph (55km/h), with conventional steering. Later versions also had novel rear-wheel steering, via a drum and cable arrangement, which slightly pivoted the rear axle and gave crab-like forward progress. Many of these armoured cars ended up in the hands of Russian revolutionaries,

and so six preserved examples of the twin-turret Austin armoured cars still parade in Red Square on each May Day.

The advent of the Great War saw Austin accept government orders for a whole range of war material, from millions of artillery shells to a variety of aircraft. Prime Minister Lloyd George ultimately recognised Herbert Austin's enormous contribution to the war effort, awarding him with a knighthood. The Belgian Order of Leopold the Second was also bestowed upon him by the equally-grateful foreign nation.

The cessation of hostilities left Austin with a hugely expanded factory, with its own railway station, power station, and foundry, and a large number of employees, now experts at aircraft construction, left with little use for their skills. Herbert Austin's team therefore took the radical step of marketing a simple light aircraft, called the Austin Whippet. This neat little Anzani-powered single-seater biplane was designed by John Kenworthy and Dr Harold Roxbee Cox, and had folding wings so that it could fit into a garage, as well as fairly large diameter wheels, so that it could be towed behind a car to the flying field – all at a cost of £275.

Several other aircraft followed: the twin-seater Austin Greyhound, costing £500 and powered by an ABC Dragonfly radial engine; the in-line Beardmore-powered Austin Kestrel; the immensely agile Austin Ball Scout; and the Austin Osprey triplane, powered by the superb WO Bentley-designed BR2, nine-cylinder rotary engine. All of these were constructed at Longbridge, along with other power units such as the 460hp V12 Austin roller bearing aero engines, designed by the Swiss Jules Haefeli.

After the war, Sir Herbert decided on a single model car policy, influenced by the success of Henry Ford's Model T, which provided a base for various bodies. Herbert's answer to the Ford was the 3.6-litre Austin Twenty, intended – like the Model T – to have international appeal. The Twenty had a good design, and was well made, offering advanced styling and features, such as an enclosed spare wheel, and a hood that became fully-concealed when not in use.

Arthur Waite soon began racing a black-painted Twenty, nicknamed 'Black Maria,' at Brooklands, and gained useful publicity. The Twenty chassis was also fitted with sports, landaulette, limousine, and tourer bodywork, plus an ingenious five-seater coupé with folding head, fully winding glass windows and again the enclosed spare wheel. The Twenty car engine was also used to power a tractor and a two-ton truck, while its chassis was the base for a Sizaire-Berwick luxury car, with Rolls-Royce-like bodywork.

To take advantage of spare factory and worker resources, and with the rapid expansion of electrical power replacing gas, a subsidiary company was established at Rugby under the name Austin Lite. This company was to manufacture complete electric lighting sets for domestic houses

The Austin Whippet light biplane, with folding wings, that Sir Herbert Austin hoped would be the flying version of his Seven. (Courtesy Ken Cooke)

end of the Second World War, and became familiar as the archetypal London taxi for many decades. A number of Sizaire-Berwick 13/26 models were also produced, using the Austin Twelve chassis. Seeing an increased demand for taxis, Herbert Austin designed his own version of the advanced Rumpler Tropfenwagen-type, rear radial-engined aerodynamic cars that had been imported and tested at Longbridge. Herbert's car featured a rear engine, front gearbox, front-wheel drive, and central steering, but, in the end, was not adopted for production.

Herbert continued to express great flexibility and fluidity of design. Still in the early 1920s, and encouraged by Arthur Waite, Herbert built a Land Speed Record car, using one of his beautiful V12 overhead camshaft marine engines, in what was a low-slung version of the 1913 twin-drive truck chassis. This was, again, ultimately abandoned, as financial pressure mounted for the Austin company.

By this time, Sir Herbert Austin had demonstrated not only his considerable business acumen, but also his instinctive design abilities, including a remarkable breadth of vision that was not always shared by his fellow company directors. He decided that the time was right for a proper small car; one to supersede the then-popular motorcycle and sidecar, but kept at a similar cost. Before he could convince doubting fellow directors of the merits of this proposal, however, he would have to prove his confidence in this plan by making his new 'baby' as his own personal project.

of all sizes, and specialised lighthouse units: the change from gas to electrical lighting was very big business indeed in the 1920s.

Unfortunately, on the car production side, the government introduced an annual car taxation formula. Based mainly on the bore size of the engine cylinders, this led indirectly to the development of slightly idiosyncratic, long-stroke engines in Britain. These engines were fairly unsuitable for export to other countries, where there was no skewing of such a fundamental engine design feature. As a result, the policy to produce only the Twenty at Austin was brought into sharp focus, and seen as a limiting factor for the future fortunes of the company.

A smaller Austin Twelve was therefore introduced in 1921, and was a considerable success. The car remained in production through to the

CHAPTER FOUR

LONGBRIDGE

HERBERT Austin had found an empty print works of fairly recent construction at Longbridge, near Rubery. It was capable of housing up to about 750 employees, and was already equipped with engines and generators, boilers, and pipework for power, lighting, and heating purposes, and sprinklers with a water supply. It was capable of being used for making motor cars within just a month or so of initial acquisition, in November 1905. The building promised good communication, room for expansion, and an unpolluted atmosphere considered essential for high quality varnish and paint finishes. Herbert's famous office was soon established on-site, which he would occupy for the next 35 years.

The first year of operations, 1906, resulted in 120 cars being built by 270 workers. 147 cars were built in 1907, involving about 400 workers, and this rose to 1000 cars in 1912 with around 1500 workmen. This rose again to 1500 cars a year, and a workforce of 2300, by the outbreak of the Great War. Austin cars very quickly gained great success, both at home and abroad – chiefly, but not solely, because of their remarkable reliability.

The fairly recently constructed, but redundant, print works at Longbridge was acquired by Herbert Austin in 1905, for the purpose of building motor cars. (Austin publicity)

Longbridge body shop, with rows of 1933 Box Saloons, and two van bodies on the right. (Austin publicity)

When the resources of the factory were turned over to the production of war material, in October 1914, there was intense pressure to organise on an immediately greater scale; the figures for workers and production almost defy belief. The private Austin Company was sold to the new publicly-listed Austin Motor Company Ltd in 1914, and early the next year Austin received instructions from the War Office to lay down and equip large workshops for the manufacture of artillery shells. This resulted in the north and west works being added

AUSTIN VILLAGE

In 1917, Herbert Austin built a village at Turves Green by importing 200 cedar prefabricated bungalows from the Alladin Co of Bay City, Michigan, USA. Sufficient numbers of these kits survived the attention of German U-boats in the North Atlantic, and were erected in blocks with 25 conventional brick-built larger houses at intervals, acting as fire breaks. Each house had three bedrooms, coke-fired central heating, a gas cooker and boiler, sink drainer and bath. They were considered fairly upmarket at the time, and laid out around roads on garden city principles, in the shape of a large horseshoe.

The garden village (later to become garden city) movement had gathered momentum at the beginning of the century, following earlier examples by socially-aware Victorian industrialists at Saltaire, Port Sunlight, and Rowntree's New Earswick. At nearby Bournville, the strongly socially-minded Cadbury brothers – who were well known to Herbert Austin – had created pleasant living conditions for workers, providing not only housing but complete community facilities.

Two children's shelters were therefore built in the streets of the Austin Village, and old farm buildings were incorporated as a village hall and clubroom. Two churches, one since demolished, also helped the village to not only provide accommodation for 1400 workers, but to also create an 'Austin' community. The bungalows themselves were initially rented out to seven workers each, with 12 workers occupying each of the larger houses, and with whole families taking over after the Great War.

The Austin Village is now a conservation area, and is surrounded by more conventional housing.

in 1916 and 1917. Large shops were also created for the manufacture of aeroplanes and aeroplane engines, lorries and armoured cars, and electric lighting sets in the new south works. A fully-equipped airfield was also laid out on land alongside. A new power station was built, as was several miles of railway sidings to accommodate materials coming in, and goods going out. A railway station was also constructed for the several thousand munitions workers.

As the Great War began, Austin employed perhaps 2000 people. When hostilities ceased, just four years later, the company employed a notable total of more than 22,000 workers, of all types and skills, spread over 220 acres of works buildings. 1906, the first year of trading, saw a turnover of £85,000. By 1918, this had increased to an astonishing £9.5m, including £5.5m worth of aircraft.

The Longbridge Factory was producing 250 cars each day by the mid-1930s. (Austin publicity)

By 1919, therefore, Longbridge had become a vast factory complex of up-to-date buildings; it was well serviced, and had a highly skilled workforce available nearby. After all, it was created in an industrial area close to Birmingham, Coventry, and other Midlands cities, housing a network of every type of mechanical and technical expertise (but especially strong in bicycles, motor cycles, cars, trucks and aircraft). It was under these circumstances that Herbert Austin had to re-launch his peacetime business.

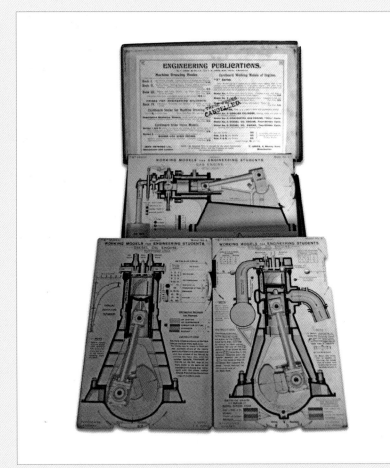

1913 Jones *Cardboard Working Models with Full Explanatory Notes*. (Author collection/Courtesy Nick Salmon)

TEACHING FIRST PRINCIPLES, JONES CARD WORKING MODEL ENGINES

At the end of the Victorian period, and prior to the Great War, there was considerable freedom of thought regarding powering vehicles and basic engine types and propellants – steam, gas, diesel oil, and 'petroleum spirit.' Engineering students, including early Austin apprentices, were taught using movable tinted card working models of sectional engines. The accompanying – rather Victorian-looking – examples by Jones of Manchester date from 1913, and originally belonged to the author's grandfather in his teaching days. They illustrate steam and gas engines, and two-stroke and four-stroke Otto-cycle engines.

Slow rotation of the exposed card disc sections, to correspond to rotating cranks and moving pistons, or to view valve opening cycles, gave explanation to each phase or period. The results were colour-coded, allowing the student to check the accuracy of his understanding.

This was cutting-edge engineering tuition for young men who might expect to work around the globe. The notes tellingly include possible locally-available fuels for the diesel engine, "introduced in 1897," as any "cheap viscous oil, lignite tar oil, fish oils, heavy petroleum residue, creosote and bitumen oil." Experiments had even included finely-sintered coal dust!

Common usage in the Great War reduced generally available motor fuels to just two types of engine propulsion: graded petrol and diesel oil. The first few UK roadside petrol pumps were not in use until 1921, however, when Herbert Austin first started thinking seriously about his little people's car.

Welfare of the workers was a high priority, and the complex featured well-equipped mess rooms, where workers took their mid-day meals, as well as recreation rooms, and technical and general libraries.

The Austin Seven was to be constructed in larger numbers than previous models, so Herbert Austin decided upon implementing 'continuous flow' production – the logical nature of which had impressed Herbert on his visits to Ford in the United States. To achieve this, internal handling and transport from his spread-out – but comprehensive – factory was essential. With each grouping of manufacturing shops acting more or less as factories on their own, the products emerging from each were then passed on for final assembly of the car on the 'production line' of the erecting shops. Continuity was assured by the superintendents of each shop being aware of the number of units required. Not every worker was impressed by this new way of working, of course, and it exposed the rift between the craftsman, who was responsible for his own work, and the production workers, who often seemed to be merely a tiny cog in a great machine. Inevitably, disputes became a common occurrence in factory life.

By the late 1920s, and in addition to goods delivered by road, no less than eight goods trains delivered materials daily. With the policy of making as many of the cars as possible in-house, there was a considerable amount of very heavy industry involved: foundries for

The heavy press shop at Longbridge, here punching out Ruby rear body panels, incorporating the spare wheel well all in one piece, as seen to the right. (Austin publicity)

SELECTIVE ASSEMBLY

'Selective assembly' is the process by which the best and most compatible components are assembled from those components available, in order to give the best end product.

Take the example of a machined piston ring, in a machined groove, in a machined piston, in a machined cylinder. It is entirely possible that the plus or minus tolerances in the machining of each separate element could happen to conspire together, giving a less than satisfactory fit when all the machined parts are put together as a single assembly. In a critical element like a piston and its rings, such variance could be the difference between a smooth-running, powerful engine, or a clattering, smoking, and rejected heap of metal. Selective Assembly requires the constant measuring and recording of the differences between the dimensions as designed, and those of the actual component prior to assembly. Such differences are frequently critical to half a thousandth of an inch.

In the example of the piston ring, measurements must be taken of: the position of the cylinder in the block, the bore of the cylinder, the diameter of the piston, the position of the gudgeon pin, the position of the top of the piston ring groove, the position of the bottom of the piston ring groove, and so on. There are at least 25 dimensions, each of which has to be known. It is then up to the expert fitter to assemble the engine to satisfactory standards, from the selection of components available to him.

Mass production techniques, involving more and more precise machining dimensions, were developed during the production life of the Austin Seven. Austin had, in any case, always used the best materials and the highest quality machine and measuring tools available, with any re-measuring adjusted to suit. Nevertheless, any engines, gearboxes, and rear axles that remained stubbornly noisy continued to be rejected upon testing. Some components, such as pairs of camshaft timing gears, had their machining tolerance 'identity' marked on until the end of production, 1939.

Selective assembly allowed Austin to maintain a consistently high build quality for his cars, with the benefits of smoother running and greater reliability than the majority of his competitors. Not only did this enhance the reputation of Austin as a manufacturer, but failures and claims in service were rare. Brand loyalty was consequentially high among customers, resulting in continued sales of products and guaranteed employment for Austin workers.

castings; a heavy press shop, with a huge 500-ton Bliss press, amongst others; light press shops making wings, scuttles, fuel tanks and body panels; a forging Shop, with noisy drop hammers making objects that ranged from a tiny autovac strap end, up to a 150lb (75kg) Austin Twenty flywheel; and a large heat treatment and hardening shop, using the latest techniques in metallurgy.

The machining shops featured rows of lathes and milling machines, mostly overhead belt driven; hydraulic tests were performed for blocks and heads; crankshafts were machined and balanced; and all was organised to flow towards intermediate measuring, testing and assembly. Completed assemblies were then tested, with rows of engines being tested on brakes, and gearboxes and rear axles, to ensure quiet

and cool running before reaching the general assembly 'tramway' lines. Once there, they were incorporated in the chassis "… at exactly the place and time, and at the proper interval of time, to ensure that the work of erection is neither hurried or delayed," as described in an imagined trip to the factory in Austin's publication *The Story of Longbridge*.

By the early 1930s, very little wood remained in the construction of the car bodies; production methods demanded greater precision in dimensions, and any leeway left for correction by the skilled coach-builders of the 1920s was long gone. Moreover, it was apparent that the finished product of the 1930s was of a generally higher standard than that of the preceding decade, and many previously skilfully crafted items were replaced by superior – and inherently cheaper – mass produced elements.

THE AUSTIN APPRENTICESHIP SCHEME

Herbert Austin was an enthusiastic advocate of progress, and the advancement of the individual worker, having himself been encouraged as a young man to embark on an adventurous and ambitious career path, after serving an engineering apprenticeship.

He had set up a factory apprenticeship scheme at Longbridge prior to the Great War, and as the company produced more of its cars in-house than many competitors, there was a whole range of skills to be learnt at the Longbridge works. An Austin Apprenticeship was thus highly sought after.

Unusually, the Austin scheme did not demand a premium payment by the parents of the potential apprentice, thereby opening up opportunities for boys from more ordinary backgrounds. Dependent

on the level of education already achieved, and the age of the applicant, the apprenticeship lasted four or five years.

As encouragement, and to reflect increasing skills, a bonus payment scheme was set up, with each individual monitored and reported upon as to their suitability or inclination towards particular departments. The development of the individual was thereby positively encouraged.

Day releases, for study and evening classes, were on offer from the Central Technical College, and from other technical colleges, paid for by Austin. Apprentices were started a wage of five shillings (25 pence) per week, with yearly incremental rises.

It was a strict regime, with a three month probationary period, and accommodation in a small hostel, set up with basic living amenities, as well as provided sports and social facilities. Approximately 250 apprentices were going through the system at any one time, and those who completed the scheme were actively sought after throughout the British Empire, and wherever Austin motor cars were sold; the long-term vision of this arrangement reinforced the close relationship between overseas dealers and the factory.

The Austin Apprenticeship was regarded something of an exemplar – so much so that the well-supported Austin Ex-Apprentices Association was set up, continuing to hold an annual dinner and other events to this day.

Architect's rendering of Nazareth House – the purpose-built Austin Engineering College for apprentices in the early days of Austin, erected in 1910. (Austin publicity)

Whilst most of the heavier factory tasks were only performed by men in peacetime, the skilled upholstery, carpet, and trimmings departments were the domain of women workers. Again, as described in *The Story of Longbridge*, these included, with the new popularity of saloon bodies, "ingenious sewing machines that stitch bands on to the fabric that lines the roof, in such a way that no seam is visible when the material is attached in position."

As the production of the Seven dwindled to a trickle in 1939, Longbridge once again re-invented itself, in order to produce the mechanical means to wage war. The company started production of 10hp Austin Utilities (nicknamed the famous 'Tillies'), K2 Ambulances, four- and six-wheel drive trucks, and militarised 8hp Tourers.

Aircraft production started in a shadow factory, with the Fairey Battle (a prewar multi-role single-engine bomber which was soon found wanting), as well as fabric and aluminium Hurricane fighters, which were far cheaper to build and repair than the all-metal Spitfires. Also built were Short Stirling heavy bombers and MkIII Lancasters, whilst Bristol radial aircraft engines were constructed in the three miles of tunnels that had been formed under the factory. Also in these tunnels were many of the works competition cars, being stored during the war to protect them from air raids.

Post World War Two, Longbridge production re-commenced under the banner 'Austin of England.'

SEVEN HORSEPOWER

There were hundreds of thousands of horses in the service of man in the late 19th century, and they all needed stabling, feeding, grooming, and shoeing. Horses also needed a lot of clearing up after they had passed by; the quantity of horse droppings shovelled up from the streets of Edwardian London each day would cover several football fields, and constituted a significant and widespread public health issue.

On the other hand, the amount of work that a single horse could perform in a day meant that – until the invention of the steam engine, followed by the internal combustion engine – there was no alternative to equine power. Given the prominence of this workforce at the time, it was perhaps inevitable that the term 'horsepower' appeared, to describe the effective power of these two new mechanical inventions; of course, it remains in everyday language more than a century later. When engine power is tested on a 'brake' – which provides a resistance against which the running engine has to work – the resistance measured is termed 'brake horse power.'

When the motor car was invented and developed as a product, the government of the day decided that the car user should pay a tax relative to the size – and, by implication, power – of the vehicle. In 1910, the Royal Automobile Club concocted a viable formula for calculating such a tax rating for car engines, but only included the total piston surface area of the cylinder bores in its determinations, ignoring the stroke of the crankshaft.

For marketing and protectionist purposes, British manufacturers like Austin were therefore commercially pressured into developing engines with smaller cylinder bores, combined with longer crankshaft strokes. This way, each engine was calculated to sit advantageously into the tax brackets labelled as seven, eight, nine, ten – and so on – horsepower engines. These titles became synonymous with manufacturers' claimed 'horsepower,' regardless of what the actual brake horse power output of their products might be.

When introduced, the RAC formula was fairly close to the reality of the power output. However, with the described methods developing throughout the 1920s, these figures became progressively further away from being relevant. Nevertheless, the horsepower rating system did not evolve with the progress of design, and was stuck with its original formula. As an example, by 1924 the Austin Seven engine, even with its fairly long stroke, produced 10.5bhp – a figure 50 per cent higher than its RAC horsepower rating, which worked out as being below an eight, and was therefore taxed as a seven.

At the time the Austin Seven was designed, the decision to use aluminium pistons, rather than cast iron, can be considered to be forward thinking and quite bold. Long piston strokes imply high piston speeds, as the piston has to move further in the cylinder to match the revolution of the crankshaft. Lighter reciprocating loads from using aluminium assisted in reducing the loads on the connecting rods and big end bearings – particularly important when subjected to the higher revs for competition work.

The British tax rating system effectively stifled design-led progress of production car engines, and British manufacturers continued to produce slow-revving, long stroke, high torque, and modest power engines as a matter of course. Little impetus existed, prior to World War Two, to change to the much more efficient overhead valve engines. These required larger diameter bores to accommodate the overhead valves, and would have inevitably moved the engines up the taxation scale.

CHAPTER FIVE

RAPID DEVELOPMENT AND THE ROARING TWENTIES

WITH EC Gordon England overseeing his own development of the competition Seven, in parallel to the factory, advances made under his eye were mutually beneficial to the rest of the company. With this set up, two lightweight fabric-bodied works racers were built, which, by August 1923, were capable of lapping the banked Brooklands track at 75mph (120km/h). This was no mean feat, the track being continually flat out for a small car, as indeed had been its original purpose – testing the competition performance of the car, rather than the ability of the driver.

There were soon three works competition sevens, with enough small differences between them to subsequently allow historical identification; all of them, however, were equipped with twin Cox Atmos carburettors, a three branch exhaust manifold, high lift cams, and slightly increased compression ratios, and were capable of

Sir Herbert proudly displays his race team at Boulogne Speed Week, August 1923. Waite/Depper are in OK 7095 'Dingo,' Kings/Brokas in OK 8945 'Opossum,' and Cutler/Hall in OL 166 'Boomer.' (Austin publicity)

sustained running at 5000rpm. All three cars were prepared for the Boulogne Motor Week in September where, racing on public roads, unfortunately two retired through lubrication troubles, and the third crashed in an accident. This failure at Boulogne led Sir Herbert to write a letter of explanation, published in *The Motor*, in which he stoutly defended racing as a means "to improve the breed." The lengthy letter also served as something of a manifesto, stating that – in Austin's view – if improvements were developed through participation in competitions, they likely could be incorporated into future cars sold to the public. Quite apart from the enjoyment of racing by the participants and the viewing public, such advances in vehicle design would be a very worthwhile benefit to all.

The lubrication problem experienced at Boulogne was a case in point. It was caused by the drop off in oil supply in the newly pressure-fed engines, in which the oil entered the crankshaft at the front and then had to overcome the centrifugal forces of the rotating long-stroke crankshaft. Finally, the oil had to reach the rearmost number four big end, by which time the pressure had tailed right off. Sir Herbert quickly resolved the lubrication problem, adding tubes to carry the oil circumferentially between the number one and two, and three and four crankshaft journals respectively. The tubes ultimately gave way to specially-designed crankshafts, with circular webs incorporating drilled

galleries. Further experimentation was carried out on the induction system by Gordon England and the Austin works, with special valves, valve springs and camshafts, cylinder head improvements and exhaust systems, and, on the chassis, Hartford shock absorbers.

Gordon England set new records at Brooklands in September, the most prominent being maintaining 79.62mph (128km/h) for a stretch of 5mi (8km). He returned to Brooklands in mid-October, entering the 1100cc class in the JCC 200 Mile Race, where he faced off against 12 other cars of 1100cc capacity, including three fast French Salmsons. With only half of the field left in the race by the end, England finished in second place behind Ramon Bueno's Salmson. The Austin lapped at 79mph (128km/h), and touched 85mph (139km/h) on the straight – an astonishing speed for a 'baby' 750cc car, plus driver and riding mechanic. Third place was taken by another Salmson, trailing three miles behind England.

Part of this success was due to the Seven running without a stop; the Austin finished as strongly as it had started, and was run carefully within its limits, at a pre-determined speed – though this was bumped up over the last few laps to 80mph (128km/h). Gordon England had reckoned that a consistent 75mph (120km/h) should be sufficient to finish the race 'in the money,' and so it had proved, with the Austin setting five records in the process.

These early racing successes, and the corresponding increase in public interest, paved the way for the little car to be considered a serious proposition. Many who had been faintly amused by the Austin Seven, when first introduced, soon had their minds changed by the Austin's successes, both in direct competition with other makes of car, and in sales numbers. These sales continued to climb steadily, giving the factory the confidence to establish even greater production capacity of the Seven as demand increased.

In January 1924, two rather rakish two-seaters were announced, named the Sports and the Brooklands Super Sports – the latter a Gordon England product, marketed by Austin. The Sports was available in that most striking and evocative of all Austin Seven colours, Kingfisher Blue, and featured electric starters and shock absorbers front and rear. Otherwise, however, it was built with standard production chassis and engines, any enhanced performance stemming from its lighter weight, a smaller frontal area – via a detachable windscreen top half – and spirited driving!

Each Gordon England Brooklands Super Sports, by comparison, was tested and sold with the guarantee of a 75mph (120km/h) top speed. The performance was gained from a high-compression cylinder head, high-lift camshaft, the usual modifications to valve gear and manifolding, and twin Zenith 30 HK carburettors. A 4.5:1 ratio rear axle was also offered. The attractive bodywork of the Super Sports was very narrow to reduce its frontal area. As a result, it required staggered seating, moving the passenger's shoulders behind the driver's, and to give the latter enough elbow room within the cockpit.

Other early variations on the Tourer – or the 'Chummy,' as the open Austin Seven would come to be called – included: a very attractive prototype Doctor's Coupé (which did not, however, go into production), a small delivery van, a commercial travellers car, and a small taxi with a single forward driver's seat.

Austin's management dealt with customer comments or complaints by referring the problems on to the relevant department. In this way, it was ensured that the quality of the product was improved, notably increasing the carrying capacity of the rear bodywork by extensions to the chassis, improving magneto performance when starting from cold, and reducing sticking valves. Oiling problems in the engine required revised piston rings, and the great variations in oil pressure between a

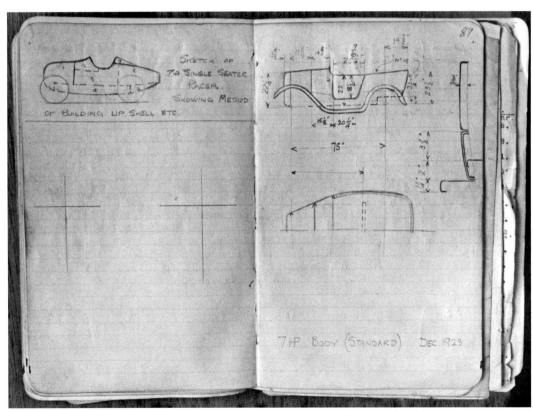

Pages from Stanley Edge's sketchbook, dated December 1923. They show detailed 7hp body dimensions, and, quite separately, "7 hp single-seater racer, showing method of building up shell, etc." (Stanley Edge archive)

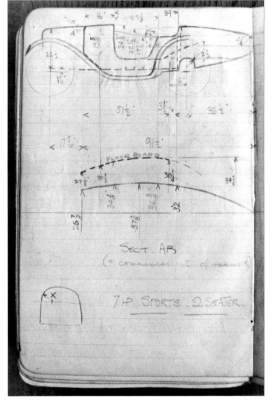

Stanley Edge sketchbook design for the "7hp Sports". (Stanley Edge archive)

cold start and normal running of the splash-fed engine were partially resolved by a projecting oil pressure indicator button, rather than a potentially misleading oil pressure gauge. Rear shock absorbers were also fitted with coil springs to avoid owners over-tightening them.

Electric starting was introduced in late 1924, and required a larger dynamo and battery. Inevitably, the minimalist original concept of the Seven started to gain a little in weight. Over-advancing the ignition –

A gazelle-like 1925 Sports. With ploughshare wings and erected hood, the model had a very jaunty and eager look. (Austin publicity)

perhaps in search of more performance – led only to rough running, as the combustion chamber characteristics did not set up the warning 'pinking' sound. This led to some early owners managing to break crankshafts, and a clutch stop had to be added to the crankcase casting to avoid clumsy drivers shearing the declutching lever taper pins of the, admittedly small, amount of clutch movement. Nevertheless, all these teething problems were responded to with swift development modifications.

Austin also started to market the Seven in rolling chassis-only form, with the radiator pre-mounted on steel 'cow horns' fixed to the chassis nose piece. Amongst the first independent coach-builders to create their own open two-seater sports bodies were Thomas Hughes and Son, of Birmingham, and Wilson Motors, of Victoria in London. These were producers of the first of a huge number of coach-built Austin Sevens, constructed mainly in the second half of the 1920s.

The reputation of the Seven had been well established by 1925, with growing waiting lists at dealers all over the country. To keep up with demand, the factory was open round the clock for parts of the working week, and a staff of 6500 worked to produce 1000 Sevens each month.

Contemporary road tests were very enthusiastic, and the car was a very agile performer by the standards of the day. This included the steering and brakes, both of which have distinctive quirks and idiosyncrasies when viewed on today's terms. The first road test, in July 1923, praised not only the liveliness and the handling, but also the attention that the Seven received from the public when seen for the first time, as a highly original design concept. The smallness of the car, combined with its excellent performance, astonished previously sceptical journalists, and was a continuing surprise to all that observed those first open road trials in public.

The handling, for a car of relatively short wheel base and narrow track, was of a far higher order than had been expected, and the road holding was considered to be very good for a car of the Seven's speed range. The suspension was reported as not given to bounce unduly over bad surfaces, and the

Paul Wood's 1925 Doctors Coupé, at Beaulieu 2016 – previously a Louis Vuitton concours winner. (Author collection)

With few purpose-built race tracks, sand racing was very popular in the 1920s. This is Southport Austin dealer Percy Stephenson on his local beach in the highly successful G E Brooklands. (Austin publicity)

Enthusiastically approaching the limits of cornering a Chummy – and a nervous moment for this driving test competitor! (Courtesy Ferret Fotographics)

springing above average for comfort. With only the driver aboard, the brand new springing was – as expected – somewhat lively, but it settled down with a passenger added, and it was reported that with a third adult the car gave an exceptionally comfortable ride. The positioning of the controls and the car's general ergonomics were also considered good, apart from, possibly, the close spacing of the brake and accelerator pedals, and the rather forward location of the gear change lever.

The restrained terminology used to describe the Seven was typical for the period, and it was clear from the initial response that Sir Herbert had a winner on his hands.

The very short clutch travel is a Seven trait that went unchanged throughout its production, and always catches out anybody who has not previously driven one of the cars. Once a driver is used to the simple technique, however, driving within the tight limits of the clutch movement becomes second nature and not at all difficult.

The steering was praised in road tests as being light and steady, and the sense of direction as accurate, which are not exactly terms one would use to describe the steering qualities of a standard Seven today, particularly on steeply cambered or bumpy roads. Steering in a straight line is influenced by the lateral 'float' of the front axle, being located by the transverse spring bolted to the chassis nose

piece, which has freely swinging shackles at each end of the spring joining the spring to the axle beam. This allows about 2in (50mm) of lateral movement, and on uneven surfaces requires that the driver make constant small adjustments to the steering wheel. Again, this is most noticeable to someone new to the Austin Seven, but entirely accepted by anyone experienced in the Seven's ways, and resolved by allowing the steering wheel to play lightly through the hands, rather than hanging on and attempting to correct every little deviation from the straight and narrow.

The quarter-elliptic rear springs of an Austin Seven also make their own contribution to the steering of the car; being fairly severely positively cambered, but with the front of the spring fixed at the chassis and the rear of the spring being fixed directly to the rear axle, the rear wheels do not spend all of their time exactly following the steered front wheels. The reason for this phenomenon is that when, for example, the Seven is being turned to the left, the body leans over towards the right-hand side. This bears down more on the right-hand spring, which, being cambered, increases in length as it flattens out under the increased load, thereby pushing the right-hand end of the axle backwards.

At the same moment, the load on the left-hand spring is reduced by the body lean, and the spring actually adopts an increasingly cambered shape, pulling the nearside of the rear axle forwards. These two actions combined, therefore, cause the axle to assist in the turning of the car; as the body leans more, the steering effort of the front wheels can be lessened, and some steering lock taken off. In fact, on a tight corner, and once a Seven has been smartly turned in, leaning over due to the in-built roll oversteer, the car may take itself round the corner with the steering wheel returned, more or less, to the 'straight ahead' position.

In a straight line on a bumpy road, therefore, the rear axle reacts to the bumps by providing little steering motions to left or right, depending on which rear wheel is moving up and which down. This, combined with the 'floating' front axle, may cause the steering to feel decidedly detached from the desired direction of the vehicle. However, after driving for just a few miles in a Seven, a novice driver, if accepting of the natural ride characteristics of the little vehicle, will soon find that steering becomes an intuitive action, requiring very little conscious input.

On Sevens that have lowered chassis, like the various sports models and post-1933 Ruby-type chassis, the rear quarter-elliptic springs have far less camber, and give better direction with less need for corrections with steering wheel movements. Very light specials, meanwhile, can all but eliminate the self-steering effect, by the use of rear springs that are more or less straight when loaded and in use.

Lacking a speedometer on the earliest cars, actual performance figures could only be described by testers in subjective terms, such as "acceleration is brisk," "hillclimbing was good," and to perform "an early gear change to maintain a high rate of engine revolutions for best results." These early test results did, however, show that overall the little car easily matched the performance of much larger contemporary cars.

The results bolstered the claims in Austin's publicity material, that the Seven could be relied upon to perform in any situation equal to established bigger cars, in higher price brackets. This was a vote of confidence in the eyes of prospective purchasers of the Seven, and a great boost to the appeal of the Seven for a wide cross-section of would-be motorists.

In an effort to describe what was, even then, a very small car, this publicity material said that under test the Seven was comfortable for two grown-ups, being "not much larger than a double bed," and "while three children or their equivalent in luggage, parcels, cricket bats, gun cases, golf clubs, or fishing tackle can be housed in the space between the adjustable front seats and the back panel of the body, and at the same time can be protected by the hood." This description in particular makes reference to the sporting activities that became increasingly popular after the Great War and through the 1920s.

There were many pressures to be faced in industrial relations at this time, not least from new working conditions and practices that formed an inevitable aspect of the expanding scale of employment demanded by mass production of goods, including, of course, motor cars. The general strike that lasted nine days – from 4th to 13th May, 1926 – had its roots in the coal industry, where a miner's wage had fallen from £6.00 to just £3.90 a week in the space of seven years. The miners were not alone, with many workers being paid less as a result of a fall in the Cost of Living Index, and the Trades Union Congress, acting on behalf of the workers, were at odds with the government. In due course, and amid genuine fears of a revolution akin to recent events in Russia, the two sides came to an agreement. This was not before, however, some ugly scenes had taken place at the gates of many industrial sites.

Continued page 56

A street in London, and a rather large guardsman tries out a Seven for size. (Author collection)

WOMEN OF THE 1920s

Across Europe and, to an extent, America, the role of women was changed forever by the Great War. The war might have demolished the optimism of the first decade of a new century – costing millions of lives, changing economies, and causing political upheaval – yet, out of the debris, a new world for women evolved at dazzling speed, with a promise of freedom that was undreamt of in an earlier age. The war had delivered voting rights to many in the United States and Europe, and, with the lure of independence via full time jobs (and careers in big cities in particular) and changes in popular culture, the social structure was completely redrawn.

In Paris, Josephine Baker, the young black exotic dancer, was the toast of the town. French beauty products, hair styles, fake tans, and thousands of what were to become recognised as Art Deco-style figures and table top lamps reflected the quite extraordinary influence of 'La Baker' – at that time the highest paid performer in the world. Also in Paris, Zelda Fitzgerald – the young wife of the novelist F Scott Fitzgerald, and akin to the female characters in his novels – promoted many different ways to live one's life, and possibilities to be explored in the future. The painter Tamara de Lempicka had fled Russia after the 1917 revolution, and began painting her stylised canvasses of very liberated women indeed; they were portrayed in adventurously luxurious surroundings, and driving themselves in motor cars. Her paintings became fashionable and distinctive works, and seemed to hold the promise of a very glamorous lifestyle, unimaginable just a decade earlier.

With the advent of free-form and improvised music, based in Black American tradition, the mid-1920s took on the title of the Jazz Age, interlinking with free movement, free dance, and a freedom of dress. The stays and corsets of Victorian times were replaced by simpler styles, with shorter skirts and far less fabric. A typical woman's dress, which in 1914 might have taken an average 20 yards of cloth, by 1926 needed only six yards of fabric. During the Great War, women working in factories had also adopted trousers for the first time. This spirit of lightness – and a reduction in over fussy design, in search of something more simple and practical – was integral with women deciding, amongst other things, to take up driving. The Austin Seven locked into this trend, partly by design, partly by fortuitous circumstances.

Many pioneer female pilots took to the air, seeking ways to express their new freedoms. Gladys de Havilland – of the famous aviation family and, later, noted to have driven an Austin Seven around the world – was one of the many female FANY (First Aid Nursing Yeomanry) ambulance drivers on the Western Front and, in 1918, had written a book on driving techniques.

The smouldering and sophisticated Tamara de Lempicka, in *Self Portrait*. She has chosen to paint herself in an Art Deco style, and at the wheel of her sports car – a far cry from the coy and submissive woman of earlier times. (Author collection)

By 1927 the number of working women had risen by 500 per cent, compared to early postwar years, and young and financially independent women opened up markets across many sectors including cosmetics and clothing, as well as smoking and mail-order. The British Rational Dress Society promoted comfortable clothing for all the new women's activities, and, with female athletes first competing in Olympic field events, buried forever the absurdities of over-elaborate formal dress. University places for girls, meanwhile, were still limited. Less than 1000 women attended all-female 'Oxbridge' colleges at the

Gladys de Havilland pauses in India to admire a camel train, on her route around the globe. (A7CA archive)

beginning of the 1920s, and women were not permitted to receive official degrees until 1921.

Led by Harmsworth's *Daily Mail*, journalism began to include more comment and opinion, rather than the simple mechanical reportage of events. From this base, tabloid-style newspapers quickly grew and fed popular culture. Widely-available popular films and radio shows arrived, where previously there had been touring theatre companies seen by a relative few. Suddenly, national celebrity was available for all to see and hear, and there was an explosion in the promotion of new lifestyle choices, and – of course – the products which went with them. Motor shows became hugely popular annual events, and along with them the promotion of motor cars in general – part of the experimental new world of the 1920s.

Amelia Earhart, Nancy Cunard, Greta Garbo, Coco Chanel, Lady Diana Cooper, Isadora Duncan, Tallulah Bankhead, Vera Brittain, the arts-driven free spirits of the bohemian Bloomsbury set, and countless others; many during this period made an individual mark on the role of women. This was not only as party-going 'flappers,' with bobbed hair and skinny clothing, but as university-educated 'bright young things', newly perceived as adventurous individuals with certain and self-fulfilled futures ahead of them. Above all, youth had gained its own identity – just the sort of person to be seen, perhaps, in their smart, new, light 'baby' Austin Seven.

A LITTLE ASSISTANCE

Autocar

A little assistance! (Author collection)

Diminutive Kay Petre, second right, is the only female racing driver in heels, yet is still dwarfed between 'Bill' Wisdom – in dark BRDC overalls – and Victoria Worsley. (Courtesy Jean-Francois Bouzanquet)

Ancienne et moderne; architect Le Corbusier's very latest 1927 Gabriel Voisin 10 CV motor car, purposely compared with his own Modernist design of the Villa at Garches, of the same year. (Author collection)

The Top Hat Saloon, here shown as a fabric-covered version, copied many details from the respected larger 12 and 20hp Austin models. This undoubtedly added to its appeal, and the popularity of the Austin Seven. (Austin publicity)

An early scoop-scuttle van displays delicate lines, and sign-writing that greatly adds to the visual appeal. (Author collection)

Herbert Austin had always carefully stated that he would carry out improvements as and when they became desirable or necessary, and this policy of constant gradual improvement to the Seven included the passing on of new developments – and a degree of novelty – to the buying public. Thus, he was able to consistently market genuinely improved models, but without the American marketing model's 'planned obsolescence' that would later dominate – particularly in post-WW2 annual motor shows, and frequently with retrograde technical features at the expense of flashy body ornamentation. Herbert Austin was not a fan of annual motor shows, feeling that they unduly influenced proper and appropriate development.

In late summer of 1926, the 6in (152mm) diameter brakes were increased to 7in (177mm), and the 26in (660mm) wheel rim diameter was reduced to 19in (482mm). This specification was retained until mid-1934, when 17in (431mm) wheels were introduced for the Art Deco-inspired low chassis Ruby Saloon. By late 1925, Gordon England had brought out the first saloon body for an Austin Seven – a fabric covered saloon on a hollow plywood box structure – and this prompted Herbert Austin to bring out his own Seven Type R Saloon design the following Easter.

Built with an aluminium skin, with a high roof to allow easy access for a public that still wore tall or elaborate hats, and "looking like a Chummy with a greenhouse on top," these first very pretty little Seven saloons have been known ever since as the 'Top Hat' model. Saloon bodies were made in increasing numbers, within a few years out-numbering the original open bodied alternatives.

The Top Hat saloon was a visually attractive car, with almost as much height of glass above the body waistline as there was solid body below; it was first, rather elegantly, referred to as the Austin Seven Coachwork Saloon. The windscreen was still split horizontally, with the top part opening as on a Chummy. The rear halves of the side windows slid forwards, for ventilation and for hand signals by the driver. The standard paintwork finish for the bodywork was black

THE BOAT TAIL

One factory-bodied Austin Seven appears to have been specifically aimed at women drivers – the 1929 Austin Seven Two-Seater, later popularly known as the Boat Tail.

There were, at this time, more than 20 different coach-builders offering specialised body styles on the Seven chassis, including the elegant Swallow with its ladies' vanity compact. Morris had also recently introduced the advanced two-seat Minor, which was not intended to be a true sports car, but did break new ground as a factory product, embodying the new concept of the attractive light tourer.

Women over the age of 21 had been given the right to vote in 1928, and these new hard-fought rights and freedoms gave rise to products that reflected women's new role in society. However, the October 1929 London Motor Show, at which the Seven Boat Tail was launched, was followed within days by the Wall Street Crash, the effects of which rippled through the industries manufacturing luxury or secondary goods.

The 1929 Boat Tail was Austin's first production two-seater since the 1925 Sports, boasting particularly good looking body styling, and a lower 'sports' profile. The car had a longer scuttle, low seat mountings, and a very pretty tail shape, the top of which was covered in fabric, the horizontal dividing waistline moulding continuing along the tops of the doors and bonnet. It also had a horizontally divided windscreen, with the top opening out; a fabric covered dashboard, with a lower rake to the steering column; and a genuinely useful boot, accessed from the removable top to the tail, or from a panel behind the seats inside the car, if the hood was folded back.

Press reports emphasised that Austin's Boat Tail was an excellent touring car without overly-sporty pretensions – perfect for the ever increasing number of women who found that an economical two-seater was ideal for their needs. Be it running up to the golf links or tennis courts, or for making calls (presumably to friends who would be pleasantly impressed by the arrival of the smart and nippy little car), the car offered a faint promotion of gentle, female snobbery – and why not? No such thoughts needed stating on paper, as the appealing Two-Seater body design spoke for itself. It remains appealing today, with a disproportionate number of surviving examples possibly reflecting the care with which they might have originally been treated by their owners.

It was a great shame that the economic climate slightly depressed this approach to quality motoring. While the Boat Tail retained the dainty lines of a vintage car, the later factory two-seater Opal APE was more multi-purpose, with rather heavier wings, a square boot, and body styling similar to the Military Tourer – an altogether more robust, masculine look.

The Boat Tail GY3507, completed in original paint colour. The red windscreen sticker denotes that it had just been driven 960 miles (1544km) by Andy and Brenda Owen, from Lands End to John O'Groats (LEJOG). (Courtesy Andy Owen)

Dire – but complete – 1932 Boat Tail found by Andy Owen. (Courtesy Andy Owen)

The pretty bodywork restored in the workshop of the late John Heath whose knowledge and skills were legendary. (Courtesy Andy Owen)

above the waistline, on the wings, and running boards. The standard range of colours were available for the bonnet and lower body sides, making for a most attractive little car. A few were later built with all-over self-coloured fabric saloon bodies.

The headlights with integral side lights were soon moved forwards, between the plated radiator surround and the front wings. However, it was pointed out by Hampshire Police that the side lights were now more than the legal maximum of 6in (152mm) from the outside limits of the bodywork. The lights were thus reverted to their previous position on the scuttle beside the windscreen pillars, then, after the police objection was legally overruled, the lights returned forward to the wings for good! Some strengthening of the frame took place at this time, to better support the rear bodywork – the saloon version of which was clearly heavier than an original open Chummy – with extra bracketry being retro-fitted free of charge by the company, in line with Herbert Austin's policies of continued development.

The van version of the Top Hat that followed is also a most delightful little vehicle. Originally as built earlier by Thomas Startin Ltd of Birmingham, it was usually supplied in primer for each individual user's livery to be painted on as required. This included the many vans in use by the Austin works, that had the familiar Austin script written on the flanks.

In late 1927, it was decided that – rather than relying on publicity from specially-built racing cars, as had been the case for the first five years – a two-seater sports car, recognisably a production works Austin Seven, should be built and marketed. The Super Sports was the result.

LIKE THE BRITISH OAK | PROVED BY TIME!

Above, right, and next eight pages: The extraordinary and innovative 1929 full colour brochure that spelled out in detail to the world the multiple benefits and lifestyle of Austin Seven ownership. (Austin publicity)

REASONS WHY

the Seven has established itself as "THE" Small Car . . . .

ITS absolute reliability as a sound engineering proposition has been definitely proved by time. This scientifically designed car was first introduced six years ago. It has since made a series of astounding performances on the road and track all over the British Empire, and on the Continent. Difficulties of bad roads and climate have been surmounted in an astonishing manner and the Seven revels in what is known as "colonial conditions."

The purchase price is remarkably low. The car is fully equipped with every essential accessory, and all front windscreens are fitted with Triplex glass as standard.

There is nothing further to buy after the initial outlay, which makes the first cost the full cost.

The Austin Seven is the cheapest car in the world to run. It gives the greatest mileage per gallon of petrol and consumes very little oil. Wear on tyres is especially light, and it is so strongly built that possible repair charges need not be considered. Because of Austin excellence in design, materials, and workmanship it is convenient in size and light in weight, making it a delight to drive and obviating parking and garage difficulties.

All Seven Days of the Week are "AUSTIN SEVEN" DAYS

The radical decision was taken to drastically improve performance of the car by supercharging the engine. After development, the Super Sports was announced in July 1928, on the back of Captain Arthur Waite's recent milestone victory in what would become known as the very first Australian Grand Prix. The bodywork was a beautiful and compact staggered-seat sports racer, with very svelte lines. It featured a subtly raised scuttle and a dropped tail that swept inwards to form a slight vertical rear line, creating a very attractive appearance.

Continued page 66

MONDAY

THAT Monday feeling—where is it if you possess an Austin Seven? When the day's duties are done this wonderful little car gives you quick and easy access to your various pursuits. If it is golf, instead of that tedious tram or bus ride and, perhaps, a long walk, the Seven takes you right to the Clubhouse, invigorated for your game. The car is always at your service to take you where you wish.

Tennis enthusiasts arrive spick and span and full of energy. In fact, you cannot fully appreciate any sport without the added pleasure of an Austin Seven.

The Fabric Saloon is exceptionally cosy in winter, yet cool in summer. The one-piece screen, opens at the bottom. In the doors the front portion of the window is lifted mechanically and the rear slides.

This unique opening of the windows controls the air circulation without draught.

THE CAR FOR PLEASURE

FABRIC SALOON. Wide doors make access easy to front and rear seats. Single piece Triplex glass front screen, which opens from the bottom. Ample room for two adults and two children. Perfect window control for ventilation and signalling. *Choice of Austin Colours.* " De Luxe". models with Triplex glass to all windows, £151.

PRICE AT WORKS
£140

TUESDAY

DURING that busy day in the City you realise the remarkable qualities of the Seven. Its acceleration, so very rapid, enables you to get away, in and out of the traffic, in safety and without difficulty. With the large brake drums on each wheel, it is possible to stop the car quickly when required without risk of skidding.

The Seven responds to the lightest touch. In rain the durable and waterproof hood, and the specially designed side-curtains can all be raised and fixed in a few seconds, ensuring complete weather protection; while the automatic windscreen wiper gives clear vision. To drive all day without fatigue, is possible because of the adjustable driving seat and well sprung cushions.

For commercial and professional men what car is so efficient for their business calls? The confidence they can place in its reliability assures them the peace of mind that is so essential for a day's work in the City.

A CAR THAT YOU CAN RELY ON

TOURING CAR with hood erected and side screens in position. Side screens may be opened half way. Two convenient recesses in dash for gloves and other small parcels. Ample accommodation under front and rear seats for tools, etc.

PRICE AT WORKS
£130

WEDNESDAY

MARKET day in the neighbouring town, where shopping is economical, is readily accessible to the Austin Seven owner. There is the additional advantage of bringing your purchases away with you in the ample space provided behind the front seats.

What has so often been a tiresome duty becomes a pleasure, and at the same time it gives you the opportunity of making the outing a happy one for the children.

From the lady's point of view there is no doubt that this is the ideal car. It needs so little effort to control; the steering is quickly responsive, the clutch is light, and the gears are easy to operate, having a gate change with a safety catch on the reverse.

On the open road it satisfies all "Milady's" desires for speed combined with complete safety. For visiting friends, on long trips or short, and the hundred-and-one other occasions when a lady needs a car.

THE SEVEN HAS NO SUPERIOR

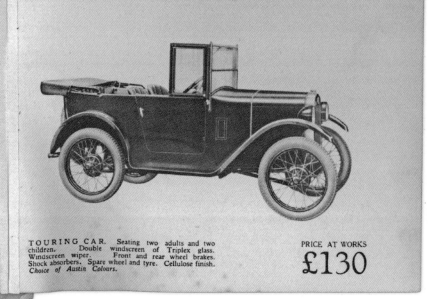

TOURING CAR. Seating two adults and two children. Double windscreen of Triplex glass. Windscreen wiper. Front and rear wheel brakes. Shock absorbers. Spare wheel and tyre. Cellulose finish. Choice of Austin Colours.

PRICE AT WORKS
£130

THURSDAY

TO those who live inland and visit the coast at holiday times, the Seven brings many extra seaside days and week-ends within easy reach. There are many who are conscious of a strange craving which only the sight and smell of salt water can satisfy. When by the sea, the most lovely coves and best bathing places become accessible and the convenient size and lightness of the car enables you to drive right down on to the sands.

The pleasure of travelling by road in your own car, is increased by the thought that the cost is less than a penny for each mile you pass. To go by train or other means would cost you more.

This delightful car can be obtained in various colours, with a cellulose finish which is durable and easy to clean. The new nickel radiator also greatly enhances its appearance.

TRULY A CAR TO BE PROUD OF

METAL SALOON. Wide doors make access easy to front and back seats. Single piece Triplex glass front screen which opens from the bottom. Ample room for two adults and two children. Supplied in dual colours. Cellulose finished. Perfect window control for signalling and ventilation. The "vizor" which gives protection against glare is easily detached when not required.

PRICE AT WORKS
£140

Choice of Austin Colours.   *" De Luxe "* models with Triplex glass to all windows.   £151

FRIDAY

THE pleasure of the theatre or dance, so often marred by having to rely on a public conveyance, is ensured by the possession of an Austin Seven, which takes you from door to door in warmth and comfort. The car takes you there to time, and the vagaries of the weather can be ignored.

Time has proved its excellence as an auxiliary car—there are many occasions when the Seven can be used much more economically than the big car. It is instantly ready for the smallest journey.

Driving by night may be disliked, but it is simplified with the Seven, the efficient headlights being mounted well forward, giving a clear vision of the road ahead. There is also a dimmer switch which enables you to leave the car with every confidence when parking.

The horn switch in the centre of the steering wheel is convenient to the hand for instantaneous warning to be given. All the controls are within easy reach.

THE IDEAL CAR

THE COUPE.   The body is metal built as far as the waist line, with fabric head.   Triplex glass front screen.   Exceptionally wide doors. Attractively upholstered and fully equipped.   Ventilators in scuttle. An ideal two seater car.   *Choice of Austin Colours.* "De Luxe" models with Triplex glass to all windows,   £151

PRICE AT WORKS

£140

SATURDAY

THE family man's day. Home early he finds his wife and youngsters have fixed things up ready for that little outing into the country. While the picnic basket is being packed, a little attention might be given to the car. The oil level in the engine can be examined by means of a dipper rod, and fresh oil added if necessary. The chassis lubricators can be given a charge with the grease gun ; it only takes a few minutes.

Soon the Seven is carrying the happy party towards the chosen spot. The ample power of the engine, together with the correct gear ratios make light work of the steepest hills.

Such pleasant hours can be yours if you have an Austin Seven, and so enjoy the freedom of the road. After a lovely day, night brings a healthy invigorated return. The car is run into its little garage, so cheaply erected in the garden, "and so to bed."

A CAR FOR THE COUNTRY

CHASSIS. This chassis has been recognised as a marvellous engineering achievement and acknowledged the world over as the successful pioneer small car. The design embodies many valuable patents. Price includes electric starter and lighting, carburetter air strangler, spare wheel and tyre, electric horn and speedometer.

PRICE AT WORKS
£94-10-0

SUNDAY

WHATEVER the occasion, the Seven is ready at short notice for the duties of the day. For visiting it is ideal, permitting many calls to be made, with the minimum loss of time.

The comfortable springing of the car, efficient shock absorbers, together with balloon tyres, enables the longest journey with a full load (three adults, or two adults and two children) to be undertaken without mental or bodily fatigue.

An outstanding feature of this car is the accessibility of all those parts requiring regular attention—whether for lubrication or adjustment. The details are so arranged that the car can be kept in the finest running condition with the minimum of time and trouble.

It is a car that has brought pleasure and satisfaction to thousands of owners in all parts of the world. It compels you to recognise the wonderful work it does.

A CAR FOR EVERY OCCASION

A FEW RECENT SUCCESSES AT HOME AND ABROAD

The Austin Seven has behind it a long record of brilliant successes. The following are a few of the most recent ones, although many others have been gained since the beginning of 1926, that are not officially recognised.

Australian Grand Prix, 100 miles	1st.
Brooklands J.C.C. 200 Mile Race, 850 c.c. class	1st and 2nd.
Western Australia, Perth, Claremont Speedway	1st and 2nd.
Johannesburg, S.A. Mulders Drift Hill Climb	1st, 2nd and 3rd.
Shelsley Walsh Midland Automobile Club Hill Climb, 750 c.c. class	1st, 2nd and 3rd.
Shelsley Walsh Midland Automobile Club Hill Climb, Racing Cars	1st and 2nd.
Victoria R.A.C. 24 hours Reliability Trial, 500 Miles.	4 finished without losing a mark
Brooklands J.C.C. High Speed Reliability Trial	6 Gold Medals.
Australia, Sydney Motor Club, Penrith Speedway	1st.
Victoria Light Car Club, Hill Climb, Wheelers Hill	1st, 2nd and 3rd.
Australia R.A.C. 24 Hours Test from Sydney, 463 Miles	5 Gold Medals.
Australia, Adelaide	Class H. Record, 63.75 m.p.h. for 3 hours.
Brooklands B.R.A.C., 75 m.p.h., Short Handicap	2nd.
New Zealand Oreti Beach. Cars up to 2,000 c.c. distance 9 Miles	2nd and 3rd.
Johannesburg, Natal Sprint Races, 25 mile	2nd.
Australian R.A.C. Sydney, Fuel Consumption Test	51 m.p.g.

A booklet, entitled "The Supremacy of the Austin Seven," gives fuller particulars of these and many other awards.

THE "AUSTIN SEVEN" — FIRST IN ITS CLASS AND OF PROVED PERFORMANCE

FEATURES and SPECIFICATION

DIMENSIONS. Full car length, 9ft. 3in. (2,821 mm.) ; Full car width, 4ft. 2in. (1,270 mm.) ; Wheelbase, 6ft. 3in. (1,905 mm.) ; Track, 3ft. 4in. (1,016) ; Road Clearance, 8¾in. (220 mm.) ; Weight (approx.) 8½ cwt. (430 kilo.) ; Height to top of screen, 4ft. 9in. (1,450 mm.) ; Height to top of hood when raised, 5ft. 4in. (1,625 mm.)

BODY. Adjustable bucket seat for driver ; Bucket seat for passenger is hinged to allow entrance to the rear seat ; Folding hood and side screens on touring model ; Ample tool accommodation.

ENGINE. 4-cylinder, water-cooled, detachable head ; bore, 2.2in. (56 mm.) ; stroke, 3in. (76 mm.). Total capacity, 747.5 c.c. ; R.A.C. rating, 7.8 ; b.h.p. 10.5 at 2,400 r.p.m. The crankshaft has roller bearings. Aluminium pistons.

FUEL SUPPLY. By gravity from 4-gallon tank (18 litres).

IGNITION. By Coil and Battery.

COOLING. Radiator and fan.

LUBRICATION. Engine lubrication is by means of a gear driven pump. Chassis lubrication is by grease gun.

TRANSMISSION. Single-plate clutch. The ratios of engine to road wheels are :—1st speed, 16 to 1 ; 2nd speed, 9 to 1 ; top 4.9 to 1 ; reverse 21 to 1. Gear changes are effected by a lever mounted centrally on the top of the box. Final drive is by helical bevel gear. The rear axle is of the three-quarter floating type, with differential and torque tube.

BRAKES. The pedal-operated brake acts on the drums of the rear wheels, and the hand lever applies brakes to the front wheels. The adjustment of both sets is extremely accessible and quickly carried out.

STEERING. Steering is of the worm and worm wheel type with provision for taking up wear. Over the steering wheel are the throttle and ignition control levers.

SUSPENSION. Semi-elliptic cross spring in front ; those at the rear are quarter elliptic. Shock absorbers, front and rear.

TYRES. Tyres are 26 x 3½in. (Dunlop Cord reinforced Balloon), and the wheels are of special wire type.

EQUIPMENT. Electric starting and lighting, automatic windscreen wiper, carburetter air strangler, spare wheel and tyre, electric horn, speedometer, licence holder, blank number plates.

ALL FRONT SCREENS OF TRIPLEX GLASS

Its purposeful stance, even when static, hinted at speed and high-performance. The car did not disappoint, falling in the 750cc class at most events. The light aluminium doorless bodywork was fixed to an ash frame, with steel wings, floorpan, and bonnet based on touring components. A small fixed step was subsequently added to assist access for the passengers, and in later versions the light flowing lines were also slightly simplified.

The initial, fairly standard, chassis and running gear were changed in 1929 to include lowered rear and front springs, a bowed front axle beam to provide for spring clearance, and dropped ends to the radius

MANUFACTURERS' WARRANTY

THE goods manufactured by the Company, and specified in this catalogue shall be accepted by the purchaser subject to the conditions hereinafter mentioned and subject to the following express warranty, which excludes all warranties, conditions and liabilities whatsoever, whether statutory or otherwise, which might exist against the Company, but for this provision, viz. :—In the event of any defect being disclosed in any part or parts of the goods and if the part or parts alleged to be defective are returned to the Company's works, carriage paid, within twelve months after delivery, the Company undertakes to examine same, and should any fault, due to defective material or workmanship, be found on examination by the Company, it will repair the defective part or supply, free of charge, a new part in place thereof.

The Company's responsibility is limited to the terms of this guarantee, and it shall not be answerable for any contingent or resulting liability, or loss arising through any defects This guarantee does not relate to defects caused by motor racing, wear and tear, misuse or neglect, or to the defects in any motor, motor vehicle, or goods which have been altered after leaving the Company's works, or which have been let out on hire, or the identification numbers or marks on which have been altered or removed. The Company accepts no responsibility for tyres, speedometers or the electrical equipment or other goods (including coachwork) not of its own manufacture.

The Austin Motor Co., Ltd., issues no warranty of the goods except as stated herein, but desires and expects that customers shall make a thorough examination before purchasing. This warranty is limited to the despatch to the purchaser without charge, except for transportation of the part or parts, whether new or repaired, in exchange for those acknowledged by the Company to be defective.

The purchaser shall, if required at the time of purchase, personally sign the form supplied by the Company, and register his name, address, date of purchase, number of car and name and address of Seller with the Company, and shall obtain from the Company a signed copy of this warranty, and shall produce same to the Company's representative for inspection in case of any claim being made. This warranty shall not be assigned or transferred to anyone unless the Manufacturer's consent in writing has first been obtained.

The purchaser shall send to the Company's works such part or parts as are alleged or claimed to be defective promptly on the discovery of the claimed defect. Transportation is to be prepaid by the purchaser, and said part or parts to be properly packed for transit and clearly marked for identification with the name and full address of the owner, and with the number of the vehicle from which the said part or parts were taken

The purchaser shall post to the Company at its works on or before despatch of such part or parts alleged to be defective, a full and complete description of the claim and the reasons therefor.

The judgment of the Austin Motor Co., Ltd., in all cases of claims shall be final and conclusive, and the purchaser agrees to accept its decision on all questions as to defects and to the exchange of part or parts. After the expiration of six days from the despatch of notification of the Company's decision, the part or parts submitted may be scrapped or returned carriage forward by the Company.

THE AUSTIN MOTOR CO. LTD.

LONGBRIDGE, BIRMINGHAM

Telegrams : "SPEEDILY, NORTHFIELD"   Telephone : PRIORY 2101—2110
Code : BENTLEY'S

479-483 OXFORD STREET, LONDON, W.1

"AUSTINETTE, LONDON"   MAYFAIR 6230

HOLLAND PARK HALL, HOLLAND PARK AVENUE

LONDON. W.11

Publication No. 657A

---

superchargers. These superchargers were manufactured under licence by LT Delaney of Gallay Radiators, and ran at a pressure of six pounds per square inch, mounted on the nearside of the engine and driven by gears. The fully counter-balanced crankshafts were machined from solid billet, with pressure-fed lubrication and $1\frac{5}{16}$in (33mm) main journals.

Production engines, using all special components, produced 27bhp at 4500rpm, and the works cars had perhaps 15 per cent more than this at higher revolutions. All the cars had three branch exhaust systems, and the considerable increase in torque of the supercharger was responsible for vastly improved performance in the mid-range and 'pulling power' of the little 750cc units, which were raced by the works and private owners. These little sports racing cars would soon be known as the legendary 'Ulsters' after their success in the 1929 Ulster Tourist Trophy race.

The slow-down in the international economy during 1928 had a variety of consequences, and a division of responses amongst social classes, with a degree of surface frivolity masking an undercurrent of unease. Increased production of cars threatened to overtake demand, leading to a price war between Austin and his immediate competitors for the small car market – this at a time for the company when the Seven represented half of all Austins produced. A significantly upgraded version of the familiar and popular Chummy had been introduced, officially labelled the AD Tourer, which shared the appearance of the earlier car but provided more room in the body, particularly for the rear seats.

The bodywork was still made up of aluminium panels fixed to an ash frame, but the radiator was higher, and the body widened at the scuttle and towards the rear, giving occupants more elbow room and

A 1927 Chummy seeks shelter where it may. (Courtesy Neill Bruce)

---

arms, to maintain their clearance under the frame rails. This basic lowering method of the Austin Seven suspension was adopted for most subsequent sports models, with only detail changes and upgrades for evolving main components. The engines were highly modified, and fitted with water pumps and French-designed Cozette No 4-size more practical rear seating. The chassis frame had minor updates, and inevitably the overall weight increased slightly. From late 1928, the magneto ignition was replaced by a coil, with the CAV dynamo replaced by a larger-output Lucas DEL-type; this design decision marked the beginning of the change from what are regarded as 'vintage' cars, to those types more redolent of typical later-1930s thinking.

In late 1928, a development of the Top Hat saloon was announced, as a revised saloon with higher radiator and neatly hinged ventilators that let into the lower part of the scuttle, to supplement the openable two-piece windscreen. Almost simultaneously, the RK Saloon – which featured a single-piece windscreen – was also put into production. The RK did, however, retain the peak-styled overhang to the body above the windscreen.

The great numbers of cars in production at this time varied in specification. Whilst standard saloons had aluminium skins pinned to ash frames, the fabric–bodied factory versions were particularly attractive, and sliding 'sunshine' roofs became available to get back to the fresh air claims of the original open Chummy.

The elaborate sales brochures produced at this time were beautifully designed, and printed in full colour. Rather than being limited to simply promoting the car, they instead offered a glimpse into a complete lifestyle for the potential Austin Seven owner. One such brochure shown here dedicates a page to each day of the week, showing the Seven's benefits to health and interests.

A Type B Coupé was also introduced in late 1928, and figured strongly in the brochure, with a dropped roofline and superbly balanced four-window bodywork. Late 1929 marked Austin's 100,000th Seven-chassied motor car, a fabric-bodied RK Saloon; a quite extraordinary achievement for any manufacturer's single design. Updated AE Tourers, vans, and saloons rounded off the decade. The factory was open 24 hours a day, with three shifts in each of the five working days, and cleaning and maintenance carried out over each weekend.

There is little doubt that the popularity and appeal of the Austin Seven was due in good part to its success in racing and other competitions. From the moment that Lou Kings threw one of the prototypes up Shelsley Walsh in 1922, a public fascination grew regarding exactly what Herbert Austin's baby car could do, and what

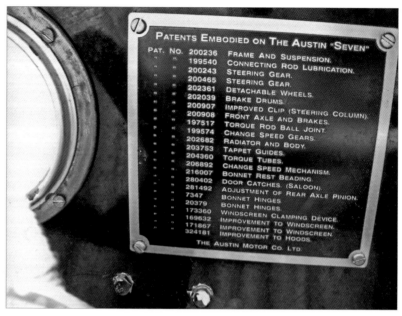

Getting the message out – the familiar list of Austin Seven patents, rather quirkily fixed to most production dashboards. Each patent on every Seven sold added to the wealth of Sir Herbert. (Author collection)

might come next. At Brooklands, many of the races were handicaps, with the tiny Austin Seven pitted against much larger cars. A bet could be placed on whether the lumbering 'big 'un' would ever catch the lightweight 'little 'un' howling ahead round the banking. The plucky little Seven attracted hordes of followers; it seemed every person in the land knew what an Austin Seven was.

Herbert Austin was a genuine racing enthusiast, and thoroughly enjoyed competition, originally through his own very effective efforts, but continuing long after he had become a well-established and successful industrialist. Paternal and philanthropic, Herbert was prepared to assist ambitious young men and women with works support in competition (declared or not). This was particularly true for otherwise-private escapades in Austin Sevens, and in many cases he provided both works cars and entry money out of his own pocket. Several private owners therefore enjoyed 'semi-works' status over many seasons, and in return Austin received both feedback and kudos for the tide of youthful enthusiasm directed at the new motoring phenomenon that was the Austin Seven.

CHAPTER SIX

COACH-BUILT SEVENS

A NATURAL part of the process of creating a motor car in the 1920s was the choice of chassis – including engine and running gear – and, probably quite separately, the choice of the bodywork.

Almost all car makers offered rolling chassis for sale, up to and including luxury brands like Rolls-Royce, Bentley, Bugatti, and Hispano-Suiza, where well-heeled buyers created their own personalised motor transport. In a trickle-down effect to manufacturers, aspirational owners of more modest offerings like the Austin Seven were given the choice of a coach-built car, and the certain cachet that came with it, even if it had rather humbler underpinnings. Herbert Austin had decades of experience with this practice, and therefore offered the Austin Seven as a rolling chassis, almost from day one.

The art of the often small and widely distributed coach-builder had developed over several centuries in the United Kingdom, and indeed included the author's great grandfather, John Morgan, operating from a small works in the 1860s in Stratford-upon-Avon, Warwickshire. After providing horse-drawn farmers' carts, and elegant and exquisitely detailed carriages for nobility and gentry, many of the age-old coach-

The elegantly balanced early pattern Mulliner Sports 7HP was available in blue or tan fabric bodywork. Note the scuttle vents. (Author collection)

building skills were equally in demand for the construction of 'horseless carriage' motor cars in the burgeoning motor age.

The Austin Seven rolling chassis, with its triangular-plan form, provided an ideal base for building a simple or elaborate coach-built body, which itself did not have to be especially structurally strong. Open bodywork was considered the norm in the early days of the Seven, and so many simple 'bath tub-type' bodies were created before saloon-type bodywork took over in the late 1920s. Saloon bodies were a lot more expensive and difficult to build, however, and by the early 1930s, production-built saloons were by far the cheaper option. In challenging economic times, and with the fashion for small coach-built cars having passed, the coach-building companies that had proliferated just a few years previously now found themselves closing at an equally rapid rate.

Gordon England was probably the earliest exponent of the coach-built Austin Seven, with his 1923 Brooklands Super Sports. In October that same year, however, Thomas Startin, of Birmingham, built a delightful small van body. Startin used a traditional ash frame with aluminium panelling, and retained the factory scoop-scuttle, bonnet, lights, and windscreen. A feature from earlier carriage days was also retained with the bottom of the rear doors curving inwards to tuck under towards the rear axle – a complication, but considered aesthetically worthwhile when constructing for the 1923 Olympia Motor Show, where the van was shown on the Austin stand.

In 1924, Thomas Hughes, a Birmingham-based sidecar manufacturer, built an ultra-light sports body out of 22-gauge aluminium – doorless and with a tiny pointed tail – for more agile customers. At about the same time, Alan Gruzellier created a one-off two-seater, and a boat tail design appeared from Wilson Motors of London; named the Burghley Sports, it was a flamboyant project with wildly flared front and rear wings on some examples. Also in 1924, a chassis was shipped to New South Wales Motors in Sydney, Australia, where it was bodied in smart two-seater form, and marketed as the Ace.

The Burghly Sports' advertising claimed statistics of 55mph (88km/h) and 50mpg. (Author collection)

The Ace's bodywork styling was highly advanced: in steel on an ash frame; with a streamlined cowling to the radiator, which was extended downwards to enclose and shroud the front suspension and radius arms; a bee-shaped tail, which predated the similarly-shaped production Austin Speedy tail design by ten years; and a shallow fold-flat, single-piece windscreen. The whole effect was a very good-looking sports car, and was the precursor to a line of Austin Seven-based cars from Australia.

The 1924 Australian-built Ace was an amazingly advanced design. (A7CA archive)

Included only for its rarity, this blurred image shows the only example of the 1926 Brighton Sports Saloon Coupé known to have been built. (Author collection)

The first saloon Austin Seven body was a fabric affair, constructed by Gordon England in late 1925. It proved very popular and, in turn, convinced Sir Herbert that he too should offer works saloon bodies. Gordon England delivery van bodies were also built to satisfy demand, as the company only built bodywork, and so was not slowed down by the demands of a mass production factory.

In mid-1926, Duple of Edgware Road, Hendon, took the concept of purpose-built bodywork a stage further, offering two bodies on the same Austin Seven base – a four-seater tourer for pleasure, and a commercial van for business use; a popular, if short-lived, idea at the time. The Duple Convertible was also built, based on a cut-down Type R saloon, but has no known production numbers.

Cole and Shuttleworth offered a pretty two-seater, with a flat-topped, pointed boat-tail body design, quite similar to that which was later built by the factory. The rear deck of this body had a top hatch opening, for access to luggage space and a spare wheel. This echoed the Citroën Clover-Leaf and other three-seater bodies, with a child seat or 'dog hole' centrally to the rear – somewhat like a dickey seat – and popular in France at this time.

The peak of Austin Seven coach-building arrived in 1927 with the Swallow Saloon Coupé, built by William Lyons. This was perhaps the highest quality product on an Austin Seven base, and irresistibly gave momentum to the career of Lyons. Duple built its first – and very attractive – two-seat Sports, which it also offered as a complete kit of parts to be assembled by the purchaser; this would be a plausible candidate for the very first 'kit car' design to fit straight onto a Seven

chassis. These early light and taut Duple bodies, with their gently sloping tails and an air of eagerness about their profile, certainly appeared to be just the job for swift motoring around the countryside – an example of the finished article looking just as good as the promotional brochure.

The coach-builder New Avon also put forth a carefully styled two-seater. Advertised as "an attractive and distinctive semi-sporting small car," it was destined for admiration by all at the tennis club, with well-balanced lines and wings of a matching slope to the tail, giving a more rakish appearance than the normal production wings. The Taylor Semi-Sports – built in London's fashionable Kensington district – displayed its up-market pretensions with a nicely shaped tail and sloping split-V windscreen, as well as details like 'snorkel' air vents mounted on top of the scuttle – as on some Swallow bodies – and snazzy contrasting two-colour paintwork. The whole effect owed quite a lot to the contemporary sporting river launches and barnstorming air racers. Taylor continued to build its range based on the contemporary and updated Seven for some years. A slightly strange, very square, two-seater with a large rear boot was built by Arc Manufacturing in the same period, costing £175, and reduced to £160 a year later.

Granville Motors, of South West London, built the Miniature Saloon, with distinctive 'faux-landau' bodywork on a standard chassis, radiator, bonnet, scuttle, and wings. A line ran around the rear bodywork at windowsill height, with landau irons breaking up the shape. Glass was limited to the windscreen, doors, and a small rear

CRAFT AND MASS PRODUCTION

The industrial revolution had, by mid-Victorian times, led inexorably to the mass production of goods, and the 'satanic mills' of the textile and other industries. The mass of workers had little to do but to constantly feed the machines, and the tasks allotted to the individual were, in many cases, reduced to single repetitive actions for the whole working day.

The late-Victorian Arts and Crafts movement, championed by John Ruskin and William Morris, rejected the shoddiness of many mass-produced objects. It also examined the mental and physical wellbeing of the worker as an individual, and looked towards elevating the worker's role back to the craftsmen of earlier times. As far back as the Middle Ages, craftsmen were grouped in guilds, with an egalitarian ethos between each group and with little distinction between stonemasons and sculptors, or leather workers and saddlers. Ruskin and Morris were driven by a nostalgia for such objects and customs, that had appeared out of folk tradition, in contrast to the artificiality of the offerings of mass production, which relied on their cheap price to sell to the many.

Intense thought began to be applied to the very nature of organised work; to the moral welfare of the worker, the general health of ever-evolving society, and the causal connections between these factors. Thomas Carlyle, Karl Marx, and others formed theories that became radical political expressions of the dilemma that faced a massed work force. Ruskin and Morris, meanwhile, championed the craft worker, who took personal responsibility for each of the objects that he himself made, usually with his own hands.

The many craft trades in the early years of the motor trade included panel beaters and coach-builders, upholsterers and trimmers, painters and finishers, and many others besides. Each of these was partly or wholly absorbed into the process of mass production within 40 years of the first viable cars moving gingerly about the unsurfaced lanes, which at that time covered most of the countryside.

Post-Industrial Revolution positions required skills in engineering, and obliged individuals to achieve competence in machining processes and fitting that were not needed – and indeed didn't exist – in earlier times. Ultimately, the Arts and Crafts movement faded away for two reasons. The first was financial, as individually-crafted goods could be broadly replicated by mass production methods at a vastly reduced price to the consumer. Secondly, the sheer weight of mass produced goods simply took over the market place, pushing crafted items into a tiny corner.

Nevertheless, the Arts and Crafts movement and its aesthetics (of which the architecture of Austin's home at Lickey Grange was a good example), did have a lasting influence in the Bauhaus in Germany, De Stijl in Holland, Art Nouveau in France, and via Frank Lloyd Wright in the United States. Most prominently, of course, it also led to the somewhat-debased mock Tudor, or 'Tudorbethan,' half-timbered house designs being erected in enormous estates, all over the British Isles. This occurred during the production life of the Austin Seven, the brochures of which offered, for the first time at an attainable cost, a lifestyle choice for the smart young up-and-coming motor car-owning family.

---

window, and the interior appeared slightly claustrophobic. At £172, the Miniature Saloon was priced similarly to its competitors, as was the pointed tail, two-seater 1927 Coupette, by Jarvis of Wimbledon.

Around this time, Mulliner of Birmingham brought out the Fabric Saloon, a two-seat coupé, and a Brougham, which was – in essence – an upper class van with coachwork built on Weymann principles, and a top-hinged horizontally-opening rear door to give access to the rear interior for goods or samples.

The following year, 1928, saw the later famous company Abbott of Farnham build three Dropheads and one Landaulet, and London-based Alpe and Saunders build at least one – by then slightly old-fashioned – Coupé.

A new look for British Austin Seven bodies was found in the KC Sports, built in Chelsea, London, and marketed through the successful and long-established Normand Garages of Oxford Street. The appearance of the KC Sports was not dissimilar to the earlier

The coach-built Jarvis Two-Seater was a workmanlike design, very well executed. (Author collection)

Australian Ace, with the bodywork sides dropping significantly below the chassis and giving a lower, less skittish, and decidedly 'late-vintage' visual appearance. The cycle-type wings were given more flowing lines at the base, and were filled with visually separate panels, in a manner similar to the later production Sports 65. These, with the rising bonnet and scuttle line, and very shallow V-shaped windscreen, represented an advance over other offerings.

The talented Jensen brothers laid the foundations of their eponymous car building empire by designing bodywork for an Austin Seven to be built by the New Avon Body Company, in Warwick. The resulting car was to be called the Avon Swan, there being plenty of these elegant birds with their royal associations on the river in that part of Warwickshire. The idea behind the Avon Swan was to produce a fairly roomy 'all seasons' body, and the venture was promoted as the 'Aristocrat of Austin Sevens.' To give the car a distinctive look, the wheels were painted white, and the body incorporated a small – but separate – top-lidded boot at the rear, on which the spare wheel was mounted. One can see that this bodywork was, in Britain, a precursor to the classic 'three box' car body style, which predominated car body forms right through to the advent of the hatchback, some 50 years later; it marked distinct a move away from the traditional vintage car shape.

Another two-seater was offered by Hoyal of Weybridge in 1928, either as a bodykit to be fitted, or as a complete car.

During 1926, Boyd-Carpenter had taken over the former Gordon England service garage in Hampstead, North London. In 1928, it introduced its own Austin Seven Boyd-Carpenter Special, priced at almost £220 and with a good looking body in the then-current style – with low body sides and a false dumb-iron cover, but also a steeply sloping tail, giving the body a slightly heavier appearance than its modest Austin origins might have suggested.

Boyd-Carpenter modified the suspension of the standard road Austin chassis in the normal 'sports' specification, and tuned the engine very carefully through the selection and machining of components. It was also the agent for the French LAP overhead valve conversion – an ingenious device that, for £25 extra cost, used push rods in place of the usual valves, blanked off the ports in the cylinder block, had an adapter for the inlet manifold, and breathed through a Claudel-Hobson carburettor. Boyd-Carpenter had many competition successes, helping to advertise its products, and a number of these well-built cars have survived, including – famously – the car raced by John Sutton over many years.

Mulliner introduced its fabric-covered Sunshine Saloon, of Weymann principle construction, in late 1928. To counter any

THE JENSEN BROTHERS

The first car Richard and Alan Jensen built was a two-seater sports based on a 1925 Austin Seven chassis. It was lowered in the normal sports manner, with flattened springs, and the sides of the bodywork taken down to a line below the Austin side members rather than perching on top. The Austin Seven radiator cowl had a stone guard and a false dumb iron cover below, which faired in and concealed most of the front suspension and provided a mounting for the number plate. The cockpit was as far to the rear as possible, with the driver's right elbow resting on the offside rear wing. This gave it an extended bonnet line, the scuttle topped with a shallow V-shaped Auster windscreen, and the spare wheel being mounted on the offside.

The visual length of this beautiful small car was extended further with long sloping wings that dropped to ultra-short running boards in a continuous line. The merits of the car's styling and quality of build were not lost on the directors of the Standard Motor Company, just down the road in Coventry. The company commissioned the Jensen brothers to design and produce special-bodied Standard cars, and the brothers' career paths took off.

By 1934, Jensen Motors had been set up for the brothers to build cars under their own company name. The firm expanded during World War Two and – subcontracted to Austin, post-war – built the bodywork of sports Austin A40s and Austin Healeys. It ultimately built its own range of Jensen sporting and luxury cars, including a collaboration with Lotus, each venture carrying forward more than a little DNA of the Austin Seven.

The beautifully designed and detailed Austin Seven special that, in 1928, set the Jensen brothers on their way to founding their car manufacturing empire. (Author collection)

GC Willis in his Boyd Carpenter, on a steep Inter-Varsity section. (Courtesy Jeremy Wood)

marketing ploy from its competitors promoting the health benefits of open bodywork, an optional sliding roof panel was offered, providing all the fresh air that the occupants needed. A polished walnut dashboard added a touch of luxury, finished off by wheels whose colour contrasted with the body. Just to cover all eventualities, however, an open fabric-covered two-seater Sports followed. Complete with a boat tail, this delicate and delightful body design was rooted firmly in the Twenties. The 1929 Mulliners had some bodies with distinctive louvred panels below the body sides in order to conceal all of the frame, somewhat like the MG M-type – at least one of which is in regular use by Marcus Gillah at the time of writing.

Swallow followed up its earlier Coupé prototypes with a coach-built open Sports, with distinctive rounded radiator cowl and bullet-shaped tail. The Swallow Saloon was introduced at the same time, and both have survived in some numbers, being a particular favourite amongst enthusiasts who appreciate the remarkable design feat of

Geoff Parker with his gently-restored Swallow Saloon, at the A7CA Warwick Rally in 2012. (Author collection)

WILLIAM LYONS, SWALLOW, AND JAGUAR

William Lyons was born in 1901, the son of a Blackpool piano dealer. Lyons had a great interest in motorcycles and, after the Great War ended, met William Walmsley – another motorcycle enthusiast, with a small motorcycle repair business. Walmsley had an idea for a sidecar that could be attached to any make of motorcycle, and devised a lightweight, streamlined sidecar body that had immediate visual appeal. William Lyons enthusiastically joined him, in 1922, to form a company at premises in Bloomfield Road, Blackpool, with the two young men each working hard on the attractive (and ultimately successful) product.

By 1926, the company had 30 men building sporting torpedo-bodied sidecars. The next year the company expanded, re-naming itself The Swallow Sidecar and Coach-building Company. By degrees, the venture moved to an ex-Great War munitions factory in Holbrook Lane, Foleshill, Coventry, and built its first car body design on an Austin Seven chassis, readily available from nearby Longbridge. This design was a very neat coupé body, and was an immediate success. The body offered an entirely different image to the standard Austin product, with William Lyons showing his great flair for design and marketing at this early stage in his career.

A rounded bull-nosed radiator cowl set the look, and imitated the overall streamlined form of the Swallow sidecars. The smooth lines continued down to a pleasing and rounded tail shape, set off initially by cycle-pattern mudguards, which turned with the wheels. Snazzy wheel discs completed the effect – the closest an Austin Seven body could come to being described as a torpedo.

The Swallow sidecars had been skinned in aluminium, and this material was also used for the car's bodywork, over a traditional ash frame. A V-shaped Auster windscreen and hood frame was tightly designed to complement the overall neat appearance, with an alternative hardtop option available at a later date. The very distinctive and pretty Swallow radiator mascot sat on top of the radiator, and high quality interior trim and seating made for a luxurious product on economy underpinnings, and was marketed at £175.

The swallow, or bluebird, was a popular emblem of speed at this time, and used by Campbell and others. The reliable homing instinct of the swallow possibly added to the subliminal sub-text of the advertising for the car.

In October 1928, a Swallow saloon was introduced with a very distinctive look indeed – a gloriously rounded and balanced body design, which incorporated a dual contrasting paint scheme with a 'pen-nib' separation on the bonnet top. This bodywork had Art Deco overtones, and the rounded corners to the side windows, large oval shaped rear windows, and naval style 'ships' ventilators mounted on the top of the scuttle are reminders that the design was contemporary with futuristic adventure-genre films of the time. Lyons' design and marketing ensured that the Swallow saloon was more at home in London's West End than anywhere else. At the same time, the tiny doors, luxury trim, tight driving position, and vanity set (complete with mirror, powder puff and face powder) included in the glove locker was an overt appeal to the fairer sex. The cars were bought in some numbers.

Changes were made for 1930, that included carefully-designed double bumpers, a divider down the centre of the radiator shell, and a louvred panel between false dumb iron covers. However, production shifted away from the Austin Seven in 1931, towards the special-bodied, Standard-based SS 1. The company name was changed to SS Cars Ltd in 1933, after which William Walmsley left the company.

The famous and rakishly-bodied SS 100 Sports followed in 1935 and – after World War Two, and now based in war-torn Coventry – Lyons changed the company name once again, this time to Jaguar, to avoid any connotations with the Nazi Schutzstaffel, or SS. Jaguar introduced the fabulous XK engine to power Lyons' new brainchild, the Jaguar XK120 – an affordable, yet glamorous, sports car. The XK120 represented Lyons' vision of great looks, high-performance, and an aspirational ownership demographic, at half the price of its direct competitors.

Announced at the 1948 British International Motor Show, the XK120 cause a sensation beyond all William's expectations. The XK engine subsequently powered thousands of Jaguars, from multiple Le Mans winners to stately Mark X limousines. Lyons was awarded a knighthood in 1956, and continued to live his entire life involved in the British Motor Industry, one of the most influential innovators of his generation.

The XK engine designer, Walter Hassan, had previously been involved with racing Bentleys, English Racing Automobiles, and the Napier-Railton land speed record assault. He later joined Coventry Climax, with his old friend Harry Mundy. Their successful FW (featherweight) fire pump concept was adapted by Keift, Cooper, and Lotus to power sports racing cars, leading to multiple F1 Championship wins in the 1950s and 60s, and Coventry Climax advertising it as "The fire pump that wins races." With neat symmetry, 750 Formula racer Tony Southgate would go on to design the 1988 Le Mans-winning Jaguar XJR-9.

A beautiful replica GE Brooklands at Beaulieu Rally 2016. (Author collection)

creating a true luxury car in miniature. The details are also to be marvelled at, from the Art Deco-influenced paintwork – incorporating a signature pen-nib division of colour on the bonnet top – as well as the unique gliding Swallow radiator cap mascot, and the ladies' vanity set inside the passenger-side glove box.

One intriguing car to come out of London's West End, in the lull before the Wall Street storm, was the 1929 Cadogan, commissioned and designed by Captain H O'Hagan – of Vanden Plas, Belgium – as something of a vanity project. For the Cadogan, the Austin chassis was lengthened by 18in (500mm), and a dramatically low coupé body built by Cadogan Motors. The front wings were close-fitted to the wheels, mounted on the brake drums and turning with the front wheels, which, in turn, were fitted with Ewart-type wheel discs. A very shallow windscreen was set well back behind the long bonnet, the whole effect being that of a much larger car; one that perhaps would have been equally at home cruising London's Knightsbridge, or chasing the Blue Train down to the South of France – if only it wasn't an Austin Seven underneath!

The KC two-seater was reintroduced in modified form in 1929, catalogued: Special, Special Sports, and Ulster-type under-slung chassis – which was to be based on the Austin EA chassis. The cheapest variant was advertised as "the best value in fast Austins," at a mere £168.

Arrow Coachworks followed up with a two-seater design by a Mr Simmonds, of Cambridge University. Arrow Coachworks went on to provide one of the most visually successful series of coach-built Austin Sevens, with many cars later being built on Austin Seven Nippy rolling chassis, supplied by the factory, as well as lengthened-wheelbase Sports Foursomes.

By 1930, a few special orders for novel designs were undertaken by various coach-builders: the Romney Coupé, built by Martin Walter Ltd; the pretty Hawk two-seater, built in penny numbers at the Matchless Motorcycle works; the pointed-tail Spear, built at Hanwell and to be marketed by major Austin dealers HA Saunders, of North London; and the T&D Sports two-seater coupé, built at Swiss Cottage, North London.

On Bedford Road, near Alexandra Palace, North London – and just around the corner from where Colin Chapman would, 15 years

Ken Wallis' wacky 1934 special used two Austin Seven frames bolted together and extreme styling. RAF hero Ken invented, built, and flew the autogyro 'Little Nellie' in the James Bond film *You Only Live Twice*. (Courtesy Ian Hancock/Ken Wallis)

later, build his first Lotus – a number of coach-built sports AE Wright Austins would be built, despite the direct competition from Austin factory-built Type 65s and Nippys.

In early 1933, AE Wright's Bedford works offered purpose-built, low-slung, two- and four-seater bodywork, in aluminium on traditional ash framing. The AEW bodywork was quite boxy, but immensely practical on long-wheelbase chassis, and – as was the style at the time – featured well-louvred panels, including along the base of each body side. For body strength, there was initially a small door on the passenger side only, and, for holding capacity, the spare

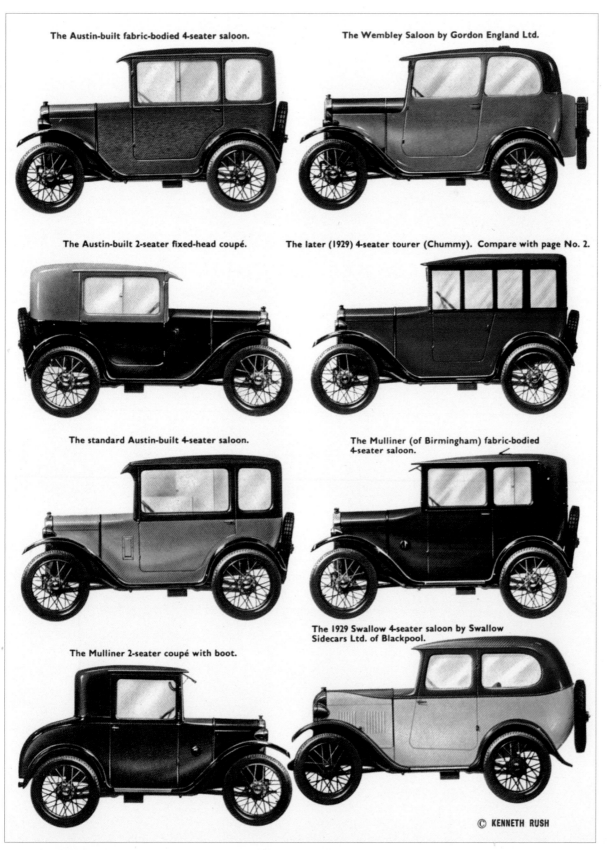

The Austin-built fabric-bodied 4-seater saloon.

The Wembley Saloon by Gordon England Ltd.

The Austin-built 2-seater fixed-head coupé.

The later (1929) 4-seater tourer (Chummy). Compare with page No. 2.

The standard Austin-built 4-seater saloon.

The Mulliner (of Birmingham) fabric-bodied 4-seater saloon.

The Mulliner 2-seater coupé with boot.

The 1929 Swallow 4-seater saloon by Swallow Sidecars Ltd. of Blackpool.

© KENNETH RUSH

wheel was mounted on the rear of the squared-off tail. Each car was individually produced, and so no two cars were quite the same, but the AEW Sevens, several of which still survive, have a certain charm of their own – though no pretensions at being café racers.

Unfortunately, however, time was fast running out for these specially-built cars; the flurry of activity in building mainly two-seater sports bodies on contemporary Austin Sevens lasted less than ten years. The coach-building of the 1920s had resulted in some beautiful little cars being built on Longbridge-produced chassis. Sadly, many of the more frail offerings – particularly the open cars – did not weather very well, and became obsolete, of little value and so left outside with little protection. Many succumbed to the elements, with their final days spent in breakers' yards.

Original coach-built sports and open tourer bodies on Austin Sevens are now rare and hard to find. However, there is a whole array of enthusiasts waiting to resurrect or recreate the rarer coach-built Sevens, many examples of which are great fun, very attractive, and always draw comment on the rally field.

The comparative studies of Austin Seven coachwork in the late 1920s, by Ken Rush, which capture the lightness of line and subtle differences in proportion. (Courtesy Kenneth Rush)

CHAPTER SEVEN

THE MIGHTY ATOM

I N 1932, the Austin Motor Company produced a new entry in a number of black and white publicity films. This film, complete with newfangled sound, focused on all the uses to which the Austin Seven engine could be put, and was titled *The Mighty Atom*.

Beginning (and ending) with footage of an Open Tourer driving down a sunlit country lane ("a familiar sight"), the film moves on to Ducks at Brooklands ("crack drivers in crack cars"), and Shelsley Walsh ("you can't keep a good baby down"). More unusual applications of the Seven power unit are displayed throughout: a Kent farmer, with a small home-built tractor for his apple orchards; a "shining monster" Brough motorcycle, with twin rear wheels; what seems to be a "kiddie car" but which turns out to be a self-propelled paint spraying unit; the launch of a marine Austin Seven Thetis motor, demonstrating the "dependable power" of the unit; and a rear-steering three-wheel mobile crane with a carrying capacity of one ton (1016kg).

An air propeller-driven "hydro-glider" (what we would now know as a hydroplane) skims over the shallow waters of the upper

The Austin Seven Engine

Austin 1930 press information on the Seven engine, with a cut-away drawing and careful description of principal performance and use features. (Austin publicity)

Severn, helping to "open up new possibilities in navigation." This is followed by the narrow gauge railway at Great Yarmouth pleasure beach, with the engine powering a train pulling a "record load," consisting of an "eager crowd of passengers." Lastly – with a nod to the fairer sex – we look at the auxiliary engine of a "graceful cutter," the sea going sailing boat helmed by a "very skilful yachtswoman."

The film ends with the statement that "we come to look upon this smallest and most versatile of Austin engines with a new respect … remember the Austin Seven engine, The Mighty Atom." The Austin works supplied many thousands of Austin Seven engines, sometimes with gearboxes, for a whole host of users.

The 1930 Austin Seagull motor launch was built by Hammersmith-based Austin specialists Maintenance Ltd, and fitted with a tuned marine version of the Seven engine on a Moorcar Boat Co hull. Tried out on the Thames by Bill Boddy for *Motor Sport*, the craft recorded 18mph (29km/h) over the measured mile, and was easy to handle. The very smart appearance was heightened by

THE Austin Seven Engine is a "high efficiency" power unit designed to give the maximum output for the minimum consumption of fuel, it generates 10·5 b.h.p. at 2,400 r.p.m., and a gallon of petrol will suffice for 40 to 45 miles.

The sturdy crankshaft, of specially selected alloy steel, is carried on two roller bearings. It is carefully tested on balancing machines before being passed for engine assembly. The lightness of reciprocating parts is a feature of an engine remarkable for swift acceleration.

The engine unit is exceedingly compact without sacrifice of accessibility to any components which may require those "little attentions" which mean so much in prolonging the life and sweet running of the engine.

The cooling system of the Seven is adequate for any task and any climate. The water passages in the monobloc are of generous dimensions, and the fan cooled radiator has a capacity of one and a quarter gallons.

Proper lubrication of a small high efficiency engine is of the first importance, and is well provided for in the Austin Seven engine design. The reservoir holds about half a gallon, and is easily removed for cleaning purposes. Oil is circulated by means of a gear driven pump which forces oil to the crankshaft, whilst other parts receive lubrication from an oily mist.

The Seven engine has definitely the smallest consumption of oil per thousand miles.

THE BROUGH SUPERIOR MOTORCYCLE

The Brough motorcycle company in Nottingham had made a name for itself with its large-engined touring models, and, in 1931, made an approach to Sir Herbert Austin to supply suitable engines for a new machine, named the Brough Superior.

The Austin Seven engine was adapted, retaining its water cooling via a pair of small radiators placed low, by the rider's leg guards, and fitted with a special aluminium cylinder head. The Seven gearbox was also retained, with shaft drive to a crown wheel and pinion set between two rear wheels for use with a sidecar.

The first example left the factory early in 1932, but the adaptation of the Austin unit proved far too expensive for motorcycle use in this way. Although it was a fascinating concept, less than a dozen were built over a period of two years.

1932 Austin Seven-powered Brough Superior Combination, with twin rear wheels. These also used an Austin Seven gearbox and crown wheel and pinion. Eight out of the ten produced still survive. (Courtesy Ken Cooke)

"Wrigley's chewing gum steadies nerves" proved useful advice for Ketring and Patsy Dare, as they managed to be the first Austin Seven drivers to ride the 'Wall of Death' at Olympia. (Author collection)

Tornado Smith is mighty close to the top of the wall at Southend Kursaal, with a lap time of under two seconds! 750 Motor Club stalwart Harold Perry looked after two Austin Sevens used there. (Author collection)

RAILWAY AUSTIN SEVENS

A number of Sevens were adapted to run on railways, and one company who specialised in railcars was D Wickham & Co Ltd of Ware, in Hertfordshire.

Wickham created two basic types. The first was unarguably an otherwise normal-looking Austin Seven, equipped with railway wheels. The second, however, was a purpose-built railcar, powered by an Austin Seven engine – much like a miniature version of Ettore Bugatti's French railcars that were making use of the exotic Royale car engine.

Wickham's railcar Chummys had solid flanged cast iron wheels and double protection bumpers at the front and rear, but of course no steering wheel, as that component was redundant on a fixed track. However, the steering column itself was retained, complete with hand throttle and advance/retard ignition levers. It must have felt pretty strange for the drivers to have no steering wheel to hang on to. Apparently, the hammering that the joints received from the rail – via the heavy solid wheels on standard-gauge railways – played havoc with the modestly sized Austin wheel bearings, so these railway Sevens were of limited use.

Wickham also produced purpose-made Inspection Trolley railcars for Columbian railways, powered by an Austin Seven engine and gearbox. These were very much more successful, serving on a line into the Andes that rose, in parts, to 12,000ft above sea level.

Austin Seven power was used in many narrow gauge railway vehicles, including a ganger's trolley noted by Viv Orchard on the

The Austin Chummy, converted for use on railways by Wickham and Co. It featured heavy bumpers and cast flanged wheels, but no steering wheel – which must have made driving one a strange experience. (Author collection)

Talyllyn line in North Wales. This was purpose-built, and had two Austin Seven gearboxes, one of which was back-to-front, to give equal performance shunting backwards or forwards. Austin Seven power was also seen on a 1940s railway ride at Chessington Zoo, and at a railway operating on watercress beds at Bere Regis. There have undoubtedly been many more examples worldwide.

The Austin Seven-powered Seagull motor launch of 1930, with the pleasing lines and varnished mahogany decking of contemporary sporting river craft. (Austin publicity)

the period fashion for varnished mahogany decks, with frames and planking of the same material – all for a price of £200.

A great number of Austin Seven engines were also supplied for other distinct uses, such as saw benches, static engines, and pump operations. This further explains the disparity between chassis and engine numbers, which, having commenced more or less in synchrony, grew further apart as the years went by. A sectionalised teaching demonstration military engine, supplied to the Army in 1939 and latterly liberated by Peter Hornby, was found to have a number several thousand ahead of the last known allocated car chassis numbers.

In 1938, Austin supplied 500 engines, gearboxes, and rear axles to Reliant Motor Co Ltd at Tamworth. These were to be used for its three-wheeler delivery van, with a single forward steered wheel carried in girder-type motorcycle front forks. Austin Seven steering columns were used with an offset linkage to steer the single central

Ray Walker's heavily truncated Seven tractor contains more original vintage Austin parts than most. Found in East Anglia, converted around WW2, and seen here at Beaulieu in 1973. (Courtesy Ken Cooke)

wheel, and the reverse gear of the four-speed gearbox was blanked off to comply with taxation legislation.

After 1939 Reliant obtained a licence to manufacture the Austin Seven engine, and developed it into a far more sophisticated unit, with stronger crankshaft and rods, and improved cylinder head design. In 750 Formula, this side-valve Austin-based Reliant engine superseded the Austin Seven engine in the early 1960s, and thereby saved the important development Formula from extinction. Reliant continued to build three- and four-wheeled cars for decades; the David Ogle-designed Ford-engined Scimitar being an original concept sports-brake much favoured by Royals. Ultimately, however, Reliant could not shake off the 'Del Boy' image of its three-wheelers in the 1990s. Sales declined, and it was a great regret of the company owners that it could not find commercial acceptance for a smart three-wheeled delivery 'Trike,' similar to thousands of vehicles favoured by Italian upmarket hotels and stores, from Milan to Amalfi.

Rear-wheel steering dump truck, with special self-warming seat. (Courtesy Ken Cooke)

An amazing Austin Seven-powered bicycle from Ireland visited Cofton Park for the 1982 Diamond Jubilee Rally. (Courtesy Ken Cooke)

FLYING FLEAS

A craze for home-built aeroplanes swept through Europe in the mid-1930s, when an apparently practical and easily constructed design was published in France by Henri Mignet. This was just 30 years after the Wright brothers had literally catapulted their aircraft into the record books, and with the rapid expansion of flying expertise stemming from the Great War, the idea of a simple and cheap 'hedge hopper' proved irresistible to a large number of young men and women. Soon, hundreds of Henri Mignet's Flying Fleas, or Pou-du-Ciel, were being built in garages, garden sheds, and even bedrooms, with Mignet claiming that anybody who could build a packing case could build one of his aeroplanes.

Like Herbert Austin with his Austin Seven, Mignet built his early HM-series Fleas in the 1920s. By 1933, he had devised a high-lift lightly loaded staggered-wing biplane, with the top pivoting parasol wing allied to a large vertical rudder. The HM 14, as described in Mignet's book (translated into English in 1935, and selling 6000 copies in the first few months), was "a flying armchair for the novice pilot."

At least eight completed Fleas were fitted with Austin Seven engines, and at least two received 'Authorisation to Fly' from the authorities. This is not to say that several others did not also take to the air in fields and meadows – after all, you had to demonstrate that the machine would actually fly before it could be submitted for Authorisation inspection!

Henri Mignet's sensational Pou-du-Ciel, or Flying Flea, inspired many to believe that they could fly – including, here, a bicycle dealer. The simple controls were sadly not sophisticated enough to prevent accidents. (Author collection)

A keen PG Woodhouse-type closely examines the tuned Austin Seven engine installed back-to-front in Charles Cooper's home-built 1935 Mignet Flying Flea. Note the Alta aluminium head and companion's fur coat. (Courtesy John Cooper)

Charles Cooper sits in the cockpit of Cooper Garage's G-AEEI Flying Flea, while young John Cooper swings the chain driven propeller to start the Austin Seven engine. (Author collection)

The Flying Flea constructed by Charles Cooper, of Cooper Car Company, Surbiton, was registered as G-AEEI, and, in bright red dope, tested at Shoreham. It was then taken to Redhill by Charles and his son John – then 12 years old – and fitted with a tuned Austin Seven engine, with an Alta aluminium cylinder head from Geoffrey Taylor's

nearby outfit. Fred Brown and J Patson (both of Peterborough), BW Millichamp (from Belton, Suffolk), and J Baylittle (Lancashire) all also succeeded in registering their Fleas with water-cooled Austin Seven power, and two others converted Seven engines to air cooling, with mixed results.

In the design of the Flea, the thrust height of the propeller was critical, and Charles Cooper's Flea had the engine mounted low and backwards, a chain sprocket in place of the flywheel, driving a two bladed propeller running on a shaft through trunnions bolted to the cylinder head. The water radiator was mounted just in front of the pilot's instrument panel, keeping the centre of gravity below the main spar of the top wing. To save the weight of an electric starter and big battery, the engine was instead started in the traditional way of swinging the prop.

13th of April, 1936, was to be the big day of the Flying Flea rally near Ashingdon, Essex. Charles Cooper was up early, and observed while he moved the aircraft around on the ground under control, then completed a couple of flying circuits of the airfield, receiving his Authorisation to Fly. Navigating by road maps, Charles then immediately flew north to the Thames, turned east down the river, then north as he reached Southend pier. He landed, joining seven other Fleas on the ground, plus one that flew over the event without trying to land. Apart from a later race day at Ramsgate, this was probably the largest gathering of Flying Fleas in the United Kingdom.

For an ultra-light aircraft, the power-to-weight ratio of the Austin Seven engine was severely limited by the water cooling, and Charles soon changed to a Henderson motorcycle engine. He tested the one against the other by attaching the tail of the Flea to a shed with bungee cords, and seeing which motive power stretched the cords the furthest – the Henderson won hands down.

Charles Cooper's three-hour round trip appears to be possibly the longest undertaken by an Austin Seven-powered aircraft. By late 1936, fatal accidents and safety fears meant that no unmodified Flying Fleas could have their Authorisation to Fly renewed, and the craze was over. Charles Cooper, along with the rest of the country, therefore put his flying ambitions on hold, as most Flying Fleas were stowed away in barns or simply scrapped.

In Charles' case, he was left with a perfectly good tuned Austin Seven engine, and, having a fired-up son with a birthday coming up, Charles decided to use the engine to create a snazzy little two-seater Austin Seven special for John Cooper. This proved to be the taproot of a whole dynasty of racing car production, including placing the engine in the rear, a game changer for Formula One design from 1959 onwards.

CHAPTER EIGHT

THE MILITARY AUSTIN SEVEN

GREAT BRITAIN

THE combatant nations of The Great War – as the First World War was then called – faced populations traumatised by the conflict and its aftermath; the huge numbers of young men killed during this period constituted an entire lost generation. By the early 1920s, there was, understandably, still no public taste for spending money on updating weapons of war. However, a changed and evolving political scene in Europe meant that the professional soldiers of the British Army, and its Empire's forces, still had to perform their public duty, and consider the future service requirements of King and Country.

Colonel Fuller, the British military strategist, had decided as early as 1919 that future conflicts would not be the static slaughter of trench warfare. His ideas were developed by Captain Liddell Hart, Swinton, and Martel, with the then newly invented tank at the centre of any land-based new military order.

The 1929 Military Mulliner MT 6249 was the 17th actual car delivered to the army. The author's 1932 version, behind, is the sole surviving 'Tropical/Export' example. (Courtesy John Blackman)

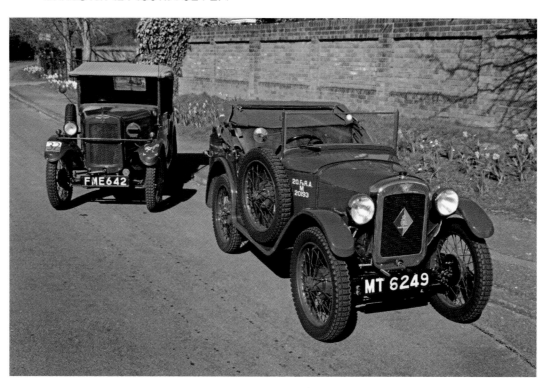

The British invention of the tank had not won the First World War, but it had provided a powerful indicator of how future conflicts might be fought, as had the rapid development of reliable military aircraft, to be used as observation and fighting machines in their own right.

One thing was clear; the horror of the Flanders mud was not to be repeated, and the limitations that came with the millions of horses involved in horse-mounted cavalry and horse-drawn transport – which had historically governed the both the speed and

The Military Trials of 1930-33, and a light and nimble Seven Mulliner Scout car of the 11th Hussars exchanges notes with the crew of a Rolls-Royce heavy armoured car, just outside Warminster. (Author collection)

Mechanisation Trials 1931. Early Military Mulliner Scout Cars, here carrying 3in (76mm) mortars as a front-line two man weapons system (!) overtake horse-mounted Cavalry. (Austin Publicity)

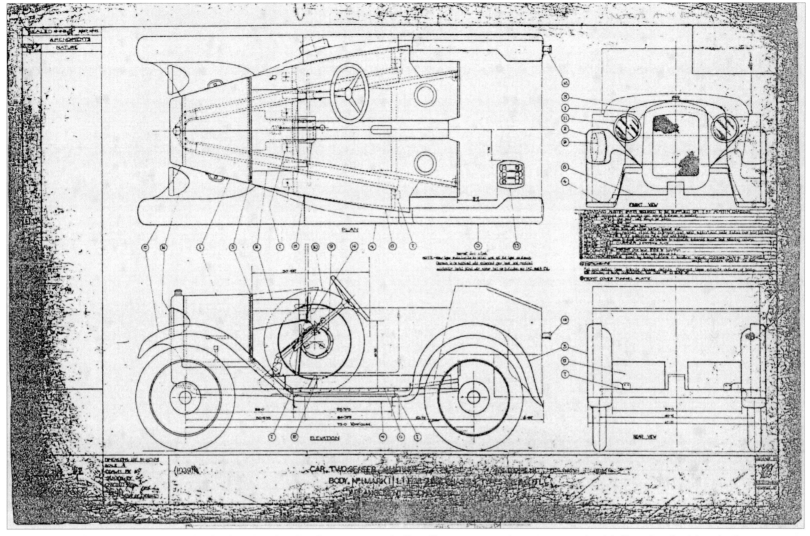

A 1929 War Department body drawing for the first purpose-built military reconnaissance car – the Mulliner-bodied Austin Seven.

daily range of all marching armies since Roman times – would have to be changed. Any future conflict would, it was reasoned, be a moving war. It would involve the rapid taking and holding of territory, and the thousands of army horses would be replaced by powered machines yet to be designed.

Ideally, all this movement of armed forces would take place so quickly, and involve such complete surprise, that the enemy would have no time to organise an effective defence. Thus, once any fixed defences had been penetrated, the invading army would proceed at speed to occupy the enemy's land. The paradox was that, in theory, this potentially deadlier type of warfare should involve far fewer casualties on both sides than the 1914-18 war.

For Britain in the 1920s, the key means to achieve all this was the 'mechanisation of the British Army.' Plans were drawn up as to

what machinery might be required, and how it might be tested and developed. The main difficulty was avoiding any big disparity in the speed of the machines, so that the whole army would advance in good order, at the same reasonably fast pace – this at a time when one newly-designed self-propelled British gun recorded a lumbering road speed of less than 2mph (3km/h). In contrast, apart from motorcycles, the Austin Seven was the fastest vehicle considered by the Army at this time!

In 1927, the 17th Field Company Royal Engineers workshops built a low, minimal (to the point of being skeletal) cross-country vehicle on an Austin Seven chassis. The vehicle returned promising results, being light enough to be man-handled out of trouble, and with a rear platform for an observer to stand upon. The War Department therefore decided that a small reconnaissance field or scout car should

Guards officers bicker over who gets to lead in the Austin Sevens. These are early low-profile 1929 Mulliners with shallow windscreens. The armoured cars are huge Lanchesters, built on six-wheeled truck chassis. (Author collection)

be commissioned and evaluated in trials – by both cavalry regiments – before committing a major advance by their Rolls-Royce and Lanchester armoured cars. The car was also to be tested by British field artillery, to take an officer observer forward and allow them to report back to the guns on the accuracy of their fire. Both of these tasks were previously undertaken by a single horse-mounted scout.

Austin had previously sold a few examples of the popular, inexpensive, and expendable Seven to the Army, and was approached again by the War Office. In April 1929, and after a couple of prototypes, the first purpose-built

The original Austin Seven Military tool-kit contains a few special items like the hub extractor, but here also includes the D-shaped wheel hub handles (part 1A4068) with which the occupants can lift the entire car in emergencies. (Author collection)

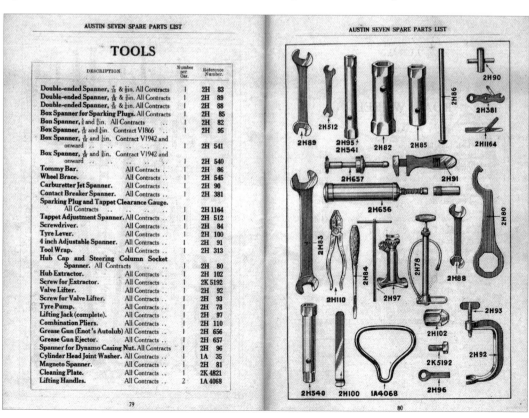

AUSTIN SEVEN SPARE PARTS LIST

TOOLS

DESCRIPTION.		Number per Car.	Reference Number.
Double-ended Spanner, ⁷⁄₁₆ & ½in. All Contracts		1	2H 83
Double-ended Spanner, ⁵⁄₁₆ & ⅜in. All Contracts		1	2H 89
Double-ended Spanner, ¼ & ⁵⁄₁₆in. All Contracts		1	2H 88
Box Spanner for Sparking Plugs. All Contracts		1	2H 85
Box Spanner, ⅜in. All Contracts		1	2H 82
Box Spanner, ⁷⁄₁₆ and ½in. Contract V1866		1	2H 95
Box Spanner, ⁷⁄₁₆ and ½in. Contract V1942 and onward		1	2H 541
Box Spanner, ⁷⁄₁₆ and ½in. Contract V1942 and onward		1	2H 540
Tommy Bar.	All Contracts	1	2H 86
Wheel Brace.	All Contracts	1	2H 545
Carburetter Jet Spanner.	All Contracts	1	2H 90
Contact Breaker Spanner.	All Contracts	1	2H 381
Sparking Plug and Tappet Clearance Gauge. All Contracts		1	2H 1164
Tappet Adjustment Spanner.	All Contracts	1	2H 512
Screwdriver.	All Contracts	1	2H 84
Tyre Lever.	All Contracts	1	2H 100
4 inch Adjustable Spanner.	All Contracts	1	2H 91
Tool Wrap.	All Contracts	1	2H 313
Hub Cap and Steering Column Socket Spanner. All Contracts		1	2H 80
Hub Extractor.	All Contracts	1	2H 102
Screw for Extractor.	All Contracts	1	2K 5192
Valve Lifter.	All Contracts	1	2H 92
Screw for Valve Lifter.	All Contracts	1	2H 93
Tyre Pump.	All Contracts	1	2H 78
Lifting Jack (complete).	All Contracts	1	2H 97
Combination Pliers.	All Contracts	1	2H 110
Grease Gun (Enot's Autolub) All Contracts		1	2H 656
Grease Gun Ejector.	All Contracts	1	2H 657
Spanner for Dynamo Casing Nut. All Contracts		1	2H 96
Cylinder Head Joint Washer. All Contracts		1	1A 35
Magneto Spanner.	All Contracts	1	2H 81
Cleaning Plate.	All Contracts	1	2K 4821
Lifting Handles.	All Contracts	2	1A 4068

79

AUSTIN SEVEN SPARE PARTS LIST

2H90

2H86

2H381

2H512

2H89   2H95 / 2H541   2H82   2H85   2H1164

2H657   2H91

2H656

2H83   2H84   2H78   2H88

2H80

2H110   2H97

2H93

2H102

2K5192   2H92

2H540   2H100   1A4068   2H96

80

The rare 1939 Dinky Toys Mechanised Army Set, this example owned by the author's elder brother, explained to a small boy the role and function of the Military Austin Seven. (Author collection/Courtesy Nick Salmon)

the rake of the steering column, and giving a commendably low profile to the whole car, which could be entirely concealed below a low hedge. A canvas hood was provided, but no side screens, or windscreen wipers for the low windscreen, were considered necessary. The scuttle-mounted fuel tank had a very large diameter filler (for pre-jerry can military-type fuel churns) and there was a system of weirs inside the fuel tank to retain enough fuel to get home in the event of the car having been completely upside down at any stage of its military travels. The scuttle

run of military Sevens were given a body by Mulliners of Birmingham, despite originally being intended to be built in Army workshops.

Sir Herbert Austin had, of course, early personal connections with the Vickers, Armstrong, and Maxim armament manufacturers, as well as close ties with the military authorities as a result of his factory's production of trucks, shells, and aircraft during World War One. The Army had used many standard and modified cars in a host of roles during the conflict, but the 1929 Austin Seven Scout car was the first purpose-designed and built reconnaissance car of any make employed by the British Army.

The Austin Seven had good ground clearance, and was light. It was so light, in fact (and keeping in mind the mud of churned up battlefields), that the early military versions had small bobbins fitted to the wheel centres. This allowed the two occupants to lift either end of the car out of muddy difficulties, using D-shaped handles and ropes with eyelets found in the tool kit. Towing eyes were also fitted to the chassis below the radiator, and to the radius arms. The rear axle had strengthening webs, and an extra-low gear ratio. The Mulliner body consisted of a simple box-like locker to the rear with a large top lid, on which were clipped two Lee Enfield .303 rifles for self-protection. The spare wheel was mounted vertically, where the driver's door would otherwise be, and there was a single – and removable – passenger's door for the officer observer.

The first cars had very shallow windscreens and seats fixed straight to the floor, requiring a sports-type steering box to lower

top was removable via wing nuts, allowing access to the dashboard, and 'knobbly' tyres were fitted. 'Mechanisation trials' took place on Salisbury Plain over a three year period, and the military Austin Seven was considered a success; ultimately several hundred of these cars, updated in-line with production Sevens, were tested against horse mounted troops. The dashing cavalry regiments the 10th and 11th Royal Hussars and the 12th Royal Lancers, in particular, were – not unnaturally – very reluctant indeed to give up their horses, to which they had been historically wedded for 300 years.

Communication between mechanical mobile forces at this time was, as between ships in the Navy, mainly via coloured signalling flags, and so equally visible to both friend and foe. The field artillery spotter Austin Sevens were intended to go forward and observe, do a quick three-point turn, then return to the – bulky, and difficult to conceal – Crossley field telephone trucks. These were connected by wire field telephone to the controller at the guns. Amazing though it may now seem, military Austin Sevens were therefore front-line vehicles!

The next development was to try to use radios for communication. These early sets, however, were large, bulky, and fragile; the No 1 Radio Set was unsuccessfully tried in three of the original Mulliner-bodied Scouts, where there was just not enough room. So, the wide scuttle Signals-bodied military Austin Sevens of 1932 came into being.

These cars had the No 1 Radio Set let into the scuttle, in front of the passenger/operator – the type's new bodywork being open at the rear, like a small pick-up truck, and packed full of batteries. A larger canvas

The RAF experimented with this 1931 wireless car to contact nearby aircraft, and – in the Middle East – RAF Rolls-Royce armoured cars on patrol. (Author collection)

The unusual crankcase of a 1932 'Tropical' spec Military Mulliner, accommodating a gear-driven water pump at the front. Army spec Sevens generally lagged behind normal examples, in an attempt at standardisation. (Author collection)

hood covered the whole area, and the spare wheel was now vertically mounted on the back. The whole contraption was surmounted by a 14ft high (3.9m) wood and wire-braced aerial on the scuttle, which could only be erected while the car was static.

These signal- or wireless-bodied cars were later deployed alongside the Mulliner Scout cars, during the Saar Plebiscite in the winter of 1934/35, as well as in the Middle and Far East, where many were equipped with special water pump engines, large-gilled tube radiators, and other 'tropical' equipment. The rapid development and reduction in size of radio equipment at this time led, by 1940, to personal two-way field radios, or 'Walkie-Talkies,' in backpacks. This made obsolete the primary need for a whole vehicle to carry fragile glass-valve radio equipment, which in any case was rapidly shaken to bits when bouncing over rough terrain in an enthusiastically-driven cart-sprung Austin Seven.

The Austin Seven Mulliner Scout cars, however, were capable of carrying two men, as opposed to a single rider on a horse, and so fared a little better. They were even trialled as a two-man weapons system, carrying either a 3in (76mm) mortar, strapped across the rear locker, or a Vickers water-cooled heavy machine gun. The limited range of both weapons unfortunately placed the Austin well within sight of the enemy!

By 1934, the War Department had concluded the trials for which the original Mulliner-bodied Scout cars had been designed, and in 1935 came up with a new and drastically different British Army specification.

This required future military Scout cars to be four-wheel drive, both forward and backward, thus eliminating the need for a three-point turn in a potentially exposed position. They were to

November 11, 1939.   729   The Light Car

The Light Car Inaugurates—

A REGISTER OF MOTOR TRIALS DRIVERS

War Office Approves of Scheme Proposed by this Journal

READERS with trials driving experience will be interested to learn that the War Office has warmly approved the idea of *The Light Car* register of experienced trials drivers for enlistment in the R.A.S.C. Negotiations with the appropriate department have been concluded. We now launch the scheme and we shall be pleased to hear from readers who would care to offer their services.

A number of driving schools has just been initiated, and there are vacancies for the posts of driver-instructors. There are also openings not only for non-commissioned ranks, but for commissioned ranks as well; in fact, the prospects in the case of suitable applicants in the R.A.S.C. are "outstandingly good," to quote the official description.

The biggest requirement of all is for ex-Service men with trials experience, as they are familiar with the drill and Army procedure. They would be posted to driving centres as instructors with very little or no preliminary training.

At the outset, readers who think that they might qualify should write to us, briefly outlining their experience and naming in particular any awards in trials they have obtained. If the application is considered to be a satisfactory one, a special form issued by the recruiting authorities will be sent to the applicant, which will ensure that the application reaches the correct destination.

All applications should be addressed to The Editor, *The Light Car*, Bowling Green Lane, London, E.C.1, and marked "War Driver" in the top left-

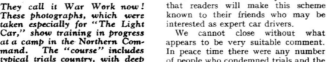

They call it War Work now! These photographs, which were taken especially for "The Light Car," show training in progress at a camp in the Northern Command. The "course" includes typical trials country, with deep water-splashes and steep grass-grown gradients as part and parcel of the route. An Austin and a Morris figure in the photographs.

hand corner. Incidentally, we trust that readers will make this scheme known to their friends who may be interested as expert car drivers.

We cannot close without what appears to be very suitable comment. In peace time there were any number of people who condemned trials and the type of young enthusiast who took part in them. On more than one occasion we were compelled staunchly to support them. We pointed out, amongst other things, that they would be urgently needed if war broke out.

We were right.

The two photographs on this page clearly reveal the kind of training through which novices are at present passed. Either of the pictures might well be mistaken for an episode in any trial you like to name, organized by any club you like to mention. The war, it is said, is making a new race of trials drivers; to put it another way, trials drivers are offered the opportunity of carrying on with the fine old pastime under war conditions. Even for men who ultimately drive heavy lorries, it has been found that the light car offers the best method of early training.

It is fitting that *The Light Car* should undertake the preparation of a Register of War Drivers. The journal has been essentially the *vade mecum* of club and trials enthusiasts; it is recognized as such throughout the country. Any clubs which are still functioning might deem it worth while to circularize their members, drawing attention to our scheme. They can be sure of our whole-hearted co-operation.

▲ 13

Experienced Austin Seven trials drivers were in great demand as instructors in the run-up to WW2; the Seven was the basic RASC training vehicle, with *The Light Car* setting up a register.
(Courtesy *The Light Car*)

have light armour, and more performance from more power. The resultant vehicle, now known as the very familiar Daimler Dingo, was a light-armoured Scout car, with a revolving driver's seat and five-speed gearbox – operating equally in both directions – and coil suspension. Recognisable derivative types, in the form of the more recent Ferret family of armoured cars, therefore owe something of their existence to the military Austin Seven. Unfortunately, few of the early Mulliner types have survived, as 'tests to destruction' formed a part of the trials.

Back in 1929, a few Gordon England Two-Seater Cup models were also trialled as staff cars for junior officers, a double rear axle Seven was tested to improve load carrying across rough terrain, and at least one Mulliner was equipped with Horstman swinging arm front suspension (Horstman were specialists in tracked vehicle suspension as used on interwar British Light and Medium tanks).

The Army had, in 1932, ordered some two-seater PD Open Tourers for general liaison work. These were, initially, simply the civilian version, but painted in prewar military Service Green (very close to Land Rover's Deep Bronze Green). However, they were subsequently fitted with uprated road springs and 17in (431mm) wheels, including lifting bobbins, along with other detail changes. These cars were used extensively for driver training, and it was the well-deserved 'go anywhere' reputation of the Seven that made them especially suitable for general military duties.

The Military Tourer APD, derived from the PD, was built solely for the British Army at home and abroad, and over 1000 were supplied from 1934, with many still in service into World War Two. Many examples that were with the British Expeditionary Force ended up being abandoned on the beaches of Dunkirk in 1940. The cars were used in World War Two for light liaison and driver training, and, postwar, a few of these Austin Seven APDs were still in use in RASC (Royal Army Service Corps) depots – their narrow width being useful between aisles of military stores at the time of the 1948 Berlin airlift.

Austin exported two batches of doorless military APDs to India, none of which have reappeared to date, but a detailed inspection of the Khyber Pass might reveal a few survivors!

As Austin Seven use after World War Two reduced, and the cars became obsolete, government surplus bulk sales allowed the purchase of many new military spares – such as crankshafts, tyres, and even complete cars. This formed the basis for many specialist Austin Seven supply companies, such as Pride and Clarke, and allowed them to thrive during the 1950s, and serve enthusiasts right up to the present, also starting the cottage industry that keeps the surprising number of Sevens running today.

Late 1930s Military Convoy training, led by a toy-like APD. Morris Commercial Light Infantry trucks follow. (Author collection)

The aftermath of war. Dunkirk, 1940, and an abandoned and disabled British Expeditionary Force APD Military Tourer is left amongst the silent debris on the beach. (Author collection)

The German Army plays serious war games far away from prying eyes, in Eastern Prussia. The numbered cardboard tanks mounted on Dixis are amusing now, but belied deadly intentions. (Author collection)

1930s German military trials of the Dixi/BMW Field Car, with camouflaged competition behind. (Courtesy Helmut Kasimirowicz)

The Reichswehr (note the RW number plates) train using military Dixis, fitted with solid windscreens with vision splits to simulate fully armoured warfare conditions. (Courtesy Helmut Kasimirowicz)

GERMANY

After World War One, the Treaty of Versailles had forbidden Germany from producing heavy artillery or other weapons of war. The country's postwar military organisation, dubbed the Reichswehr, was limited to light cars such as the Automobilwerk Eisenach Dixi DA-1, which started production in 1927 and was very similar to its contemporary the Austin Chummy. Being left-hand drive, however, the Longbridge-designed Dixi engine was a mirror image of the normal Austin version.

The BMW motorcycle company took over Automobilwerk Eisenach the following year, and with it production of the Dixi. In early 1929,

at around the same time that the War Office in Britain had devised the specification of the Mulliner Scout, BMW came up with its own military vehicle by modifying a production DA-2 design. This new vehicle incorporated a simple two-seater open body, front cycle wings that turned with the wheels, and a scuttle-mounted machine gun. These cars carried an assortment of panniers and a basket-weave quiver on the side, to store long-handled signalling flags for practicing manoeuvres.

One of the German brains behind this effort was Heinz Guderian. Guderian had taken great note of the freely-published works by several

A rare photograph showing that in Germany the Wehrmacht (note the WH registration number) used its Dixi BMWs for general liaison duties through World War Two. (Courtesy Helmut Kasimirowicz)

An American Austin, converted by the US Army with a multiple-barrel anti-aircraft gun and balloon tyres on tiny wheels. Production apparently stopped at just the one. (Author collection)

Group of 1941 Bantam Jeep prototypes of surprisingly familiar shape. (Bantam publicity)

British military theorists, on avoiding the entrenched stalemate of the First World War. Taking this to heart, it was he who came up with the famous 'Blitzkrieg' or 'lightning war' plan of attack – aptly named, and forged in the electricity of the new art of radio communications and the fire of the internal combustion engine.

The German generals were forced to play out their war games in Eastern Prussia – far away from prying international eyes – and, having been banned from producing tanks, made do by building wooden tank replica bodies to be mounted on their Dixis. Crews were trained, relying only on vision slits, to communicate with flags and – later on – radios. Later, they transferred their machine guns to the famous BMW high-speed military sidecars that were loved by post-WW2 filmmakers.

With its military ambitions, the development of weapons and logistical vehicles was heavily financed by the Nazi government. After Dunkirk, in 1940, the victorious Wehrmacht must have been bemused to see that the British Expeditionary Force was still using Austin Sevens as forward communications vehicles.

UNITED STATES

By the late '20s, the United States Army had taken note of the European fashion for minimal, ultra-light cross-country military vehicles, such as the Austin Seven. In 1933, a stripped-down Seven (built in Butler, Pennsylvania, by The American Austin Car Company) was fitted with enormous balloon tyres and triple machine guns on a simple rear

deck. Possibly the same Austin Seven engine was then taken by Master Sergeant Melvyn Wiley and Colonel Robert Howie, and mounted in the back of an extremely low-profile, simple platform chassis, on small wheels. The vehicle was equipped with a forward-facing machine gun, operated by the two occupants lying full-length on their stomachs – hence its nickname, 'Belly Flopper.' It was remarkably similar in general concept and appearance to the Mini Moke, which the British Army flirted with as a lightweight, low-profile airborne vehicle, some four decades later.

Flying 1941 Bantam Jeep, towing a 75mm field gun during trials at Fort Belvoir, Virginia. (Bantam publicity)

American Austin became American Bantam in 1935, and in 1938 the company lent three standard Austin Seven-based solid disc-wheeled Bantam Roadsters to the National Guard for trials. As a result of favourable reports on the three little cars, in June 1940 Charles Payne of Bantam put forward his own original design proposal to the US Army. He suggested an order of special small reconnaissance vehicles broadly based on these cars, and unknowingly sparked a revolution in car design.

The specification was soon agreed, and included two driven axles and a maximum wheelbase of 6ft 8in (2.0m). However, of the 135 manufacturers approached, just two replied – Bantam and Willys-Overland – and only Bantam agreed to build the prototype cars within the extremely short specified time limit of 75 days. As a result, Bantam was inevitably given the order.

The Bantam-built prototype field car already looked astonishingly Jeep-like when delivered and tested. Unfortunately for Bantam, however, observers from Willys and Ford were allowed to be present at the trials, and the rest is history. The 1500 cars of the initial contract were split three ways, between Bantam, Willys, and Ford, and it was only a matter of time before the two larger companies effectively took over the production. 2675 Bantam BRC 40 'Jeeps' were eventually built, many being sent to Russia, and a few delivered to the UK for use by the British Airborne Division and 6th Armoured Division in the North African Campaign.

Willys and Ford went on to build tens of thousands of their own versions of the Bantam design. Just as the tank had been the primary new vehicle type to come out of the First World War, so the Jeep was the new vehicle type to emanate from World War Two. Countless 4x4s and SUVs on the road today therefore owe some of their ancestral DNA to Bantam – via the Jeep – and so to the Austin Seven.

CHAPTER NINE

RACING SUCCESS AND INTO THE 1930s

TOWARDS the end of the 1920s, a number of fundamental changes were made to the Seven. All by way of improvements to the specification, rather than change for change's sake, these alterations had the result of, over a three year period, a radically different basic-type Austin Seven being made available to the public. The principal base model moved from a short chassis, narrow open body, three-speed magneto ignition machine, to a longer, wider, steel saloon body, with a four-speed gearbox and coil ignition.

The first of these changes was made in late 1928 – by which time 68,000 cars had already been completed – by moving from magneto ignition to Lucas coil. In October 1930, after more than 140,000 Sevens had been built, the first RN Saloons, with steel bodies on a longer-wheelbase 6ft 9in (2.05m) chassis, were introduced. A year later, the three-speed gearboxes were replaced by a four-speed constant mesh gearbox, and the electric starter motor was moved from its position on top of the gearbox and inside the cockpit, to be relocated under the bonnet, in front of the driver's foot pedals.

The chassis was extended to the rear, the whole front two-thirds of the frame remaining much as it had previously. The wider rear required that the rear axle was also widened, gaining track width to better support the heavier rear bodywork, and was assisted by strengthened chassis extensions sitting inside the rear quarter-elliptic springs. The radiator also was increased in height, to balance the visual raising of the car waistline, with the result of the whole vehicle becoming slightly more bulky.

Within a few short years, therefore, the Austin Seven as a product had changed. It had perhaps put on a little weight, but was a better and more civilised motor car to show for it. This was a sentiment the public clearly agreed with, as, despite international economic difficulties causing demand for cars to tail off, no less than 45,000 Sevens left Longbridge in 1930-31, and more than 20,000 in 1932. This, in comparison with the 1929 production peak of 26,450.

With the technical changes at the end of the 1920s, the Austin Seven also lost some of its original visual lightness. Instead, a more rounded body shape was complemented by fuller profile wings. When the Vintage Sports Car Club was set up just a few years later – both

The new range for 1930 included the nicely proportioned, long scuttle 'Two-Seater' (later named the Boat Tail), the 'Fabric' Saloon, with fully openable screen, and the four-seat 'Tourer.' (Austin publicity)

The Austin Seven—Models

The "Two Seater"

A "nippy and natty" little model, with appearance in line with its performance.

The wide doors give easy access to comfortable seats and the car is both a sporty proposition and thoroughly comfortable conveyance, too. There is ample luggage space, and the spare wheel—included in equipment —is neatly stowed away. The hood and side curtains afford ample protection when in position. The colours and colour schemes are most attractive.

The New "Fabric" Saloon

THIS new fabric saloon of special non-drumming construction has increased roominess. The elegance of the new lines makes it a more dainty carriage than before.

Visibility is remarkably good, and light and ventilation are excellent.

Both saloons have slightly sloping one-piece windscreens, with a very ingenious device for securing the screen in an open or closed position.

The "Tourer"

HERE is "the little friend of all the world." When the hood and side curtains are erected this model loses none of that smart appearance which distinguishes it when in fine-weather trim.

The well equipped fascia board possesses two small recesses, convenient for gloves, small parcels, etc.

Both the comfortable front seats tip up and are adjustable.

15

Austin's original detailed spare parts lists, such as this 1932 Military Scout car example, hold invaluable information for enthusiasts, restorers, and historians alike. (Author collection)

marking and mourning the passing of 'vintage' motoring – it set a date of December 1930 as the end of the vintage era. This date is certainly reflected in the case of Austin Seven design.

The success of the Seven had not gone unnoticed by other motor manufacturers, particularly William Morris, and it is a point worth debating as to why it took so long for competitors to mount a challenge against Herbert Austin's little Seven. It is perhaps a measure of the success of the Austin Seven's original design concept that, while it was selling like hot cakes, there were few alternatives to it that could be imagined, other than a straight copy. Such a move would hardly be British, and possibly infringe upon the patents that Herbert Austin so jealously guarded – to the real benefit of both the factory, and his personal bank balance.

It is possible, too, that the great fuss that the public made of the Austin Seven upon its introduction, and the subsequent individual identity that the little car fostered, in effect suppressed the ability of potential competitors to believe that they could possibly do any better. Herbert Austin had anticipated the demand for his tiny – but practical and economical – Seven in 1922, and perhaps his competitors could not see any other direction that small family motoring could take, until more than half a decade had passed.

By 1928, however, William Morris had done his homework on the market for a car with horsepower akin to the Seven, based on his own success in the market for larger family cars. Morris, at this time, was selling many more cars than Austin in the popular mid-horsepower range. It had recently updated the famous Bullnose, as well as taking over Wolseley – the rival company – and, importantly, its Birmingham factory.

The statistics from 1927 show that while sales of 12hp cars were increasing nationally in Britain – by about 15 per cent, per year – figures for 8hp cars were doubling year on year. What's more, Austin Sevens accounted for almost 50 per cent of all sales in the 8hp cars range that year, and there were (correct) expectations of even greater sales in 1928-29, of more than 20,000 Sevens sold per year. On top of the promising sales forecasts, fuel duty had been increased in 1928, further favouring the small car.

Finally, William Morris decided the time had come for a car to take on Austin's Seven. That May, the Morris Minor was introduced. It has to be said that the Morris Minor was a good car, with an 850cc overhead camshaft engine, better brakes, and a slightly larger body – so, a higher overall specification – and this all for a similar showroom price of an Austin Seven.

Singer, too, built large numbers of its own 845cc small car, and the other British firms of Triumph, AC, Jowett, and Trojan – along with the inexpensive 9hp Clyno – all offered very cheap alternatives to the Seven, in an attempt to cash in on the market that the original car, by its very concept, had created.

The Austin Seven, by this time in 1928, was available at £99 for a rolling chassis, £135 for a Tourer and £150 for a Saloon – all very similar prices to the slightly more advanced, but perhaps less charismatic, Morris Minor. With the motor trade talking of little else but these 'baby' cars, William Morris felt perhaps over-confident, and decided to increase the price of the Minor by £5 across the whole range in time for the London Motor Show – now known as the British International Motor Show.

The successful Barnes Brothers, with the 1929 'Harlequin' Ulster.
(Austin publicity)

Whilst the others, including Clyno, followed suit, Sir Herbert Austin's master stroke was to announce that the price of a Seven was to be dropped. With the price of a chassis down to £92, this allowed the many coach-builders with vehicles based on Seven chassis to also drop their prices accordingly.

A somewhat red-faced William Morris was forced to change course, and his rather hasty price increase of a few weeks earlier was put into immediate reverse. His Minor range dropped back down to figures very similar to the price of a Seven, and this embarrassment marked the beginning of a small car price war.

However, it may also be true that the advent of rivals to his Seven – which closely coincided with the group of improvements that can be considered the 'baby' growing up – inspired or obliged Herbert Austin to take stock, and to revitalise the Seven in preparation for its second decade of production.

Many of the changes and improvements to the Seven are difficult to pin down to specific chassis numbers, as there was always a degree of overlap. The written specification of an individual model may or may not, therefore, have included all of the available modifications that its date of manufacture might indicate. It would seem that certain features appeared as stocks became available, such as vent flaps fitted into the sides of the scuttle (at about the time when one-piece windscreens were first adopted), and the differences in the design of the peaks above the windscreen. Differences in the dashboard layout have been noted for the same reasons, and, when

speaking today, many owners will reveal one or two specification anomalies about their own Sevens.

Factory stoppages by particular tradesmen did not assist in the steady and consistent production that was all but demanded by the continuous-speed production lines. Many cars were therefore sold that were not compliant to the company sales brochures, to a greater or lesser degree. Then, with disruptive strikes by workers concerned about the loss of hard-fought-for employment rights, Longbridge stopped production for several weeks in early 1928. Herbert Austin was reluctantly obliged to threaten dismissal in order to get his workers back and order restored, and the losses incurred, together with an increased and improved specification – such as Triplex safety glass – were reflected in a small price increase.

In marketing terms, the need to tempt the public with a new product had swung momentum away from simply improving in small increments, as had been Austin's policy from its earliest days. Instead, it was in vogue to have introduce a new or different model each year, announced at the London Motor Show – a move that was against the grain of Herbert Austin's own ethos. Morris had also introduced the concept of a basic 'starter' model in the company's range, to be supplemented with a deluxe model that cost significantly more, available if the purchaser wished to spend extra for additional features. This pattern of marketing increasingly became accepted by the public as the norm; for the manufacturer, the profit margins on the deluxe versions were greater, and the buyers were tempted by salesmen who could, in effect, offer a more custom-made specification for each individual car.

The Austin Seven derivatives in France and Germany had become very successful, and Herbert Austin was certain that the American market would also respond to the Seven, even though there was no apparent demand at the time. Both Ford and General Motors were truly international companies, and their European representatives were very familiar with the light and small cars that were widely available. However, the executives of each company back in the States were equally aware of the demands of its own market.

Against the odds, therefore, but still convinced of the viability of producing a light economy car for America, Herbert Austin set out on a path that had a far from satisfactory conclusion. First with American Austins, and later with the US-produced Sevens restructured and re-badged as Bantam, Herbert led both shareholders and workers on a roller coaster ride of varied fortunes for most of the 1930s.

The general and world-wide economic depression that followed the 1929 Wall Street crash had obliged the Labour government of the day – led by Ramsay McDonald – to channel enormous sums into providing for the unemployed. The great majority of those who found themselves

Nobby Spero in 'Mrs Jo Jo' – the ex-Gordon England No 2 racer –
leads a field of other Sevens at Brooklands in 1928.
(Courtesy Ferret Fotographics)

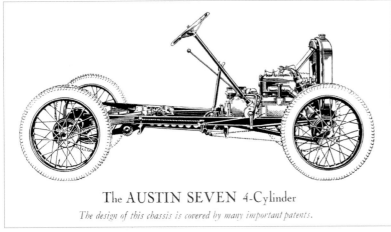

The **AUSTIN SEVEN** 4-Cylinder
The design of this chassis is covered by many important patents.

The 1930 chassis with ball change gearbox. (Austin publicity)

however, a buffer effect on the car industry, as those able to purchase a motor car were not amongst the sectors most affected by the initial stagnation of the economy. The shareholders in Austin continued to do well, with the production of the Seven accounting for more than half of the 43,000 cars – of all types – produced in that year.

Technical changes were made to the Seven, such as coupled brakes, which allowed all four brakes to be applied simultaneously, by either the foot pedal or the hand brake, or – in an emergency – both together. A longitudinal light channel section, set on its side and perforated with lightening holes, was also riveted between the middle and rear crossmembers, giving a stiffer mounting for the handbrake, compensator cross shaft centre bearing, and adjuster. This stiffened structure gave more bite to the feel of the brakes, and the improved brakes were needed for the extra weight of the whole car.

The scuttle-mounted under-bonnet fuel tank was increased in capacity by a gallon, by making its base horizontal rather than sloping, and leg room was increased for the back seat passengers. The recommended load capacity for the car also increased, from 30 to 36 stone (405lb), and made possible by upping the gauge of the steel floor.

Ingenious pneumatic seat squabs were introduced, in design rather like a jumping cracker firework, with a serpentine layout of inflatable rubber tubes (these are possible to almost replicate by taping together tyre inner tubes). The front seats, meanwhile, were tipped forward in order to gain access to the rear seats. The door windows were changed from two-piece horizontal sliders to a single piece of glass, raised and lowered by winding handles, and the top hanged opening windscreen was operated by an over-centre lockable lever handle. Both the Seven Tourer and the new Seven Saloon were marketed at a similar price to the Morris Minor two-seater, at £130, while steel-bodied vans were offered at £7 less.

Sevens continued to be raced and used in other competitive sporting events throughout this period. In March 1928, Gunnar Poppe – captain of the London Welsh rugby team – took a normal tourer, fitted with a 13½-gallon fuel tank, from Austin's Piccadilly London showroom to Edinburgh and back. He covered the 790mi (1271km) journey in just under 21 hours, driving virtually non-stop and pausing in Edinburgh for just 15 minutes before beginning his return journey.

Poppe and SV Holbrook took two Super Sports prototypes to the Shelsley Walsh Hillclimb in July, Holbrook climbing in a brisk 63.6 seconds, while on the same day 'Slippery Ann' – a supercharged Seven racer – managed 57.4 seconds, driven by Coldicutt. At Pendine Sands in August, the two Super Sports were in the same hands, and this time recorded a win and a second place result, lapping at 60mph (96km/h) and touching 84mph (135km/h) on the straights.

out of work were vulnerable unskilled, or semi-skilled, men who had little job security to start with. Unemployed numbers continued to increase, passing the two million mark by late 1930, representing an unacceptably large percentage of men available for work. There was,

Captain CK Chase and his two relief drivers, HB Parker and HD Bland, at Montlhéry, Paris, after raising the 24-hour record to a 65.98mph (106.18km/h) average including stops. (Austin publicity)

and economy race, popular at the time, with Waters missing the win by one lap. The light little Cup-bodied car achieved this speed at a fuel consumption of a mere 46.39mpg.

Dingle, with JH Wilson as co-driver, managed 306.4mi (492km) in the Essex Motor Club Six-Hour Endurance at Brooklands, in May. Also at Brooklands, the 'up to 850cc' class was full of Sevens in the important JCC 200-Mile Race at Brooklands in July. Gordon Hendy was joined by AE Walter, Coldicutt in 'Slippery Ann,' HC Spero in 'Mrs Jo-Jo,' Dingle, RF Walker in XW1581, and Chase in the 24-hour record breaker.

Various troubles were experienced by some entries, mainly from cylinder heads and head gaskets, but Spero consistently averaged a whisker under 60mph (96km/h), winning the class from Walter. Chase had his oil pump spindle break, and scalding oil blew out of the engine to burn his arm severely. He pushed the car home, only to find himself out of the time limit.

Continued page 105

CK Chase took his 1927 200-Mile Race-winning car, now with a Thomson and Taylor-tuned motor, to Montlhéry. There, he attacked long distance records that were held at the time by Peugeot, at the very modest average speed of less than 41mph (65km/h). With co-drivers HB Parker and HD Bland, Chase set off in appalling weather, averaging over 67mph (107km/h) for the first three hours. Parker and Bland then took over for the next five hours. At midnight, Chase got into the Austin again but, after another two and a half hours in pouring rain, was alarmed to suddenly lose his sight. It was only by good fortune that he avoided crashing at speed, and managed to creep back to the pits where he collapsed and was replaced by Bland. Chase's sight only returned after rest.

After beating the previously held 750cc 24-hours distance record after only 15½ hours of running, Chase decided to finish with a flourish. He gave the little car its head and, incredibly, averaged more than 80mph (128km/h) for the last four laps – setting new 12 hour, 1000km, 1000mi and 2000km records, and covering 1584.32mi (2549km) in 24 hours, at an average speed of 65.98mph. A quite extraordinary achievement. The speeds achieved on the banked tracks – where, even when straw bale chicanes were installed, the Austins were still flat out for most of the lap – do demonstrate the car's amazing reliability, and bear comparison with the speeds achieved by Austin Sevens in current vintage events even today.

In June 1928, Hendy won a 75mph Brooklands Short Handicap race at 80.20mph (129km/h). Dingle and Waters, in a Gordon England Brooklands and Cup respectively, ran in a 150-mile speed

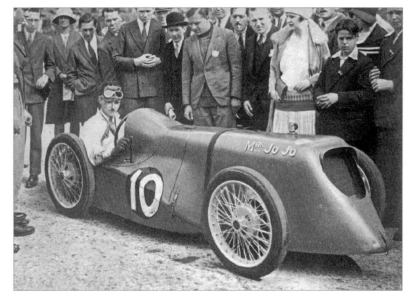

The famous photograph of HC Spero at the wheel of Mrs Jo Jo, having won the President's Gold Plate at Brooklands. (A7CA archive)

THE AUSTIN SEVEN ULSTER

The two-seater sports, now popularly known as the Ulster, evolved from the 1928 Super Sports, which had staggered-seat bodywork, a swept up scuttle, and a pretty pointed tail that dropped towards the rear and contained a horizontally-mounted spare wheel. The 1928 supercharged engine claimed to produce only 27bhp at 4500rpm, and the 75mph (120km/h) maximum catalogue speed was little different from the unblown Brooklands model of a few years earlier. These modest figures were, however, proven to be over-cautious, with the works car exhibiting a speed of 84mph (135km/h) in the 1928 Ulster Grand Prix, at the hands of the Barnes brothers.

For the 1929 version, the bodywork was similar in appearance but slightly widened, allowing side-by-side seating. The upswept scuttle had gone, with the bonnet line instead simply following through to the top of the dashboard, and the tail profile was made a little higher at the rear. The suspension was lowered over 3in, following 1928 racing experience, by fitting reverse-camber rear quarter-elliptic springs and a similar reversed profile front spring, which, in turn, required forged drop ends to the radius arms in order to clear the underside of the chassis side rail. This type of suspension became the norm for the various sports Austin Sevens which followed.

The rear axle ratio was still the standard – and rather high – 4.9:1, but the three-speed gearbox featured a high intermediate, or second, gear to assist dig out of corners on a road course. With a stronger crankshaft and connecting rods, the engine could safely reach the higher revs made available by the better breathing that a larger Solex carburettor afforded it – possibly producing up to 38bhp at 5500rpm or above.

With these cars in the roster, the 1929 racing season was highly successful for the works entries, including – famously – the 1929 Ulster Tourist Trophy Race, in which the Austin Sevens had led for hours, much to the delight of the crowd and the acclaim of the motoring press. The little pointed-tail sports racing cars were thereafter called Ulsters and, in latter times have been the

Ex-RAF Meteor jet fighter pilot Reg Nice proudly shows off his immaculate production Ulster (KR 8320) at the 750 Motor Club North Herts Rally, Melbourne in 1972. (750 Motor Club archive)

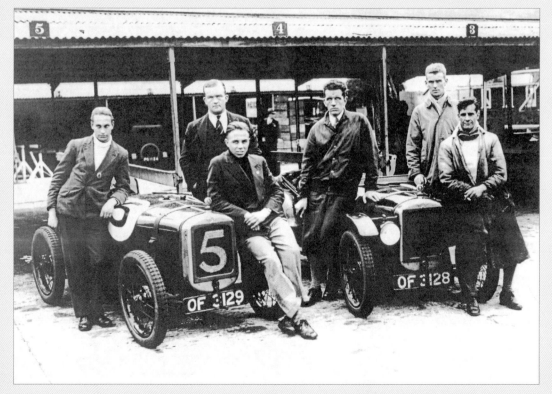

A good day at the office? Apart from Gunnar Poppe, the works Austin team regards the photographer with less than enthusiasm. (Austin publicity)

subject of countless specifically-built replicas or 'specials.' These have varying degrees of authenticity and accuracy of detail, dependant on the intentions and pockets of their enthusiastic owners.

Buoyed up by this success, new factory cars were built for the 1930 season, with distinctively different and deeper rear bodywork to allow the spare wheel to be mounted vertically across the car, just behind the rear axle, with a metal cover fixed down over the body with a leather strap. The seating remained side-by-side, with a cushioned bodywork edge around the doorless cockpit to save banged elbows, whilst the continued development of the engines was accompanied by experiments with lower rear axle ratios.

The increased-capacity fuel tank was mounted above the legs of the driver and passenger, and profiled to form the outer skin of the scuttle bodywork, thus eliminating any unnecessary duplication of metal. The driver was provided with an externally-mounted hand fuel pump. The radiator was slightly higher, as on production Sevens, and maintained Herbert Austin's policy of closely matching his racing models to what was available for the buying public. This special factory racer became known as the Ulster TT.

For the first outing in the 1930 JCC Double Twelve, Arthur Waite was partnered with the Earl of March in one supercharged car, and Frazer-Nash and Gunnar Poppe occupied the other. An unblown Ulster was also entrusted to the experienced Barnes brothers. All ran well, but on handicaps were outpaced by the works MG Midgets.

At the Irish Grand Prix, Frazer-Nash placed third overall, while Poppe retired with engine problems. Waite narrowly missed out on second, behind the Riley of Victor Gillow, when he was wrongly flagged down by a marshal and finally finished a frustrated fifth.

The team had high hopes for its return to the Ulster Tourist Trophy in 1930, and three supercharged cars were entered. The Austins were very fast, benefiting from engine development upgrades, but only Gunnar Poppe was able to finish, and in fifth place, despite being quicker than the previous year's average. Frazer-Nash suffered a blown engine, and it was here that Arthur Waite sadly endured the bad accident in which his jaw was broken, signalling the end of his racing career.

The engine problem experienced by Frazer-Nash stemmed from a failure at the interface of the block with the crankcase. This, in turn was due – it was thought – to additional internal stresses caused by the high supercharger boost pressure that was now being employed by the fitting of special gears to increase the rotational speed of the blowers. The experimental use of higher-lift camshafts, and the stiffer valve springs to control them, may have also contributed to the added stresses; subsequent similar failures in more modern times often cause horizontal cracks to the standard aluminium crankcase, just below the level of the stud fixings for the cast iron block.

The Ulster engine blocks were quickly given heavier base flanges, and an extra thickness of aluminium was added to the top deck of the crankcase, with two additional studs employed. The problem was cured, thus freeing up the potential of these powerful early engines,

Adli Halabi, in the ex-Mike Eyre Orange TT Ulster at Beaulieu, collects his award from Clive Hadley and Mike Featherstonehaugh. (Author collection)

Plenty of information and much to do – the busy cockpit of David Howes' TT Ulster. (Author collection)

estimated to be some 46bhp at 6000rpm. This performance was soon demonstrated, when SCH 'Sammy' Davis was substituted in for the injured Waite at the September BARC meeting, and promptly turned in laps at above 90mph (144km/h). This naturally raised anticipation for the imminent BRDC 500-Mile Race to an all-time high.

Arthur Waite was well enough to act a team manager for the 500 miles, and great care was taken over the preparation of three cars. The first was to be driven by Sammy Davis, with the Earl of March as his partner, the second piloted by Gunnar Poppe and Charles Goodacre, and the third under the care of Barnes and Crabtree. Waite had rehearsed the whole distance before the race, and was confident of the speed required to achieve success with a carefully-measured performance.

The race started in rain, Davis lapping at 83mph (133km/h), in contrast to Philip's unblown Boyd Carpenter Austin's speed of 75mph (120km/h), still pulling and holding 5000rpm on larger 27⅕in diameter tyres. Sadly, a piston seized on Poppe's car, and Crabtree lost all his cooling water. The March/Davis car, however, still flew round the course, being chased by intimidating 'blower' Bentleys, Bugattis, Talbots, and Sunbeams (the Austin pit stops took some time, due to having ordinary filler caps for its two fuel tanks and twin oil tanks).

Being pressed towards the finish, Davis replied with a flourish, turning in successive laps at over 87mph (140km/h) – the driver huddled down below the scuttle level, and holding on to the lowest and shortest line possible around the banking. The Earl of March/ Davis car just held on to the lead, crossing the finish line having averaged no less than 83.4mph (134km/h), whilst the thundering and spectacularly-driven Benjafield/Hall Bentley had to settle for second place, just over six minutes behind after 500mi.

The winning car was taken back to Brooklands a few days later and driven by Davis and Charles Goodacre. There, the 12-hour distance record was attacked, and set at 81.71mph (131km/h) despite the pair having to stop to repair a broken petrol pipe. The endeavour also set 13 International Class H (750cc) records, to the credit of Waite's team. The works development Ulster was then used by Charles Goodacre to take four more records at Brooklands, and it would appear that it was this car that was re-bodied as a 'one-and-a-half-seater,' and taken by Sir Malcolm Campbell to Daytona Beach. There, he achieved a two-way record of 94.06mph (151km/h) – still some way shy of the magic 100mph (160km/h).

The 1930 500-Mile Race win remains the most famous victory by a 'proper' Austin Seven, with Waite able to claim that the car was running well within its performance envelope. Such was the popularity of the win that demand for the production Ulster shot up, and the factory

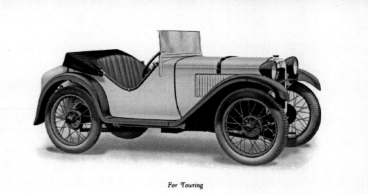

For Touring

In Racing Trim

1931 Sports Model brochure, showing distinctive and popular cream/ green paintwork, but… "any reasonable colours to order without extra charge." (Austin publicity)

responded with a menu of specifications for Austin's premium sports offering, to suit each buyer's requirements.

The production Ulster, marketed as the Austin Seven Super Sports model, was available from early 1930 in two basic specifications – a blown or unblown road car, with full-length touring wings, and a competition blown version with optional separate cycle-type wings. All variations and options had an individual price tag.

The bodywork of the car was marginally wider, and the blown engine was offered in a milder state of tune, giving 33bhp at 5000rpm. True to Austin's original 1923 advertising, the car was sold both as a sports car and for racing, and, being built on the original short and light wheelbase chassis, the production Ulster became (and remains) the most popular of all Austin sports cars. The car combined agile, true vintage performance with robust production bodywork that was superior to most coach-built efforts of the same period, few of which have survived.

For serious private racers, motors up to works specification were made available, and the availability of unblown engines – but with pressurised lubrication and coil ignition – provided many owners with a thoroughly reliable and tractable high performance little car. The model also featured a cast iron head, based on Ricardo theories of the value of turbulence in the charge to enhance combustion particular to the Austin side-valve configuration. The rear axle ratio was changed from the standard Chummy 4.9:1 to a lower 5.22:1, sourced from the 1929 military axle and requiring a larger banjo casing for the lower-ratio crown wheel and pinion. This transformed performance, particularly assisting acceleration off the line, as well as pick up out of slower corners and top end flexibility.

The exploits of all the private entries of Ulsters over 70 years – both pre- and post-World War Two – would fill a book on their own. They are the most competitive two-seater sports built by Austin, and seen in countless weekends events, in the UK and elsewhere, throughout the year.

In his 1930 road Ulster, Graham Beckett marks his turn-in point for Pardon Hairpin at a damp 1998 Prescott meeting. (Courtesy Ferret Fotographics)

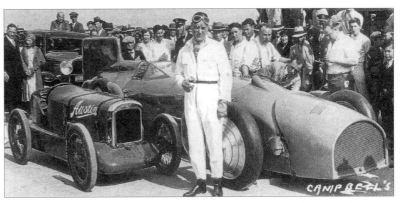

Daytona Beach, Florida, USA, January 1931. Malcolm Campbell stands with the works offset single-seater, alongside the LSR car 'Bluebird.' (Austin publicity)

A relatively minor accident occurred at Kop Hillclimb, near Princes Risborough, in 1925, where a spectator in an unauthorised location had his leg broken after a Bugatti slid off the road. There was such an outcry in the press around this incident that the government of the day banned races and speed events from taking place on public roads on mainland Britain. After some time had passed, the RAC looked at running on closed road circuits elsewhere, and, harking back to the old Gordon Bennett events of an earlier era, decided to hold a 30-lap, 410mi (659km) Ulster Grand Prix in Northern Ireland in August.

The Barnes brothers were entered in a new semi-works, un-supercharged two-seater sports, registered ER3410. With Sir Herbert Austin watching, to evaluate this new major event, they managed to place 16th after a crash. Their lap time of a modest 48mph (77km/h) average proved too low, but gave Sir Herbert food for thought as to what would be required to keep his Seven in the public eye.

At the 1929 Brooklands Easter Monday meeting, Kaye Don and mechanic Charles Cooper broke the track record in a Sunbeam, leaving it at over 131mph (210km/h), and before long the Barnes brothers were out again in the JCC Double Twelve race in May.

Held at Brooklands, this was the first 24-hour race to be staged in England, run in two 12-hour stints to avoid disturbing the locals in their nearby Georges Hill mansions. The event featured a traditional Le Mans start, with the cars lined up in a row on one side of the track, and the drivers on the other side, running across the track, erecting the hoods, and starting with electric starters. The hoods were furled after ten laps had been completed, and 29 cars finished of the 52 that started.

The Barnes duo averaged just under 49mph (78km/h), and covered 1080mi (1738km) in a continuous run, with no breakdowns or unplanned stoppages. This was an excellent performance for a 750cc side-valve vehicle, and they repeated this success at the end of June by winning their class in the BARC (British Automobile Racing Club) six-hour endurance race at over 50mph, again with no stoppages.

Holbrook and Poppe took part in the popular sand racing of the Southport 100-Mile Race with two supercharged works cars. Poppe then later managed a lap at the Phoenix Park Irish International Grand Prix with a speed of 66.70mph in a blown car, which raised eyebrows as this was his first major race. Sadly, he ran out of fuel, and – together with his mechanic – then pushed the car to the pits and frantically re-fuelled. He then dashed around the course, hitting the barriers at least twice, but ultimately finishing with the highly respectable average of almost 62mph. The other supercharged car, driven by Sullivan, also finished.

These rather hectic performances were not exactly what Herbert Austin was looking for when promoting the Seven. Appointing Gordon England as team manger seemingly did the trick, however; he used his experience and gravitas to ensure that, at the upcoming Ulster RAC Tourist Trophy, the works Austins would be better prepared, and run on strictly team terms.

For this event, the four Sevens in competition – two normally aspirated and two supercharged – were based at Harry Ferguson's works in Belfast. However, the superiority of the blown cars became apparent over the Ards course, where they were 10mph faster than the un-supercharged versions. To remedy this, additional superchargers and engine parts were rushed over from Longbridge to equip all four entries.

The Tourist Trophy was run over 410mi (659km), constituting 30 laps of the 14-mile circuit, and the handicapper gave the smallest class, the 750cc runners, a five lap start. Entries in the event included Coldicutt, Holbrook, Archie Frazer-Nash, the Barnes brothers (who were lent a works car in place of their earlier version, which was up for sale), and the amateur R Heyn. The latter withdrew, however, as his mechanic was ill and he did not wish to spoil his amateur status by accepting professional assistance.

The four little Austins were the crowd's favourites, being loudly cheered each time they passed by. Holbrook took an early lead, while Barnes averaged 55mph, including a lap at almost 60mph. After ten laps – or a third of the distance – Holbrook, Frazer-Nash, Coldicutt, and Barnes still headed the field, in that order, and mostly in pouring rain.

Frazer-Nash increased his average to above the magic 60mph mark, before Holbrook crested 61mph – the Austins genuinely

Continued page 109

RUBBER DUCKS

At the close of 1924, the FIA (or, the Fédération Internationale de l'Automobile) banned riding mechanics in Grand Prix events. This was despite arguments put forward by Arthur Waite that the driver had enough to do keeping his eyes on the road without looking at the car's instruments, and Sammy Davis suggesting that a passenger can look behind for fast-approaching cars, without the need for the driver to consult mirrors if fitted. Having to only provide a driver's seat meant that the two-seater racing cars became obsolete during the second half of the 1920s – there were, however, still many examples with double-width bodywork – and monopostos came into their own as pure racing cars, with two-seaters consigned to separate sports car regulations.

Over the winter of 1930/31, the Austin Motor Company decided to build a single seat 750cc vehicle, with the aim of being the first to reach the magic 100mph (160km/h). This was in the face of stiff opposition from MG, who already had a small overhead camshaft engine of suitable capacity. Austin still wanted the single-seater to look like just another Austin Seven, and to retain the side-valve engine, A-frame plan for the chassis, quarter-elliptic springs at the rear, and transverse front spring. The bodywork, however, would be entirely special, and streamlined to offer as much benefit to performance as possible.

A special version of the Seven frame was built, and, to achieve a low profile but avoid the radius arms fouling the chassis, shorter radius arms were instead fixed to the outside of the chassis rails, running forward to an early-pattern solid front axle beam. The key to getting the driver's seat set low in the car for a low frontal area – rather than him sitting perched above a central propshaft – was to move the propshaft to the driver's left side. An offset axle was then manufactured, with the crown wheel and pinion angled using a specially-cut CWP set, to take the drive line parallel with the nearside chassis rail. The engine and gearbox were then similarly angled in the frame on special mounts, to keep the drive line straight and the crankshaft and torque tube in line. This simple design solution to create an in-line drive train avoided transmission losses, which would otherwise have been caused by angularities in the propshaft joints.

The engine was similar to that of a racing Ulster, but with different crankcase cast mounting lugs, a mechanical fuel pump driven from a gear on the camshaft, and a bevel gear drive to the front off-side of the crankcase, to a large vertically-mounted Zoller 3 supercharger. The engine underwent further development over a four year period, but performance was frequently compromised by

A 1931 chassis drawing of the works blown record-breaker that would evolve into the Dutch Clog, or Rubber Duck racers. Note the short front radius arms compromising solid beam axle geometry – solved later by the jointed tubular axle. (Austin publicity)

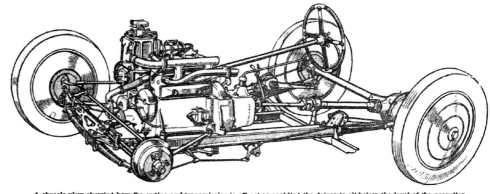

A NEW AUSTIN SEVEN RACER
A Particularly Interesting Car with Off-set Engine and Transmission

A chassis view showing how the engine and transmission is off-set so enabling the driver to sit below the level of the propeller shaft. Note also the vertical mounting of the supercharger and the mounting of the front spring under the axle.

cylinder head sealing problems, with gaskets blowing due to the high boost pressure that the supercharger provided. Additional cylinder head studs were fitted, and the iron blown Ulster-pattern cylinder heads changed to special aluminium heads, held down with no less than 25 studs of ⅜in (9mm) diameter, and Roots-pattern superchargers adopted.

The single-seater body enveloped all the mechanical components, as far as possible, leaving only the wheels and parts of the suspension exposed. The low seating position was made possible by the offset transmission, and made for a very compact, neat little car, in the style of contemporary Land Speed Record breakers, with very small frontal areas.

The rounded nose enclosed the water radiator, which had gills ducted around its rear edges to expel the heated air as quickly as possible, through the bonnet sides and top – this again copied from LSR practice. Finally, the long rear pointed tail had a high streamlined head fairing.

The first of these cars was built purely as a record breaker, with discs covering the wheels and streamlined sponsons between the front and rear wheels, similar to the exquisite 1929 three-ton Irving-Napier Golden Arrow, driven by Seagrave at Daytona to a world record of over 231mph (371km/h). The new car first appeared in public when driven by Poppe at the popular Easter meeting at Brooklands, and was nicknamed 'Yellow Canary.' By this time, however, Eyston had already raised the record to over 100mph (160km/h) in his MG 750, at the banked Montlhéry track near Paris.

After a couple of unsatisfactory outings, Leon Cushman managed to beat the MGs' record, setting the British International flying start kilometre and mile records at 102mph (164km/h) and 100.67mph (162km/h), respectively. The Austin was, therefore, the first 750cc machine to exceed 100mph (160km/h) on British soil. Within a very short space of time, however, Lord Ridley easily broke the Austin records driving his amazing little Ridley Special, with speeds of 105.42mph (169km/h) for the mile and 104.56mph (168km/h) for the kilometre. Ridley's car had an exotic one-off, twin

Leon Cushman in 'Yellow Canary,' in intermediate nose form, attended by Alf Depper and Ral Appleby. The works team of 'Rubber Ducks' evolved from this successful car. (Austin publicity)

Contemporary toy Austin Sevens, the slush-moulded Yellow Canary by Taylor and Barrett and Arcade's Bantam Coupé. The Dinky APE Tourer is correct in blue, but all real military APDs had flat radiators. (Author collection/Courtesy Nick Salmon)

overhead cam, supercharged engine that owed something to Bugatti in design. It was equipped with Laystall Engineering Co crankshaft, camshafts, timing gears and precision crown wheel and pinion set, and had a low bodyshell similar to a Thomas 'flat iron.'

Lord Ridley then hurt himself quite badly in a crash while trying to better his own figures. The extraordinary Ridley Special was rarely seen again in public, but does still exist today.

Gwenda Stewart then took the Austin to Montlhéry, and broke four records – the fastest at 109.129mph (175km/h) for five kilometres. Later, this very quick and brave lady driver carried out testing on lightened versions of the record breaker, to be used for track racing.

Three of these shortened and simplified single-seaters were built to a similar specification, but without the wheel discs and streamlined sponsons. With their sloping noses and high head fairings blended into short tails, they had a distinctive 'push along toy' appearance, and were nicknamed 'Dutch Clogs' or 'Rubber Ducks.'

In October 1931, the streamliner – driven by Cushman – and the ambitious Austin team – complete now, comprising three Duck racers with Barnes, Driscoll, and Charles Goodacre in the cockpits – all retired with overheating troubles on their first time out. Later, however, Cushman and co-driver Pat Driscoll took a whole clutch of British distance records in the streamliner, including those for the 500mi and six hours, the latter at 90.12mph (145km/h).

The works Rubber Duck design was effective enough at record breaking, and on a high-speed banked track, but when they were entered for hillclimbs, two inherent design limitations became very apparent. Firstly, the cockpits were tight, and the controls were placed awkwardly for the inch-perfect positioning required by drivers looking to shave milliseconds off hillclimb times. These cramped and uncomfortable cockpits particularly compromised performance for taller drivers. In addition, the conflicts caused by incorrect geometry of the front suspension, with short side-mounted radius arms and rigid axle beams, flared up badly when the greater steering input required for sharp cornering caused the inside front wheels to leave the road, and stay airborne around corners.

This latter problem was solved on the later Austin single-seaters, with the adoption of a fabricated tubular front axle beam, which included a rotational joint that allowed the two halves of the beam to rotate slightly, and to act independently of each other. This vastly improved front end performance, and made the cars more controllable in general. At this point, the Duck racers had reached a development ceiling, above which it was all but impossible to advance without a re-design of the engine architecture to overcome the thermal problems inherent in the block design of a small side-valve engine.

The Rubber Ducks team cars were raced hard for several seasons, after which one was sent to New Zealand (to return to the UK in 2002, for the Longbridge rally) and one to South Africa, where it was modified by Doug Riet with a one-off front swing axle arrangement and a sloping Ruby radiator cowl, which did little for its appearance. It was returned to Martin Eyre, in the UK, in the mid-1990s.

The unique ex-Doug Van Riet modified Dutch Clog, with Ruby radiator cowl and swing axle front suspension, was raced by Martin Eyre at Goodwood Revival. (Author collection)

The Ards TT, with one of the Team Ulsters taking the Dundonald Hairpin. (Austin publicity)

racing amongst themselves, and delighting the spectators. This continued, Frazer-Nash managing 62mph before Holbrook responded with an average of more than 63mph; all conducted over a proper road course with cambered roads, varying surfaces, and natural hazards still in place.

There was momentary drama as Coldicutt spun twice at the notorious Quarry Corner, damaging the tail of his car but resuming without dropping a place. Frazer-Nash now led Holbrook, but by 2:00pm it was apparent that the larger and faster cars – in particular Caracciola's Mercedes – were eroding the Austins' lead. Campari's Alfa Romeo overtook the smaller cars by lap 26, and the Mercedes did the same a lap later. Frazer-Nash finished a magnificent third, and Holbrook placed fourth at a shade under 60mph (96km/h).

Caracciola was impressed, and his observation was that the Austins were "wonderful; I take my hat off to those little midget cars and their brave drivers." Surprisingly, Herbert Austin was also able to truthfully claim that none of the Sevens had been touched by a spanner during the race; this was a significant achievement and not, he hoped, one that was lost on the buying pubic.

Thus, the legend of the Austin Ulster was born. The name was quickly adopted in the wake of the Ards success, and a line of sporting Austin Ulsters was introduced with bodywork and specification closely following the instantly famous works cars.

VSCC Scottish Trial, 2016. Peter Kite tackles the 'Burn' at Coulter in his 1930 Ulster Replica, with suitably watery results. (Courtesy Gary Clarke)

THE MACLACHLAN SPECIAL

The base of this fascinating special was an early Gordon England Brooklands that had been successfully raced by Austin sales director RM Papelian in America, in 1926. Having been brought back to England, it was acquired by ANL Maclachlan, who not only used it extensively as his sole means of transport, but also won the 1100cc class at the 1927 Inter Varsity Hillclimb, at Ewelme Down, and was awarded a 'gold' in the 1928 Lands End Trial.

The car was enthusiastically driven to its limits, with a genuine top speed of 80mph (128km/h). In recognition of its young driver's efforts, the engine was bench-tested at the Austin works, and found to give 28bhp at 4700rpm when using a 6.8:1 compression ratio Ricardo alloy head.

As with other fragile lightweight sports bodies, after 25,000mi the GE Brooklands body broke up in a terminal way, and Maclachlan decided to convert the car into a quasi-single-seater sprint machine. He rebuilt the running gear, constructed a light ash frame over which Rexine was stretched, and installed a small petrol tank on the floor of the passenger's side. He then spent 18 months in South Africa. Three events were tackled with the car in this form, with an 1100cc class win at Lewes Speed Trial, a win on a Portsmouth dirt track, and a third place finish at the October 1931 Brooklands Mountain Circuit race, at 58.2mph (93.6km/h).

The engine was converted to blown Ulster specifications, using a No 4 Cozette, one of Geoff Taylor's 'Alta' aluminium cylinder heads, and sprint fuel. Another run of events resulted in a 1935 Shelsley

ANL Maclachlan in the Maclachlan Special, at speed in the 1938 Lewes Speed Trial. The car is in its intermediate body form, and still on early 19in wheels. (Courtesy Ferret Fotographics)

The complete engine and blower installation of the Maclachlan Special. (Author collection)

that was compromised by wheelspin and sideways motoring, and a "far too light" back end. To complete a good day, and for helping Austin win the Team Prize, Austin encouragingly gave Maclachlan one of the works' spare 25-stud blocks, slipper pistons and cylinder head!

That winter, a new single-seat body was constructed by Harringtons of Hove, in aluminium on a light steel frame, and with an ingenious – and readily detachable – one-piece bonnet and radiator cowl. The definitive engine was built up combining the works components with the original Brooklands camshaft and BLIC magneto.

After all the years of development, the performance of the new 1936 machine fully matched expectations, returning a Shelsley Walsh Hillclimb time of 44.04 seconds, and a Lewes Speed Trial time of 20.23 seconds. The end of that season saw the radiator altered, to pull the top of the cowl further back and improve the appearance and balance of this now black-painted miniature monoposto.

Maclachlan experimented further with wheel and tyre sizes for different courses, and ran for three seasons prior to World War Two. The quasi-works engine, blown at truly substantial pressure, threw 'Tiddler' down the road staggeringly quickly – reaching 80mph (128km/h) in 15 seconds. A strong effort at Brighton in 1937 brought him victory, beating Bert Hadley in the works Twin Cam and Denis Evans in his Q-type sprint special, in the 850cc and 1500cc racing car classes.

The car was carefully greased and put into storage during the war, and it was not until 1948 that 'Tiddler' again emerged, blinking in the daylight. Maclachlan ran the car run at the famous Luton Hoo event, and had the immense satisfaction of recording a personal best of 42.94 seconds at the Shelsley Walsh Hillclimb. The car is currently a regular runner in the safe hands of historic racer Martin Eyre.

Walsh Hillclimb best time of 45.6 seconds, and another celebrated win at Brooklands Mountain Circuit.

Having seen how the works Austin single-seaters performed, Maclachlan teamed up with his friend Jim Elwes to yet again rebuild 'Tiddler,' as he had called his project car. This time, however, it was to be a light, simple, purer single-seater, with "some real punch" coming from the addition of an 800cc Centric 17psi supercharger, mounted in front of the engine with a 40mm Solex carburettor and all-new induction system.

An Ulster front axle beam was set to give increased castor; rear springs were flattened and double clamped above the frame rails; 8in (203mm) brakes were installed, with a more robust actuation system; and there was a change to 17in (431mm) wheels. This newest configuration was ready for the September 1935 Shelsley Walsh Hillclimb, but a disastrous blow-up in practice saw the team frantically rebuilding the engine overnight, at the friendly Austin Experimental Department, with new block, head and pistons. The reward for this hard work was a 45.5 seconds run, despite handling

CHAPTER TEN

AUSTIN SEVENS ABROAD

DIXI AND BMW

SIR Herbert Austin had already exported many Sevens through the Berlin-based company of Koch and Weichel. In 1927, however, he was introduced to the German-domiciled industrialist Jakob Schapiro, with whom he opened discussions about building his successful small car under licence within Germany.

Schapiro controlled a number of companies, including Automobilwerk Eisenach (operating under the name Dixi), which had already been manufacturing French Decauville cars under licence. Nevertheless, he was on the lookout for potential new car markets.

Dixi had become owned by Gothaer Waggonfabrik, after a forced merger, and the version of the Decauville built under its care was originally called a Wartburg, after the prominent castle of the same name at Eisenach. By 1927, the company offered two excellent larger car models, but was experiencing slow sales due to the economic climate in Germany at the time. As a result, a small 'peoples car' was an attractive proposition, but – due to testing and changing financial times – only if it could be put into production very quickly.

Sir Herbert soon negotiated a deal with Gothaer Waggonfabrik, allowing it to manufacture versions of the Austin Seven exclusively for Germany and Eastern European countries. This would use German raw materials, and result in an anticipated production of 2000 cars – as a minimum – each year, rising hopefully to 10,000 cars per year.

At first, both complete Austin Seven cars and complete kits of parts were sent to Germany, to enable the required production resources to be set up. By the end of 1927, however, the factory had started producing purely German versions of the car, with mirror-image engines, gearboxes to allow for left-hand drive, and metric-threaded fixings. Once production had become settled, most of the ancillary components were also changed to German manufacture, with a Solex carburettor replacing the usual Zenith.

The cars were called Dixis, and the first model labelled as the 3/15 PS DA-1 – 'DA' standing for Deutsche Ausführung, or 'German Version,' and with taxable and actual horsepower denoted by the '3/15.' About 6000 Dixi DA-1 Chummy-lookalikes were built by the end of 1928. Many additional chassis were also supplied to German coach-builders, including Sindelfingen, Buschel, Ihle, and Buhne, over a five-year period. As in England, Germany was experiencing a high point in the fashion for coach-built types.

There were tourers, roadsters, coupés, and sedans in similar styles to Austin's counterparts, but with detail changes to suit German fashion and taste, and – with the exception of DKW – the Dixis had soon largely conquered the small car market.

With the restructuring of industry in post-WW1 Germany, there were many pressures put on established individual firms. BMW (Bayerische Motoren Werke), of Munich, had evolved from Rapp Motoren Werke – founded in 1913, as a manufacturer of marine and industrial engines. In a similar way to Austin, it was obliged to expand its activities enormously during the war, building large and complex Austro-Daimler aircraft engines as a sub-contractor under the dynamic and young engineer, Franz Joseph Popp. In 1916, the expanded company changed its name to BMW GmbH, and then – by degrees – to BMW AG, still managed by Popp.

At the cessation of hostilities, BMW found itself in a similar situation to Austin – left with a huge factory, equipped with enormous facilities and under-employed workers of every skill set and type. The Treaty of Versailles was intended to ensure that Germany did not build weaponry or machinery with which it could again wage war. As a result, BMW was left in a depleted state, reduced to building components for railways and aero engines on a very limited scale.

The company began to build engines suitable for trucks and general industrial use in 1922, and, at the same time, produced an efficient and multi-purpose air-cooled flat twin 500cc power unit. Used as a motorcycle engine, it was destined to completely change the company's fortunes.

A local motorcycle company that was using the flat twin 500cc was acquired, and, apart from the engine, the machine was redesigned from first principles. The resulting machine was the shaft-drive BMW R32 – the antecedent of countless thousands of successful racing and touring BMW motorbikes ever since.

The company also returned to constructing aircraft engines, but there remained a need for a mass-produced car. Seeing the success that Dixi was enjoying with its Austin Seven-derived little car, BMW successfully bid for the company in 1928. Dixi became a self-contained subsidiary of BMW, the cars being re-badged as BMW Dixis. The following year, the Dixi name was discontinued, and the BMW 3/15 DA-2 was introduced with coupled brakes and a lower 5.35:1 rear axle ratio, giving sparkling hillclimbing performance and acceleration.

The classic BMW logo – of the circle, quartered into the blue and white of the Free State of Bavaria (reversed, however, as it was illegal to use national symbols as a trademark) – was first introduced as a car badge. A contemporary advertisement showed the badge as a revolving aeroplane propeller, starting the myth of the true origins of the now-familiar badge. The bodywork had a characteristic square,

Glitzy and over-restored, this type of 1928 BMW Dixi 3/15PS DA1 Two-Seater was also used for racing and by the military – but never, ever with chrome plated wheels … (Author collection)

squat feel, exaggerated by the use of distinctive horizontal slats to the bonnet sides. It also had slightly wider coachwork than the parent Austin design, with more than faint echoes of the French Rosengart, especially in saloon versions.

The usual range of body types were continued, including sedans, sports two-seaters, cabriolet two-seaters, coupés, phaetons, and delivery vans. Several hundred 3/15 PS DA-2 military field cars were also produced, some with mounted machine guns, and supplied to the re-emerging German army.

Keen types started to race and hillclimb the cars, and the factory won a team prize in the 1929 Alpine Rally. Eyeing the success of the British cars, BMW brought out the two-seater 3/15 DA-3 Wartburg. The new car had similar chassis-lowering modifications to the Austin Ulster, a fold-flat windscreen, a high-compression cylinder head, a re-jetted 26mm Solex carburettor, and tubular manifolding. An additional interesting and advanced feature was present in a 'signalling ring,' fitted to the steering wheel and giving fingertip control for electrical semaphore indicators, headlights, and horn – quite probably a world first for ergonomic wheel-mounted controls. The very pretty bodywork had a beautifully-pointed tail, somewhat like a cross between an Ulster and a Speedy, with the spare wheel mounted vertically on the passenger's side, away from the exhaust system.

The DA-3 has to be considered to be a very important model. This car was the first in a long line of sporting BMW cars, and the twin vertical oval radiator openings first seen on these little cars is now a signature feature of all BMWs. Although never achieving the racing success of the Austin Ulster, it did give BMW a direction for sports car development, and the continued international success of the marque has since established the place of the DA-3 in history.

The DA-4, which followed, retained much of its parentage from Austin, but featured independent front suspension, giving a much more compliant ride with – in theory – greater directional stability, something that was previously woefully lacking. The

BMW independent set-up retained the transverse leaf spring, but did away with the front axle beam. Instead, the stub axle assemblies were directly fixed to the ends of the springs, with slightly reduced wheel diameter mitigating the wheel jacking effects to a degree, although the wheels were capable of working at fairly extreme angles.

A further development of the DA-4 retained the ageing Austin-based engine, in modified form, and was designated the AM-1 (standing for Automobile München, or Munich). This car had the strange independent front suspension of the DA-4, and a twin transverse spring swing axle system at the rear. It was apparently not considered a success!

Following huge success with subsequent BMW motor cars and motorcycles, BMW introduced its own version of a completely new 'Mini' in 2001. This move continued the hallowed and valuable Mini name, stemming from that first Cooper–Austin built in 1937, before evolving into the iconic Mini Cooper in the early 1960s. At the time of writing, the super successful Mini brand range continues to be built by BMW at Cowley, with the Cooper suffix still reserved for the brand's top performing models.

ROSENGART

Lucien Rosengart was, in 1928, the managing director of Peugeot France – one of the very earliest motor car manufacturers – and an acquaintance of Sir Herbert Austin, through the 'societé anonyme' Austin tractor plant from the early 1920s. During this year, he

A 1932 BMW/Gebruder Ihle 600 Sports, based on Dixi/BMW components with semi-productionised bodywork. It exhibits the first twin-nostril BMW nose treatment, still a BMW design trademark today. (Courtesy Nick Salmon)

commenced manufacturing the Austin Seven in a disused part of the Peugeot factory, under the name of 'Rosengart;' it would seem that, like Herbert Austin, Lucien Rosengart was in a position to autonomously pursue personal projects, within the organisation of his factory.

Lucien had been born in 1881, and initially followed his father into the family precision engineering business. After returning from service in the army, he set up his own workshop in Belleville, Paris, to produce bolts, nuts, and other standard fixings for established cycle, motorcycle, and car companies. By 1909, his business employed some 60 skilled men. By the outbreak of the Great War, Rosengart had expanded to a second factory, producing parts for railway rolling stock, and a range of dynamos and electrical products. To assist in the war effort, he teamed up with André Citroën, producing artillery shells in an even larger factory – again, in parallel to Herbert Austin's activities during that period.

At the cessation of hostilities, Rosengart was able to assist Citroën financially, and, in exchange, took on the lucrative role of managing Citroën's factory. Along with this came the inception of the revolutionary Kégresse half-track, the beloved vehicle of France's North African and Saharan colonies, and the successful Citroën 5CV.

Peugeot, also in financial difficulties after the Great War, now called upon Lucien Rosengart's expertise. Once again, he was again able to come up with a viable financial package, and in return took on a directorship in the Peugeot Company. Lucien continued to have innovative ideas for various products, including a small auxiliary engine to power a standard bicycle – a type of personal transport still synonymous with the French – and a dynamo-powered battery-less torch that lit up when squeezed.

The Peugeot Quadrilette and Citroën 5CV had little future development left in them by the mid-1920s, and Lucien Rosengart saw an opportunity to grasp the 'holy grail' for automotive manufacturers at that time – a new small car for the masses – in the recently introduced Austin Seven.

Rosengart therefore approached Sir Herbert Austin, and a similar deal to Dixi was arranged. A number of Seven rolling chassis were sent to France for evaluation, and Rosengart acquired the old Bellager factory at Neuilly-sur-Seine to the north west of Paris. This factory formed a part of Rosengart's termination terms with Peugeot, and a showroom was set up on the Champs-Élysées under the upmarket name Élysées Automobiles. Austin continued to supply various parts while the Rosengart factory was still establishing itself, and a change to metric threads – to take advantage of Lucien's existing products – was followed by French-supplied starter motors and dynamos.

The LR1's first body type was a three-seater – long familiar to the French with the 1920s Citroën 'Cloverleaf' and the open-bodied three-seat Amilcars – with all metal bodywork below the waistline and fabric covering above. Wheel discs, supplied virtually from day one, were a very distinctive and 'chic' feature, and all-over 'jazz'-patterned fabric interiors were set off with hardwood door cappings and dashboards to give a very distinctive, and unmistakably Gallic, feel. Right-hand drive was retained, easing the production process, and the engine crankcase casting was emblazoned with 'Rosengart,' cast in full-length lettering.

In the LR2, range coil ignition replaced the gear-driven magneto, and a forward-facing starter was used instead of the earlier rearward-facing item, with its more complex mountings. Saloon, coupé, and tourer versions were also added, and – now firmly established – the factory engaged in a series of sporting events. Borrowing an Austin works Super Sport, the company disguised it with Rosengart badging and competed in a hillclimb near to Grasse – the elegant centre of the French perfume industry, just north of Nice. The driver,

Derek Sheldon's very attractive and immaculate 1930 Rosengart LR2 two-seater coupé. (Author collection)

Colin Ring takes a good look at a restored 1929 Rosengart Cabriolet – an early precursor of the 'three box' body style, including a boot – at a 1990s 750 Motor Club Beaulieu Rally. (Author collection)

a M Vinatier, not only won the 750cc class, but also beat the 1500cc and 2-litre times for good measure!

Thus encouraged, M Turel – a Rosengart dealer from Lyon – devised an extreme long distance trial to demonstrate not only speed, but reliability. An apparently ordinary L2 saloon was to be taken off the factory production line, and on a circuitous route from Lyon, north via Bourg-en-Bresse, through Burgundy, to Dijon, and back again to Lyon. The car was to be briskly driven four times each day, for a total distance of some 900km (550mi) every day. M Turel and his co-driver, M Lecot, set off. The 20,000km mark was passed at the beginning of September, they had reached 50,000km by the beginning of October, and 100,00km before the end of November – an extraordinary feat, and with no noted mechanical troubles.

The intrepid pair were fêted by the press and caused quite a stir, establishing the little Rosengart as a weapon of choice for the many long distance rallies. These events were a beloved fixture of pre-WW2 French sporting motorists, steeped in the tradition of France's heroic marathon events dating from the earliest days of motoring. At the other end of the spectrum, the rural French community was in need of local carriers – which might involve cargo of anything from a hay bale, a sack of apples, or a pig. This demand saw the range of bodies extended to include basic saloons and tourers, as well as a van, later with an extended chassis frame, somewhat like the English Ruby types, and with half elliptical rear springing.

The two-seater Coupé, the Torpedo, and the Coupé Spider were available in a range of top-end specifications, labelled 'luxe' and 'grand luxe.' At the other end of the market, a basic two-seater – the R5 – was offered, with steel body, a bench seat, and naked wire wheels. This was priced at less than 12,000 old French francs, and claimed to be the cheapest 'proper' car in Europe at the time.

The rally competition heritage of Rosengarts was enhanced by successful outings on the 1930-31 Paris-Nice and Paris-St Raphael rallies, the Bol d'Or, and the highly prestigious Grand Prix des

Frontières at Chimay, close to the Belgian border, where an R5 competed.

At the same time, Rosengart ventured out and introduced a six-cylinder version of its Seven engine. This resulted in a capacity of just under 1100cc, with the greater power being exceeded by the increase in torque of this little, long stroke 'six.'

In-line with developments in England however, the next step in Rosengart's evolution was the long-wheelbase LR4. This included an increase in track, giving a much roomier body envelope, whilst the rear axle was redesigned with a long propshaft and no torque tube, as had become the design convention of the day. Many detail improvements were made to the engine; the water manifolding was improved, sump capacity was increased from two to three litres – in response to the long distances frequently travelled in the spread-out countryside of France – and engine mountings reduced in number from four to a tripod of three.

For 1932, the LR44 – a smaller-engined version of the 1100cc LR4 – was introduced. The next year, the again-improved range was designated LR45, LR47, and LR49.

The 1936 LR4N2 marked a complete change in the look of the bodywork, with a cowled radiator grille similar to a Delahaye, and long horizontal 'speed lines' giving the car a definite Art Deco feel. Pressed steel 'easy-clean' wheels were also fitted, similar to those used by a score of other car manufacturers. The range, with its redesigned

Mademoiselle Simone des Forest and the Rosengart 4CV in action during the Frejus Plage 500-metre sprint special section. She won her class in the Paris-Saint-Raphael. (Courtesy Jean-Francois Bouzanquet)

bodies, had shaken off all vestiges of 1920s body shapes, and were really quite stylish. The generic Supercinq ('Super Five') name still referred to the smallness of the car, which was available in various body types, including the commercial traveller saloons – the latter having been championed by Sir Herbert Austin from very early days.

The LR4N2, and its derivatives, were built in some numbers for the next four years, and production even continued into the Second World War, with two new models having the, then advanced, concept of independent rear suspension. Postwar, in 1950, 747cc Austin-type engines were fitted to the LR4PL. In 1952, this was followed by the LR4SA Ariette, with a very typical French cabriolet body of the day resembling a Panhard Sports, and its charming small saloon sister, the Coach Ariette, a number of which are happily in the hands of preservationists. Later versions of these modest little runabouts were built using Panhard flat twin engines, and the evolutionary break from the Austin design, some 30 years previously, was complete.

AMERICAN AUSTIN AND BANTAM

With the Austin Seven in full production, Herbert Austin again looked across the Atlantic for a possible market. In April 1927, Austin's export manager, PM Papelian, arrived in New York with the latest saloon Seven, which he proceeded to drive to Detroit

IT WON'T BE LONG NOW!

Soon the American Austin can speak to you for itself. Meanwhile a Merry Christmas and a New Year filled with Happiness and Prosperity from this Bantam-Car and the

AMERICAN AUSTIN CAR CO. · WOODWARD AT GRAND BOULEVARD · DETROIT · MICHIGAN

Pre-launch Christmas publicity for the eagerly-awaited American Austin. (Author collection)

in order to test American reaction. A few Sevens had already found their way to the US, but some sort of angle was required to convince a sceptical public of the value of such a tiny lightweight car. This was particularly a tricky task in the States, where the average weight of a car was considerably more than a ton; the economic arguments were weaker there than in Europe, as large and commodious American-built cars were cheap, and the difference in petrol costs inconsequential.

In late 1928, Sir Herbert and Lady Austin sailed to New York with four Austin Sevens in the hold of their ship, which went on display at the New York Automobile Show. This was typical of Herbert's direct hands-on approach, and, in June 1929, the American Austin Car Co was set up. It was to be under entirely American management, and in no sense an Austin subsidiary, with ex-General Motors executive Arthur Brandt directing. A deal was done with financier Elias Ritts, of Butler, Pennsylvania, to purchase an empty factory in the area, with Ritts expecting that the Austin Seven might soon do for Butler what the Model T Ford had done for Detroit.

However, with no local expertise, any necessary changes and development to the English Austin – principally consisting of re-styling the bodywork, to suit it to the American market – had to be carried out in distant Detroit. In the edgy prevailing financial climate of September 1929, the almost complete absence of activity at the Butler factory started conspiracy rumours of a possible scam, to rob investors and erode local confidence, despite the well-briefed local press making reassuring noises. This was all happening at the very worst of times, and the Wall Street Crash – just a few weeks later, at the end of October – almost called time on the whole enterprise.

Nerves were calmed by a New Year Butler Board of Commerce banquet honouring Sir Herbert Austin and Arthur Brandt, with the latter announcing to the local dignitaries that production would be starting imminently. He stated that "if we were to organise another company to start making automobiles at this date, I would call it extreme folly, but we do not feel that the Austin [Seven] is just another car; we are convinced it has a distinct future."

The launch of the American Austin, in three body styles, took place at the Hotel Shelton in New York, and coincided with the National Automobile Show, where it caused a sensation. Amidst media frenzy, literally thousands of dealers tried to sign up this new and novel little car, viewing it as a possible saviour in the depressed climate. Cadillac agents in particular, and for obvious reasons, were keen to have an economy car to offer the buying public.

The reality of getting the car into production again took months, and it wasn't until the end of May 1930 that Butler-built Austins finally rolled out of the factory doors. These were priced at about the same

as the larger Ford Model A, but cleverly marketed as 'the world's first economy car.'

If Sir Herbert's original Seven had been the right car at the right time, then just as surely the reverse was true of the American Austin. With the purchasing power of the average American family man declining month on month, and cheap secondhand cars readily available, the Austin Seven was not seen as a necessary – or even desirable – expense at all. Those that did buy, however, turned into local celebrities overnight. The car itself was viewed with amusement, but also quickly with affection, and many japes presented themselves; Austin Seven owners often returned to find their previously parked cars moved mysteriously to ballroom entrances, up hotel steps, and into local public gardens.

For publicity stunts, and in a mirror image to the single-seat Flying Flea in Europe, the super-lightweight and home-flown Aeronca high parasol wing two-seater aircraft was matched with the Austin Seven in movie newsreels. The diminutive Austin otherwise found itself frequently contrasted with large limousines in films, magazines, and newspapers. Whilst all this was apparently good publicity for Austin, it had the unfortunate and unwanted side effect of undermining the

A Bantam converted to a cable ferry at Pudding River, Oregon, by merely replacing tyres with flat rubber traction bands and adding third cable pulley cradle above. (Author collection)

confidence of the buyer. The car was taken less and less seriously as a practical automobile, and finishing up as the butt of far too many jokes.

By the end of 1930, only 8500 cars had been produced, and the accounts recorded a loss of more than a million dollars. Fewer than

The 1930 American Austin Coupé is a beautifully proportioned car, seen here with a Model A Ford. (American Austin publicity)

1300 cars were built in 1931, and bankruptcy loomed. The factory closed in the spring of 1932, with almost 1500 incomplete cars inside the factory gates.

A young self-made entrepreneur called Roy Evans then appeared on the scene. Having a large automobile dealership in the South, and with finance already in place, Evans bought the 1500 unfinished cars, and paid to have them completed. Once finished, they were shipped to Florida and, discounted to less than $300 each, quickly sold in their entirety.

Evans then arranged to finance the factory's suppliers and re-started production, completing 3845 new cars and vans by the end of 1932. Updated styling and uprated engines saw over 4500 vehicles of all types sold in 1933, including a new Coupé Suburban, but production had declined again by the end of 1934, despite rethinking demand for small commercial panel vans and pick-ups.

The 35-year-old Evans was still convinced of the desirability of a really small car, and arrived at a new deal. Going to Butler's mayor and the company's major creditors, he acquired all the assets of the American Austin Car Co. At the same time, he also negotiated with British Austin to be granted exclusive distribution rights for territory east of the Rocky Mountains, and went to Fiat for total US representation for its newly-announced baby car, the Topolino 500.

Meanwhile, the excellent – but otherwise idle – Austin machine shops at Butler were used by the superlative race car designer Harry Miller. Miller had been the director of engineering at American Austin, and used the shops to build several of his radical four-wheel drive Gulf Oil Indianapolis specials, as well as the racing hydroplane 'Miss Canada.' He was retained by Evans at the company for a new design project.

The American Austin Car Co – which had used a bantam as its logo – was re-organised as American Bantam in June 1936. The company was re-financed, and the product range given re-styled bodywork to give the

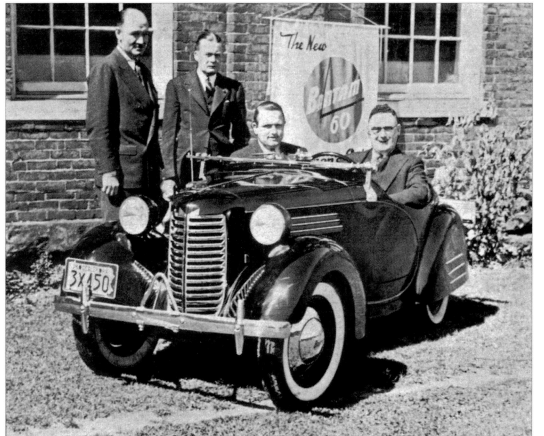

The principals of American Bantam Car Co in 1939, having shipped the first 50 chassis to Melbourne. From left: Gill, Fenn, President Roy Evans and Australian Production Manager Cameron. (Bantam publicity)

When the American Austin hit the Hollywood boulevards everyone wanted to be in on the act – this is Keystone Cop Slim Summerville trying a Coupé for size. (American Austin publicity)

impression of new vehicles. Sadly, however, no new Harry Miller engine was present. A new coupé, roadster, and panel truck, all with new wings and curved radiator grille, were made ready for the 1936 National Automobile Show, but instead Bantam chose to hold the cars' launch at a hotel. This proved to be a smart move; the media were full of the still-novel little cars, and, eight years after the first launch, an improved economic climate allowed a new public to become totally beguiled by the offerings – motoring in miniature, rather than in a joke!

Bantams had also been sold in Australia, and plans were initially made to assemble 50 cars in Sydney. Plans even extended as far as to assemble cars in the UK (at Chiswick, west of London), Belgium, and South America.

In the USA, meanwhile, careful financial planning had led to the cars being the cheapest on the American market, and the improved engine – now with pressurised oil system – gave genuine 60mph (95km/h) performance. Disappointingly, however, output for 1938

Buster Keaton with his sons at MGM studios, in a Roadster that appeared in several of his films.
Note the detachable wheel rim design. (Author collection)

1931 American Austin Roadster actually in snazzy blue and yellow 'Art Deco' contrasting paint. (Courtesy Underwood)

Mechanically, the cars were like later Rosengarts and Dixi/BMWs – being mirror-image versions of the English original – though the rear axles were of quite different design and construction, with brake diameter increased to 8in (20cm). Electrical equipment was naturally of US manufacture, and wheels of 18in (55cm) diameter with detachable rims and 3.75in width section tyres. Under Roy Evan's ownership, the 1932/33 versions had various facelifts. Bantam badging was implemented, and, later, the gear drive to the dynamo was replaced by a more conventional (for the time) rubber V-belt, and the timing case altered to take the distributor.

Sir Herbert Austin had originally been paid two dollars royalty on each American Austin sold. However, it appears that this financial arrangement finally came to an end as the Bantam design changed, and the rear suspension was altered to half-elliptical springing. The product was deemed to be sufficiently removed from its original design, and the arrangement was voided.

By the time that car production ground to a halt in late 1941, the United States had already entered World War Two. In addition to the production of some 2500 Bantam Jeeps, the Bantam Company produced thousands of trailers and torpedo propulsion motors for the war effort. In all, just over 19,000 American Austins were built, and about 4250 American Bantams. The company was finally wound up in 1955.

American built Sevens proved attractive to the Hot Rod Movement, but sadly only the small and light car bodies were commandeered. The rest of the car was often scrapped, akin to events in the United Kingdom in the late 1950s, where the well-intended – but ill-considered – Ministry of Transport tests for old cars caused countless perfectly good Austin Sevens to go to the crusher. Many American Austin Sevens and Seven specials were, however, raced on the East Coast, on dirt roads, hillclimbs, and shale ovals, helping to spawn the mighty Sports Car Club of America.

was only about 2000 cars. Modifications followed in 1939, and included a four-seater Speedster, and a Station Wagon that had novel two-stage springing, which lowered the chassis and softened the ride.

New models in 1940 included a Hollywood coupé and Riviera sedan. These cars were amongst the best small cars built anywhere in the world, but ultimately the Bantam business model was no longer viable, and had run out of steam. About 6700 Bantam cars and small trucks had been made over a period of two and a half years, but every vehicle built had involved a loss of $75 each.

All was not entirely lost, however. Previously, in July 1938, the Pennsylvania National Guard had been thoughtfully provided by the factory with two Bantam roadsters when it went on its summer training manoeuvres. These small and light vehicles performed well as field cars and – as had been first demonstrated by British Austin Military Scout cars in trials nine years previously – the Seven's versatility inspired the officers in attendance to consider potential new roles for such vehicles in the future. "I believe that this car has great possibilities for military work," reported Major James F Leech – and that part of the Austin Seven story is separately told.

AMERICAN AUSTIN AND BANTAM – THE CARS
The Sevens produced by American Austin had body styling performed by Alexis de Sakhnoffsky of the Hayes Body Company. Allowing for the parameters within which he worked, a remarkable transformation of the rather quaint English Seven bodies was achieved. Looking very powerful, with longer bonnets, shallow windscreens, and solid disc wheels, the de Sakhnoffsky designs were outstanding.

SPORTS CAR CLUB OF AMERICA
In October 1929, the month of the Wall Street Crash, the Overlook Automobile Racing Club was formed. This group took its name from the wealthy Collier family's country estate in Westchester

George Weaver in a 1938 road race, driving the ex-Campbell Record Breaker, stripped of its body fairings, and on late Ruby 17in (431mm) wheels. The car still awaits re-discovery. (Author collection)

County, New York, where the three Collier brothers, and their friend Tom Dewart, laid out a simple road racing course. Here, they ran home-made motorcycle-engined 'buckboards,' in European 'Grand Prix' style – with named corners, rather than the traditional American dirt or paved ovals, with turns simply numbered 'turn one', 'turn two' and so on.

In 1933, they rather ambitiously adopted the grandiose title of the Automobile Racing Club of America. By this time they had graduated to mostly imported European sports cars – the quickest an MG, then a Henderson Special – but, importantly, Allen Quinby, Tom Stewart, and Langdon Quinby all drove sports Austin Sevens. More people joined in, and what had started as a loose-knit group of enthusiasts became a well organised and effective club. Its stated aim was to encourage road racing, with a breed of automobile and amateur sportsmen based on the essentially English model – "road racing for amateurs."

By 1934, Miles Collier had set out the simple unpaved artificial course of Sleepy Hollow. A lengthy three-hour event followed, attended by none other than Bill Mitchell, the automobile designer who would later work at General Motors and famously design the Chevrolet Corvette. Austin Sevens, driven by J Marshall and Alan Beavis, were up against Bugattis and Amilcars, the Austins finishing fifth, seventh, and eighth that year, including Mrs Conway's left-hand drive American Austin.

1935 saw the Austin Sevens out again, with Anglophile Alan Berris competing at the Climb to the Clouds Hillclimb at Mount Washington in an ultra-skimpy Austin. In 1937, George Weaver raised eyebrows by arriving in none other than the unique ex-works Donald Campbell Daytona record-breaking Austin Seven, now fitted with 17in (431mm) Ruby wheels. These small Austins made regular and competitive appearances for two more years.

1939 saw ARCA founder Miles Collier go to Le Mans with a streamlined MG – the first US entry since 1921 – and postwar he competed in the event as a co-driver, with his friend Briggs Cunningham, through to the late 1950s.

The ARCA was 'inactivated' after 1941, due to Pearl Harbour. The several Austin Sevens that had been present at the very start of the club remaining to be competitive and a part of it right to the end. After the war, ARCA Austin Seven driver George Weaver, special builders John Reuter and Lem Ladd, and others, formed the new car club The Sports Car Club of America, or SCCA for short. The group organised race meetings across the continent, along European lines and for mostly European cars, and remains the road racing organising body in the United States today.

EXPORT VARIANTS

Almost from the date that the Seven was announced, Austin built and supplied many thousands of rolling chassis to coach-building companies in the United Kingdom and abroad. Many of these rolling chassis, as with a number of export specification cars, incorporated features specific to the country or the company concerned.

Legislation in Australia favoured the import of rolling chassis to be bodied by local firms, and Austin sent out Sevens as chassis-only, or with sets of factory wings and scuttles to order. The range of larger Austins were already being bodied by Holden, and, with the introduction of the Seven, Holden produced a neat body, very similar

The 1935 model Holden Sports Tourer, which was built on a complete chassis shipped out from Longbridge, and fitted with 16in (406mm) wheels. (Courtesy Nick Salmon)

to the English Tourer, but easily distinguished by a bolder waistline moulding round the rear of the body. A two-seater followed with similar detail, Holden going on to continue with Ruby-like versions right through the 1930s.

Also in Australia, the exotically-named Latrobe company built a Chummy-like body with an emphasised waistline moulding, as well as a two-seater sports with an Ulster-like pointed tail and cycle wings. An attractive design for a two-seater sports car – not unlike the British Boyd-Carpenter, with dropped body sides, a sloping radiator, V windscreen and pointed tail – was laid down in the late 1920s. Called the Meteor, it formed the basis for a number of replicas by New South Wales Motors, Richardson of Sydney, and Flood of Melbourne. A number of examples of this design have been restored or replicated in recent times.

A number of Sevens were exported to Japan in the early 1930s, and one or more of these was examined by Datsun – the precursor of modern Nissan. A number of Austin rolling chassis were also bodied in Japan to comply with its taxation class, which was based on overall vehicle length. There was an announcement in April 1934 that Japan intended to sell these Seven-based cars for a mere £50 each in Australia and the colonies. This caused Herbert Austin to, in turn, immediately try to procure one

Ron Jones climbs the 3300 feet of Table Mountain, Cape Town, not surprisingly using only first gear, and taking over ten hours to get to the top and under two for the descent. (Austin publicity)

Berlin Motor Show 1934 with Sir Herbert Austin standing between Adolf Hitler and Col Waite explaining the Willys-Overland assembled left-hand drive Nippy. (Helmut Kasimirowicz)

of the Jidosha-Seizo-built (and Yokohama-based) cars, via his area representative Crane Williams. The first Japanese built car to arrive in Australia was swiftly purchased, and straight away shipped back to England for evaluation. Freddie Henry recalled its arrival, and the poor 'orange peel' finish of its green paint.

Herbert Austin was astounded to note the various borrowed features present on the badly-finished vehicle, which had, even in 1933, no shock absorbers fitted. The ride, in consequence, was very unstable. The engine had a one-piece iron block, and the rear axle used worm drive. It had adopted the late Rosengart's half-elliptic rear springs, the Dixi's engine layout, and American Austin styling. For whatever reason, however, Austin decided not to pursue any infringement of patent.

The original name for the delivered car was Datson – meaning 'Son of DAT', formed from the initials of the Japanese backers – but was changed to Datsun after Nissan took control of the company, as apparently the original name sounds like a very impolite word in Japanese! After World War Two, Nissan subsequently built the Austin A40 under licence, and continued to do so until, in the 1960s, it built the first of its own designs. A senior Nissan executive acknowledged in a 1979 interview that "we were taught how to build cars by Austin," and "Nissan was built on Austin technology."

In the mid-1930s, many Longbridge-built left-hand drive 'export' Rubys and Nippys were offered in Germany by Willys-Overland, which was Austin's concessionaire in the territory. Perhaps surprisingly, the well-proven 'export' left-hand drive Military Mulliner Scout cars and AP Military Tourers were also put on offer by Austin, to countries considered to be 'friendly' towards Britain, with publicity and sales brochures inviting enquiries.

1935 Datsun two-seater Tourer undergoing restoration. (Author collection)

CHAPTER ELEVEN

VILLIERS, JAMIESON, AND THE TWIN-CAM RACERS

MURRAY Jamieson was an immensely talented young design engineer who, after a glittering academic career, first joined the Green Engine Company at Twickenham in 1925, before joining Amherst Villiers in June 1928, to work on Raymond Mays' supercharged 1922-based Vauxhall Villiers hillclimbing special. It is accepted that the car engine supercharger has its origins as an air blower for the blast furnaces of late 19th century industrial America, and certainly, superchargers were fitted to a few car engines in Edwardian times. However, it was their application – in lightweight form – to fighter and bomber aircraft in the Great War that demonstrated the value of forced induction, directly geared to engine speed, to provide potential increases in both top end power and – equally importantly, when in an automotive application – greater torque in the middle rev range.

The 1922 Vauxhall was of Harry Ricardo's design. It was equipped with a 3-litre four-cylinder engine, and to this Amherst Villiers added a large, vertically-mounted supercharger at the front of the engine, allowing Raymond Mays to record a time of 42.4 seconds at the Shelsley Walsh Hillclimb in 1933. Charles Amherst Villiers was one of that rare breed of artist-engineers who could often rely on their own intuitive aesthetic judgment, should mechanical conundrums require more than mere mathematical calculation to resolve.

Villiers' start in the industry had come in 1922, modifying Mays' hillclimb machine, a Cognac-sponsored Bugatti Brescia, and a very fast AC-based special. He turned out a prodigious amount of work over his career, from aircraft design and exhibition-standard portrait painting, through to a spell at Douglas, in California, working on space missions. He even designed a horizontally-opposed 3-litre Formula One engine in the 1970s.

As a result, Murray Jamieson had, in Villiers, a mentor who passed on enormous confidence, and a breadth of vision that inspired innovative design. Together, they colluded on the design of a small supercharger for a production Austin Seven EA Sports, or Ulster, that had apparently been made available to Villiers by Sir Herbert Austin, who had been impressed by Villiers' expertise and results. Villiers and Jamieson both favoured a twin-rotor Roots-pattern supercharger layout, for its efficiency and its allowance for potential development. A gear-driven Jamieson-penned Roots-type blower was installed in the white painted Ulster, together with a special cylinder head and block, and suitably profiled camshaft.

The car was then taken to Brooklands, where – with the young Murray Jamieson driving, and with the Austin works team present – it proceeded to lap at an astonishing 99mph (159km/h), with full road equipment; a speed far quicker than the equivalent works car. This caused consternation amongst Stan Yeal's works Austin team, who were aghast and suspicious of this young Londoner, and how he could possibly have shown them a thing or two about the performance of their own Cozette-blown Sevens.

Murray Jamieson's performance could not be ignored, however, and Arthur Waite negotiated with Villiers and Jamieson for the latter to join Austin in the Experimental Department, working exclusively on competition cars. Soon upon his arrival, and working with Bert Hadley and Len Brokas, he was instructed to produce the ultimate side-valve single-seat racer for Austin. The works team, meanwhile, continued to race and refine the Rubber Ducks, which became more reliable, though little quicker.

By early 1932, MG had increased the flying mile record to 118.83mph (191.23km/h) at Pendine Sands, thereby raising the bar to a level that those at Austin knew was impossible to beat with its Rubber Duck's engine, no matter how efficient and streamlined a body was used. Tests had shown that on any sensible and available

BERT HADLEY

Bert Hadley – of solid Birmingham stock – was born in 1910, at Stirchley, near Bourneville. At 14 years old, he was instantly smitten upon seeing a Gordon England Brooklands Austin Seven in a local dealer's showroom – the family soon after buying a Tourer, in which young Bert quickly taught himself to drive.

A visit to the Shelsley Walsh Hillclimb further fired Bert's ambitions, and he took up an apprenticeship at 'The Austin' in early 1927, working in ten different departments before being placed in charge of four Austin Seven engines on test. There were 50 engines on test at any one time, all running 'on full noise,' with the usual fun and games amongst the young crew of the test house. After about three years, and a rather tense interview with Sir Herbert, Bert was asked to report to the Experimental Department. There, he was placed under Alf Depper and chief mechanic Len Brokas, relishing the build process of racing engines, including the Campbell Daytona record breaker.

Bert's first participation in a race was as a mechanic to Charles Goodacre in the 1931 LCC Relay Race, where the Austin team won. He regularly drove the works Ulster-type cars to Brooklands for high-speed testing, and formed a lasting friendship with Goodacre.

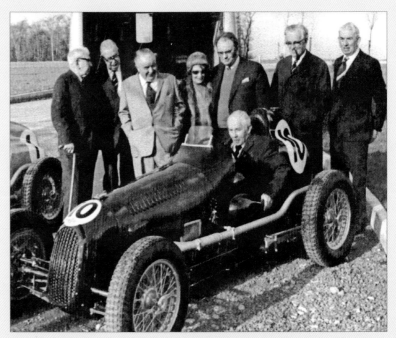

1974, with Tom Wheatcroft at Donington – the first and only time the Austin works team had been together since 1939. From left: Ral Appleby, Pat Driscoll, Bert Hadley, Kay Petre, Tom Wheatcroft, Charles Goodacre, and Jim Bramley (publicity), with Arthur 'Charlie' Dodson in the Twin-Cam. (750 Motor Club archive)

Bert worked closely with Murray Jamieson on the blown cars, and later on the Twin-Cam. Testing revealed the geometrical difficulties of the front suspension, and Bert was impressed by Jamieson's quick solution to the problem, introducing the rotational joint in the tubular front axle.

Bert was invited, one memorable day, to try the Side-Valve on Brooklands Mountain Circuit, managing to beat the established works driver's times. After some drama in his first official race for the team, and misplaced harsh words with Lord Austin, Hadley became a regular driver of the single-seaters. Ultimately, he became the fastest driver at Austin, having a particular synergy with the Twin-Cam single-seater, and surviving – by incredible fortune – an engine blow-up at Brooklands that deranged the steering at full chat. He gained innumerable class wins and handicap results in both hillclimbs and races, including the last race at Crystal Palace in August 1939, at the very brink of World War Two.

In May 1941, Bert took up the position of an inspector of labour supply at Cheylesmore, in Coventry. After the end of the war, he co-drove one of the sensational Jaguar XK120s at Le Mans with Leslie Johnson, lying in third when the clutch broke up in the final hour. He later joined Stirling Moss and other Jaguar, Jowett, and Austin Healey works drivers in highly successful 1950s record-breaking and racing exploits.

In recent times, the Prewar Austin Seven Club honoured Bert Hadley by naming its highly-acclaimed sprint and hillclimb series The Bert Hadley Trophy.

Bert Hadley is well out of the cockpit as his Twin-Cam turns in at Crystal Palace, October 1938. (Courtesy Ferret Fotographics)

tyre size, the existing rear axle ratio of 4.5:1 would require the Duck engine to rev to 7000rpm – an impossible speed. Alternatively, if the supercharger boost was raised further, in order to pull a higher axle ratio, the over-stressed engine would merely be awaiting disaster. Any adverse publicity from such an event was something that the factory dare not risk.

The answer was to try a fresh approach, with Murray Jamieson heading a design team with a layout that – from first principles – represented the ultimate solution for the side-valve layout. All areas were re-examined, evaluated, and set out to eliminate all of the inherent limitations of the Duck engine, which, in its most highly developed form, delivered about 56bhp at 6000rpm. The ambitious target for the new project, which was achieved, was an honest and usable 70bhp at 7000rpm, with even more power, together with increased torque, available in short bursts for sprint events.

The bottom end included a fully counter-balanced stiff $1\frac{11}{16}$in diameter bearing crankshaft, in a highly reinforced complicated cast-magnesium crankcase, and, with the Roots-type blower, the available engine speeds were safely raised. To accord to Herbert Austin's strictures, the bore and stroke dimensions were kept the same as an ordinary Seven engine, along with the spacing of the bores and the length of the connecting rods. The camshaft also rested in its familiar location, at the top nearside of the crankcase.

The oiling system included a dry sump, with both supply and return galleries cast into the crankcase – including pressure feed to the tappets – and connecting rods that needed to be asymmetric to clear the camshaft lobes. The cylinder block casting was equally complex, incorporating more reinforcement, improved cooling transfer and porting, and extra studs between the block and crankcase. 32 studs were used to fix the special aluminium cylinder head, which had combustion chambers based on the Duck design, with twin 14mm spark plugs per cylinder. The drive for one magneto and the water pump was via a detachable Ulster-based timing gear front, and the vertical supercharger turned at twice engine speed, via a bevel gear drive off the front of the crankshaft. The second magneto was on the nearside, its gear drive stacked off the cam gear.

The beautifully-built and detailed engine was fitted into a Duck chassis, and, for record breaking purposes, a one-off light streamlined bodyshell was mounted. The body shape incorporated a very low fully-ducted nose and tail, and low mounted fairings in front of, and behind, each of its four wheels. This was very much in the LSR design spirit of the day, helping to keep down frontal area. A long slim tail – to cut down on turbulence and, hopefully aerodynamic drag – was also fitted, with a variable horizontal aerofoil section for downforce and traction.

Murray Jamieson in the fully developed 120mph (193km/h) Record Side-Valve, from which evolved the Side-Valve racers. (Austin Publicity)

Jamieson himself first drove his new creation at Montlhéry in October 1933, achieving 119.30mph (191.99km/h) for 10km, and five and ten mile Class H 750cc records – gathering much information from his highly-instrumented motor car in the process. In the heated atmosphere of Austin's great rivalry with MG, these records were soon broken by motorcyclist Denly, in a works MG. With Pat Driscoll driving, however, the Jamieson SV Austin pushed back, breaking the World 1km record, and taking it to 122.74mph (197.53km/h) on the beach course at Southport. This was despite a very nasty cut to Driscoll's nose, when the timing thread rode up over the low streamlined body.

After much debate, it was accepted by Austin that, for record speed attempts, the limitations of a side-valve layout – similar in most respects to the little prototype Seven of 1922 – had probably been reached. The lovely Jamieson side-valve machine was therefore subsequently rebuilt as a contemporary circuit racer.

The Duck chassis was retained, but, due to the known handling difficulties caused by the front suspension (brought about by using short side-mounted radius arms and a stiff one-piece beam axle lifting inside front wheels on corners), a new tubular front axle was designed, which incorporated a rotating bearing towards the nearside. The effect of this was to allow each wheel, attached to its own half of the tubular axle, to pivot quite separately from the other wheel. This change instantly gave vastly improved cornering, and gave the drivers more confidence in attacking hills. Centre-lock wire wheels were fitted for the first time, together with larger finned brakes, but cable brake operation was favoured over hydraulic actuation.

The overall offset Duck transmission was retained, and a completely new bodyshell was designed that resembled a cross between the latest Grand Prix Mercedes and – with a nod across the Atlantic – the distinctive contemporary American dirt track midget racers. The shape of the bodyshell had tightly-fitting vertical slab sides, with a cut away cockpit cleverly moulded into a pretty rounded nose. Complete with a curved dash cowl and delicately shaped tail, the whole thing was simple but attractive, and much copied in later years by enthusiastic special builders.

The chassis rails were allowed to run outside the bodywork, and – together with the partially-exposed suspension and wheels – this added greatly to the overall pleasing aesthetic functionality of this new little racer. A four-speed close-ratio gearbox was fitted, and the performance of the developed engine in a light car, now with good handling, was a revelation.

Running on alcohol, and with a blower pressure of 24psi, the robustly detailed engine ran up to 8500rpm, at which point it delivered no less than 85bhp. Pat Driscoll drove the car, now known as No 2, from mid-1934 onwards as the class of the field. The car was sent to Germany for Baumer to use in continental events, and another new car for Driscoll prepared for the 1935 season. Further development allowed even greater revs for sprints, where the Austins excelled. However, sustained high throttle openings at high blower pressures ultimately took their toll of the engines on longer courses, where the inherent cooling difficulties of the side-valve layout became the performance-limiting factor.

Notwithstanding some excellent results, it was recognised by Herbert Austin that a pure racing engine, that owed less to its Austin Seven heritage than previously, was the only way forward for the 1935 season. The enthusiastic and talented Murray Jamieson was therefore given free rein for a radical design solution – and this time for the whole car.

Jamieson, totally immersed in race car design, was familiar with the work of innovative designers like Gabriel Voisin and André Lefèbvre who, in the 1920s, had produced the Voisin Laboratoire, with its monocoque aluminium body structure and WW1 fighter aircraft-inspired agility and feedback to the driver. He was also aware, however, of various largely-German experiments, like Auto Union, with rear engine designs, and LSR projects. The pure design ethos of reducing the weight and total number of elements, by incorporating

Middle period works Austin race development in a nutshell. Entered in the 1934 LCC Relay Race were: Goodacre's Ulster (2C), Parish's yellow Rubber Duck (2B), and Pat Driscoll in the Jamieson Side-Valve racer. (Author collection)

WV Appleby and Tom Brown, two young engineers, were seconded to Jamieson to work on the project. The chassis layout was to reflect the well-known Austin Seven A-frame, with quarter-elliptic rear springs and a beam front axle, in order to be presented to the public as an identifiable variation of available showroom models.

The chassis employed longer than standard channel section side members, a tubular crossmember in front of the engine, and a forged 'banjo' crossmember between the rear spring mounts to support the front of the rear axle torque tube. It also featured a pressed-steel middle member, supporting the front of the seat, and a stiff scuttle mounting the steering box on a very short steering column, with an intermediate rod to a bellcrank on the frame, then forward via a steering rod to the front axle. A tubular crossmember at the rear supported the 25-gallon pressurised fuel tank in the tail, which employed a hand pump. The rear quarter elliptics employed trailing tie rods to avoid rear spring 'wind-up' on acceleration, and the fully floating rear axle utilised a double reduction gear to reduce the size of the crown wheel, giving a total rear axle ratio of 5.5:1.

The wheels were again centre lock, but of smaller diameter and with low pressure tyres. In anticipation of the high speeds to be achieved, 12in (304mm) brakes were installed on the front and 10in (254mm) on the rear, the drums heavily finned with vented back plates and careful fully-compensating enclosed cable brake activation. The front axle

Continued page 133

more than one function for each component, was very evident in Jamieson's solution.

Jamieson's radical design, as recorded later by both Charles Goodacre and Freddie Henry, was an ultra-low aluminium monocoque, with a rear-mounted twin overhead camshaft two-stage blown 750cc engine, producing 150bhp (up to 200bhp when ultimately developed). The driver semi-reclined between slim sponson fuel tanks fitted between the wheels, with low drag surface radiators and adjustable aerofoils mounted front and rear – all this some 27 years prior to Colin Chapman's game-changing monocoque Lotus 25. Very sadly, no design drawings of Jamieson's momentous concept seem to have survived.

When Sir Herbert Austin returned from abroad and was presented with these boldly extreme proposals, he was somewhat taken aback, mostly concerned about the safety of his works driver in such a device. After due consideration, Herbert decided that a front-engined car was far safer for the team drivers, was probably more controllable, and better fitted the marketing of the Austin Seven. As a result, a modified version of the Jamieson Side-Valve racer was decided upon, fitted with a twin overhead motor of all new design.

Jamieson, who has been described as the presiding genius in the circle in which he moved, used this new brief to create the most charismatic small prewar racing car built in the United Kingdom. Astonishingly, the Jamieson Twin-Cam Austin Seven of 1935 still remains as the last true single-seater racing car designed for a front-line international racing formula, by any British volume car manufacturer.

Overleaf, left: Murray Jamieson's exquisite design drawing of the Austin 750cc Twin Cam racing engine. Drawn by hand in pencil on cartridge paper, the commitment of the engineering parameters for dimensional setting-out demonstrates an extraordinary mind. (A7CA archive)
Overleaf right: Longitudinal section of the Austin 750cc Twin-Cam racing engine, showing the novel gasket-free cylinder block to head sealing arrangement. (A7CA archive)

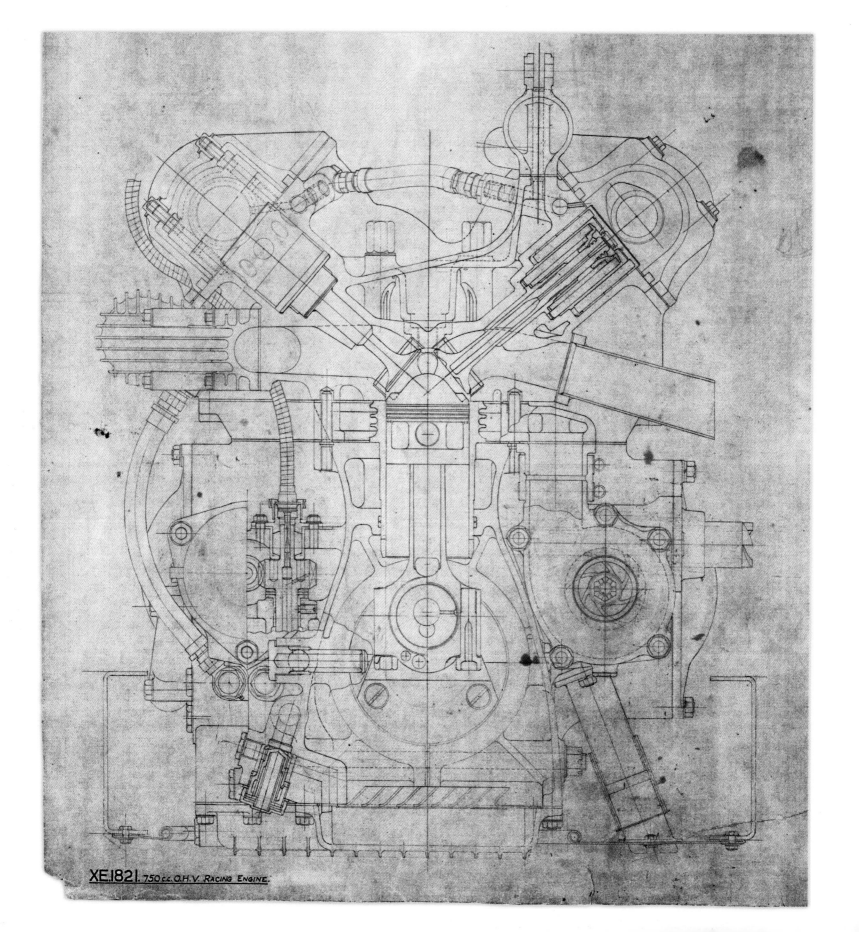

XE.1821. 750 c.c. O.H.V. Racing Engine.

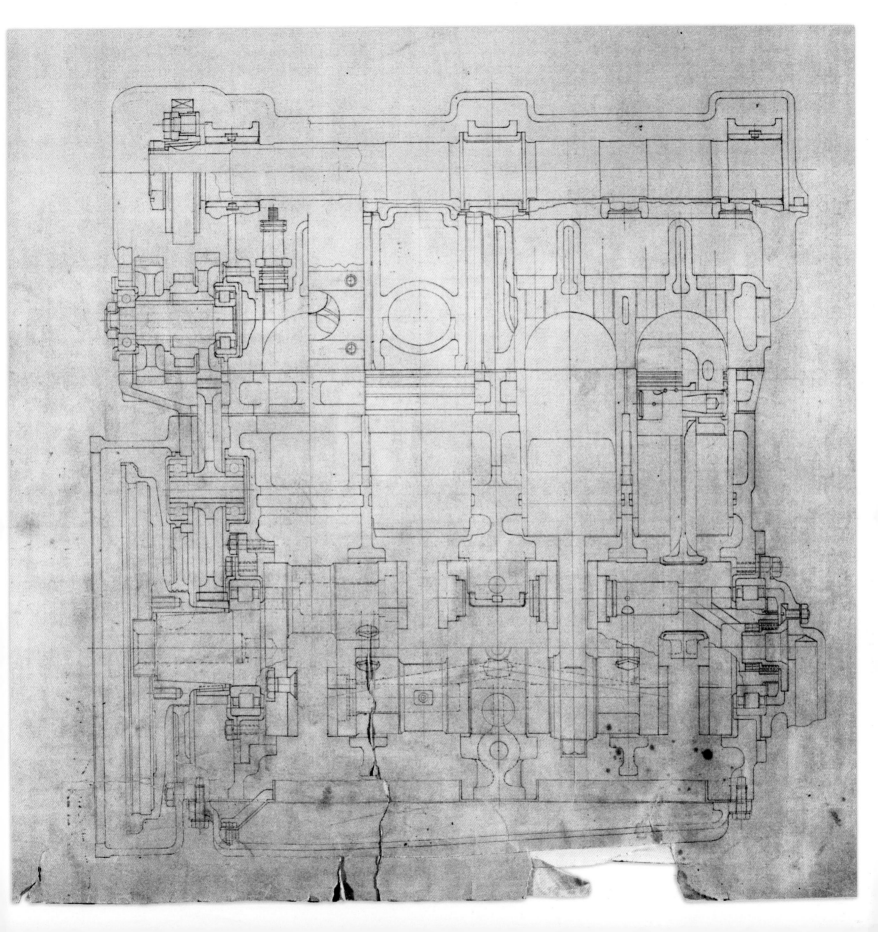

PAT DRISCOLL

Austin works driver Pat Driscoll was born in 1900, and started his competition career racing on Norton motorbikes, winning his first race at Brooklands in 1922. Having converted to cars with a Lea-Francis Hyper, in a 1931 race he stopped to assist SCH Davis – who had crashed – and impressed Austin team manager Arthur Waite. Waite invited Driscoll to co-drive with Archie Frazer-Nash in a works Ulster in that year's Brooklands Double Twelve, where they retired with a seriously cracked block.

Driscoll drove a new Zoller-blown Duck in the Brooklands BRDC 500-Mile Race where, despite the cramped cockpit, he strapped himself in and lapped at 94mph (151km/h). Encouraged by Waite to go for the Class H six-hour record, Driscoll insisted on starting early, despite thick fog, and secured the record at 90.12mph (145.03km/h), and being upgraded to the number one works driver in the process.

Driscoll's racing bike experience was invaluable; on his advice Norton-like conrods were machined, reliably raising the available engine revolutions per minute by 1000. With this benefit, Driscoll's Duck lapped at 102.48mph (164.92km/h) at the Brooklands Easter meeting, then over 103mph (165km/h), backed by Barnes and Goodacre. Driscoll also drove the long tailed car at Southport, taking the Class H flying kilometre record at 122.74mph (197.53km/h), despite his being cut by the timing thread and sustaining a nasty injury. At the Shelsley Walsh Hillclimb, he won his class at 46.16mph (74.28km/h), despite bending the standard gearlever. Once again at Brooklands, he set a class Mountain Circuit lap record of 72.87mph (117.27km/h), which he then raised, with the new tubular axle installed, to 74.95mph (120.62km/h).

The Twin-Cams were ready for 1936, but Driscoll span out at Brooklands when his foot became jammed on the throttle. Then, at Madresfield Speed Trials, and unknown to Pat, Murray Jamieson had locked the differential, leaving the car difficult to control. He also

retired at Donington's Empire Trophy Race with a broken Scintilla magneto. At the Brighton Speed Trials, he had run the works Side-Valve engine up to 10,500rpm – some way beyond what was thought possible for these motors.

The 1936 Backwell Hillclimb near Bristol saw Driscoll entered in a twin rear wheel Twin-Cam. However, in the wet, and possibly due to the combination of twin rear wheels and low tyre pressures, he was sent violently sideways into a tree at speed. The car folded around the tree trunk, badly injuring Driscoll and bringing his brilliant racing career to a premature end.

Partially blind for almost two years from his head injury, Pat moved to his beloved Hayling Island and took up competitive sailing. He was a keen cyclist until well into his seventies, and is remembered as an absolute gentleman.

Pat Driscoll, in a works Rubber Duck, hands over the sash to Barnes in the 1938 LCC Relay Race at Brooklands. (Author collection)

Lively 1932 Brooklands poster. (Author collection)

A beautiful Geoffrey Goddard study of the Twin-Cam, exposed to display its glittering detail. (Courtesy Ferret Fotographics)

was again tubular in two parts, and incorporated the lessons learnt on the Side-Valve racer. Again, it featured a joint with an internal roller bearing, allowing each part of the axle to act independently of the other without compromising the steering or suspension geometry, and tie rods in tension under braking were fitted above the chassis side-mounted radius arms.

Allied to a stiffer frame, both the transverse leaf spring and the rear quarter elliptics were allowed to be fairly soft. Along with multiple disc dampers, everything pointed towards a more compliant and modern suspension philosophy, while also reflecting the improved road surfaces upon which competitive events were, by then, being held. The engine crankcase was solidly fixed to the side rails of the chassis, to assist in the avoidance of 'lozenging,' and

the open propeller shaft was fitted with steady bearings to avoid any propshaft whip.

A single plate clutch with five toggles and fifteen springs was used, and the integral four-speed gearbox was designed to be alternatively fitted with straight pinions or synchromesh gearing, depending on the type of event – synchromesh being available on the top three gears for hillclimbs or short course racing. Later hub fittings were added for twin rear wheels, for extra grip on tight or steep corners. The twin overhead camshaft engine was, of course, of interest at the time, and has continued to fascinate enthusiasts and historians ever since, gaining almost mythical status in the interim.

The ambition of Jamieson to create, from first principles, a new engine that would far surpass all previous designs of this small – but important – 750cc capacity class acted as a spur. The clarity of his proposals, complex for the period, are readily apparent in both his design drawings (which reward diligent study) and in the finished engines. The engine was intended to run at extremely high speed, and upper limits on piston speed dictated a short stroke. The short stroke, in turn, allowed a generous cylinder bore diameter, with a large diameter hemispherical combustion chamber, into which the raised piston crowns would intrude to give a very high compression ratio. The large bore also permitted large-diameter valves, which were needed to give sufficient breathing at high engine revs.

The other part of Jamieson's brief was to eliminate, by design, the obvious engine features that might potentially jeopardise reliability caused by any short-comings in lubrication and cooling. Such issues could negate the team's joint efforts by causing the car to fail to complete a race or other competitive event.

Jamieson decided in his compact design to do without conventional gaskets in the principal joints, and to tackle the thermal difficulties presented in a highly-stressed racing engine from the disparity between adjacent metal masses, which created internal stresses due to uneven heating and cooling. This meant doing away with the large mass of metal otherwise contained in the adjoining faces of the cylinder block and the cylinder head, which defied even temperature control. One only has to consider the incoming cool fuel mixture, ignition, and the expulsion of the heated exhaust gases – all going on within millimetres of each other, more than 60 times a second, in each of four cylinders – to appreciate the difficulty and complexity of this task.

Jamieson and his little team were determined to resolve it, however. It was decided to leave the top of the block open, with the four wet cylinder liners projecting a full 1¼in (32mm) above the outside edge of the block. A cylinder head was to be made from RR50 metal, and to have its bottom face machined out as much as possible to give maximum unobstructed flow of coolant between. As can be seen on the drawings, a spacer sandwich plate – also of RR50 metal, of

slightly less than 1¼in (32mm) thickness – was then placed between the block and the cylinder head, with a rubber joint washer between head, spacer, and block. This was to give a waterproof joint when compressed by the head being pulled down over four studs spaced equally around each cylinder. In practice, this design was found to be entirely reliable and presented no problems, a metal-to-metal gas-proof joint being formed between cylinder liners and cylinder head.

The Twin-Cam rear axle and suspension and cockpit, the chassis design showing complex cross-members and robust handbrake detailing. (Courtesy Ferret Fotographics)

Twin-Cam cockpit detail illustrating the beautifully machined offset gated gear change with stubby lever, propshaft and pedals. Driver ergonomics were a big improvement over the Rubber Ducks. (Courtesy Ferret Fotographics)

Through experimentation it was found that, with the designed blower pressure, the inlet valves could potentially be considerably larger than the exhaust. However, the original design drawings show inlet and exhaust valves of similar diameter, which is how the engines were probably built, though there are detail variations to each unit.

Three element wire valve springs were used to avoid overstressing, and very wide cam faces were employed to avoid overload – the camshaft lobes acting on short inverted bucket plungers clear of the valve stems, to eliminate any sideways load whatsoever on the latter. The twin overhead camshafts and supercharger drive were gear-driven off the rear of the engine, with variable gear sets to change the supercharger speed and boost – up to one and a half times engine speed, giving 22lb boost from the Roots blower fed by a large SU carburettor with a single float chamber to the side.

The careful work on the drawing board was matched by evolving theory and calculation within the little design team; the planned rev range of the engine exceeded its knowledge of the available contributing data, and testing a built engine was going to be vital to development. One fundamental known factor was that the fully-counterbalanced crankshaft, machined from solid billet, fell short of completely balancing the rotating part of the connecting rod. Experiments were carried out with three different magneto suppliers, and dry sump lubrication was decided to be essential, not only to guarantee supply under the centrifugal forces of long corners, but to enable sufficient cooling of the engine oil. Such was the calculated combustion heat transfer from the cylinders and pistons, an oil cooler being fitted behind the radiator.

The crankshaft was carried in two roller bearings, one at each end, with a plan bearing in the centre. Lubricating the crankshaft bearings and big ends was performed via an oil gallery into the front of the crankshaft. This fed into the bearings via an ingenious arrangement of steel washers, with precision-ground faces, transferring the oil from an essentially static source to a rotating one, while still maintaining 100psi oil pressure throughout the oil system.

After initially running the engine without the supercharger in place, the blower was fitted and the engine ran smoothly, recording 90bhp at the considerable engine speed of 8000rpm. Experiments with different piston crown shapes, compression ratios, and spark plug positions soon gave 110bhp, and the motor would happily rev past the 8000rpm mark without difficulty, or encountering any feared unusual effects.

Jamieson first tried out his brainchild at Donington, in late 1935. Its performance exceeded even his expectations, and assembly of the second and third cars were immediately put in hand for the

Tom Murray Jamieson test driving a Twin Cam. Tom enjoyed testing his creations and could test drive as hard as drivers of Hadley's calibre. (Austin Publicity)

1936 season of sprints, hillclimbs, and short and long distance races. Works drivers Pat Driscoll, Charles Goodacre, and Arthur Dodson were set to drive the new machines, while Bert Hadley was given the Side-Valve racer. Lord Austin launched the new Twin-Cam racer at a reception at the Grand Hotel in Birmingham, telling the press of his belief in competition design 'improving the breed.' Unfortunately, however, the first outing at the Brooklands track was rained off.

The three Twin-Cams ran at the 1936 JCC 250-Mile International Trophy Race at Brooklands in May, but – almost disastrously – a connecting rod broke on Driscoll's car, with flying metal denting his helmet and holing his oil cooler. Goodacre and Dodson also retired due to misfiring, the former with magneto problems and the latter with oiled up plugs due to an erratic blower valve. The Shelsley Walsh Hillclimb followed, but all three OHC (overhead cam) cars suffered once again, unable to rev cleanly. At the County Down Trophy race, in Ulster, Goodacre was soon out once again, with a broken throttle, and Driscoll followed. Dodson, however, drove brilliantly, averaging 83mph (133km/h), and bettering the previous lap record, only to spoil his run by breaking down.

The main problem was identified as piston crowns burning out and collapsing through the mixture becoming too lean – a fault not evident when running on the test brake – and it was to take the whole season to be finally cured. The SU carburettor representative suggested that

CHARLES GOODACRE

In 1930, Charles Goodacre joined Austin as an improver mechanic in the Experimental Department and, by degrees, became an all-round works driver, taking part in trials with Grasshoppers, races, and hillclimbs from 1930-37.

The youthful Charles was teamed with Gunnar Poppe in the works 'Harlequin' two-seater at the British Racing Drivers Club 500-Mile Race in October 1930, where the car retired with a seized piston. Then, in the following year's event, with the ex-Yellow Canary Rubber Duck, all suffered bodywork damage on the rough banking.

Earlier in 1931, Charles had delivered a works-prepared Ulster TT replica to Signor Trevisan, which the pair drove around Italy in the Mille Miglia, coming in a creditable second in the 1100cc class, and 34th overall – to the great pleasure of Herbert Austin. Tantalisingly, a second Austin Seven was entered in the Mille Miglia, by a certain Enzo Ferrari, but this car does not appear to have made the start.

The 1931 Tourist Trophy at Ards, Belfast, saw Goodacre place 8th in Class H and 17th overall, after which the works Ulsters were not entered again as a factory team. By that September, Goodacre was competing in the Rubber Duck, and the following May competed at the notorious and fast AVUS banked track in Berlin, coming second to Barnes in the 750cc Class. More works single-seater and development Ulster drives followed, with Goodacre almost matching the very quick

Brooklands, 1937, and the Austin team's supercharged single-seaters sit in the sunshine. Kay Petre is in the Side-Valve, with Charles Goodacre and Bert Hadley in Twin-Cams. (750 Motor Club archive)

Bert Hadley, not only in the number of appearances for the works team, but in speed too.

Goodacre and Rod Turner drove one of the three-bearing crank Grasshoppers at Le Mans in 1935, but retired in the early hours. The same thing happened there in 1937, with Buckley as co-driver. The October 1937 Crystal Palace meeting was the first ever television-broadcast outside motor race, and Bert Hadley and Charles Goodacre competed in BRG Twin-Cam Austins. Goodacre led most of the final, only for Bira and Dobson, both in ERAs, to overtake on the last lap.

This was to be Charles Goodacre's last race for Austin, although he did later make appearances at the wheel of a works Grasshopper in the MCC Exeter Trial and, post-World War Two, gave very well-received talks to motor clubs. Charles was honoured by the 750 Formula, with the main championship award being named the Goodacre Trophy.

---

the single float chamber system should be augmented with a second float chamber fitted in-line across the engine, so that any fuel surges to left or right when cornering would be cancelled out by the opposite float chamber coming into operation. The root of the engine problem, therefore, lay in the very high cornering speeds achieved by the low slung racer, riding on wider, softer tyres and efficient suspension. It

is possible that Murray Jamieson was simply not a hard enough test driver for the problem to show up earlier.

The 1936 season continued with difficult races at Donington, then at the Madresfield Speed Trial, where the OHC Austins swept the board and considerably lifted team spirits. At Blackwell Hillclimb in July, however, disaster struck when Pat Driscoll's single entry crashed

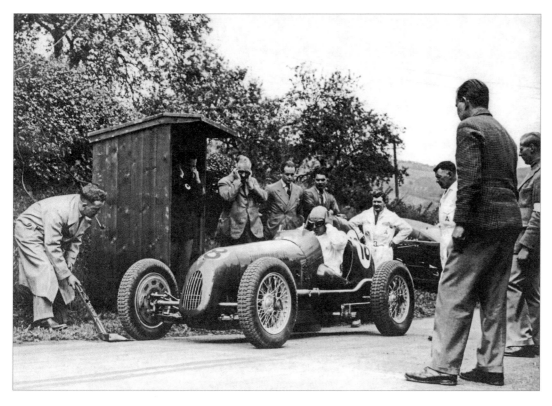

Hold onto your eardrums! Bert Hadley adjusts his goggles as he prepares for take-off at Shelsley Walsh in a Twin Cam. Note the partially cowled nose to assist warming up. (A7CA Bert Hadley archive)

Shortly after, Bert Hadley established a new record at Craigantlet Hillclimb, then, at Shelsley Walsh Hillclimb, Austin swept the board in the 750cc class, with Goodacre beating Baumer, Hadley followed in third, with RF Turner fourth. Dodson then set a series of records at Brooklands – six International Class H, the fastest being 50km at 118.51mph (190.72km/h), and seven British, including the flying kilometre at 122.74mph (197.53km/h).

Despite finishing the 1936 season on a high note, the mixed fortunes of the expensive Twin-Cam racer caused much debate back at Longbridge, where it had been acknowledged

badly. Pat was severely injured, and the incident, tragically, finished his front-line driving career.

When a Twin-Cam was running cleanly, the noise was glorious, the power impressive, and the handling sweet. This was soon demonstrated when a single car was made available to German driver Walter Baumer, for the (typically continental) almost eight-mile-long Frieburg Hillclimb, which rose over 2500ft (762m) and had no fewer than 83 corners.

Baumer took the Austin up in eight minutes 43.2 seconds, taking 33 seconds off the 1100cc record, and beating the best 1500cc time by a clear 15 seconds – an astonishing performance by any standards.

that – whilst any serious racing project must take time to develop – there was pressure to withdraw the OHC cars from competition. Sadly, this led to Murray Jamieson deciding to leave, feeling that his talents might be more appreciated elsewhere. He moved to ERA, a pure racing team with fewer politics, and focussed entirely on its Voiturette-class single-seaters.

For 1937, Austin decided to continue with the two surviving Twin-Cams and one Side-Valve, but to limit entries to the more high-profile national events. Things did not start well, with a pit fire at Donington badly burning Arthur Dodson, who remained out of competition driving for the remainder of the season. Charles Goodacre, with the role of team leader, and the ever-faster young Bert Hadley drove the British Racing Green Twin-Cams, with Kay Petre driving the works Side-Valve racer painted in her personal racing livery of pale blue.

The Coronation Meeting at Donington in May 1937 was held on a glorious sunny day. An ecstatic Goodacre won the first three races,

The 'Austin' bridge at Donington Park in 1937, with the works Mercedes W125s roaring through below. (Author collection)

KAY PETRE

Canadian-born Kay Petre twice broke the Women's Outer Circuit Record at Brooklands – first in a Bugatti at 129.58mph (208.54km/h) and later, in a monster 10.5-litre Delage at 134.75mph (216.85km/h). In the latter, her petite figure required a special small seat, and extended pedals.

Herbert Austin was so taken with Kay that she was offered a place in the works team, on driving merit alone, racing the blown Side-Valve single-seater as the only female driver on a genuine works team at that time. Always immaculate in tailored pale blue silk overalls, and with cars painted to match, Kay was a distinctive attraction. Not surprisingly, she accumulated crowds of fans as Austin's 'pin-up girl.'

She drove at Brooklands, Crystal Palace, Donington, and Shelsley Walsh, where – always turning in a fast performance – she won the Ladies Challenge Trophy in 1936 and in 1937, with a record ascent of 43.78 seconds. In 1937 Kay drove a Grasshopper at the Le Mans 24-hour race, and in the Paris to Nice Rally. She then travelled to South Africa with her own Riley, and was given a test drive in one of the mighty rear-engined Auto Union Grand Prix cars – a considerable honour and mark of respect for her abilities.

Sadly, her racing career came to an abrupt and disastrous end when practicing at the 1937 Brooklands BRDC 500km Race. Reg Parnell took his MG Magnette too high when overtaking on a banking turn, and slid down into Kay's Side-Valve Austin. The Austin overturned, and threw Kay out at 100mph (160km/h). Kay was badly injured, and did not drive competitively again.

When, eventually, she recovered, she became the *Daily Graphic*'s motoring correspondent, and postwar was Austin's colour and trim adviser, including her work for the 1959 Mini interiors.

Always good for publicity, Kay Petre poses in the works Side-Valve single-seater, while Bill Rogers and Bob Simpson try to give a convincing push. The tail of the Austin transporter truck is visible on the right. (Courtesy Jean-François Bouzanquet)

Bert Hadley at Shelsley Walsh in a Twin-Cam; this was an attempt with twin rear wheels, which are under enormous power and already spinning. Note the multiple detail differences – signs of continuous development (A7CA Bert Hadley archive).

Reg Parnell, who had been fined in July for causing an accident, lost control of his MG at about 90mph (144km/h) as he was attempting to pass her, higher on the banking. Kay was thrown out of her Side-Valve, and suffered facial injuries and a concussion. A considerable recovery time followed, and the incident marked the end of her – hitherto glittering – racing career. Chastened, the remaining Austin team retired from the race – first Hadley with engine problems, then Goodacre with a broken trackrod. In the last event of 1937, at Crystal Palace, Goodacre took a third behind Bira and Dodson, both ERA-mounted.

before the 100-mile main event – one that would be almost impossible, on paper, for the Austins to win. The Austin team nevertheless roared off, in the order of Hadley and Goodacre leading, with Kay Petre following closely behind. Tensions rose as the race continued, and the bigger cars behind inexorably began catching them, lap by lap. Then, quite unexpectedly, it started to rain.

The larger cars were naturally obliged to slow down, but not so Hadley and Goodacre, who began to stretch out their lead. Seven laps from the finish, Hadley retired with a broken oil pipe. Goodacre motored on, however, at an average of over 61mph (98km/h) on the road course, and recorded his fourth win of the day. One driver, and one car, had swept the board – an extraordinary achievement, bringing great publicity to Austin and silencing any noises from Longbridge about the value of racing.

The next month saw a visit to the Shelsley Walsh Hillcimb, where Bert Hadley recorded a 40.83 second run, to Raymond Mays' new record of 39.02 seconds in his personally-developed ERA, and Austin won the Team Prize. At Brooklands the team excelled once again, winning the 240km Light Car Club Relay Race at over 105mph (168km/h), including stops. This was despite Kay Petre having to contend with an oil gauge leak dripping scalding oil onto her legs for 50 laps.

The September BRDC 500km race, also held at Brooklands, proved tragic for the Austin team. Kay Petre was badly hurt in practice when

The Austin single-seaters naturally evolved, and photographs show a variety of fuel, oil, and radiator fillers. Small developments were made to the radiator cowls and cockpit sides, depending on the requirement for outright speed at Brooklands, or the agility and visibility needed to aid precise placing on hillclimbs.

More good results were obtained in 1938, but in May came the news that Murray Jamieson – by then in the employ of ERA – had been killed in an accident at Brooklands. A Delage and a Darracq had tangled close to an embankment, where only a paling fence protected the spectators, the Delage crashing through and killing Jamieson and another spectator. Jamieson's death extinguished a star that had flashed brightly across British motorsport for a decade. He had contributed immeasurably to Austin's Seven competition history. As Denis Jenkinson later wrote, had he lived, Jamieson would have surely had a fundamental influence on motorsport after World War Two.

Bert Hadley had, by 1939, developed into a formidable driver, and came second only to Rolt's ERA at Donington in the British Empire Trophy race, where Dodson's Twin-Cam suffered an unexpected cylinder head problem. At Crystal Palace in July, Hadley won a heat of the handicap Crystal Palace Cup race, then – after a thrilling final – just conceded first place to Mays' ERA.

With war clouds gathering in Europe, Bert Hadley was again at 'the Palace' in August, this time for the Imperial Trophy event. He easily

took the 20-mile sprint at a touch under 56mph (90km/h), before driving like a man possessed in the final, throwing his Twin-Cam round the track a full 2mph faster than ever before, and winning. This ended, with a flourish, the racing career of Herbert Austin's little jewel of a race car, and the Twin-Cams were then pushed quietly into the darker recesses below the Longbridge factory, to await better times.

Amherst Villiers survived the war, and continued with his illustrious career. Raymond Mays, after the success of ERA, went on to found British Racing Motors in the late 1940s, under the auspices of Alfred Owen's organisation. The BRM engineered by Tony Rudd (himself owning a Seven Box Saloon) went on to win the 1962 Formula One Driver's Championship, with that celebrated and terribly British Austin Seven Chummy owner, Graham Hill.

Culmination. The Austin Seven Twin-Cam now in Rod Spollon's ownership, pictured at Château Impney. (Courtesy Rod Spollon)

CHAPTER TWELVE

A PROPER CAR FOR £100

PRESS announcements for new cars were still national headline news in the early 1930s, and small 'proper' cars were gradually reducing in costs in these hard times, with the Holy Grail being the ability to sell a car for £100. There was, of course, nothing noteworthy about this round figure as far as production costs went, but a £100 sticker in a showroom was every car salesman's dream – as was the commission cheque that would come with it.

Press speculation that Austin was about to market a £100 Seven was initially rebutted by Herbert Austin. However, this denial was used by Morris – Austin's wily competitor – to announce that *he* would soon be building such a car, the economy model two-seater Morris Minor. Having surveyed demand, and realising that fabric-bodied saloons had now had their day, and were losing popularity, Herbert Austin instead announced price reductions and fundamental upgrades to the Seven range. The central model of this range would be the Saloon, to be built on the new long wheelbase, 6ft 9in (2.06m) chassis, with various logical technical upgrades. Despite unemployment still rising in 1931, Austin sold over 21,000 Sevens over the course of the year,

The Dalai Lama was given this Austin Seven Tourer on his 14th birthday. Note the Tibetan number plate. (Courtesy Ken Cooke)

The versatile Seven vans were used for various duties, such as transporting the increasingly common traffic signs on the nation's highways, performed by both the AA, and, as seen here, the RAC. (Author collection)

and the Morris Minor failed to become the force to topple the Austin Seven from its position of popularity.

The times were really quite tumultuous and frenetic; public appetite swayed wildly, with the middle and upper classes looking for the very latest 'new thing' – whether it was a dance craze, a style of clothing, music, or motor cars. As in modern times, folk of more ordinary means followed the trends whenever they could. Such changing values were exhibited in the sudden decline of the myriad specialist coach-builders that had built considerable numbers of special bodies on Sevens. With the notable exceptions of Swallow and a few others, virtually all of these had disappeared by 1931, with only 750 Austin Seven rolling chassis being supplied out to 'the trade' in that year.

It had very quickly become the norm to regard the saloon as the ordinary car, and the two-seater – whether Sports or Semi-Sports Tourer – as a rather specialised product, and probably not first choice except among a small minority of the public. This is not to say that racing, hillclimbs, and endurance trials were not of interest to the public – they were, and the public still flocked to spectate at such events whenever they were held. This was viewed as a valuable form of advertising, as long as – Herbert Austin stated – two criteria were met. First, the public had to be able to easily recognise the competition Seven as just another variation of the standard family product, which formed the vast percentage of the showroom sales. Secondly, the Seven had to remain to be successful in competition.

The new long-wheelbase RN-type Seven saloon was a proper four-seater. It was upholstered in leather, had new wings and running

'Thunderclap,' the Ulster-based, scoop scuttle Chummy-bodied ex-Barnes brothers' Seven that Charles Metchim ran for 16 hours in the 1933 Le Mans 24-hour race before the steering broke.

boards, stylish louvres on the bonnet sides, and plated centres to the wheels, to give visual emphasis. As recognition of the original, and continuing claims to the healthy aspects of motoring, a sliding sunshine roof was installed as standard. The new long wheelbase Seven saloon, now known universally as the Box Saloon due to its fairly square proportions, in fact retained a good sense of visual balance. Where the original Chummy looks light and delicate, the Box sits more solidly on the ground – admittedly with a heavier look, but also with a more robust appearance. A 'de Luxe' version was introduced in the October, and, as with previous models, van versions were load-rated at five hundredweight (560lb/254kg). The Austin Seven de Luxe

THE 65 SPORTS AND NIPPY

With the Ulster body design looking decidedly dated by 1933, and demand high for sports two-seaters that were slightly more serious than the lightweight Boat Tail, an entirely newly bodied car was announced – the EB 65 Sports (alluding to its speed). This was a sports touring car with no pretensions towards serious competition work or racing (although the works did have a trials version). Several components were naturally similar to earlier EA Ulsters, and the model was based on a long-wheelbase chassis frame, lowered in the normal sports way.

The body design was particularly appealing, and – with the driver set well back – combined the long bonnet of the Boat Tail with a generous cockpit, and a cleverly conceived and originally designed well-rounded tail. It would have been easy for this latter shape to appear clumsy and bulky, but the 65 exhibited an individual and distinctive look. It also had the added benefit of entirely concealing the spare wheel, and providing a commodious luggage space, accessed from behind the forward-tipping seats.

The model's wings, floor pan, bulkheads, and bonnet were made of steel, while aluminium was used on ash framing for the main bodyshell, and a fully top-opening windscreen, fitted with twin wipers. The front wings were styled as domed cycle wings, but with infill splash panels and with the low bonnet height adding some purposeful elegance to the overall appearance and stance of the car.

The engine had a 1½in (38mm) diameter big end unpressurised special crankshaft, which was machined all over and balanced

Leslie Hore-Belisha, on the right in a silk top hat, demonstrates his new-for-1934 invention – an illuminated 'Belisha beacon' at pedestrian crossing points – to Freddie Henry, the amused driver of a Sports 65. (Courtesy Ken Cooke)

statically and dynamically, as well as plain skirted pistons, on fully floating gudgeon pins, and a high lift camshaft. The block and EA-type cylinder head were of 'Chromidium'-quality material, with tulip-shaped valves and double valve springs. A deep-ribbed sump of one gallon (4.5l) was used, along with a Zenith 30 VEI downdraught carburettor with a 21mm choke tube, a close-ratio gearbox, and an 'export' wide fan belt and pulley.

The exhaust was routed beneath the car, allowing generously wide doors that covered over the chassis sides, and gave unusually good cockpit access for even tall drivers. About 250 examples of the car left the factory.

With body-building methods evolving from hand-built to mass-produced, in 1934 the aluminium on ash frame construction was changed to entirely pressed steel bodywork over a similar ash frame, with small changes to allow for the different production methods. This bodywork is very complex, and therefore expensive to replicate.

At this time, the car's title was changed from 65 to Nippy, and the model continued in production until, it is thought, 1937. The Nippy is a most attractive and practical small sports car; it is robustly detailed and has a good number of survivors, many of which are still in use on a regular basis.

THE NIPPY SPORTS TWO-SEATER

Austin dependability is combined with speed in this graceful sports model. Many special features are incorporated including a high compression engine with down-draught carburation, high lift camshaft, special valves, etc. The sports gear ratios are 5.6, 8.38, 13.3 and 21.9 to 1 (with synchromesh for top, second and third). Other features are bound road springs, spring arm steering wheel and a sports front axle, giving the lower centre of gravity which contributes so much to the remarkable road stability of this lively little car. The hood is fully effective and readily erected when required. The spare wheel is carried in the tail where there is also ample space for luggage, and pneumatic seating in best selected hide, an electric windscreen wiper, Triplex toughened screen and automatic return direction indicators are included.

PRICE AT WORKS £142

The Nippy Sports Two-Seater. (Austin publicity)

The 1933 de Luxe Saloon of Mervyn Hoyle, in both natty period attire and with full accoutrements! (Author collection)

Saloon was a very good seller, at £125, and comprised one in every four Austin cars built.

Sir Herbert was certain by early 1932 that a corner had been turned in the economy, and that a period of renewed prosperity was ahead. The industry was encouraged at this time by Ford's announcement of a new small car, to be built in its new state-of-the-art factory at Dagenham, on the Thames estuary, to the east of London. Ford's new model – though small – had a 950cc engine, and was rated at 8hp. It was a significantly larger car than Herbert's Austin Seven, and its styling, not surprisingly, owed much to its transatlantic origins.

On the back of the United States' entry into the Great War, and via the almost surreal skyscrapers, fashions, and – particularly – films of the 1920s, American influence on the popular mind of Europe was immense. As a result, images of the vast number of motor cars in the big American cities set the United States as the leader of the popular motoring movement in the minds of many.

The production Ford Eight – as it was marketed – had a swept back, painted Art Deco grille covering the radiator, and generally graceful sweeping bodywork lines, including a sloping windscreen lifted straight from its American cousins – at a time when Austin was still persevering, doggedly, with a vintage vertical plated radiator and a vertical windscreen. All this, and the two-door version of the Ford Eight was priced at only £120. It was exceptionally good value, designed and built to take advantage of the Dagenham mass-production line. What's more, the new Dagenham factory was able to dedicate its time almost entirely to this one single product.

By contrast, Austin was busy still making a much bigger range of Seven variations. In 1932, the company built about 15,000 saloons, 1000 tourers, and 1000 sports cars and chassis, as well as some commercial vehicles. One wonders whether, on the day of the announcement of the new small Ford, Herbert Austin paused for a reflective moment in front of the photograph of Henry Ford on the wall of his office, to look Henry Ford in the eye! There was, however, still a degree of snobbery at the time, that led some to look down on those buying a Ford; the

This 1933 Box Saloon, here reduced to its constituent parts exactly 50 years after manufacture, was successfully rebuilt by Tony Theobald, and is alive and well. (A7CA archive)

Continued page 148

TRIALS

Trials of the performance of motor cars have taken place since the dawn of motoring, with the reliability trials of 1894, and the activity has taken many forms. There have been mixtures of paved road and off-road sections, simple hillclimbs or driving tests, 'classic' trials, production car trials, specialist mud-plugging trials, and the more 'official' RAC National Trials Car Formula. Some very early trials would now be described as very long-distance road races, taking place on whatever road surfaces the competitors encountered en route.

Herbert Austin was well-versed in the publicity attached to this most strenuous of disciplines, and its ability to show off the versatility and reliability of his products. Austin tested his Sevens initially on Lickey Hill and the surrounding roads and, in July 1922, Lou Kings took the 670cc show car (registered OK 2950) up the – then loose – surface of the Shelsley Walsh Hillclimb in 89.8 seconds. At the end of the year, the same car was driven by the experienced J Falahee in the MCC Exeter Trial. This comprised travelling from Staines, through Salisbury and Yeovil, then back to Staines via Dorchester, taking in some timed sections along the way, including difficult country hills.

These early excursions, and the Colmore Cup run by SUNBAC, convinced Austin to increase the engine size of the car to 747cc (though exactly when is open to debate), and, at the MCC Lands End Trial of 1923, Falahee won a bronze award.

E G Bromhead's Chummy won a second class award in the 1924 Colmore Cup, and ten Sevens took part in the Lands End Trial, winning three golds, a silver, and three bronze awards; clearly, Austin Sevens showed their suitability for this type of competition. The Mid-Wales RAC Small Car Trials also attracted Gunnar Poppe in a works car, but he retired with magneto troubles. The tough MCC Edinburgh Trial started in Barnet, and continued into Scotland via a night run up the A1, returning through the difficult terrain of the Lake District. All four of the Austin Sevens entered gained gold awards – a considerable achievement.

Countless other awards were won by Austin Sevens in these types of events while the car was in production, and this started a real tradition. The Austin Seven was almost embarrassingly successful as a trials car, not only in its class, but in overall awards. Numerous Sevens now appear in similar current events run by the VSCC, and for some years, the 750 Motor Club successfully ran Austin Seven Trials Formula events. The works Grasshoppers continued to perform well during the 1930s in more specialised mixed surface trials.

The trials driver who epitomised the private Austin Seven entrant was surely Harold Biggs. Harold had used a 1930 Seven (registered EXF 601) in a JCC High Speed Trial at Brooklands, having chopped

The October 1938 Mid-Surrey Automobile Club Expert Trial run over Exmoor. The works Grasshoppers BOA 57 (Scriven), COA 121 (Langley), and BOA 58 (Buckley) await the start in Dunster marketplace. (Courtesy Ferret Fotographics)

the roof off, fitted LMB swing axle front suspension, and using a set of cycle wings when regulations allowed. He then built a more specialised car post-WW2, in company with off-road specialist Tom Lush and JV Bowles, on a 1932 long wheelbase chassis, and fitted with a 1934 engine with a Whatmough Hewitt alloy head and Scintilla Vertex magneto.

Bill Boddy wrote of the vehicle, "a very trim car this, in its correct Austin orange, with fuel tank from an Amilcar." The light, but sturdy, body was built by Maltick of Wandsworth, with provision for twin rear spare wheels, and hand controls added for clutch and throttle. A deeply dished steering wheel was installed, with a long fly-off handbrake, and carefully-placed cockpit leg padding. Two metal cut-out badges of red-painted cows were placed, one either side of the bonnet, paying homage to the Hammersmith pub where much time had been spent discussing how to take over the motorsporting world!

The car provided decades of trialling fun for Harold Biggs, with countless trophies won. Later owned, and enthusiastically used, by Cliff Bradshaw, and its current keeper Graham Fullalove, the distinctive Biggs Special is still a regular visitor to 750 Motor Club events.

Arthur Mallock was a keen Austin Seven trials exponent, writing for the national magazine *MotorSport*, and of course penning *750 Motor Club Bulletin* articles like 'A poor man in search of motorsport,'

Harold Biggs pauses during the build of his eponymous Biggs Special. Note the 'Red Cow' bonnet emblem. (Courtesy Grahame Fullalove)

A 1950s trials Chummy protests violently to a relentlessly long special stage, as the occupants prepare to take cover. (Courtesy Mike Peck)

in which he describes the most simple of minimal cars, and encourages a careful reading of regulations – for example, in search of lightness, a 'spare wheel' in the final instructions might be of any size and might not include a tyre, unless a tyre was specifically demanded!

Colin Chapman, of course, also started his glittering motorsport career with an Austin Seven based trials car. The Lotus Four was a Ford-engined Austin Seven-based car. The engine was moved so far back, for traction on hills, that it had two 5-gallon (22l) jerry cans fixed under the bonnet, in the front of the engine bay, filled with water to give better road handling between hills or special sections. These were then emptied again to move the centre of gravity rearwards, and more effectively attack the hills.

Ken Delingpole and Ron Lowe, both trials enthusiasts, also built their first few Dellow specials on Austin Seven chassis in 1947. With reasonably civilised bodywork and weatherproofing, they found a small but enthusiastic market. In a move towards production, and to replace

the Austin frames, Dellow found ideal high-quality government-surplus chrome-moly tubes, which were originally RP3 rocket tubes fitted to ground attack 'tank buster' Hawker Typhoons. The Dellows proved to be genuine multi-purpose enthusiast's cars, and were driven by Peter Collins, Tony Marsh, and others. They successfully competed in trials, MCC rallies, and the Circuit of Ireland.

With its long stroke, the Austin Seven engine produces plenty of torque for its capacity, and the lightweight nature and good ground clearance of the Seven makes it a natural choice for trialling. Classic trials have traditionally had a continuous following, and Austin Sevens have always had a numerically strong showing in the entries, being more than able to hold their own; the cars achieved not only class awards, but performed well overall. Historic motoring events of all types continue to have huge numbers of participants and public onlookers, and Sir Herbert's little baby is the weapon of choice for those starting out, as well as for the more experienced.

THE GRASSHOPPER AND SPEEDY 75

With long-chassied production 65 Sports unlikely to be successful in serious competition, the works looked to create a successor to the Ulster, and keep the Austin brand in the public eye. The Ruby was, by 1934, the standard production saloon. This chassis, with its upswept rear extensions, was therefore used as the basis for the new cars. The chassis lent itself to allowing more weight, in the form of twin spare wheels and a slab-type fuel tank carried behind the rear axle – a most

useful attribute for trials where loss of traction was a frequent limiter on slippery hills.

The suspension was lowered in the usual sports fashion, and a low-ratio rear axle fitted, along with a close-ratio Speedy-type gearbox and an enclosed remote change mechanism – this was necessary, as the seating position was so far rearwards as to make a direct gear level far too long for a rapid change. The body shape, driven by the rear slab tank and long bonnet, was of akin to the design of a conventional MG-like sports

A rare sight, as five Grasshoppers gather in 1995 at The Bear, Rodborough Common. (Courtesy Michael Dorsett)

car of the period. The factory wavered, however, regarding retaining the traditional upright radiator shell – having already just introduced the Ruby – before adopting that from the Austin Ten Ripley Tourer.

The engine is the most advanced Austin Seven sports motor, with one main advance being in the design of the Duck-type combustion chambers. There was also more robust detailing of the fixing to the crankcase, and more generous water circulation to improve the eternal thermal difficulties of the closely grouped side valve layout – quite possibly the work of Harry Weslake.

A good result in the Lands End Trial encouraged an entry at the 1935 Le Mans 24-hour race, where three Grasshoppers were joined by the Harry Ferguson-run Speedy 75, driven by Carr and Barbour. In the event, the latter finished second-to-last, but beat the sole remaining Grasshopper (driven by Dodson/Richardson) to average almost 50mph (80km/h) for the 24 hours. This was by no means a poor performance for a 750cc machine.

Subsequently, the cars had belt-driven Centric 125 superchargers mounted on top of the forward part of the cylinder heads, fed by an SU carburettor above that required a bonnet bulge to be added for clearance. These bulges varied in design detail, and provide useful clues when attempting identification.

The works continued development on the unblown engines, and, after the 1936 Le Mans 24-hour race was cancelled, the team returned to the event in 1937, only to suffer centre main bearing failure on all three cars. They were, however, successful at the Donington 12-hour sports car race. These cars were then converted to high-chassis trials specification, by fitting straight front axle beams and Military Seven-type road springs all round, before being sold to Scottish trials specialists under the name 'Tartan Grasshoppers.'

The works and Scottish Grasshoppers were immensely successful in trials, aided by the increased torque and power of the deep-breathing

blown engines, and these important – but rare – cars are today highly prized by their current owners.

The EK 75 Sports, or Speedy, was a beautifully bodied two-seat sports car, with flowing lines and a 'bee'-shaped tail on a long wheelbase chassis. It was produced in small numbers, some unused bodies being assembled and sold by Coopers of Putney. The steel floor pan was unique to the type, and the bodywork was the first to use the Art Deco-style open-able bonnet side vents, rather than 'vintage' louvres. As with the Nippy, the Speedy was offered in left-hand drive form at the 1934 Berlin Motor Show, and had its finest hour at the 1935 Le Mans 24-hour race.

1935, Le Mans. Two of the three Grasshoppers on the Austin team (No 60 & No 61) and the lone Harry Ferguson-prepared Speedy (No 62) trickle down to take their places for the start. The Speedy would return 75 years later. (Author collection)

name continued to carry the burden of the Model T, which, in spite of its success, was regarded as 'cheap.'

1933 saw the use of a new four-speed gearbox, with double helical third and top gears, and the old-fashioned updraught carburettor of 1922 finally gave way to a better side-draught Zenith on an integral hot-spotted inlet/exhaust manifold, for better warming up and more efficient and smoother running. The fuel tank was moved to the extreme rear of the car, taking advantage of the void behind the rear axle in the larger bodywork, and freeing up under-bonnet scuttle space for a battery and toolbox. This also added to the 'civilising' effect of separating the passenger facilities from the functioning and mechanical parts of the car. The fuel, no longer being gravity fed, was pumped from the rear tank by an AC mechanical pump fixed to the lower nearside of the engine crankcase, and driven by an arm that reached inside to its own cam in the rear of the camshaft.

The other tidying up of the mechanical duties entailed moving the electric starter motor from inside the passenger compartment to a mounting, cast into the crankcase and under the bonnet. The starter ring on the flywheel was therefore also moved from the rear to the front face. A by-product of this move was a much increased ease with which the driver could check the ignition timing; the flywheel markings for this being visible by removing a light pressed-metal flywheel cover, rather than the whole starter housing. The brake drums were increased in width simply by altering the shoes and drums, and controls were improved.

A new type of the two-seat Tourer, the Opal, was offered. This model was to be in production for seven years, with contemporary updates, and constituted one of the longest runs for a Seven model. Performance for the saloon was given as accelerating to 49mph (78km/h) in a quarter mile, with a kerb weight of ten hundredweight two quarters (533kg). The production Seven of the early 1930s was available in cheery, friendly colours as standard: Royal Blue, Maroon, and Opal Blue for Tourers; Light

Maroon, Light Royal Blue, and Light Auto Brown for Saloons. The de Luxe Saloon was offered with Opal Blue or Fawn lower panels and black upper parts, these combinations being particularly pleasing.

In 1933, Austin built an amazing one-third of all the cars produced in the car industry in Britain, and over one-third of all Austins produced that year were Austin Sevens – the vast majority of them de Luxe Saloons. This was a period of high production and stability of a proven product, although much experimentation was also taking place at Longbridge, with automatic or semi-automatic gear systems, and, particularly, with the Hayes infinitely-variable transmission.

Synchromesh in the top three gears was introduced in August 1933, by which time chassis numbers of Sevens had almost reached 180,000, over a production period of some 11 years. Pressure was nevertheless growing from sales staff for an updated-looking version of the Seven. Sir Herbert railed, however, at the idea of needlessly altering his small car concept, simply to pander to a change in popular aesthetic taste. After much discussion and debate at the highest level, and including – of course – all senior production staff, the decision was taken in late 1933 to radically change the entire concept of Austin's small family car. The whole vehicle was to be upgraded towards being a direct competitor in the 8hp to 10hp class, and be able to carry four adults plus a modicum of luggage. The body design was also to be revised to

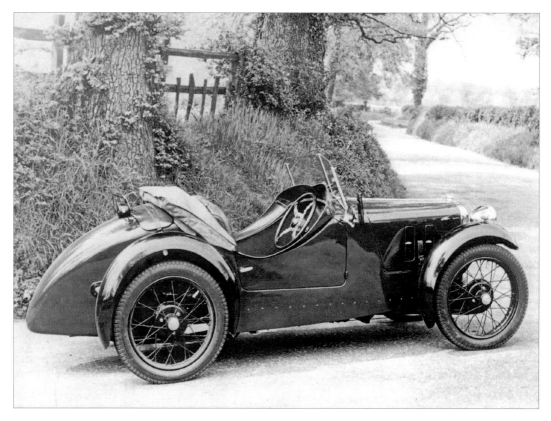

The press Speedy Type 75, photographed in a Warwickshire lane, with the elegant tail and distinctive cockpit cowling shown well. No sprint car, the Speedy was, however, highly successful at Le Mans. (Austin Publicity)

a more current streamlined Art Deco shape, and the result was to be the brand new Ruby, Pearl, and Opal range – the latter needing to be altered very little, apart from its radiator and bonnet.

The Society of Motor Manufacturers and Traders, of which Austin was a primary member, had made a ruling that any new models were not to be announced prior to 13th August the year before. The somewhat conservative Sir Herbert took the opportunity to vent his feelings on the subject of styling change, when announcing his new models at the August 1934 press launch:

"It is an unfortunate fact that the public demand for change does not always allow us to derive the full benefit of settled design. Whilst I appreciate the advances these new models represent, it is not without a tinge of regret that I see the passing of our familiar radiator shell, which has been associated with the name of Austin since the founding of the firm."

Continuing in a slightly moderated tone, he added, "The most notable changes that have taken place are the fitting of a newly-designed radiator shell, the introduction of sweeping lines, lengthened bonnets, the absence of projecting fittings, and the fact that equipment is now unified and becomes a definite part of the vehicle construction … I recollect that when we met in Paris, during last year's Motor Show, the principal speakers gave me to understand that our old radiator shell was the one obstacle in the way of unlimited sales."

The speech was hardly a snappy promotional spiel, and was not entirely reflective of the advantages of the new Ruby design.

The Austin Seven frame rails had increased in section by degrees, and were increased again for the heavier Ruby bodywork. Two substantial rear-pressed steel and inverted U-section outriggers were added to support the extra weight at the rear. This came with the added benefit of providing chassis mountings for shorter arms to the

The long-wheelbase Ruby chassis was more robust than earlier types, and featured upswept rear outriggers to support heavier bodywork, a fuel tank, and a fold-out luggage rack. (Austin publicity)

friction dampers, thus improving their effect, and less camber on the road springs lowered the chassis by 2in (50mm).

The most obvious styling change was the adoption of a fully-cowled radiator surround – the Austin wings badge carefully curved over the top face – and the radiator filler under the bonnet. Openable air vents were also added, complete with miniature 'speed line' chromed die-cast handles, to the bonnet sides. The new windscreen sloped backwards at the top, just like its rival the Ford Eight, which was a feature welcomed by any driver that previously used a car with a vintage vertical windscreen; when driven at night, particularly with rather feeble standard Austin Seven headlights, all one could see in a dark vertical windshield was the glaring reflection of the headlights of every car following.

The Ruby windscreen, which retained the top opening facility, was blended into the roof. The top silhouette line flowed back over the car, dropping down the rear and flowing backwards at low level – in complete contrast to the tucked under carriage-style tail of the earlier Box Saloon.

Separate covers had been offered for the exposed spare wheel on Box saloons, but on the Ruby the spare was partly recessed into the rear bodywork, with a shallow cover that incorporated the rear number plate. A cleverly-designed scissor-action two-position fold-out luggage grid was also concealed behind the spare wheel cover, and mounted directly off the newly introduced chassis outriggers. This

This early Ruby with narrow window frames at Beaulieu displays the excellent retractable rear luggage rack design which allows the spare wheel cover to be re-fitted when carrying cases or hampers. (Author collection)

allowed cases or trunks to be carried externally, even with the spare wheel cover replaced, and added considerably to the practicality of the Ruby as a family car. Many examples were still performing this function 30 years later, well into the 1960s, as many period films attest.

A further radical change was – for the first time in the story of the Seven – to move away from 19in (482mm) diameter wheels, and the adoption of 17in (431mm) wheels for the Ruby. Together with the lower riding chassis, this lowered the centre of gravity even with the heavier bodywork. It is interesting to note that road construction and finish had kept pace with the availability of family road transport, allowing the use of smaller radius wheels and tyres, without a loss of comfort. The front suspension of an Austin Seven, employing leading arm suspension, makes it prone to a jolting upward 'flick' on poor surfaces, mitigated by a large rolling radius tyre.

The 1934 Ruby's doors had light angular window frames, to provide a larger area of glass – this to be changed later to the more familiar all-in-one pressings, broadly similar to the previous Box Saloon doors. The rear passenger space side windows were side-hung from the leading edge, and could be opened a few inches with a miniature version of the windscreen over-centre catch (a feature that was next seen on Alec Issigonis' Mini Se7en, in 1959). The Art Deco styling of the Ruby range was reflected in a compete change in the style of sales material; the new clean 'Odeon Cinema' lines were a world away from the rather prosaic earlier promotional material on the coffee tables in any Austin dealership. It may seem difficult now to describe an Austin Ruby as 'streamlined,' but that is what they were in 1934!

The four-seater Open Road Tourer was priced at £108, and, at last, an Austin Seven was made available for £100 – just 12 years after its introduction – in the form of the most basic two-seater Opal. Possibly in order to use existing stock, the early Opals retained the vertical-chromed radiator, and was heavily promoted at the magic £100. It was certainly a very useful sales pitch, even if minor extras took the price tag slightly over.

In 1934-35, Austin built more than 77,000 cars, including 22,500 Sevens. The Ruby saloon remained the cheapest in its class, priced at £120, with the Ruby fixed head saloon at £112. The Pearl cabriolet – a new model type, which featured fixed side windows and upper body like a saloon, combined with an almost full-width fold-back canvas top that allowed for proper open air motoring – meanwhile, was sold for £128.

The new range was sold with deeper section black wings, and body colours that included Dove Grey (which proved very popular), Black, and Westminster Green. Car tax was dropped from £1 per one rated horse power, down to 15 shillings (75p), in January 1935. Despite fears

Continued page 154

COOPER SPECIAL NUMBER ONE

Charles Cooper and Kaye Don were motorcycling friends and when Kaye started racing cars, Charles, who was the better mechanic, stepped in to help him at Brooklands and, later, with the Silver Bullet Land Speed Record contender at Daytona and Southport.

Charles had built a Flying Flea home-built aeroplane, powered by a tuned Austin Seven engine. After it had been grounded in 1936, and was therefore useless in its current form, Charles decided to build an Austin Seven special for his son, John, using the Flea engine. The engine was on an Austin chassis, number 179,358, and the car was lowered with flattened springs and a cranked, rather than bowed, front axle beam that narrowed the front track. Charles copied the new Austin Seven Speedy's wasp tail, and added the latest Ford Eight radiator grille to create a sleek and individual body shape, painted a mid 'Cooper Blue.'

15in (381mm) tyres had just become available with the advent of the Fiat Topolino – a car which was subsequently to play a crucial part in Cooper's fortunes, with the post-war 500s – and so Charles made up some 15in (381mm) rims on Austin centres. This was the first time that this size wheel was used on an Austin Seven, lowering the car and the gearing, and giving better acceleration, braking leverage, and road holding. Close-fitting mudguards were mounted directly onto the brake back-plates, with a Brooklands silencer and fishtail to the exhaust, and Brooklands leather straps to hold down the bonnet.

John Cooper, who was still only 14 years old, quickly caught the motor racing bug in this little car, driving on the Brooklands infield roads with his friend – the young Donald Campbell – and getting a ticking off for venturing out onto the banked track.

The Cooper Special Number One, as it was called (and designated C1 in the log book), was subsequently used for grass track racing, and sprouted a supercharger. This blower lasted until the early 1950s, when – owned by one young couple – the car was repainted cream, with maroon wheels, and

Charles Cooper, standing centre, built the Cooper Special Number One for son John's 14th birthday, using the tuned Seven engine from his grounded Flying Flea and the first 15in (381mm) wheels. (Author collection)

The Cooper Special Number One accelerates out of the sun-dappled Pardon Hairpin at the 2013 VSCC Prescott Speed Hillclimb, with the author at the wheel. (Courtesy Iain Mansell)

driven to Berlin and back on a honeymoon. After more adventures, and a period at rest, in 1992 it was rediscovered as a barn find by the author, and restored with John Cooper's enthusiastic help.

Charles and John Cooper founded the Cooper Car Company in 1946, finding a market ready for their inspirational rear-engined monoposto racing car, equipped with a 500cc motorbike engine. The expansion of the company was assured when 500cc racing transformed into the international Formula Three, and the de facto nursery class for aspiring racing drivers. During the 1950s, Coopers expanded rapidly, first into sports car racing, then the 1500cc international Formula Two by 1958. They were soon winning Formula One Grands Prix, becoming 1959 and 1960 F1 World Champions with Jack Brabham.

This coincided with the introduction of the Issigonis Mini, and, a year or so later and tuned by John Cooper, the iconic Mini Cooper was born – a powerful brand name, still.

ALEC ISSIGONIS, THE LIGHTWEIGHT SPECIAL AND AUSTIN SE7EN

Alec Issigonis was born in 1906, in Smyrna, South Eastern Turkey, to a Greek father (a comfortably-off engineer) and a Bavarian mother. He developed into a highly-energetic, but thoughtful and open-minded, young man. He arrived in Britain from troubled Turkey in 1923, and studied engineering at Battersea Polytechnic while following motor racing.

It appears that his first Austin Seven was a Gordon England Cup, and Issigonis' design instincts were immediately set into motion with his love for this diminutive and light device. His second car was a new blown 1930 Super Sports GH 1645. He entered trials and hillclimbs, with some success, and became friends with Jack Duller, who prepared cars in West Hampstead. By degrees, his Sports Austin was modified – the forward chassis was stiffened by stressing the

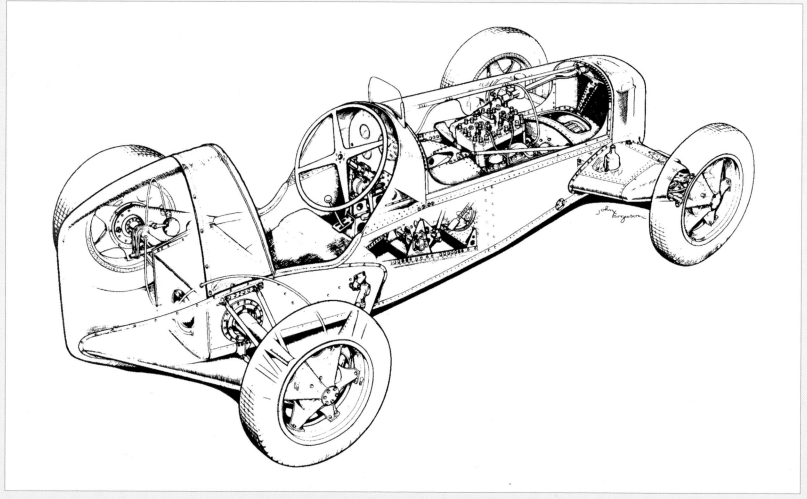

John Ferguson's very fine 1937 cutaway drawing of the Lightweight Special, as originally fitted with the 25-stud ex-works supercharged engine. (*Autocar*)

The Issigonis Ulster which Alec modified by stiffening the bonnet sides and forming a semi-monocoque structure, to great benefit in handling and performance – lessons well learned. (Author collection)

Alec Issigonis' Lightweight Special at Oulton Park. (Mike Ware)

Dowson to create a state-of-the-art stressed-skin sprint car. They named the car the Lightweight Special, drawing plans full-size on the garage walls.

Inspired by André Lefèbvre's structural designs for Voisin, and, visually, by the W25 Mercedes, the Lightweight's two-ply/aluminium sandwich flanks were joined by dual-purpose elements of structure: the blower casing, crankcase, differential mount, seat pan and undershield, main bulkhead, and a few cross tubes. Front suspension comprised rubber rings in a cross tube, while the rear used rubber loops in tension, both ends contained within fairings and readily adjustable by the addition or removal of rings and loops. Austin Ulster brake drums were integrated into Bugatti-inspired cast-electron 16in (406mm) wheels, with cable-operated actuation.

By now a good friend of Murray Jamieson, Issigonis shared information with the designer, and so obtained a blown Ulster engine, incorporating full works SV parts, including a 32 stud block and head, plus a complete spare of the same specification. For sprints, a tiny fuel tank was mounted forward of the engine, and a Seven gearbox was operated by a stubbly gate change lever. Weight was a mere 587lb (266kg), of which the engine and blower accounted for 252lb (114kg) – this contrasting with a works Twin-Cam that weighed in at 1092lb (495kg).

When Lightweight and Twin-Cam met for the first time, at Prescott in 1939, the George Dowson-driven Lightweight recorded 50.64 seconds to Buckley's 49.23 and the flying Bert Hadley at 47.76 seconds, both driving Austins. Just five weeks later, World War Two broke out and the Lightweight was tucked away in one of Dowson's barns.

As a design exercise it was masterful, setting standards that few others would ever reach and still retains an almost mystical aura. Issigonis and Dowson successfully competed in many early postwar sprints and hillclimbs, Alec by now working for Morris Motors, where he designed the torsion bar-suspended quasi-American-styled Morris Minor – a bestselling family car, with a very long production run. Interestingly, the main competitor to the Morris Minor at the time was the Austin A30, a car that itself has a claim to being the first true monocoque, incorporating no sub-frames, and that was first marketed as the new Austin Seven.

Issigonis' main claim to fame was to come in 1959 when, with BMC, he conceived the super-compact family car now known as the Mini, but available then as the Austin Se7en, in true homage to Sir Herbert Austin's lightweight original, and with its wheels at all four corners.

bonnet sides and radiator, and converted into a single-seater by covering over the passenger's space. He divided the front axle beam, widening the track by 4.5 inches (114mm) in the process, and moved the engine back, before fitting a Zoller blower in place of the original Cozette.

Issigonis was by now also designing monocoque chassis structures with inter-connected suspension – both these principles would re-surface later in his career – and set out with George

At last! After twelve years of production, an Austin Seven for £100.00 – "price at works." (Austin publicity)

OPEN MODELS

THE OPAL TWO-SEATER

This handy little car meets the demand for a general purpose vehicle, seating two and involving the minimum capital and subsequent outlay. Although its price is so remarkably low it embodies all the essential features which render the Seven pre-eminent value. These include synchromesh for top, third and second speeds, pneumatic cushions, five-lamp equipment with dip-and-switch head-lamps, instrument panel light, spare wheel cover, moulded rubber floor mats, fume excluders, leather-cloth upholstery and simplified controls. There is a Triplex toughened windscreen, the side-screens and hood are efficient and convenient and there is ample luggage room behind the bucket seats.

PRICE AT WORKS £100

that this change might hit sales of the Seven, in reality there was such a public appetite for motoring – in all its forms – that any effect was entirely lost within sales figures across the range. Austin benefited from increased demand for its larger 10hp models, which this class moving towards being the norm for family motoring.

In 1935, more than 27,000 Austin Sevens of all types were sold, marking the highest figure ever achieved by the model, and the trend towards the four-seater saloon continued, with it becoming by far the most sought-after model choice. There was, however, a brief surge in chassis sales for specialist sports bodies, with 1400 rolling chassis leaving Longbridge over the course of the year. This was the high point of Austin Seven production; with Ford's Dagenham factory getting into its stride, an executive decision was made to offer the basic four-seat Ford Eight saloon for just £100 – not surprisingly coinciding with the beginning of a decline in sales of the Austin Seven.

The Ford took a further two years to overtake sales of Sir Herbert's well-developed baby, which was equally tied to the popularity of the slightly larger 10hp class, in which Austin already had an ever-increasing market share with its larger models.

In 1935 too, Austin doubled its previous figures for exported vehicles, so whilst the Austin Seven story was beginning to run its course, other markets were making demands upon the factory. The complexity of overseas manufacturers needing to build cars under licence had passed, with those same foreign manufacturers beginning to design cars themselves, to cater for their own home markets.

The economic market ebb and flow in 1936 led to a softening of home demand for motor cars. Sales of smaller classes remained strong, however, and again some 23,500 Austin Sevens were built, with the Ruby range having fully-panelled doors and a slight re-profiling of the sloping windscreen. A major change was also made to the engine, with a third crankshaft bearing being introduced, in the interests of smooth running and greater safe power delivery. The cylinder head design was reviewed by Harry Ricardo, and given a higher compression ratio and smaller 14mm sparking plugs positioned closer to the exhaust valves, for better

The RAC made good use of late model APE Tourers as patrol cars. (Author collection)

burning of the charge. Semi-Girling brakes were adopted to increase stopping power, this then needing to be resisted on the front axle beam through use of heavier front radius arms running back to the chassis.

The 1937 political map of Europe was changing rapidly, with a fascist dictatorship in Italy, Spain in the grip of a civil war, and the threatening Nazi party having come to power in Germany. At the same time, all leading nations were hurriedly increasing armament production. To the common man, it seemed little time at all since

Europe had extricated itself from the Great War. The hope of the bright young things of the 1920s had been largely snuffed out by the Wall Street Crash, and the recovery of the early 1930s was now once again threatened by another conflict.

The shortage of manufacturing materials resulting from these preparations, and the increased costs of labour, put a strain on the pricing of motor cars. To maintain market share, a reduction in the manufacturers' margins was made where available. A delicate balancing act followed, trying to anticipate buying habits in a changing market and planning accordingly, the general increase in motoring at the time masking – to an extent – the potential future sales of any particular model.

Whilst 23,000 Sevens were again sold in 1937, this number of sales remained stubbornly static, while sales of other classes – and, in particular, Ford's share of these classes – rose enormously. Sir Herbert and his directors recognised that there was no Austin product to fit between an Austin Seven, available only in two-door form, and an Austin Ten with four doors. By July 1937, Austin had a new car concept for launch.

Sir Herbert again arranged for a press release, and gave a carefully-worded speech outlining his new proposal: "Today is an auspicious one for the company, in so much as we are introducing – for the first time since 1922 – another small car: the Big Seven. My thoughts naturally go back to a day 15 years ago, when I introduced to a somewhat sceptical meeting of pressmen the first Baby Austin. Conditions at that time were somewhat less favourable than they are today. The company, along with the entire country, was suffering from the economic aftermath of the war. Many of those who should have been in a position to judge did not view the advent of the Baby with any degree of confidence. How wrong they were is, of course, a matter of history.

Continued page 158

The Austin Seven

A road Ulster crew carefully climbs a loose shale special stage of the 1937 Lands End Trial; goggles up, fags on! (Courtesy Ferret Fotographics)

Ruby publicity promised plenty of fresh air for families. (Austin publicity)

LESLIE BALLAMY AND SWING AXLE FRONT SUSPENSION

When Leslie Mark Ballamy – born in 1903 – was just 17 years old, he set off travelling with an equally enterprising friend. Moving across France, and around Europe and the Middle East, Ballamy worked as a sometime song-and-dance act, interspersed with motorcycle and car maintenance.

Returning to England at the end of the 1920s, Ballamy opened a small garage and repair shop in South London, inventing and trying out various motorcycle suspension systems, including stiffer girder front forks to improve handling. He then moved on to cars, and in 1933 experimented with improving the front end of his Austin Seven to provide a simple and cheap form of swing axle independent suspension. At that time in Britain, only Alvis and Sunbeam offered independently-sprung front wheels, the rest were stuck with solid beam axles.

Whether it was entirely an original idea we will now never know, as the 1931 Peugeot 201 also employed a swing axle-type front suspension with a transverse spring. Leslie's Austin Seven conversion

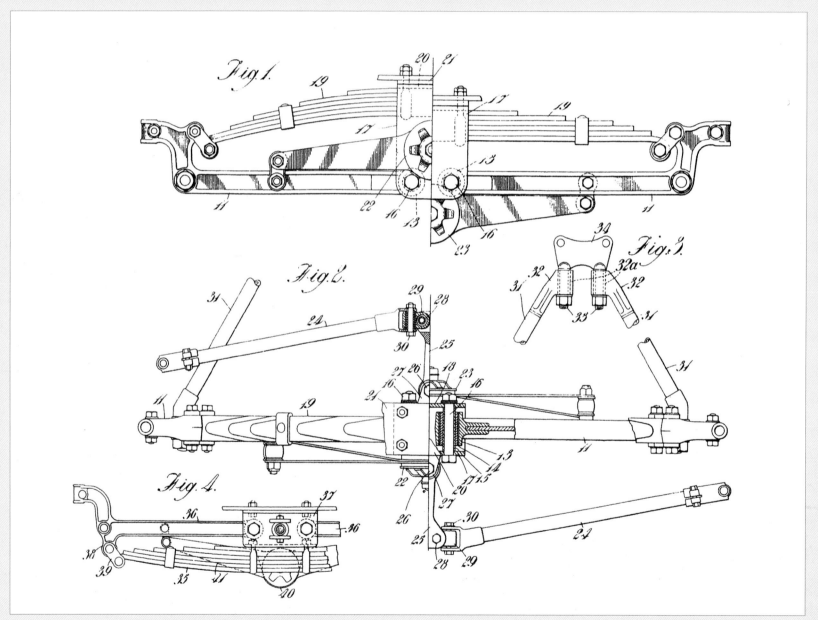

1934 LM Ballamy patent drawing of the Austin Seven swing axle system, including a version with a spring below axle to lower the car. (Courtesy LMB)

was made very simple by the fact that the Seven already had divided radius arms, rather than a single piece V-shaped yoke as on most other cars. As a result, it required only the cutting in half of the axle beam, and the two halves fitted with welded-on bushes, pivoting on a specially fabricated bracket fixed to the chassis nose-piece.

The steering track rod also had to be divided, and the two halves pivoted from the same bracket to avoid conflicts in geometry, and, in November 1933, *The Autocar* published a drawing of the Ballamy system. Freeing each wheel to react to the road surface or cornering gave an entirely different ride to a Seven, as well as improving road-holding. A big part of this was achieved by eliminating the lateral float of an ordinary Seven front axle on its spring shackles. This vastly improved the car's steering, and inspired confidence in the driver.

Leslie set about building the multi-purpose Ellembee Austin Seven special – named after his own initials, 'LMB' – based on a 1928 Chummy, which he used to great effect in all kinds of competition. This special included an increase in front track of 4in (100mm), generating a huge increase in cornering power, and – allied to a standard, but narrower, rear track – very good directional stability.

The Ellembee had a modestly-tuned engine on a stiffened chassis, which, again, highlighted the benefits of the swing axle front end, and specially-built wire wheels with Michelin RLP tyres. The body was paint-coated paper-maché, over a Zeppelin-like lattice metal framework. In this good looking, high performance little car, Ballamy won a special award in a Brooklands High-Speed Trial, at an average speed of 72.3mph (117km/h).

Les Ballamy indulges in a little kerb-clipping, demonstrating the capabilities of his fully independent swing axle front suspension when fitted to a Ruby – with both wheels upright. (Courtesy LMB)

Bill Boddy and others commented very favourably on this proven design, and soon LMB swing axle suspension was fitted to a raft of cars, including: Sir Malcolm Campbell's Ford V8 Coupé, his brand new Ford Model C, as well as his 10hp and larger Ford Saloons; Conan Doyle's 1925 Grand Prix Delage; cars for Whitney Straight and Dick Seaman; a 3-litre Bentley; and a Type 37 Bugatti. Ballamy also marketed swing axle conversion kits for Austins, and small Fords under his LMB label.

When Sydney Allard built a hillclimb/trials special in 1936, it too had LMB swing axles. This car was so successful that all production Allards into the 1950s also employed similar front ends, including Allard's own Monte Carlo Rally-winning car. The suspension was particularly effective in mud-plugging trials cars, where a softly rated version allowed each front wheel to maintain contact with the ground under extreme conditions. The historic Biggs Special still retains its pre-war LMB components.

The characteristics of front swing axles – which, for simplicity and economics, originated in the Austin Seven axle beam – remove the interfering effects of one wheel's movement at one end of the axle beam upon the other. This effect was explored at length by special builders, as well as post-World War Two producers of small high-performance cars in the United Kingdom, and particularly within the 750 Motor Club.

Swing axle suspension undoubtedly placed more stress on standard Austin Seven kingpins, and Colin Chapman used swing axle front suspension based on modified small Ford components in most of his Lotus cars. This continued up until 1957, when he believed that steering kick from gyroscopic forces on the revolving road wheels had become a limiting factor on his ever-increasingly fast, but light, cars.

There was a good deal of debate on the merits – or otherwise – of swing axles throughout the postwar period, and it is a debate that continues to this day. Hundreds of other club-level sporting cars continued with the system. Some later examples used longer swing axles cut from two axle beams, running past each other to pivot, not in the middle of the car, but on the far side of the chassis frame. By doing so, camber change to the front wheels was reduced when under extreme cornering conditions.

The knowledge provided – both in the United Kingdom and beyond – by the apparently humble swing axle front suspension, from the Austin Sevens of the 1930s through to others in the 1960s, is immensely important, and cannot be overstated. Design terminology of more modern suspension systems still include the words 'effective swing axle length' to explain the geometry of camber change, and is a readily-understood phrase.

The Austin Seven in its final production form, from the catalogue. The type two New Ruby, with fully pressed steel doors, three-bearing Ricardo high-compression engine, and Girling brakes – but still true to the original concept. (Austin publicity)

The Austin "New Ruby" Saloon

A new engine, with the crankshaft carried by three bearings, giving increased power and sweeter running, and more powerful brakes are among the improvements in the latest edition of the world-famous Austin "Seven," which now gives even better performance and still greater comfort.
Wide doors, low floor and new adjustable front seats give easy access. There is accommodation for four adults and both front and rear seats have pneumatic cushions.
Door windows are enclosed in a single-piece frame and the fully-moulded quarter windows wind open for ventilation. The spare wheel and luggage carrier are enclosed in the rear panel. The de luxe model has a Pytchley sliding roof, full-width bumpers and full equipment.

ROYAL Blue, Maroon, *Westminster Green, Black or *Ash Grey are the standard colours and upholstery is in *best quality leather.
Triplex glass is fitted to windscreen, side and rear windows and equipment includes automatic-return direction indicators, electric windscreen wiper, *sun visor, remote control rear blind, driving mirror, luggage carrier, luggage straps, foot-operated dip-and-switch headlight control, door locks, door pockets, draught and heat excluders, bonnet and scuttle ventilators, and a *Pytchley sliding roof. Head and side lamps and other fittings are chromium plated.

* The fixed head saloon has seats and squabs upholstered in leather and cellulosed headlamps with chromium rims. It is without bumpers and the items marked with an asterisk (*).

21   Prices on Page 23

"The Big Seven, which I am introducing today, is built on the unique experience we have gained in building over 300,000 Sevens, an experience that I think you will agree counts for a lot. When I tell you we are very satisfied with the performance of the Big Seven and its market possibilities, I think that will count for something to the Austin family, and does not in any way supersede the famous Baby. It is our opinion that the time is opportune to introduce a car that in size, running costs, accommodation, and price comes between the Seven and the Ten.'

By outlining the gap in the market, Sir Herbert was showing his hand in perhaps an unwise way, almost declaring to the world that the days of the Austin Seven were numbered. The four-door Big Seven Forlite followed general Austin Ruby lines, with a triangular chassis plan, transverse springing to the front beam axle, and quarter-elliptic springs to the rear. However, it had a wheelbase of 7ft 3½in (2.2m), a wider track, both front and rear, and a newly-designed 900cc four-cylinder engine. This gave it sprightly enough performance, and with almost 2000 cars being sold in its first year of production – perhaps trading in the past name and reputation of the Seven – it can be considered to be an initial success.

The Big Seven is today still regarded as perhaps a bit of an enigma – perhaps the same enigma that Sir Herbert alluded to in his speech at the launch of the model. The Big Seven was, and still is, a perfectly good motor car, but it looked the work of a committee, each putting together one little element of the design and hoping for the best. The Big Seven is perhaps not an inspired concept from a single mind, and therefore lacks the charisma of the Austin Seven.

History may have treated the Big Seven unfairly, always compared to the original Seven, and inevitably always having a less-than-favourable hearing. The Big Seven looks so similar in appearance to several other cars in its 8hp class that its lack of identity was, and will always be, a handicap in evaluating the type. It also has no pretensions

The Austin Big Seven was by no means a bad car, but had lost the individuality that marked out an Austin Seven from the rest. (Austin publicity)

of any sporting legacy, and so, again, falls short of the adulation and affection handed out to its elder, but more agile, sibling.

The original Seven was given a sturdier rear axle, with full Girling-type brakes, in July 1938. By this time, however, sales of the Austin Seven were in serious decline – an alarming situation for a car trade that had geared up for expected constant future expansion. This was dealt with

THE BRETTELL 100MPH SPECIAL

Later a British Spitfire pilot in World War Two, E Gordon Brettell commissioned Monaco Garage of Watford to build a sprint and hillclimb single-seat Seven in 1936. The result was a very individual, purposeful looking, and well-built device.

It was based on the Marquis de Belleroche's Ulster chassis, the rear springs being double clamped above the frame rails, which in turn were fitted with aluminium blocks to prevent crushing or distortion. This arrangement was arguably superior to the original Austin set-up where there is no direct connection between rear springs and frame rails, the springs being fixed only to underside plates. Otherwise, the chassis was normal Sports fare, but with springs and steering arms highly polished to hopefully show up incipient failure – Brettell was clearly interested in safety as well as speed.

A Cozette-supercharged Ulster engine was fitted, featuring a rare bronze Whatmough-Hewitt head, and at some point a Powerplus blower was tried. This required the radiator to be moved forward, giving a nose heavy – but not unpleasant – appearance, and retained even when the Cozette was installed again. The eternal conundrum of where to mount the steering box in an Austin single-seater was resolved by fixing it to the frame rail, the steering wheel therefore being angled in the tiny 17½in-wide (444mm) cockpit. The shapely tail was formed largely by the 10-gallon (45l) fuel tank immediately behind the driver's seat.

Running on a mixture of 50/50 methyl alcohol and benzole, and fitted with a close-ratio four-speed gearbox, the Brettell could reach 80mph (128km/h) in third and a genuine 100mph (160km/h) in top. Brettell won the 1937 Brooklands Easter Mountain Handicap in the vehicle, as well as a 1938 Whit Monday Campbell Circuit race. Despite being a careful driver, he later broke his arm in a race when, to great consternation, he went over the top of the banking.

On the outbreak of war, Brettell joined the RAF as a No 92 Squadron Spitfire fighter pilot. Emboldened by the successes of the Battle of Britain in 1941, the RAF took to flying sweeps over France, taking the fight back to Europe and trying to goad the Luftwaffe into responding. This was – of course – a calculated risk, and that September Brettell survived an encounter with no less than nine Messerschmitt Bf 109s at 13,000ft (3962m) over St Omer. The Germans turned for home as Brettell, who had by now half blacked out from a serious head wound, limped back to Hawkinge.

After his recovery took almost a year, Brettel began flying with the No 133 Squadron of Spitfires, and again found himself over France, escorting newly arrived B-17 bombers. The Squadron became hopelessly lost in dense cloud, and disastrously low on fuel. 12 Spitfires were lost, and Brettell was again lucky to survive, becoming a prisoner of war in the notorious Stalag Luft III – now enshrined as the setting for the film *The Great Escape*.

Brettell was integral to the escape plans and had already burrowed out under the wire once, but had been recaptured. In March 1944, he was one of the 76 men who passed through the tunnel named Harry to freedom. With another escapee, the men got as far as Poland, but were again captured at a document check at Schneidemühl. Brettell, along with three other recaptured POWs, was taken to Danzig, where all four were shot. Brettell's luck had finally run out, along with 46 others executed after the mass escape.

The Brettell Special lives on as something of a memorial to an extraordinary generation of young men.

E Gordon Brettell's oddly proportioned – but very effective – Cozette-supercharged Special, which would win many speed events prior its creator being killed during World War Two. (750 Motor Club archive)

RUNNING ADJUSTMENTS

Decarbonising ; Valve Grinding ; Brake Adjustments

THE adjustments set out below are all that the owner will find it necessary to make to keep the car in good running order.

Valve Tappet Adjustment.

To ensure that the full power of the engine is obtained and to maintain silence in the valve operation, it is essential to keep the tappets correctly adjusted. To make this adjustment, remove the valve cover, and have the engine turned slowly round with the hand starting crank.

While each valve is closed there should be between the valve stem A (illustrated) and tappet screw B a clearance equal to the thickness of the thin blade of the "tappet clearance gauge," ('004 in. with the engine hot). If the clearance is other than this, it can be adjusted by loosening the locknut C and raising or lowering screw B, being careful to tighten up the lock-nut when the adjustment is completed.

A special spanner is provided in the tool kit for this operation. Check this adjustment when the engine is hot.

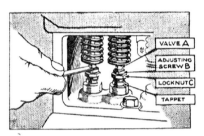

On Sports Models the most efficient setting of the tappets is that which gives a clearance of .004in. **when the engine is very hot.** It is not easy to make the necessary adjustments when the engine is really hot—there is always the danger of burnt fingers and hands—so to compensate for the expansion due to a hot engine, the tappets should be adjusted when the engine is cold, thus :—inlet .008in., exhaust .010in.

Cleaning Combustion Chamber.

To secure the maximum efficiency from the engine it is necessary to remove the carbon deposit that will have formed on the surfaces of the combustion chamber. This should be done after about 2,000 miles running.

54

Valve Cotter Pin.

When the cylinder head is off for this job, it is advisable to take this opportunity of grinding-in the valves, although this will need a longer time for the work to be carried out. In any case, it is recommended that after about 4,000 miles the work of grinding-in the valves should be undertaken.

First drain the water through cock under the radiator. Detach the top water tube from the head. Disconnect the high tension wires from the sparking plugs. Remove the nuts holding down the head. Then take hold of the head at each end and lift it off.

This should be fairly easy to do, without damaging the joint washer, which, in the ordinary course, may be in a condition to be replaced.

When working at the partly dismantled engine a spanner or perhaps part of the engine may be dropped on to the "live" starter terminal, thus causing a short and possible damage. Therefore, disconnect the battery cable at the battery for safety.

Removing the Carbon.

When the head has been removed the valves and tops of pistons will be exposed to view. All dirt or deposit should be removed by carefully scraping with a sharp tool.

Before grinding-in valves it will be necessary to remove the inlet pipe, and exhaust manifold and carburetter. Then disconnect the carburetter control, and the air strangler wire. The valve cover with its washer, can be removed on undoing the two milled nuts.

Each valve spring must be lifted by means of the special tool provided to allow the cotter pin to be withdrawn. Then remove the spring. The valve is now free to be rotated on its seat when the tappet screw has been lowered clear of the stem. After the valve is cleaned a little grinding

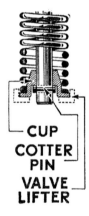

CUP
COTTER
PIN
VALVE
LIFTER

55

The original Austin Seven handbook included excellent drawings to assist in home maintenance. These sketches were replicated in the popular Nicholson and Pitman after-market versions (Austin publicity)

by reducing margins all round, with sub-contractors and suppliers being down-ordered. Only 8500 Sevens were sold in 1938, and about 8000 Big Sevens, a far lower number than had been forecast only months previously.

Looking round for other purchasers, Austin had entered into a contract with the Tamworth-based Reliant Engineering Co Ltd, in March of 1938, to supply 500 Austin Seven engines for the three-wheeled 8cwt (approx. 406kg) Reliant van and truck. These vehicles proved to be very successful, and production continued post-World War Two, leading to a continued business link between the two companies.

Many hundreds, if not thousands, of Austin Seven engines were used in other applications, including boats, planes, and trains, as well as beautifully sectionalised engines for demonstration and educational purposes, with many sent to the British Armed Forces.

Into 1939, and war with Germany was now firmly on the horizon. A mere 800 Austin Sevens were built in the first three months of the year, and a just few later, including mostly van types. Production finally came to a halt in July 1939, by which time almost 300,000 Austin Sevens had been produced.

CHAPTER THIRTEEN

A 750 CLUB – IF NEEDED

A S the Austin Seven production slowed to a trickle in 1939, Bill Boddy, the influential 24-year-old editor of *MotorSport*, decided that there was sufficient enthusiasm amongst the mainly young drivers of Sevens to start a club. There had already been a short-lived club for Austin Seven owners formed in 1926, and another within the Longbridge factory in the mid-1930s. Little was heard of these, however, and Bill Boddy's idea was to cater for drivers of competition Sevens, which at the time were being out-performed after being lumped together in a class with larger cars.

Bill wrote, "In view of the fact that class divisions, which are becoming increasingly popular in trials, usually start at up to 1100cc, the Austin Seven as a 747cc side-valve car is apt to be out-classed in its older form, as owned by a large body of enthusiasts. The obvious cure seems to be to found a 750 club, exclusively for Austin Seven owners, and run sensible trials for those fascinating babies, possibly permitting entries from such things as the inevitable Morris Cowley and the 850cc M-Type MG on occasion. Quite an interesting one-make club should result, because so many variations of the Austin Seven exist, mostly of sports-type body,

750 Motor Club founder Bill Boddy in his eponymous 'Tramfare Chummy' at the 1939 Committee Cup Trial. Note the abbreviated trials-pattern wings, and the scrutineer's insistence on Bill's 'knobblies' being used at the front! (Courtesy Ferret Fotographics)

while probably more conversions are based upon its chassis than any other."

There was an immediate response, and an inaugural committee was formed in March 1939, where it was decided that owners of Austin Sevens, Big Sevens, and Eights could be members, with owners of other marques admitted as associate members. The first 750 Motor Club event was held in April 1939, with a rally of 31 cars at Virginia Water, followed by 15 Sevens on a day run to Stonehenge. Other events soon sprang up, including supporting Dancers End Hillclimb and Markyate Hillclimb, a day run to Bournemouth, and the first Committee Trial: "Hills to be of a non-chassis breaking nature[!] suited to cars of moderate power."

A spares bureau was run by AS Head, and Bill Williams answered technical enquiries regarding what might make a Seven go reliably

BILL WILLIAMS AND CAMBRIDGE ENGINEERING

Londoner, LM 'Bill' Williams, born in 1903, worked for some time at Austin during the middle period of Austin Seven production. Upon leaving, he founded Auto Conversions, at Willesden in North West London, specialising in sporting Sevens in the style of the J2 MG. Shortly after the 750 Motor Club was formed in 1939 – with Bill Williams as Chairman – he relocated to Cambridge Road, Kew Green (behind the Coach and Horses), changing the business name to Cambridge Engineering.

Williams was following something of a British tradition of specialist small car builders – occupying the otherwise empty stable buildings attached to public houses. At Kew Green, he was almost within walking distance of the 750 Motor Club's regular pub meetings at The Red Cow and The Abbey Hotel.

In the 750 Motor Club, Williams answered members' technical queries, and had already built several successful Austin Seven specials, including those for Ken Jarvis. He also marketed Ulster-type axle beams, steering box wedges, long brake levers, and various other simple but essential components. He worked on John Moon's quick Nippy for Godfrey Oxley-Sidey – a pretty blue special, built with the last Nippy body to leave Longbridge – as well as a low-built Cozette-blown special for himself while he worked in the aircraft industry during the war.

The monoposto supercharged Austin built for Ken Jarvis by Bill Williams, using the ex-Almack engine. Seen here at Beechwood, where a Best Time of the Day in its class was succeeded by a comprehensive blow up! (Courtesy Ferret Fotographics)

Bill decided to concentrate on special components and customer cars, and gave up competing himself (perhaps adding some gloss by saying that he felt that he had an unfair advantage, being a 'professional' in a strictly amateur club). He had also acquired some ex-works Ulster parts that had remained at Longbridge, and, during the 1950s, he developed his business to feed the craze for building Austin Seven specials. His booklet, *Rebuild your Austin Seven the Cambridge way*, cleverly described his comprehensive service, instructions, and opinions on what the special builder could expect from the finished product. At Kew Green, Bill and his helpers would spend quite a lot of time 'talking specials' with young enthusiasts, even if – like the author – they left after a couple of hours chatting, having only bought a set of double valve springs!

In 1958 Bill Williams' book *Austin Seven Specials* was published and devoured by the devoted, just as Pat Stephens' own earlier work had influenced 750 Formula. Bill's book did, however, cause the 750 Motor Club to publish a 'clarification' addendum on some of his technical advice. In the same year, it was announced that Cambridge Engineering was under new ownership, and Bill's ultimate Austin Seven special – the LMW – was completed. This was a beautiful and low all-enveloping coupé, on a tubular ladder chassis powered by an ex-works blown 25-stud engine. The body superficially resembled the just-announced Lotus Elite, though with faired-in headlights, but was in fact closer to an earlier Peter Kirwin-Taylor design for a Frazer-Nash, stabled at Brentford just round the corner from Kew Green.

Bill was seen at many contemporary events in this car, which is currently in the safe hands of Williams' expert, Stuart Ulph.

In addition to all the short and long chassis 'Auto Conversions' and 'Cambridge' J2-type production bodies he supplied, Bill Williams built the well-known and highly successful one-and-a-half-seater, with cast 'Aerolite' wheels, for Peter Almack. The offset single-seater for RR Willis followed,

then a two-seater W Special, with Bill's signature sloping Austin radiator, for Bill de Selincourt. A similarly-styled single-seater for Ken Jarvis came after that, along with at least two others – all of which are of considerable interest, and almost all of which have survived.

The refined coupé lines of Bill Williams' LMW Special, powered by an ex-works 25-stud engine. This was the ultimate 1950s Austin Seven Special. (Author collection)

The same car, barely recognisable, at Prescott in May 1949. It is driven by Ken Jarvis and fitted with the cast Aerolite wheels from the Almack car and an ex-Cutler 25-stud works engine. (Courtesy Ferret Fotographics)

possessed. He battled through to the lead in the works Austin Twin-Cam single-seater, beating the ERAs – of twice the engine capacity and power – in the process, to win by almost a whole lap. Little did they know, the crowd had just watched the last circuit race in Britain for more than six years; a few days later, Germany invaded Poland and triggered Britain's declared obligation to enter into war against Germany.

World events had overtaken the simple pleasure of playing with Austin Sevens, and, for the second time in just over two decades, Longbridge was turned over entirely to production for the war effort. Meanwhile, the East works shadow factory had played host to a surprise – and ominous – visit from General Erhard Milch, head of aircraft procurement for the German Luftwaffe, just a few weeks previously.

The whole of the Midlands was bombed heavily in the war, including the organised and systematic blitz on Coventry in November 1940, when – in addition to about 1000 deaths – many car, truck, and aircraft factories were hit. As workers crouched below, listening anxiously to the BMW engines of the Heinkels (desynchronised to confuse the defences), some surely knew that there was a measure of Austin Seven DNA in the overhead threat. Longbridge itself was singled out for a minor daylight raid in early 1941, with several workers killed. Herbert Austin insisted on attending the upsetting funeral for these workers, catching double

Peter Clark in Marcus Chambers' 'White Rabbit,' at the 1938 Lewes Speed Trials. Later owners included Dick Prothero and rally star Roger Clark, and it is currently in Rodger Dudding's collection. (Courtesy Ferret Fotographics)

quicker – and unwittingly started a far-reaching hallmark of the 750 Motor Club, which was to freely share information with fellow enthusiasts. Little did Bill Boddy know at the time, he would still be writing to the *750 Motor Club Bulletin* well into the next millennium, more than 79 years later!

Typical fixtures on the entry lists of early events include five Nippys, three Ulsters (including that of Holland Birkett), several specials (including Smith's super low-ratio double gearbox Seven), a four-seater, two AEWs, an Arrow, a GE Brooklands, a Military two-seater, a Ruby, and many Chummys in various stages of tune. The Imperial Trophy was held on 26th August at Crystal Palace, and Austin Sevenists amongst the large crowd witnessed Bert Hadley driving like a man

Stuart Ulph in the 'Ironside' and Olly Sanders in the 'Willis' offset single-seater – both Bill Williams-built Specials – wait to go out at Curborough for the Austin Seven Spring Practice Day in 2017. (Author collection)

A great number of cars were lost to bombing in World War Two; many wrecks were used as Home Guard road blocks, or wheeled onto potential invasion glider landing sites. (Author collection)

A poignant reminder of World War Two air-raids; an Austin Motor Co ARP steel helmet from Assembly Blocks A and B, Longbridge. (Author collection/Courtesy Nick Salmon)

The first post-war production A30 'Austin Seven,' beside Freddie Henry's Chummy. (Courtesy Ken Cooke)

pneumonia in the process. He never recovered, and died from a heart attack on 23rd May 1941, aged 74.

Sir Herbert was active in the factory until the very end, and, having a rolling programme for future products, had signed documents approving the designs for new cars planned to go into production as soon as the war was over. His funeral procession led past the factory, with many thousands lining the route to his final resting place – the little churchyard adjoining Lickey Grange, overlooking the huge empire that he created at Longbridge in the valley below. Lady Austin would be buried with him just a year later.

The Seven had saved the Austin company in 1922, and for the design and production of the Seven – plus payments for his many patents and overseas licences – it is understood that Sir Herbert Austin ultimately received about 12 million pounds, an unimaginable sum at the time, and the equivalent of almost half a billion pounds today equating to about £1500 per car.

The young men and women of the newly formed and rapidly growing 750 Motor Club had decided to try to keep the club going during this time, helped enormously by Billy Boddy's efforts to continue to publish *MotorSport*. Meetings continued to be held, and even some short competitive runs were organised, with many participants driving in uniform. One unlawful quarter-mile sprint, held on a public road on a nice Autumn day, had to be abandoned when two elderly ladies appeared picking blackberries. Oblivious to the occasional burst of frenetic driving, they steadfastly refused to move out of the way of the Timekeeper!

The July 1941 Chessington Rally attracted Rivers Fletcher, Sam Clutton, John Wyer (later of Aston Martin and Gulf fame), Peter

Monkhouse, John Bolster, Forrest Lycett, Bill Boddy (of course), Lawrence Pomeroy, and George Roesch. They were joined by the rest of the usual 750 crowd, and no less than 160 people sat down for tea.

The Rembrandt Hotel in Kensington was used as a lunchtime base throughout the war, with film shows. In 1943, with the tide starting to turn in favour of the Allies, a regular 'brain trust' was started, with panellists such as Leslie Ballamy, EC Gordon England, HR Godfrey, Cecil Kimber and Kay Petre. It was chaired by George Eyston or Lord Brabazon, and attended by members including Marcus Chambers, Denis Jenkinson, the actor and racer Jack Warner, and even a young Roy Salvadori.

At the end of the war, there were thoughts at Longbridge about restarting production of the Seven as a cheap stop-gap model, and – in France – Rosengart began building its side-valve engines, as Reliant were later to do.

In the summer of 1945, Rivers Fletcher organised the 'Cockfosters event' – an unofficial sprint around the unfinished Cat Hill Belmont Housing Estate, to show off to a motorsport-starved public. Amongst other entries were: Tony Rolt and Bob Gerard in ERAs; John Dowson in the Lightweight Special; Lord Brabazon's aero-bodied Fiat; and – to the delight of the crowd – John Bolster, who managed to spin his Bolster Special, Bloody Mary. Penny Rivers Fletcher's Austin Seven two-seater was the course car.

Sprints were held at Cofton Hackett (the Austin test track near Longbridge), and, as it was realised that Brooklands, Donington Park and Crystal Palace were closed as venues, the ideas of racing on wartime airfields took shape. In June 1946, the VSCC held a race meeting at such a location at Gransden Lodge. Trials, grass track racing, sprints, and hillclimbs could be held at more informed locations, and these types of events heralded a complete change – both in motorsport, and in the number of ordinary individuals that could expect to compete.

Gone forever was the 'right crowd and no crowding' mentality of the wealthy elite of

Ian Webb, in a 1930 Ulster Replica, kicks up some soft going in the 2016 VSCC Welsh Trial, as the front wheels claw the air. (Gary Clarke)

prewar Brooklands. The 750 Motor Club and the motorcycle-engined '500 Brigade' both promoted affordable motorsport. Redundant air-fields, with smooth runways and huge run-off areas, provided a very safe racing environment compared with road racing on public roads, as was still practised on the continent. With money short, any motoring had to be really cheap. In the United Kingdom, in the 1940s, that meant an Austin Seven.

175. Clive Lone's 1946 'Tiger Kitten', a successful 500cc Formula car, was a complete Austin Seven chassis turned upside down and JAP engine added. 'Kitten' was the first 500 to climb Prescott in under 50 seconds. (Courtesy Ferret Fotographics)

Major Arthur Mallock was based at Tholthorpe Airfield in September 1947, where he almost single-handedly organised a real race meeting. No record of the illicit meeting exists, as this was a condition of accepting any entry! Arthur's multi-purpose Austin Seven special was shared with his great friend Jack French, and lapped at 58mph (93km/h). The pair were on the podium four times in six races. Other cars in attendance at the 'race that never was' included Tyrer's BMW, Slater's ERA, and Reg Phillip's Fairley – which won a handicap race.

Eager would-be racers were clearly not going to wait for a purpose-built race track, when literally dozens of almost unused airfields were potentially available all over the United Kingdom. The ex-US bomber bases of Eastern and Southern England in particular had tempting combinations of concrete runways and perimeter tracks.

The 750 Motor Club met regularly at The Red Cow, Hammersmith, from 1947 onwards. It was there that Holland (Holly) Birkett came forward with an idea for an inexpensive set of parameters for Austin Seven racing, intended to equalise performance at a modest level and allow road cars to compete in races, initially outlawing the use of trailers. Holly's proposal was to encourage un-supercharged, mainly two-seater, sports cars – including multi-purpose cars, production Sports Sevens and Chummys – to allow as many people as possible to race.

The new category was named 750 Formula. To qualify, the prospective cars had to include certain Austin Seven parts: the

Continued page 170

Jeff Sparrow in his home-built Austin Seven-based 500 'SMS,' at Prescott in 1948. The car was powered by a Rudge Ulster engine, and had all independent suspension, and A7 swing axles at the front. (Courtesy Ferret Fotographics)

ARTHUR MALLOCK, BREN, BOMBSK, AND U2

Major Arthur Mallock is one of the most important personalities of British motorsport. Born in 1918, he was – by 1938 – a regular officer in the Royal Corps of Signals, and until 1980 worked as an electronics engineer at Hanslope Park, the Government communication centre, living just a few miles from Silverstone in nearby Roade.

As a boy, he built Meccano racing cars, bicycles, and simple valve radio sets, before a visit to Lewes Speed Trial brought him into life-changing contact with John Bolster's 'Bloody Mary' Seven special, with its Austin Seven front corners. Arthur was already planning his own Seven special as he cycled home. He bought his first Austin Seven at 17, costing him £3, and followed it up with a

Arthur Mallock and Jack French in 'Bren,' showing that its LMB front swing axles are working to good effect in the 1946 Jeans Gold Cup Trial. (Courtesy Ferret Fotographics)

Jack French in Simplicity (left) warmly acknowledges his great friend Arthur Mallock passing in WJ 1515 the legendary Austin Seven-based 1172 Formula car – the first of hundreds of Arthur's U2 race and hillclimb racers. (Courtesy Richard Mallock)

Gordon England Cup. He built his first special on a 1932 van chassis, lowered with a Williams kit, and, with rudimentary tuning, entered it into the Hartlepool Speed Trial in the short summer of 1939. After volunteering for pilot training, he met Jack French in 1942, and began an immediate friendship.

Postwar, Mallock built a trials car called Bren, which was almost the equal of an ex-works Grasshopper at a 1946 Trial. The car that followed was named Bombsk, built by Jack and Arthur in Jack's soon-to-be-famous green shed. This was based on a road-legal Austin Seven chassis WJ 1515, with an almost standard engine, plus a Marshall supercharger, and minimalist bodywork. This skimpy device created a sensation at the 1947 Northern Experts Trial, when Arthur beat Ken Warton, who was, at the time, acknowledged as being the supreme trials competitor. Unbeknownst to those present, however, was that shortly before the race, Arthur – with the car in race spec – had already won two races at the Tolthorpe Yorkshire secret 'race meeting that never was.' With the bodywork tidied up by Jack, Arthur also competed at 'the black market sprint' at Luton Hoo, where police took names and (still rationed) petrol samples of the runners – a hurried switch of Arthur's twin fuel tanks saving the day!

WJ 1515 was equally at home at hillclimbs, sprints, races, and trials, and, after a brief and dismal attempt at 500cc racing in a CRM, the old Austin-based car had an 1172cc Ford engine from Arthur's road car fitted for the 1953 1172 Formula inaugural season. By this time, Mallock's

sons Raymond and Richard had been born (both destined to become influential in the motorsport world), and Arthur continued to use WJ 1515 in evolving forms in 1172 Formula racing. Ever quicker, and almost catching the Lotus Elevens, Arthur shared his experiences and expertise in writing for the *750 Motor Club Bulletin* and motoring magazines.

Finally, in 1958, the running gear from the car was transferred from the Austin Seven frame to a purpose-built space frame christened U2, after a body-building advert of the period, to run in 1172 Formula and various other categories. The 'Mallock U2' name was shortened to just 'Mallock,' and the cars built under this name have shaped British amateur motorsport from the 1960s onwards, in Clubmans and other categories, and driven by luminaries like Hugh Chamberlain, Max Mosley, Frank Sytner, Andy Priaulx, and Harvey Postlethwaite.

With Arthur's passing, Richard and Sue Mallock now head Mallock Sports and Racing, and Ray Mallock RML Motorsports, with wide-ranging international facilities and services, including BTCC, Le Mans, and Group One.

The Mallock effect on British motorsport is incalculable, and without Arthur, his example, and his encouragement, the UK would not have enjoyed the same vibrant postwar club racing scene. Before Arthur sadly passed away, the author had the honour to organise, with the Mallock family, the 1993 celebration of his 75th birthday at Silverstone. Arthur led a parade of U2s and Mallocks on the track for one last time.

JACK FRENCH AND SIMPLICITY

Jack French did more for the budding amateur motorsport enthusiasts than any other postwar individual. He led by example how to put Austin Seven dreams into reality, writing down his experiences and sharing his expertise; he exemplified the 'IE,' or 'Impecunious Enthusiast' – a person of limited means, as described and enshrined into the sporting regulations of the 750 Motor Club.

Chapman's complete dominance of the 1951 750 Formula racing season, with his Lotus Mark III, led to a rapid decline in interest by dispirited would-be 750 Formula racers. Jack French stepped in, and busily wrote up encouraging articles in the *750 Motor Club Bulletin* to show that good-to-excellent performance could be readily achieved in an Austin special by sticking to certain simple rules: lightweight, including all rotating masses; sound, simple engineering for a reliable engine; correct gearing; adequate brakes; and good weight distribution.

He wrote – in highly entertaining style – about the everyday trials and tribulations of special building, including two false starts of his own making. In doing so, he inspired a whole generation of young men to follow his progress, and to create for themselves small, sporting cars suitable for race trials, hillclimbs and sprints for very little money and – equally importantly – not too much time. He also passed on names of useful firms to carry out essential tasks like straight-forward machining and metal treatments.

His earlier articles would be re-read for decades to come, and formed the nucleus of the 750 Motor Club *Special Builders Guide*, later expanded to become *Design for Competition*, and also spawning the *Austin Seven Companion*, still published by 750 Motor Club. At the core of his principles, at a time when Austin Seven spares of all types were cheaply available, was the selection and use of only what was the most appropriate for the intended job. With the need for only the most modest of workshop equipment

Martin Eyre at the VSCC Curborough Sprint circa 1972, driving Jack French's rebuilt and quick Formula car, 'Roberta.' It was light, had low rolling resistance and produced approximately 38bhp. (Courtesy Ferret Fotographics)

– when historically scarcely anybody even owned an electric drill – Jack answered members' questions personally, and much of this information also reached the pages of the *750 Motor Club Bulletin*. Jack also gave talks to centres up and down the country.

Jack and his friends created a car in just five weeks and, as it was ultra-simple, named it 'Simplicity.' Arguably, this was to be the most influential postwar Austin Seven special of all. Arthur Mallock contributed the unboxed short-wheelbase frame from his own special, named Bombsk, which already had Ruby rear outriggers to support the rear including fuel tank and battery, and had more effective short late friction shock absorbers. A rare 1931 narrow-track rear axle, with a 5.25:1 crown wheel and pinion, was suspended on flattened springs with the main leaves inverted. At the front, a standard 3ft 4in (1.02m) track LMB Austin-based swing axle sat below a flattened spring bearing directly on the axle beam. Front dampers were initially dispensed with.

The engine was, at first, almost standard. It was fitted 2in (50mm) further back in the frame for better weight distribution. This was soon replaced with a tuned splash-fed 1930 Chummy unit that

incorporated Jack's ideas on maintaining high induction gas speeds to provide greater mid-range torque for good acceleration, and was allied to smaller rear wheels to lower gearing for the short events anticipated. The stark doorless bodywork was squared off at the rear, and the long bonnet opening allowed good access to both sides of the fireproof bulkhead, to get at engine, gearbox, all controls, and instruments. The four speed Nippy box was later swapped for a three-speed Ulster, simply to save more weight.

Tuning information was mainly aimed at the amateur motorcycle fraternity around wartime, and Jack experimented with very effective re-grinds of standard camshafts to get more overlap and better breathing. Together with flatter radius and shortened tappets, he supplied these in a steady stream to other members for years. Above all, he was totally against adding more complication or weight, and his blunt lessons were sometimes difficult to accept amongst the more aesthetic followers of club motorsport.

Simplicity – the car – was campaigned relentlessly by many drivers throughout the 1950s. One of Jack's extreme weekend jaunts took place over 700mi (1126km) on pre-motorway roads, and incorporated events in Norfolk and Davidstow in Cornwall, before returning to Gloucestershire! Simplicity won its last contemporary race at Silverstone in 1962, in the hands of Arthur Mallock, after which it was retired.

Jack wrote that he had never driven Simplicity faster than 80mph (128km/h) to win races. His gearing equated an engine speed of 6000rpm, which he knew he had to reach two-thirds of the way down any particular straight of any particular circuit, or he would never get to this top speed at all, through being over-geared. The car was developed in-period with king-pin tension stays and other experiments. By 1957, the car was lower, had a wider front track, and was fitted with smaller diameter – but slightly wider – tyres (effectively Mark II specification), including a slight negative camber to the rear wheels. Apparently the axle casings bent by accidentally dropping the whole car!

After the car was retired, Jack fettled away, removing brake back plates, drilling and paring other parts down to a minimum, Zeppelin-like drilled diagonal steel strips zig-zagging across the otherwise open bottoms of the frame rails, and revising the steering with a single piece trackrod in front of the radiator. Upon Jack's passing in the 1990s, this assemblage was put together by Martin Eyre and Tim Myall to VSCC front beam axle specifications, enjoying a new lease of life and a new fan-base. This was followed by some years in Barry Clarke's hands, prior to Graham Beckett acquiring the car in 2015 – Simplicity motors on.

chassis side members, rear axle, engine crankcase and block. There was freedom in other areas both to allow existing modified cars to compete, and to encourage the development of ideas.

750 Formula was an instant hit, and was very well supported with a healthy mix of old sports and racing Austin Sevens, various specials on traditional lines, and a few stripped Chummys. With nationwide interest in the club, it was evident that there were many groups of far-flung Austin Seven enthusiasts, spread far and wide. It was Leslie Ballamy who came up with the idea of separate and ultimately semi-autonomous centres that were set up to cater for local groups.

At a time of fuel shortages, rationing, and a postwar scarcity of commodities such as tyres and batteries, any local help from a like-minded enthusiast was of huge benefit. Many ordinary households lacked even a telephone, so a regular local meeting place and a

A full field of early 750 Formula cars leaves the grid, watched by a huge motorsport starved post-World War Two crowd. Goggles were the sole concession to driver safety. (Author collection)

Ironside in his distinctive Williams Special VB 7571 at VSCC Silverstone, May 1953. The car still has a busy life in the capable hands of Williams' expert, Stuart Ulph.

Early post-war appearance of 'Mrs Jo Jo' at the 1947 Prescott event, in new paint and modified bodywork, the driver not protected in any way. (Courtesy Ferret Fotographics)

August 1953, Ron Grimsley at the NSCC Silverstone event in his very effective 750 Formula car. Ron uniquely won the Goodacre Trophy for two successive 'Austin' years – 1952 and 1953. (Courtesy Ferret Fotographics).

Meetings for discussions, talks, and film shows were held, as well as local events, put on under the umbrella of the club; trials; both daylight and night-time Rallies; jaunts up mountains; driving tests; gymkhanas; and road runs. Essentially, anything where you could have a good day's fun in an Austin Seven, or a similar small car.

Membership of 750 Motor Club passed the 500 mark in 1951. This was the year of the Festival of Britain, with the United Kingdom putting on a show of its products and successes to a world audience, and celebrating the identity of its people. There was full employment, but most home-produced goods were headed for the export market. The *Bulletin* was enlarged and better produced, advertising popular night trials, and speed trials at Tarrant Rushton that attracted 50 entries. The Birkett Six Hour Relay Race granted national status – a considerable coup for the strictly amateur club – and scores of talks were given on all sorts of motoring topics.

By 1953, more than 1000 people had joined the 750 Motor Club. It was at this tipping point – as the value of an Austin Seven fell to a very low level – that the newly-identified 'teenager' began to become interested in Austin Sevens in a big way, and came along to meetings. Just as had happened after World War One, there was a huge social impact from the effects of the Second World War, and the shared trauma of Auschwitz and Hiroshima searched for public expression.

As with all national trends, the reasons for the youth upsurge of the 1950s are complex; there was a new young Queen on the throne, clothing was no longer the same as that worn by their parents, popular music had become owned by young people, and there was a new sense of identity around youth culture. Mid-fifties Rock 'n' Roll was a critical element, and it is easy to see in retrospect the effect of James Dean and Marlon Brando films, Elvis Presley's music, John Osbourne in the theatre, Lionel Bart musicals, the young free-thinking Abstract Impressionists in art … The list is endless and self-evident, and provided radical new philosophy for the young, which evolved into a continuous celebration of youth that is still with us.

monthly *Bulletin* were priceless, and expansion of club membership accelerated fast. Local centres were put on a proper financial footing by headquarters – military terminology ruled, post-World War Two – and soon there were more than two dozen centres and many more local groups organising themselves on behalf of the national club.

HOLLAND BIRKETT

Charles Bulmer, writing in 2009, said "The quite irresistible force behind the postwar revival of 750 Motor Club was the Fleet vet and special builder Holly Birkett. He had a passion to understand fundamental engineering principles, particularly about tyres, handling, steering, geometry and suspension, and translate this to the brainstorming group … which often included Jack French, Arthur Mallock, Tom Lush (of Allards), Bill Boddy, and Jenks [Denis Jenkinson]."

Holly felt he was on an educational mission to convey all this to 750 Motor Club members, through its monthly *Bulletin* and meetings. He was equally determined that there should be somewhere for the impecunious to use this knowledge competitively, leading first to the invention of 750 Formula, then the Ford Ten-based 1172 Formula, the Eight Clubs Association (whereby a group of motor clubs shared circuit costs), and the 750 Motor Club National Six Hour Relay Race. In this way, the club rapidly became the meeting place and forcing ground for an entirely new element in motorsport. Young engineers and other young enthusiasts, who had bright ideas but little money (like Colin Chapman and others), began to take over what had previously been a pastime for only the privileged few.

After more than a decade of hands-on work for the 750 Motor Club, Holly, in 1961, succeeded Colin Chapman as non-executive Club President. Just two years later, however, the Club's euphoria following the inaugural 1963 National Austin Seven Rally at Beaulieu was cut cruelly short by the news that Holly – who was also an enthusiastic amateur pilot – had died in an aircraft crash at Le Touquet, along with his wife Margaret.

The 750 MC National Six Hour Relay race was renamed The Birkett in his honour.

A young vet named Holland Birkett flings his Austin Seven round Pardon hairpin at Prescott in 1948. (Courtesy Guy Griffiths)

"Bodywork optional!" Geoffrey Render in natty head gear, string and braces, in the savagely lightened blown sprint Ulster that he shared with his younger brother (and British Sprint Champion) David. (Author collection)

Postwar political educational reforms saw a building boom in schools and higher educational buildings. The small boy who grew up in the forties and fifties playing with his train set and tinkering with Meccano, whilst perhaps not one of the select few who then went on to university, often became one of the enthusiastic many attending excellent technical colleges and polytechnics. This fed the then vast British car and aerospace industries. To such a boy, the early acquisition of cheap mechanical transport was a natural part of growing up.

New motorcycles became affordable in the 1950s, but for the aspiring young British motorist, Austin Sevens represented not only very cheap transport, but also very simple mechanics and an abundance of secondhand spares. Scrapyards in every town were filled with largely prewar motor cars, of which Austin Sevens were well represented. Late model Austin Sevens were kept in sparkling condition, and still used as normal family cars up to the late 1950s and even into the 1960s, before the creation of motorways. There were a larger number of lesser specimens readily available for very little money – indeed, on leaving school at 16, the author bought a perfectly good 1934 Ruby for 20 pounds out of his second month's wages.

The *750 Motor Club Bulletin* carried members' classified advertisements that ultimately ran to four pages, including Northwood's Austin Seven Spares, Cambridge Engineering, Lotus in 1952 ("a complete service to the special builder"), and many other

The great Austin Seven enthusiast Mike Ware and his passenger are well out of their seats urging
'Thunderbox' on to greater things on the 'Exeter.' (Courtesy Mike Peck)

useful engineering contacts. In 1953, Pat Stephens wrote *Building and Racing my 750*, which quickly sold out and was reprinted several times.

A lot was happening at once, and a craze erupted for building Austin Seven specials, fuelled by the success and popularity of 750 Formula and the idea that you could build yourself a snappy little sports car. The 750 Motor Club eventually got involved with marketing its own fibreglass shell, but it was sensibly left to Microplas of Surrey to make and market the Stiletto – believed to be the first British shell.

Evening meetings were now held twice a month at the large Abbey Hotel road house on the North Circular Road, North London (and a safe distance from the bikers in The Ace Café at Stonebridge Park). Film shows and talks took place, with an overflowing car park of Sevens, specials, and occasional more exotic intruders. On warm summer evenings, 750 Motor Club members bent on looking at the latest specials had to be forcibly rounded up to go inside, to avoid the invited speaker addressing an empty room.

750 Motor Club and VSCC types had, by now, started careful restorations of early Sevens, and the historically minded turned to re-examining the credentials of the Austin Seven as "the motor for the millions," and originality for its own sake gained adherents. Roland Harrison had first written *Austin Racing History* in 1949 – and this

A JAP Twin-powered Austin Seven-based road legal special lines up at VSCC Prescott in 1962. Note the lack of front brakes. (Courtesy Ferret Fotographics)

was to be reprinted several times – but it would not be until 1968 that Bob Wyatt published the results of lengthy and careful research. His magnum opus, titled *The Austin Seven* was also reprinted many times.

750 Motor Club centres developed a healthy rivalry, encouraged by the Board of Directors. Centre teams entered driving tests, trials, sprints, and races with their own emblems proudly displayed, nowhere more so than in the annual Six Hour Relay Race, where, in 1959, a team famously consisting only of Austin Seven Ulsters took part.

New *Bulletin* advertisers, meanwhile, included Withams Spares, Laws of Lewisham, Southern Cylinder Services, Giesler Balancing, Bowden Engineering and West London Repair (who rebuilt Austin

Continued page 177

COLIN CHAPMAN, LOTUS, AND THE AUSTIN SEVEN

Immediately after the Second World War, there was a great hunger among young returning service personnel for motorsport of any kind. Many had become proficient at driving trucks, cars, and motorbikes for the first time, they had technical training – having looked after tanks, aircraft, and ships – and had experienced excitement in foreign places that they would not have otherwise visited. Motorsport, in all its various forms, had immense appeal for this generation. However, in times of austerity, and with little money or machinery to go round, it came naturally to them to make use of whatever was readily available – and there were plenty of cheap Austin Sevens about.

At this time, Colin Chapman was an engineering student in his late teens, who belonged to the University of London Air Squadron. He built a multi-purpose trials Austin Seven special, the body of which was in a box form, and fabricated from alloy-faced plywood, immediately making his special stiffer, more controllable, and better at negotiating the off-road sections of the events in which he took part. After a short-term commission in the RAF, he built a second Austin Seven-based – but Ford Ten-powered – trials car that also introduced him to circuit racing. He won the first race in which he took part, and, not unnaturally, was immediately smitten.

He joined the British Aluminium Company at about the same time that the 750 Motor Club announced circuit racing for a Formula Championship specifically for Austin Sevens – or cars built

The very first Lotus, a trials special on a 1930 Saloon chassis, seen here in 1948 on its third registration plate with Colin (far right) and Hazel Chapman (far left). (Courtesy Cliff Bradshaw)

The 1950 Walsingham Trial; Hazel Chapman has Graham Hill as a passenger, with Colin Chapman in the back as bouncer. The Chummy was by now Graham's, bought from Hazel on the proviso that she could enter the occasional event. (Courtesy Mike Peck)

The 750 Formula was for two-seater sports cars, and stipulated that an Austin Seven un-supercharged engine, rear axle, and chassis side members had to be used, but allowed freedoms elsewhere. Using his knowledge of aircraft techniques from the RAF, and lightweight materials from his employer, Colin laid out a stiff light chassis, with boxed-in side members and tubular cross members. He used compliant (later marketed as 'soft-ride') springs, a swing axle with Ford Eight beam at the front, telescopic dampers to replace the vintage friction discs, and a smooth torpedo body, with a rounded nose and tail, minimal frontal area and a full undertray. This last item was reckoned to add 7mph (11km/h) to the car's top speed, compared with an exposed chassis with a floor on top. Colin worked with Michael and Nigel Allen to build one racer each, but in the event only Colin's car was close enough to completion to start the season (although the Allen brothers shared the driving).

Having studied Ricardo, and collaborated with Australian Derek Jolly, Colin devised a method of dividing the two siamesed inlet ports and creating four inlet ports on the Austin's block, thereby releasing enough power to run at 6500rpm. This yielded a track speed of 97mph (156km/h) – at least 18mph (28km/h) faster than any of the other runners. The Austin aluminium crankcase was solidly mounted in the chassis to aid stiffness, but when this caused engine trouble rubber mountings were substituted, so losing the chassis-bracing effect and alarming Colin at the difference in cornering speed. His fertile mind solved that problem by the addition of a lightweight inverted cradle of small diameter tubes above the engine – the first but not the last appearance of a space frame on a Lotus.

The Lotus Mark III was immensely successful, and such was its superiority that it almost killed 750 Formula racing stone dead, even before it had started. Dividing the inlet ports was banned for the next season, and the Formula was largely saved by Jack French's series of articles in *750 Motor Club Bulletin*, showing how a racing Austin Seven special could be built using a selection of readily available bits from the local scrapyard.

It may only be speculated about how many lessons were learnt by Colin Chapman from playing with Austin Sevens. By examining Chapman's evolving designs, it is not too far-fetched to believe that distinct Austin Seven ingredients went into his psyche, only to return in later configurations of successful Lotus concepts. He must have been impressed by the minimal number of components in an Austin Seven, with the quarter elliptic springs locating the rear axle as well as being the suspension medium, thereby performing two jobs in one. This became one of Chapman's favourite design features. Anybody that has tried to modify an Austin Seven chassis for greater

up from Austin Seven components – was to be held in 1951. Colin immediately started devouring all the books that he could find on the subject, and had long discussions with all the established motor racing personalities that he could meet, impressing all with his unusual level of enthusiasm, verve, and drive – Colin had found his métier.

He named his 750 Formula car 'Lotus', for reasons which still remain secret, and, as it was his third car design, it became the Lotus Mark III. Blueprints of Colin's original drawings survive, and show an unusually detailed layout, beautifully drafted, and demonstrating a number of considered choices in the Austin components actually used.

Colin Chapman (race number 12) makes a smokey start in his Lotus Mark III, at a 1951 Silverstone 750 Formula race – a season that the Lotus completely dominated. (750 Motor Club archive)

performance has to fight a constant battle of adding components, such as lowering links or additional mountings for new damper points, against the penalty of complexity and weight.

Herbert Austin initially tried to do completely without items like shock absorbers, electric starters, and windscreen wipers. This helped to keep costs down, and Herbert only added them when it became evident that they would show an improvement. With Chapman, weight was a priority. Every component was weighed and recorded in Chapman's notebook, and the quote "There is nothing as light as nothing" is often attributed to Colin. 'The competition starts with the receipt of the rules' is the mantra of the lateral thinker, and Colin Chapman was forever looking eagerly at exploiting any loopholes in the regulations. This continued right up to the end of his career, when he was continually frustrated by the crushing of his innovations through more and more stifling legislation.

Chapman recognised the advantage of 'designing in' light weight when using a modest power unit like an Austin Seven, or any other proprietary power unit that was equally available to the competition. In the case of Lotus, this would later relate to the use of Ford Tens, MG, Coventry Climax, and ultimately Cosworth and other engines. Lotus exemplified the use of lightweight stiff space frames that allowed more compliant suspension, with the wheels spending more time properly in contact with the ground, as first seen in the Lotus Mark III. This ethos served Colin well, as did input from Peter Ross, Mike Costin, and stress engineer Gilbert 'Mac' McIntosh – all from de Havilland Aircraft Co. Their work was invaluable, and contributed to meteoric advances in race car design in period.

The use of minimal and efficient space frames, allied to compliant suspension, saw British chassis design pre-eminent over continental opposition for more than a decade, and this spark contributed immeasurably to the impetus of British supremacy in motorsport up to the present.

The advantages of real aerodynamics became a Lotus must; as we have seen, the homogeneous whole bodyshell form adopted for Lotus Mark III was a direct benefit of the Austin Seven triangular frame plan, with no outside excrescences requiring additional cowlings. The simple triangulation of the front suspension, within a nose piece of limited width, allowed a minimal cross-section torpedo shape and good aerodynamic penetration.

Colin's first trials car gained performance from its plywood box body stiffening the frame, and the ground-breaking full-monocoque Lotus 25 Grand Prix cars followed in 1962. Early lessons regarding engines being used as stiffening structures – that Colin first learnt with the Lotus Mark III – were ultimately seen to have made a great effect, when the Cosworth DFV Formula One engine was itself specifically designed as the rear half of the all-conquering Formula One Lotus 49. Most, if not all, of these innovations were also seen elsewhere, but Colin's exposure to all the early and basic lessons in car dynamics must inevitably have sown the seeds of his brilliant design approach, which resonates even today.

When designing the famous 'wobbly-web' cast magnesium wheels (copied from a Chance Voight aircraft wheel, and first seen in 1956 for his super lightweight Formula Two Lotus Twelve), Chapman found himself in need of a deeply-threaded wheel nut. It had to be quite long, and so not completely buried in the 'wobbly' folds, to be finely threaded, and to have sufficient 'bite' with the magnesium that no further locking devices were required. He found that he already had some wheel nuts to this precise specification knocking around – ordinary Austin Seven wheel nuts fitted the bill exactly, and were still in use six years later on Jim Clark's Grand Prix-winning monocoque F1 Lotus 25.

Young John Haynes stands proudly behind his newly-constructed Austin Seven special in 1958. Haynes went on to found his world-renowned publishing house from these modest beginnings. (Author collection)

The author in 1958 with 'Hot Box.' The cycle wings, drilled front shock-absorbers, painted registration, and air intakes for brakes and carburettor constantly demanded spirited driving! (Author collection)

wire wheels in smaller diameters, and with lighter wheel centres). The *Special Builders Guide* was published by the club. Fibreglass body manufacturer advertising included Convair, Autoplex, Heron, Simplast, and Ashley Laminates, which was a long-lived company.

Eric and Graham Broadley's Austin Special sits proudly at Beaulieu '750 Graduates' display with Lola Sports 2000, Lola T70 and Broadley designed Ford GTO behind. (Courtesy Ken Cooke)

In race organisation, the 750 Motor Club was an inaugural member of 'The Eight Clubs' – a group formed specifically to spread the financial burden and risk of organised race days. It also formed one third of 'The Trio,' with the closely-connected Club Lotus (Chapman was 750 Motor Club President) and the 250 MRC, which ran tiny motorcycle-engined cars before the invention of karting.

In August 1956, an advertisement for the small book *Building a 750 Special* appeared, pricing the title at five shillings (25p). This was placed by a Mr John Haynes of Sutton Valence in Kent – the precursor of the many millions of Haynes manuals sold worldwide.

While the Suez crisis of 1956/57 caused the cancellation of many events, 750 Motor Club membership was now heading towards 2500. By way of a change, and a sign of the times, the Walsingham Cup trial – normally

JOHN MILES

When John Miles was 17 years old, he bought a 1936 Austin Nippy and went along to a 750 Motor Club Red Cow meeting, to listen to a talk given by Colin Chapman. Just six years later, John was driving a works Formula Three Lotus for Chapman, and, by late 1970, had competed in 15 Grands Prix for Team Lotus. This included driving the FWD cars, and the initially tricky Lotus 72, before he walked away after a falling out with Chapman, following the shocking death of Jochen Rindt at Monza. Prior to that, John had rebuilt a rare 1926 Super Sport, and developed a feel for chassis engineering. He says that racing the low-powered Austin was "amazingly good training for using every scrap of power, speed, and grip in faster cars."

In early 1963, John founded the Sports Austin Register, to gather together and record details of all surviving examples. That July, the first National Austin Seven Rally took place at Beaulieu, and accelerated popular interest in Austin Sevens for their own sake. John Miles' Register expanded to include all Sevens, becoming the Austin Seven Register, which held its first AGM at Brooklands in 1964. After his professional driving career, John became a highly-respected development engineer and journalist, his gift for profound evaluation of suspension systems benefiting manufacturers and readers alike.

John re-purchased his earlier Super Sports and re-visited its racing potential, commissioning the first new Austin Seven crankshafts from Gordon Allen in Slough, and providing the Austin Seven tuning collaborator Stuart Rolt an indestructible bottom end basis for development. An Oulton Park win in 1975, with Martin Eyre driving, heralded a new safer age for rare and valuable competition Austin Seven engines.

Latterly, John Miles delivers fascinating talks on his life's motorsport experiences, and, like Chapman, John has instituted an annual 750 Motor Club award for technical excellence, innovation or young driver promise. John is a Vice President of the 750 Motor Club, and continues to build up performance Austin Sevens purely for pleasure. One of his

latest contributions is more fundamental re-thinking of 95-year-old handling problems – the well-reasoned answer to which is to lengthen the standard Austin Seven steering arm by a relatively small amount … "the most worthwhile modification that I have made to an Austin Seven for 50 years!"

John Miles at a 1963 750 Motor Club Debden race meeting in his Super Sports. (Courtesy John Miles)

Development still continues – John Miles separates roll stiffness from high front bump rate by widening the mounting base for transverse spring, adding rollers and separate lateral location. (Courtesy John Miles)

"Oh! The indignity!" This short wheelbase Box Saloon at Mallory Park illustrates the way in which Austin Sevens were enthusiastically used by young owners in the late 1950s. (Courtesy Ferret Fotographics)

exclusively an Austin Seven event – allowed Les Needham to compete in a brand-new BMW Isetta bubble car!

In 1957, the club had cause to celebrate Stirling Moss' great victory in the British Grand Prix at Aintree, driving a Vanwall. Stirling always been a great friend of 750 Motor Club, and the Vanwall had a new frame and suspension that had been designed by Colin Chapman just five years after racing his Austin Seven, a body by Frank Costin, and was spannered by Derek Wooton – all 750 Motor Club men. For good measure, Chapman's beautiful Lotus Elevens won its class and the Biennial Cup at Le Mans too – it was the beginning of great things for British motorsport.

The Ford Ten 1172cc side-valve engine was a lot less fragile than the Austin Seven unit, and 1172 Formula racing allowed much greater scope for budding car builders than the restrictions of 750 Formula. Not only that, but with an 1172 Ford Formula car you could pit both your creation and your driving skills against Ford-powered Lotus Nines, Elevens, and Sevens – an attractive idea to any aspiring Colin Chapman. Indeed, this was the very path taken by Eric Broadley of Lola, design engineer Len Terry, F1 engine builder Brian Hart, and countless others.

There was, at the same time, a group led by Frank Tiedeman – himself the enthusiastic owner of a quick Austin Ulster – that wished

A typically crowded early '60s 750 Formula field at Eight Clubs Silverstone. Abbot leads in his sophisticated special, amongst equally extreme Austin Seven-powered racers. (Courtesy Ferret Fotographics)

to rid themselves of the limitations of a sports car Formula, with wings, lights, and road paraphernalia. Instead, they built and competed in single-seat racing cars, naming the result the Monoposto Formula.

An enormous number of Austin Seven specials were built in the late 1950s, and were a common sight on the roads. It is a fact, however, that for every three or four specials started, perhaps only one was ever completed. The number of (admittedly mainly inferior condition) Sevens that were dismantled at this time is sad to contemplate now. In 1959, an Austin Seven could be scrapped and destroyed for the price of a set of new king pins; it was frequently cheaper to go and get a better complete car from the scrapyard, and perhaps swap over any good bits from the 'scrapper.'

The sheer number of poor condition cars that were dismantled by special builders, and the parts stored in sheds and garages, has contributed greatly to the amount of original spare parts for Austin Sevens that still exist today, in far greater numbers than any other prewar car. Each main element of an Austin Seven (engine, gearbox, back axle, etc) is light enough in itself to be picked up and carried by one man. This, along with their small size, made storing Austin Seven parts – for half a century or more – very easy!

As the 1950s turned into the 1960s, a number of events conspired to change the way in which an ordinary Austin Seven was viewed. In May 1958 the Austin Healey Sprite small sports car was announced, followed in 1959 by the Issigonis Mini, the van version of which cost

TEAM SIGMA AND THE WORDEN

Team Sigma was one of the prominent groups of 750 Motor Club enthusiasts formed in the late 1950s, initially joining forces to build a car specifically to win the coveted Goodacre Trophy. Graphic designer Mike Featherstonehaugh paired up with the Ford design and development engineer Harry Worral in 1957, and together they built the successful and pretty GRP (Glassfibre Reinforced Plastic) streamliner-bodied FW Special. This resembled a pared down Lotus Eleven, and had a super-light space frame built over its long-wheelbase Seven chassis.

This GRP car body was subsequently marketed by Speedex as the 'Silverstone.' The distinctive Team Sigma colours were all-over white, with a 4in-wide (101mm) Valspar 'Burnt Orange' stripe down the body centreline – paying homage to the works Austin Ulster's orange paintwork.

For 1959 the pair were joined by Tony Densham of Sutton Re-bore Co and engine specialist Keith Dixon, who had himself raced a fast Ulster. Inspired by the earlier build principles of Colin Chapman and Jack French, the Worral/Densham Worden – a radical ultra-light slipper-bodied car – was intended to be a big single leap forward in Austin Seven racing, rather than incremental development. A pair of long-wheelbase frame rails formed the bottom members of a super-light space frame, the flat soft rear quarter elliptics set 4½in (114mm) higher than the frame rails by cranking the latter, damped with telescopic Konis. At the front, a Big Seven axle beam (with its larger king pins) was split as a wide track swing axle, with springing and damping by inclined Lotus Eleven coil spring/damper units.

The Keith Dixon-tuned Worden engine employed a splash-fed crankshaft, modified Ulster-pattern camshaft with the largest possible inlet valves on short tappets with all non-Austin modern ancillaries, twin 1⅛in (34mm) side draft SUs, and a state-of-the-art Lee Racing Motors (LRM) aluminium cylinder head. After some test runs, the bodywork was lowered and the driver was reclined. This resulted in the smallest possible frontal area, offering good air penetration from a single tapering plan form – matching the Seven chassis and with no compound curves, this was a new shape in Austin Seven racing.

At the first Silverstone meeting of 1960, Tony Densham drove away into the distance. Such was the astounding supremacy of the car and its pilot that it was decided that Tony would continue to drive until the Goodacre Trophy was secured – after seven consecutive victories – at which point, Harry Worral completed the season with another four wins.

So great was the leap forward in performance that the Worden could lap Club Silverstone more than five seconds faster than the quickest 750 specials of the previous season. It dominated in a manner not seen in 750 Formula racing since Colin Chapman's Lotus Mark III ten years earlier. As with Chapman, the effect was again to challenge the established order of a stable Formula class that was, at that time, more related to the enjoyment of the sport than to the advancement of science.

As a bit of light relief, a year later, Team Sigma supported Pierre de Villiers, who – having taken his narrowed-radiator Ulster to Italy, and winning the historic Coppa di Monza – acquired the one-off space frame C-Series F1 Connaught, and entered it for the 1962 Indianapolis 500. Its veteran driver, Jack Fairman, just failed to qualify. It was a very entertaining jape, but is put into perspective by being in the same year that Colin Chapman took his Len Terry-designed Lotus 29s for Jim Clark and Dan Gurney, Clark narrowly missing a win in his rookie year.

On the right, Peter Hornby lines up in the Worden, with then 750 Motor Club Chairman Mike Featherstonehaugh in the FRA – a 1990s development of his original FW Special. (Author collection)

"What could possibly go wrong?" An exceptionally well ventilated Austin Seven crankcase. (Courtesy Dave Edroff)

less than £400. Mainstream Formula racing cars went rear-engined, with front-engined cars becoming technically obsolete and immediately outdated. Then, in 1960, Ernest Marples' dreaded MOT testing of older cars was introduced. Despite the very best of intentions, this wiped thousands of Austin Sevens off the roads, to be scrapped rather than dismantled, much to the alarm of many Austin Seven enthusiasts.

The 750 Motor Club, however, expanded its activities further, with a dedicated core of Austin Seven enthusiasts organising club events and rallies; the perception of the Austin Seven and its historical place in social history and motorsport began to be viewed in a new light.

CHAPTER FOURTEEN

ANTIPODEAN SPECIALISTS

WITH strong connections to Australia going back to young Herbert Austin's first forays in the 1890s, and with the lasting influence of Col Waite's 1928 win in the first Australian Grand Prix, the Austin Seven has always enjoyed a high profile in the Antipodes. In turn, enthusiasts and mechanics in remote Australia and New Zealand, being somewhat isolated, gained a deserved reputation for resourcefulness and innovation – virtues effectively forced upon them, being so far from the mainstream production factories of Europe, whilst still being a part of the British Empire. A large number, including Jack Brabham and Bruce McLaren, were to greatly influence the path of Formula One Grand Prix racing from the late 1950s onwards.

Austin Seven racing specials were built in Australia, including examples based on modified Aces and Meteors from the mid-1920s, to compete in open classes or Formula Libre, on both paved and loose surface tracks, and initially on a mostly ad hoc basis. One such Seven surfaced in the 1930s, as the Ulster-based car of South Australian Ron Uffindel. With little limitation in the way of regulations, and showing great freedom of thought, Ron divided the inlet ports to give an eight-

Australia's Ron Uffindel on dirt and in a mighty hurry, in his eight-port engined Ulster-based Seven. (Austin publicity)

BRUCE MCLAREN'S ULSTER

When New Zealander Bruce McLaren was only nine years old, in 1946, he contracted Perthes disease. This affected his thigh bones, and he spent almost three years at a special school, with his legs encased in plaster. Bruce's father, Les McLaren, ran a small garage at Remura (a smart suburb of Auckland, on the North Island), and so Bruce spent much of his spare time around a great variety of machinery being serviced and repaired. The latter frequently required temporary fixes, when replacement parts were not readily available.

In the early 1950s, Les McLaren bought a 1929 Austin Ulster in bits, with the intention of rebuilding it for competition and possible sale. This took a year, by which time young Bruce was helping out, and had become entirely hooked on the idea of driving it himself. Assisting with the rebuild, he was learning all about the little Austin as he went along. Unfortunately, when Les first drove the Ulster in anger, he did not take to it at all. Bruce successfully pleaded for the car to be kept, for him to use, and he spent the next year going over the car again – with the odd trip out – until he was old enough for a driving licence. Just days after his fifteenth birthday – in 1952 – and with his licence in his pocket, Bruce drove to the beach-side Muriwai Hillclimb, beating his friend Phil Kerr (driving an Austin Nippy) to win the class.

The Ulster was modified by degrees; a lowered Big Seven front axle with front-mounted track rod was fitted, along with smaller wheels. When the cylinder head cracked, Bruce replaced it with a higher compression Ricardo-pattern 1936 head, the combustion chambers of which he filled with bronze weld and re-profiled. Fitted with twin SU carburettors, the Ulster, stripped of mudguards and lights, was timed at 87mph (140km/h) for the flying quarter mile, being held in top at 6000rpm. The Ulster was sold in 1955, and Bruce shared the use of an Austin Healey, until one day at an Ohakea airfield race, when Bruce practised a whopping seven seconds a lap quicker than Les.

port head, and to transform the available power and torque of the side valve by eliminating intake port robbing, and delivering a smooth power band.

This car was subsequently acquired by Derek Jolly, who ran it in stripped-chassis form, placing the radiator behind the engine for better weight distribution for hillclimbing. In 1950, it finished second at Balcombe – in front of many more powerful cars – and recorded 81mph (130km/h) at Bathurst. Derek Jolly then visited England, sending his eight-port block Austin engine ahead of him,

and into the eagerly awaiting hands of Colin Chapman, who had been corresponding with Derek on the design of Lotus Mark III. With its Ulster body replaced, and now in Jim McDonald's hands, the Uffindel car raced on, transferring to Graeme Steinfort in 1972 and raced in historic events throughout Australia.

'Australian rules' Austin Seven racing became very popular during the 1960s, and, unlike the British 750 Formula, Australian regulations allowed the cars to run with superchargers and to be stripped of wings, lights, and other impedimenta. The result was cars that became

Bruce and 'Pop' McLaren pose with their modified Ulster in 1955, showing the Big Seven front axle and small diameter rear wheels. Phil Kerr's Nippy can be seen across the road. (Author collection)

Bruce McLaren's Ulster and John Cooper's Cooper Special Number One at the Norman Foster designed McLaren Headquarters, Woking, England. (Author collection)

'Pop' McLaren decided to call it a day and concentrate on Bruce's driving career.

Bruce was, by now, exchanging letters with Jack Brabham, and bought a bobtailed Cooper T39 sports racer from Jack in 1956. He ran with Jack in a two-car team of Formula Two Coopers in the New Zealand Grand Prix, and was subsequently selected to become the first NZGP 'Driver to Europe' – a scheme designed to give a New Zealand driver experience with the best in the world. Bruce quickly became a part of the works Cooper Team, then – following Jack Brabham's example – founded McLaren Racing in 1963. The company built fearsome 'big-

banger' Can-Am sports cars, winning the championship five years in a row. Bruce was sadly killed in a testing accident, but McLaren Racing, in a lasting legacy, took its first F1 championship with Fittipaldi in 1974, then its second with James Hunt driving in 1976. Victories also followed at the Indianapolis 500, and further F1 world titles in the hands of Lauda, Prost, Senna, Hakkinen, and Lewis Hamilton in 2008.

The McLaren Ulster is another candidate for the most influential Austin Seven post World War Two, along with the Lotus Mark III. It is spectacularly symmetrical that the engine for the current road McLaren Supercar is built by Ricardo in Sussex – the very same company that designed the 1936 Austin Seven cylinder head that the young Bruce McLaren experimented with over 60 years previously.

Today the McLaren Ulster is proudly displayed amongst the Can-Am and Formula One cars at the Foster + Partners-designed McLaren headquarters building.

more highly developed and significantly quicker than their European cousins. In 1967, John Whitehouse shipped his Austin racer to Britain, altered in detail to comply with 750 Motor Club rules, and was instantly amongst the very quickest home-brewed Sevens. This inspired Tony Johns – who had worked in England, and spread barely-believed stories of his 50bhp, 100mph (160km/h) racing Seven – to organise an five-car Australian 'raid' in 1981. For two months, the cars competed half-way round the globe, amongst VSCC and 750 Motor Club compliant cars, in races and sprints.

Archetypal Australian specials are offset to the left-hand side, but retain the conventional crown wheel and pinion set in modified axle casings. Front axles are Sports-based, with soft but well-damped springing complementing chassis stiffened by the tubular steel body frame. This arrangement allows the vintage Magneto-pattern engine to be moved rearwards, in the interests of better weight distribution and traction, and a forward-pointing Roots-type supercharger to be mounted on an aluminium cast gear cover between engine and radiator, driven by a spur gear from the camshaft.

The Royal Mail delivers to the New South Wales outback in an unusual early Australian-bodied Seven.

Titled *A Seven in the Antipodes* – although the driver may have another word for it. (Austin publicity)

The simple log intake manifold is combined with a Brooklands-style exhaust manifold and short tailpipe; late Ruby Ricardo-pattern heads were favoured by most. The whole effect is very workmanlike, stripping the components down to a minimum and wasting no volume in the compact and light bodywork.

The quickest of the Australian visitors was Tony Johns, and in winning four races at Cadwell Park, he managed to lap some six seconds quicker than the fastest British car present, leaving the 750 establishment rocking on its heels, but nonetheless chuckling in appreciation.

CHAPTER FIFTEEN

LONG HAUL SEVENS

IT is an interesting facet of being human that some slight – and apparently insignificant – chance happening in childhood can fundamentally influence our adult lives. When young John Coleman was in bed, suffering from influenza, his parents bought him a copy of *Tschiffely's Ride*. This book detailed the story of a journey that started in 1925, travelling from Buenos Aires to New York by horse. Along the way, the journey involved crossing the Andes into Chile, visiting Inca ruins in Peru, and making his way through Central American jungles, Mexico, and finally on to Texas, the Mississippi Delta, and – after two years on the road – New York.

Some 20 years later, John – who had owned a number of Austin Sevens – rescued a 1925 Chummy, registered MO 6320. Something clicked; the date of the car's manufacture coincidentally matched the date that Tschiffely's journey took place. John decided, more or less on impulse, that he would replicate the journey that had lived on in his mind ever since childhood.

Carefully preparing the car, and with encouragement and support from that great Austin Seven enthusiast Lord Montagu, and Austin Motor Co, John set off for South America by boat in late 1959. The

Lord Montagu congratulates John Coleman after his epic 13,000 mile (17,702km) trans-continental adventure through South and North America. (750 Motor Club archive)

task ahead was immense – the passes into Peru ascended to 18,000ft (5486m), where the car would run short of oxygen, what modest power there was would be reduced by 40 per cent, and the water in the radiator would boil at a far lower temperature.

John had decided that prudence was his password, and to always be mindful that, with no physical back-up, rocky road surfaces would be tackled at modest speeds to keep stresses and strains on the car to a minimum. Nevertheless, his story would contain extreme heat, rain, winds, and electric storms – not to mention less-than-friendly individuals, jungle tracks, sandstorms, insects, possible tropical diseases, and border police that grew incredulous each time he had to recount his intended destination. He was obliged to avoid Columbia, and to take a boat from Ecuador to Panama. A few weeks later, he crossed from Mexico into the United States. Despite this, John and his Chummy ultimately covered at least 13,000mi (20,921km).

Famously John then wrote about his fascinating and dangerous journey in *Coleman's Drive*, published in 1964. The last stretch of more than 2000mi (3218km) – from the Mexican border to New York, after his adventures in South and Central America – is skipped over in the last couple of pages, partly due to somebody en-route stealing his photographs!

With history repeating itself, John's book was in turn read by Vince Leek, who half-jokingly talked about it in 2003, with a group of fellow Austin Sevenists who had driven to Gibraltar. As a result, a plan was

hatched to take six Austin Sevens to Buenos Aires, to follow Coleman's route. They would cross the Andes, to drop down to Santiago on the Pacific, then north to La Serena in Chile, then double back on a different route over the Andes passes via Cordoba and back to Buenos Aires. This totalled about 3000mi (4828km), and from sea level rose to an altitude of 4784m, or about 15,000ft.

In January 2005, John Coleman saw the party off: Richard and Marlies Bishop in a 1938 special, George and Joy Mooney in a 1934 Cambridge special, Peter Peeters and Andriana Ruiz a 1926 Chummy, Frank and Jane McDonald a 1929 Chummy, Allan Fullalove and Geoff Cox a 1932 Box, and Vince Leek with Chris Parkhurst in a 1930 Chummy.

The cars were each modified to some extent, with 12-volt electrics and lockable compartments, steel crankshafts, careful choice of gear ratios and back axles, and with shared spares distributed between them. Their many adventures on the way, and the interesting people they met, are recounted in *Austins over the Andes* by Vince Leek, published in 2008.

The Austin Seven had been taken on epic journeys almost from its very introduction. The first-ever around the world Austin Seven trip was accomplished in a Chummy by Gladys de Havilland – the plucky 1920s 'new woman' of the aircraft-building family. Sir Herbert Austin enthusiastically waved Gladys off in 1928, and must have been

The most travelled Cambridge-bodied 1934 special in the world; George and Joy Mooney picnic at Beaulieu in 2016 with their trans-continental Austin – having traversed North and South America, and the whole of Europe. (Author collection)

even more delighted to welcome her back the following year after a gruelling trip … One could hardly imagine better publicity for the Seven.

Gladys set off westwards by ship to New York, then made her way across the United States – all the time visiting Austin dealers on stretches of what were still primitive, barely-paved roads. Upon reaching San Francisco, she went by ship to New Zealand, then on to Australia, where she feared that at "any moment the Seven would fall to pieces, so intense was the shaking over the rock-strewn roads." Crossing over to India, where the roads were found to be mainly in good condition, both car and driver were next given a trial by intense heat. Both survived the challenge, and moved back through Europe, with the car coping well in mixed conditions through Italy and France.

Having crossed Australia, south to north, in 1929, Hector MacQuarrie and his friend Dick Matthews (both New Zealanders) then successfully circumnavigated planet Earth in McQuarrie's Seven. Macquarrie wrote about their experiences in his second book, the 1933 title *Round the World in a Baby Austin*.

Starting in Wellington with an Austin Seven named Emily, their route went east across the Pacific, but came to a premature end when the ship sank taking Emily with it. It is still waiting to be found again, 3mi (4.8km) down on the ocean floor! A month later, and having recovered their composure, they purchased Emily II. Herbert Austin's good wishes were cabled to them as they left, via Tahiti to San Francisco. Travelling south, they stayed at one-dollar-a-night 'auto camp' cabins – the forerunners of motels – and the coastal Spanish Missions, visiting the Los Angeles Bantam dealer in Hollywood. They became bored by the lack of alcohol (due to the Prohibition), were awed by the Grand Canyon, and found Texas petrol 'delightfully cheap.' They then went south to Daytona Beach, where Campbell had recently set 750cc records in the special works Seven, then up the East Coast to New York.

Taking the Cunard Line's ocean liner RMS *Aurania* right into London, Emily II was delivered in a crate back into the country she left barely six months previously. Fully checked and serviced at Longbridge, she was soon travelling south to the French Riviera, and on to Mussolini's Italy. The intrepid travellers enthusiastically explained to any quizzical enquirer en-route that the GB plate on Emily II stood for 'Gor Blimey!' – the car being laden down, with springs flattened by a tent, camping equipment, bedding and spares.

The car crossed the Adriatic to Albania, then to Istanbul, traversing unsafe bridges by moving bits of deck where parts were missing. Then it was on to Palestine, Damascus, Baghdad, Persia, Afghanistan, India, and Malaya, before being shipped back into Australia at Darwin. It was

The Hector Macquarrie/Dick Matthews trans-global Chummy 'Emily II' is examined by aboriginal Australians sporting boomerangs and extravagant headwear. (Courtesy Ken Cooke)

Clive and Sheila Ball smiling and happy at Dover in 1972, on their return from a 47,000 mile overland tour journey round the world – Clive had set out seven years earlier as a single man! (750 Motor Club archive)

an extraordinary journey, and all written up in British public school prose. Their journey is, politically, impossible to duplicate today.

In slightly more recent times, Clive Ball spent *Seven years with Samantha* – the title of his book, and containing the name of his Seven – setting out from England for Australia in late 1965 in a 1929 Aluminium Saloon Seven. He then travelled onwards to New Zealand in 1970, still in Samantha, but this time with his new Australian wife Sheila – showing just what a dangerous pastime Austin Sevens are!

Clive's outward journey was almost entirely overland, across Europe and Turkey to Jerusalem, then via Kuwait to Karachi, and through Malaya to Darwin. From there, he turned west and followed the Australian coast down to New Zealand, Honolulu, Vancouver, then right down through South America, before shipping from Buenos Aires to Barcelona, and back home. It comprised a colossal mileage, and was more of a world tour than a circumnavigation.

Other mega journeys in Austin Sevens include Brian Milton's drive down Africa, and Graham Parkin and Roger Shea, who drove from the UK to Australia in 1969 and 1971, respectively. In 1982, Tom Newsome decided to emigrate from Melbourne, Derbyshire, to Melbourne in Australia, driving the 1937 Austin Ruby, named Egbert, and taking in the sights along the way. Tom's journey across France to Italy was via Andorra, and thence to Austria via a trip to Naples. Soon, it was a zig-zag route to wherever Tom's fancy – and Egbert's wheels – took them. A few de-cokes later, they finally made the trip overland to Australia.

In 2006, Route 66 was tackled by a group. Then, in 2007, three 1930s Austin Seven Saloons – namely Rusty, Dusty, and Crusty – echoed the Peking to Paris run of exactly a century earlier, performing an epic 7500mi (12,070km) dash from Beijing to Paris in just 42 days. A third of their route, which closely followed the original old roads, consisted of barely-paved surfaces. The crews were the prime movers Vince Leek, Chris Parkhurst, and Stan Price, paired with co-drivers Steve Briggs, Mike Jones, and Johnny Johnson. Over the journey they traversed China, Mongolia, Russia, Latvia, Lithuania, Poland, Germany, Belgium, and France – an amazing feat of endurance for mature motor cars and their mature chauffeurs.

There was a return of the main players to the Argentine in 2009, for a run starting in Buenos Aires and taking in the southernmost tip of South American at Tierra Del Fuego, then round the coast and back to Buenos Aires to total 5000mi (8046km).

In 2013, three Austin Sevens again retraced the whole 11,000mi (17,70km) described in *Coleman's Drive*, traversing two continents and twelve countries in four months. The cars this time were: Stan Price's light and simple 1932 RN Saloon, Dusty; the 1933 RP de Luxe Saloon, Bertie (owned by Jack Peppiatt and Amanda Peters, and with 12-volt electrics and semi-Girling rear axle); and Feisty, a 1929 Chummy that had previously completed the Argentinian trip in the hands of Diana Garside and husband River Dukes – the latter introduced to the pleasure and pain of Austineering on the Route 66 trip. Some running repairs were determined prudent on the 80-year-old Sevens upon

Left to right: Peter Peeters from Geneva and Steve Berg from Fribourg, both with Nippys, Iain Mansell and his 65, and Steve Bradford-Best with his Nippy. Photo taken during a pause at Interlaken during Eurotour 2012. (Author collection)

arrival in Lima, with many locals enthusiastically helping out, before the cars set off again, and the crews were welcomed visitors to South American classic car collections.

In July 2012 Eunice Kratky and Guy Butcher set out in their 1928 Austin Chummy from Baltimore, USA, for Alaska. Once there, they then travelled down the West Coast, through Central and South America, to Punta Arenas at the southerly tip of Chile. They managed the 18,000mi (28,800km) journey in seven months, raising money for a children's charity.

The 750 Motor Club has successfully organised many 1000mi (1609km) Austin Seven Anniversary John O'Groats to Lands End runs (or LEJOG, for short) to celebrate the 1922 birth of the Seven. The very quickest non-stop cars are in the 18-hour bracket, and this 1000-mile event has come to be a standard unit of measurement for serious long haul exponents.

Travelling long distances in an Austin Seven has become a very popular pastime, with continental 750 Motor Club 'Eurotour' runs attracting dozens of entries, and necessitating a waiting list; the limiting factor for the organisers is not the enthusiasm of the Seven owners, but simply the logistics of finding enough suitable hotel rooms for entrants en route.

The Austin Seven, with its light weight, low gearing, good torque, and rugged simplicity is an ideal vehicle for tackling the Pennines or the Alps, and every proposed run is still immediately over-subscribed – Sir Herbert would surely approve.

EILEEN AND KEN COOKE'S DINGO

Ken and Eileen Cooke are two of the most familiar faces in the postwar world of Austin Sevens. What came to be named Dingo (after Col Arthur Waite's first Seven racer) was, in 1965, a complete 1930 Chummy that had been reduced to a pile of bits.

GF 4762 was rebuilt, the bits first running together again in unison in 1975 in the 750 Motor Club Brooklands Centre San Marino Rally, which involved 25 Austin Sevens and a baggage support van. For Ken and Eileen and their two youngest children, this was their first trip abroad of any kind, and was a huge adventure.

Apart from some navigation problems, the drive to San Marino was trouble-free. On the return, however, 19 spokes broke on the newly-rebuilt wheels, along with one rear spring. These were all repaired from 'communal' spares, and, with 2500 Austin Seven miles (4023km) covered in one go, Ken and Eileen were hooked!

Monte Carlo and Liechtenstein followed, then joining 30 other Sevens for the 750 Motor Club's 50th anniversary – taking in five capitals in five days to replicate Bill Boddy's road test. 1992 marked the 70th anniversary of the Austin Seven, with 60 examples embarking on a tour of seven countries, Dingo still behaving well. East and West Germany were next, then the south of France, Sicily in 1998, then Gibraltar in 2003. John O'Groats to Lands End was bested in 32 hours 18 minutes, Eisenach was visited, and capped off with a trip to the Dordogne alongside the Tacot Club Calaisien (twinned with the 750 Motor Club).

In 2006, Route 66 beckoned. Vince Leek (in his 1929 Chummy), George and Joy Mooney (in their lovely Cambridge special), Richard and Marlies Bishop (in their special), and Stan Price (in his 1934 Box Saloon), all organised by Diana Garside with River Dukes, in memory of her father's lifelong, but sadly never realised, ambition. Disembarking with the cars in New Jersey, six days were spent checking the cars and driving to Chicago, via the Butler American Austin and Bantam factory.

Then it was 2500mi (4023km) west along the 'Mother Road' – a total of 13 states, and every mile punctuated with waving and good wishes. The journey included side trips to the Grand Canyon and Las Vegas where, as always, they were warmly greeted. As Kent put it, "the best thing that we have ever done!"

Mechanical problems among the five Austins were limited to one burst tyre, and one dynamo failure. Unlike the others, Dingo was still running on its original crankshaft, rather than a Phoenix. It already had coupled brakes, with a simple modification to improve the balance of the rears, and the front brake cams had been filed down to improve the lever action – the work of a Saturday morning. One front spring leaf was removed by Ken, to give a more level ride attitude when loaded for a long journey. A central 'trough' on top of the tunnel was added to keep a torch and other travel items handy, along with a map shelf below the dashboard and a lead light socket. And that is it – apart from those small convenience additions, Dingo is equipped as standard, and as it left Longbridge.

Since 1975, the original Austin crankshaft, which has never been re-ground, has now done another 153,000mi (246,229km) in Eileen and Ken's hands. According to Ken, "the bearings are quite oval, but give plenty of room for the lubricant to get through!"

That may sell Ken's careful preparations short, for, in 1978, Ken and Dingo raced for two and a half seasons in 750 Motor Club Austin Seven races. This was a series largely instigated by Ken, to show just what a versatile little car Sir Herbert created. Dingo did not win any races, but Ken did once get awarded 'Driver of the Day' – something of an understatement!

Ken and Eileen Cooke pause on Route 66 in their ever faithful and much travelled Chummy 'Dingo.' (Courtesy Ken Cooke)

CHAPTER SIXTEEN

THE 1950s AUSTIN SEVEN SPECIAL BUILDING CRAZE

FOR a dozen or so years – straddling the 1950s – there were hundreds, if not thousands, of Austin Seven specials under construction. As noted by Jack French, many of those started remained unfinished; sometimes for years, sometimes forever.

Companies sprang up overnight to cater for the new craze, and established businesses like Cambridge Engineering were joined by Lotus and others, offering comprehensive services for all special building needs. The advent and success of 750 Formula had given a great boost to the hobby of special building, and the next surge came in 1953, with the introduction of GRP (glass reinforced plastic) bodies, promising an affordable modern looking road sports car for all.

Ultimately, this would lead to the development of the British kit car industry, as, at that time, self-assembly of a motor car did not attract purchase tax. This was a crippling additional expense, aimed at restricting the home market for factory-built cars, the majority of which were destined for the export market, to pay back the war loans that had kept the United Kingdom afloat and fighting in World War Two.

Postwar British production sports cars were highly desirable, particularly in the United States. With William Lyons' ground-

The Dick Morris special – a nicely detailed 'middle period' homebuilt example, which made a recent welcome return visit to the UK in the enthusiastic hands of owner Luc Wynen. (Author collection)

breaking XK120 of 1948, and the subsequent all-enveloping streamline-bodied Austin Healeys, Triumph TR2s, and MGAs, these new glamorous body shapes became the thing to have or to aspire to. As 90 per cent of the production was exported, and purchase tax added to the remaining ten per cent, these sports cars were way out of financial range of the average young enthusiast. The solution was, clearly, to build one yourself.

The first – and admittedly stumpy – GRP Stiletto bodyshell was followed by a fair imitation of an MGA, moulded by both Ashley Laminates and Falcon Shells. The Super Sabre, and the pretty Heron shell used on Divas, were also vaguely styled after contemporary sports cars.

Robin Read's Dante showed what could be done with single-curvature aluminium with the Clubman all-enveloper – a clever design by Jim Shaw. This exploited the stiffening effect of a single curved panel, on which the edges were either fixed or – if free – reinforced with light tube, producing a plough-share wing form that had echoes of 1920s Austin Seven rakish wing shapes by Burley. A number of Dantes ran in 750 Formula.

Just as professional coach-builders had found the Austin Seven chassis to be an excellent platform upon which to build a specialised little sports car in the 1920s, so 30 years later Herbert's baby again became the inspiration behind many enthusiastic projects. This time, however, the work was mainly carried out by amateur engineers.

The thought of a modern-looking sports car was beguiling. The all-enveloping bodies looked far more convincing on late long-wheelbase chassis, though there were many disappointments waiting for any special builder naïve enough to believe that all that needed to be done was to take off the old Austin body and replace it with a GRP shell. The better examples worked well enough, and a number have survived. Even the occasional 50-year-old unused GRP shell still appears on the scene.

The lure of building a practical small sports car from an Austin Seven was pervasive, and those generally looking for genuine

The Ashley Laminates/Falcon Shells MGA-like GRP-bodied specials of Andrew Waring, Mark Vincent and Iain Mansell line up together at Beaulieu in 1999. (Courtesy Ken Cooke)

CAPA

Spurred on by a hilarious talk by John Bolster in December 1945 to members of the Bristol Aeroplane Company Motor Club, Dick Caesar and some enthusiastic collaborators came up with a cheap, mainly grass racing, Formula.

Having been racing stripped Austin Seven chassis amongst themselves since 1933 on Joe Fry's estate (by chance, in parallel to the Colliers brothers' activities on the other side of the Atlantic), Caesar, Adrian Butler, Price, and Aldridge – from whose initials the CAPA name was derived – came up with some simple rules of engagement.

A maximum weight was set at 9cwt (~457kg) to protect the track surface, no road-equipped cars were allowed, and one gallon (5l) of fuel and smooth tyres on the driving wheels kept speeds and costs low.

Austin Sevens, which were available for five pounds, naturally formed the majority of the entries, with a few appearances from GN, Morgan, and Morris cars thrown in for luck. An amusing time was had by all prior to the World War Two airfield-based tracks coming into play, and CAPA spawned many successful and important hillclimb and circuit racing cars and personalities.

Frank Walker in his stark – but, more importantly, light – short wheelbase CAPA racer, at Purton in 1948. Note the small motorcycle fuel tank. (Courtesy Ted Walker/Ferret Fotographics)

CAPA grass-track racing in 1948 at Purton, near Bristol. This was an inexpensive motoring competition, and very popular. (Courtesy Ted Walker/Ferret Fotographics)

Providing a tow-start for a 1948 CAPA Austin racer, fitted with Morgan sliding pillar front suspension. (Courtesy Ferret Fotographics)

Bill Boult's neat and quick 750 Formula special at AMOC Silverstone in 1955, about to be gobbled up by a passing Bentley. (Courtesy Ferret Fotographics)

performance found that – as demonstrated in sprints, hillclimbs, trials, and 750 Formula racing – a Seven was fastest of all, with as little bodywork as possible. That simple fact also partly explains why special building became so popular. Remove the Austin Seven body, incline the steering column with a wedge, bolt on a seat, and you have a ready-made CAPA type racer (see sidebar) in the space of a couple of hours. Further improvements were generally simple, cheap, and quick: flattening the springs to lower the centre of gravity and reduce roll oversteer; immobilising one front spring shackle to stop the front axle beam from moving sideways; carefully overhauling or improving the brakes; swapping an updraught carburettor for a later side-draught, or an SU; and so on. The effect of each on an Austin Seven will be felt by the driver as soon as it is done.

Being a 'special,' the car does not need to comply with anybody's ideas except that of its creator, and does not need to be considered finished at any stage of its life. This, naturally enough, leads to ever-evolving iterations of improvements whenever its builder chooses. The degree of satisfaction that can be readily obtained by special building is like any form of self-expression – addictive. Many of the steps to improve performance on a simple car can each be dealt with on a Saturday morning, with incremental improvements. Not that this stops more advanced Austin Seven specials from being thought out as a cohesive whole – as always, the objective and purpose should ideally be decided upon before cutting any metal – and most successful specials are well thought-out entities, even if allowances are made for future development.

By 1956, Les Montgomery, a Bromley furniture maker and Seven enthusiast, was making a neat ash-framed aluminium-panelled lightweight body that was all single curvature. It included a shapely and distinctive tail that tapered to the diameter of the rear-mounted spare wheel. The body could be fitted to both short- and long-wheelbase chassis, and, within a couple of years, Les had expanded his business, Super Accessories, to include all kinds of performance equipment.

Like Cambridge Engineering, Bowden Engineering (in Devon), and several others, Les Montgomery published a special builder's guide to make use of his own products. Included was basic advice on renewing any worn or broken components, adding re-made original-pattern replacement parts sourced from a variety of cottage industry engineers. By 1962, virtually any Seven rolling chassis item was available from a number of suppliers.

These parts were, of course, also in demand for rebuilding standard Austin Sevens. With the cross-over from predominantly building specials in the early 1950s, to restoring more and more original cars from the mid-1960s onwards, demand has swelled – and been met – for newly-engineered Austin Seven replica spares.

Whatmough-Hewitt, Alta, and Ricardo-pattern Aluminium Cylinder Head Company alloy cylinder heads were available prewar, but post-World War Two a whole industry sprang up, offering a wide range of cylinder heads, finned deep sumps, simple inlet and exhaust manifolds, and valve chest covers – many cast in alloy by the Horeston Foundry in Derby. The full-race Dante Austin Seven engine – with all its alloy bits and pieces – is a pretty good imitation of an exotic be-finned Miller race engine. It gave the enthusiast something to lust after, and certainly changed the normally modest under-bonnet look to something more purposeful.

Robin Read of Dante was highly supportive of 750 Formula, organising a front-running three-car team with Roy Lee and Peter Dawe, later becoming Colin Chapman's sales manager at Lotus, and author to a number of motoring books. Unfortunately, by May 1959, Robin's Dante business had gone into liquidation.

Picking up the ball, Read's sales employee, Jem Marsh, formed the Speedex company, and began offering a very similar range of products for Austin Seven specials. His range also included distinctive cast alloy road wheels, and a simple two-seater body with separate wings and a nose cone. This body proved to be very popular, and Jem won the 1959 Goodacre Trophy in his 'works' Speedex. We were to hear a great deal more of Jem Marsh, who, in 1960, collaborated with Frank Costin to build the first plywood-chassied Marcos. Early examples of these were

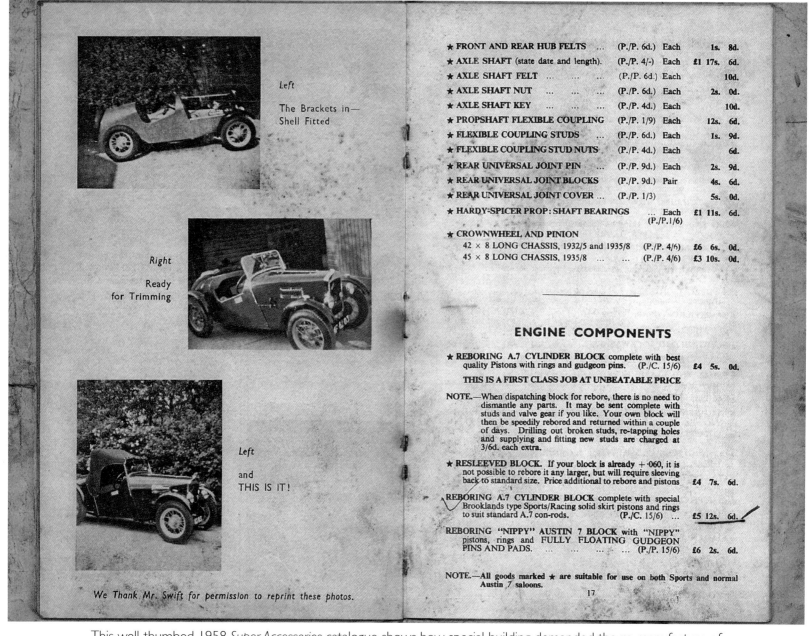

This well-thumbed 1958 *Super Accessories* catalogue shows how special building demanded the re-manufacture of vital standard Austin parts – a valuable cottage industry that continues today. (Author collection)

successfully raced by John Sutton, Jackie Oliver, and Jackie Stewart. The Dennis Adams-design fastback Marcos was followed by Volvo-powered 1800s, and the Mini-Marcos was the sole British finisher at Le Mans in 1966. A whole range of Marcos models followed, including Le Mans cars and innovative composite bodywork, and Jem raced on into his 70s in historic events, always retaining his original interest in Austin Sevens.

Pat Stephens' 1953 book *Building and racing my 750* was a bestseller, and included, in honest detail, his mistakes during the build process as well as his success, along with a guide to performance. His hand-held timing of the Stoneham Special of 8.5 seconds to 50mph (80km/h) was the equal of a Triumph TR2, and faster than an MGA!

Modified Chummys were raced in 750 Formula by Sid Marler, John Michelsen, Derek Wooton, and others, and many 'Hot Box Saloons' were seen on the road and in trials. Some enterprising souls even devoted time to extracting more power from the engines of Ruby Saloons, notable examples of which sported bright yellow or red

Jem Marsh in his pre-Speedex, pre-Marcos days, on Trengwainton's narrow surface in 1956. The radiator is almost completely blanked off to assist warming up for this short dash up the hill.

The Cowley twin plug head and twin Weber carburettors on the inclined engine of Mike Featherstonehaugh's aerodynamic ultimate FRA Austin special, built in the mid-1990s. (Courtesy Ken Cooke)

paint jobs years before Sevenists Graham Hill and George Hulbert's Speedwell company gave the same colour treatment to its racing A35s.

Notable amongst other early 1950s 750 Formula proponents were Bill and John Wilkes, Dave Rees, the Millard brothers, Lionel Hockney and Johnnie Moore, Bryan Small, Adrian Wontner, and Derek White. Each of these individuals moved on to greater things, but all had a hugely enjoyable time building quite simple competition cars from Herbert Austin's parts bin.

As the 1960s dawned, more complex ways of tuning the Seven engine evolved; first came the all-conquering Worden that married all modern ancillaries to prewar fundamentals, then Dave Boorer's high-revving Keith Dixon engine in DEB. In 1965, the Goodacre Trophy was won by Jim Yardley in his appropriately-named Complexity (as a passing salute to Jack French's Simplicity of a decade earlier), in which the Austin engine was laid down on its side, dry sumped, and the car run on small-diameter wide tyres. It was a car of minute frontal area compared to a VSCC-spec Ulster, and some distance from Austin's original concept. Twin plug cylinder heads featured on Bill Cowley's highly-developed engines, the timing of each individual plug firing sequentially to maximise efficiency and extracting even more power, and at higher engine revs than had been thought possible just a few years previously.

All this development came at the cost of wrecked original Austin components, and overlapped the realisation amongst many that this state of affairs was not sustainable. The 750 Motor Club therefore altered 750 Formula rules to allow Reliant engines to be used with any gearbox or rear axle, and 750 Formula racing went from strength to strength, the current iteration using almost stock Fiat 1100cc engines. 750 Formula remains the longest-lived national racing Formula, having a history longer even than Formula One.

The Austin Seven special building craze of the 1950s was enormously successful in spawning a huge competition heritage for the UK. This was quite apart from the countless hours of pleasure and basic engineering education that it gave to a whole generation of enthusiastic young men and women, at a time when such opportunities might have otherwise been denied by the ravages of war, and the austerity of the hard won peacetime that followed.

This was a phenomenon almost unique to the British Isles, and if it came at a cost of otherwise unused and unloved small motor cars, the advances and advantages were reward enough in human terms.

CHAPTER SEVENTEEN

RENAISSANCE

THE Austin Seven had come to something of a turning point in its history by 1960. A great many had been scrapped, as is the order of most things mechanical, having come to the end of their (very) useful lives. The youngest Seven by then was a secondhand car, over 20 years old. Many had already been destroyed in World War Two, and even more were continually written-off in road accidents; the national rate for road accidents being more than eight times higher than today, per vehicle road mile travelled.

Some Sevens, however, were still giving good service as family transport. Many, too, were in the hands of younger enthusiasts and modified for trials or racing, or rebuilt as specials, and a relative few – including historic cars – were owned by VSCC and 750 MC Members, who understood and respected their importance. As they moved into history, the place of the Seven in the romance of early motoring and sporting achievement became yet more self-evident.

The MOT's ten year test seemed to focus the realisation that there was a threat to future use of the Austin Seven as a road car. What's more, the possibility steadily grew that rare and increasingly valuable

What could be built in 1925 can readily be built almost a century later – all coachwork can be repaired or reproduced. (Author collection)

examples might be lost to the scrapyard, simply on account of the ignorance of their current owners.

The good sense of seriously competitive racing with 30- and 40-year-old components was avidly discussed. This was partly fuelled by the extraordinary achievements of 750 Formula, where a 750 special could hold 7000rpm in top at Silverstone – a solid 100mph (160km/h). The cars competing, however, had fewer and fewer Austin parts left in them.

The author was present – wide-eyed and delighted – at the 1961 750 Motor Club Welsh Harp Wiggle Driving Tests, when Club Chairman Mike Eyre first appeared with the works Orange TT Ulster. The car was fresh from a beautiful restoration and received all-round acclaim, the first of several important cars that Mike collected to form into a Seven collection. A surviving works Twin-Cam was exhibited on the 750 MC stand at The Racing Car Show in its second year, where Stuart Rolt complained about its general condition. At Château Impney, a Grasshopper surfaced to general amazement and surprised expressions of pleasure. All around, there was a much-debated sense that Austin Seven history was not only truly important but also under threat, and that something urgently needed to be done.

Other groups joined together, and, with the majority of 750 MC membership coming from southern counties, a new club was set up in Derby in 1962. Solely devoted to the Seven, the new group was named The Prewar Austin Seven Club, distinguishing it from the postwar Austin and BMC offerings that, for commercial reasons, shared the Austin Seven name.

By late 1962, 750 MC's Mike Ware, John Thorne, and Viv Orchard had decided to hold a rally the following summer exclusively for Austin Sevens, in an attempt to get as many cars and owners together in one place. This caused great excitement, and the event was ambitiously titled the 750 MC National Austin Seven Rally, to be held in the grounds of the home of the supportive Lord Montague, at Beaulieu Abbey.

The driving tests at Beaulieu require considerable concentration. This is Robert and Fenella Leigh in 2013. (Courtesy Nick Salmon)

The stripped Ulster of JF Harris, running as a racing car at the 1964 VSCC Silverstone event, and cornering fast enough to generate significant tyre deflection. (Courtesy Ferret Fotographics)

John Miles gave more focus to the movement in early 1963, by founding a register for all surviving Sports Austin Sevens with his cousin John Hinchliffe and John Thorne. After a highly successful July Beaulieu Rally, where 300 Sevens turned up on the day, and together – perhaps – with the publicity from John Coleman's recent epic drive from Buenos Aires to New York, the world of the Austin Seven suddenly lit up again very brightly. This light was never again to fade.

The Sports Register was soon expanded to include all surviving Austin Sevens, including rolling chassis and even just frames with a number or a log book. The first AGM of the Austin Seven Register was held in 1964, at the

The 750 Motor Club Beaulieu Rally always brings out individual ways of displaying your Austin Seven, in this case a long wheelbase Tourer. (Author collection)

There are always short- and long-chassied Austin Sevens, patiently waiting their turn to be re-built and to start their lives all over again … (Author collection)

A 1978 10,000km record attempt, at a then empty Goodwood. Col Waite drops the Union Jack as Stirling Moss takes the first stint in the Ulster replica, watched by Chris Gould (on the left), Vince Leek, and original works Austin race drivers. (Courtesy Chris Gould)

in 1967, Pat Kimber set up a specials register. 750 Formula regulations evolved, too, allowing competitors to field a 750 Formula car that didn't contain a single Austin Seven component.

At the 1968 AGM of the Austin Seven Register, of 400 members, a demand was made by 25 members present (and about 35 non-members) for the Board of 750 MC to give good reasons for the Austin Seven Register to remain within the club. This demand marked the beginnings of some division within the postwar Austin Seven movement, and emotions were high. There were, it seems, many misconceptions about the intentions of those who did not share, or adequately express, differing viewpoints. In some ways this was not a bad thing; many splinter groups set up all over Britain as small local Austin Seven clubs in their own right, and catered for modest-sized groups, operating at various levels and enthusiastically organising themselves. In other ways, the lack of a common voice for a hobby about which people held surprisingly strong views meant that a degree of the power of joint representation was lost. Inevitably, many Seven groups unwittingly duplicated other enthusiasts' efforts.

It was not until The Austin Seven Clubs Association was formed in 1968 that a common bond was truly re-established and all these threads were pulled together again. This voluntary and most important organisation happily remains respected, valuable, and

750 MC Brooklands Centre. John Pitchers regularly included 'Register News' in the *750 Motor Club Bulletin*, and the book *Coleman's Drive* was published.

By 1965, 750 Formula allowed Reliant 600cc-engined cars to compete. This significantly reduced the numbers of Austin Seven-engined cars on the grid, but Jim Yardley and Bill Cowley each built super little 'ultimate spec' Austin-engined cars that turned out to be spectacular performers. Austin Seven specials had been frowned upon at some early Beaulieu rallies, but this changed over time, and,

At the Goodwood 10,000 mile (16,093km) record attempts. Vince Leek (standing on the left) talks with Col Waite (seated), along with Freddie Henry, Ron Norwood, Pat Driscoll, Bert Hadley, and their wives. (Courtesy Chris Gould)

The VSCC Lakeland Trial, 2015. Jock Mackinnon, in a 1930 Chummy, climbs the slippery 1-in-4 gradient 'Drumhouse' section at Honister Slate mine. (Courtesy Gary Clarke)

vigorous today. The A7CA began publishing a numbered quarterly booklet of all things Austin Seven, made available to all A7CA clubs for their own distribution. The cover design is based on prewar Austin Seven handbooks, and coloured grey. For that reason, it is known today generically as 'The Grey Book' or 'Grey Mag.'

In 1968, too, Bob Wyatt's ground-breaking book *The Austin Seven – The Motor for the Million, 1922-1939* was first published, and this painstakingly researched and scholarly work became an instant bestseller. It was reprinted several times, and remains one of the best studies of Sir Herbert's baby. The book was eagerly devoured by Sevenists of all persuasions, and is still a standard reference work, having been written whilst many of the main players were still alive.

People began to talk about 'The Austin Seven Movement' as a rare example of enthusiastic dedication to the single model of a manufacturer, rather than to the make as a whole. It was reflective, not only of the variety of types of Austin Sevens, but also of the vast range of activities for which the Austin Seven is still an obvious choice. Where once they might have been spread apart by their differences of approach or interests, so the world of Austin Seven restorers, historians, special builders, Sunday potterers and polishers, racers, sprinters, distance drivers, and socialisers came together as one appreciative and mutually supportive group.

The original manufacturer's *Austin Seven Owner's Handbook* on use and maintenance was augmented by the excellent *The Austin*

VSCC Welsh Trial 2016. At Cwm Whitton Farm, Stephen and Tina Fathers (in an Austin Abbot special) look to be displeased at having 'landed in it.' (Courtesy Gary Clarke)

Seven Book by RT Nicholson, which used many of the former's original illustrations and. 1935 this was joined by Goodwins' *The Book of the Austin Seven*, published by Pitman, which spanned the war years. This was still in such demand in the 1950s that it was reprinted each year, up until around 1962, and gave many a young enthusiast valuable information about the workings of a Seven. The 750 MC later published *The Austin Seven Companion*, incorporating much of the established running information, as well as sections on improvements, performance, and get-you-home tips. It is still in print at the time of writing.

Austin dealers had all but run out of new spares for Sevens by the late 1950s, but brand new ex-government surplus items – even crankshafts and crown wheel and pinion sets – were available from dealers such as Pride and Clarke in Balham, South London (immortalised in the film *Blow-up*), and Jack Dalby at Kirby Wiske. The standard spares that had initially been re-made, mainly to feed the special builders of the late 1950s, became in great demand for the restoration of early original Austin Sevens. The attrition caused by the building of specials was more than counter-balanced by the availability of re-manufactured spares, which has now been in full swing for more than 50 years. The scale of this cannot be matched by any

A delightful study, as two immaculate 1980s family Austin Chummys mingle with fellow road run entries for a pleasant day out in like-minded company. (Courtesy Neill Bruce)

FITZMAURICE SINGLE-SEATER

Amongst the more recent examples of successful hillclimb Austin Seven specials is engineer Michael Fitzmaurice's single-seater. Michael loved large cars, like his Jensen Interceptor and Rolls-Royce Silver Cloud. On a whim, in 1990 he bought a single-seat short chassis unblown Austin Seven, very nicely built on traditional vintage lines by Adrian Purnell.

Michael entered six VSCC sprints and hillclimbs in 1991 and was hooked. At the Shelsley Walsh hillclimb, he achieved a respectable 52.18 seconds on his first attempt, crossing the line at 6200rpm on a standard crank! This marked his start on an interesting 25-year adventure with the little special, continuing to develop the car but keeping entries within the VSCC's strict rules and guidelines, and maintaining its period looks – emulating the amateur hillclimb heroes like Brettell and Maclachlan of the inter-war years.

The car was built on a boxed short frame, and originally had a 1930 engine that Michael rebuilt, a standard gearbox, a three-piece rear axle, a sports front beam, and hydraulic brakes. A Jack French 1937 head and re-profiled camshaft were fitted, along with a single SU, four-to-one exhaust, and full-flow oil filter – "all pretty basic stuff." Wheels were changed to 17in (431mm) diameter, with 400 front and 450 rear tyres, and a close-ratio three-speed gearbox acquired.

After an enjoyable season in this specification, Michael built up a heavily-supercharged engine (which passed so much air that it sounded like a bass organ pipe), and experimented with twin rear wheels. This was not easy engineering on a Seven axle, but the car and driver started to fly.

Michael was now really enjoying his sport, and getting serious about systematically attacking Austin Seven records. Over the course of two decades, his tally includes – amongst others – the VSCC records of: 1996 Prescott, at 45.85 seconds; 2002 Loton Park, at 67.51 seconds; 2005 Wiscombe Park, at 49.95 seconds; and 2006 Shelsley Walsh, at 39.06 seconds. He also claimed an award for Fastest

Time of the Day by a Vintage Car at the VSCC 2004 Wiscombe Park, and has held numerous PWA7C records, including 1997 Gurston Down at 43.58 seconds.

The definitive blown engine and drivetrain specification makes for interesting reading:

- Modified vintage crankcase, coil ignition, Chummy distributor with cockpit A/R controls, block + .80 thou.
- Crankshaft is pressure-fed Phoenix, custom-made extended nose piece for oil feed, camshaft and blower drive, external oil filter and adjustable pressure relief valve.
- Renault 4 con rods, custom turned three-ring flat top pistons.
- Modified Ulster-type cylinder head with 18mm plugs (warmed up on soft plugs in cold weather), camshaft re-ground Chummy.
- Crankcase, block, and head modified for extra studs.
- Blower: Chinn Roots-type, chain-driven, boost varied by changing sprockets, 1¾in (44mm) SU carburettor with dual float bowls.
- Fuel: Methanol/hydrocarbon blend, delivered by high volume electric pump.
- Cooling: Pump-assisted thermosiphon, dry-decked with three radiators.
- Gearbox: Vintage A7, three-speed, custom close-ratio gears, remote gearlever.

Michael Fitzmaurice at the 1991 VSCC Shelsley Walsh Hillclimb, with the original charming and period-looking Adrian Purnell-built single-seater. (Courtesy Michael Fitzmaurice)

- Clutch: Lightened A7 flywheel and clutch plate, cast iron linings, four-speed type release bearing.

By way of highlighting the care and dedication needed to compete with such a specialised device, at this level and for so long, Michael also divulges that apart from chassis tuning, tyre pressures, etc, the blower boost, fuel blend, spark plugs and cockpit-controlled ignition can all be changed to suit the demands of different events and track conditions.

At the time of writing, the Fitzmaurice Special is resting.

Sporting twin rear wheels and developed in the manner of all self-respecting specials, Michael hurtles into the blind and wooded left-hander at Wiscombe, on his way to Vintage Car Fastest Time of the Day. (Courtesy Michael Fitzmaurice)

other prewar motor car – the current Austin Seven support industry is widely spread and thriving.

Would that it could the same could be said of Longbridge and the originally-British volume car industry. In 1960, Britain was still the second biggest car manufacturing nation, but by 1974 Britain had slumped to sixth place and this slide continued. Derek Robinson, known to the popular press as 'Red Robbo,' was the convener of the Amalgamated Union of Engineering Workers at the Longbridge plant, by then under the control of British Leyland. In 1979, he was sacked from the company for publicly opposing a rescue plan to save the company from collapse. This plan had been proposed by the newly-appointed Chairman, Sir Michael Edwards, and was a bitterly disputed critical point in mutual mistrust and poor industrial relations.

By contrast, just seven years later, a Japanese car maker opened a large new assembly plant in Sunderland and heralded a new car manufacturing pattern. This was an ironic full circle, as that Japanese company was the flourishing Nissan, and in its roots were, of course, the immortal Austin Seven.

CHAPTER EIGHTEEN

USING YOUR AUSTIN SEVEN TODAY

FOR any prospective owner, membership of one of the several Austin Seven clubs will lead him or her into a body of friendly, helpful fellow enthusiasts with a genuine camaraderie, whether they're a duke or a dustman! The survival of some 9000 known Austin Sevens, with possibly 2000 more in various stages of undress or decrepitude, is a tribute to the original concept, to the design, and to the quality of the materials used. Thanks must also go to the several excellent manuals and instruction books on maintenance and rebuilding Austin Seven engines and running gear – subjects well covered and outside the scope of this book.

It would also be careless nowadays for a Seven to be written-off completely. Very many are rebuilt, simply because of the numbers of spare engines, gearboxes, and axles that can be found at auto-jumbles, or in the hands of other Sevenists. There is a vast and knowledgeable army of Seven enthusiasts, offering all services to the Austin Seven owner, and all the most frequently needed parts are readily available, along with sensible and discrete upgrades.

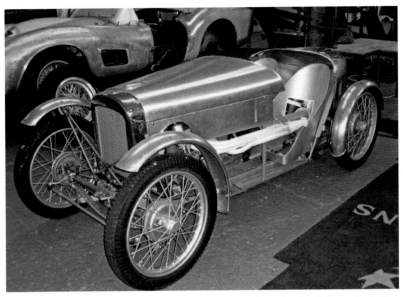

There is still much pleasure and satisfaction to be obtained from building Austin Seven specials – this 1926-based car of the author was bodied by Mike Harris after the contemporary French Amilcar. (Author collection)

"There is nothing as light as nothing" – careful reading of the regulations for this 1971 VSCC Driving Test clearly paid dividends. (Courtesy Ferret Fotographics)

The inherent problem of usual oil leaks between the engine block and crankcase has, at least, ensured that the light steel open section chassis – gently coated for some decades in oil and road dust, and having no box sections to harbour rust – is usually in good enough condition to require few repairs. The splash-fed engine, meanwhile can absorb a fair amount of misuse without seizing up solid. The author has seen ordinary Austin Seven engines still in daily use that, when dismantled, had oily crusty coatings inside the crankcase that had to be removed with a chisel!

Great numbers of Sevens were dismantled during the special-building craze of the 1950s, and were thereby saved from being scrapped. As a result, there are still good numbers of spares for ordinary Sevens, and particularly for the 1930s models.

The two acknowledged weak elements of a Seven are the original crankshaft and the rear axle half shafts.

The crankshaft, due to whip between the two end bearings, is constantly stressed even with normal driving – it is not a case of 'if' the standard crankshaft breaks, but 'when.' That said, there are modern crack-testing techniques or new stronger replacement crankshafts available, and there are well documented cases of standard two-bearing crankshafts lasting over 150,000mi (241,401km). Later, three-bearing crankshafts wear out the narrow centre bearing, which needs replacement at perhaps 5000mi (8046km) intervals, and so is unlikely to worry too many contemporary owners of normal mileage cars.

Mike Morley's beautifully engineered special attracts admiration at the 750 Motor Club National Beaulieu Rally. (Courtesy Ken Cooke)

The rear axle's weak-spot is the keyed taper between the half shaft and the rear wheel hub, which relies on the axle end nut being kept very tight. The castellated nut may have its working face lightly filed, to allow the split pin to get into the next castellation. Never, ever back the nut off to get the split pin in. Any looseness, and with torque reversals the hardened key gets 'worked' in its slot in the taper, and the half shaft is spoiled or breaks. The fix is to fit and lap in the taper

Mallory Park 1978 John Ward in his lightweight and small wheeled Chummy wins the Austin Seven race in some style. (Courtesy David Edroff)

very carefully onto its hub. Some people, particularly 'long-haul' exponents and racers, advocate using modern 'Loctite'-type products, or, again, modern replacement half shafts are usually regularly available, though produced in batches.

The most frequent critical area on a newly-discovered Seven is the condition of the bodywork. Later and lower value models have the most complicated – and therefore expensive – bodywork to repair or replicate. The condition of the interior and trim is proportionately very expensive on late models, too. For this reason, many otherwise-standard Sevens in very poor order, or existing as chassis, are inevitably re-bodied in a simpler style or used for replicas of perhaps more interesting bodywork – although this practice is frowned upon in some quarters. Ulsters are particularly popular as multi-purpose vintage-style sports cars, either on short chassis – as they were originally – or bodied as very practical long-wheelbase chassis 'Ulsteroids.' The affable Chris Gould is acknowledged to have decades of experience on these, and has written extensively on the details of conversions and authenticity. A nice Ulster, even with GRP bodywork, is impossible to tell from the real thing without a good deal of investigation.

Because the front two-thirds of an Austin Seven chassis is so similar, whether it started life as a short or long-wheelbase car, a long-wheelbase frame can be readily shortened, and a narrow rear axle then fitted. This is frequently done, as the long-wheelbase frame rails are more plentiful and stronger than on earlier cars.

The original Ulster bodywork is aluminium on a timber frame, and has only a few compound curves, whilst a Nippy bodyshell, being originally mostly compound curvature steel pressings, is inherently the most complicated and expensive sports body to replicate. The really attractive early vintage two-seater coach-built sports cars, like the Gordon England Cup, have been replicated in some numbers. Although expensive, the results of these are lovely to behold, and are surely one pleasure of re-creation, as few truly original examples have survived.

A practical hand throttle. (Author collection)

Vintage van bodywork types, frequently sign-written to reflect the taste of the owner, have also been created, and are often very effectively displayed at rallies and other events with a selection of the trader's offerings.

A few 'repro' Swallow sports and saloons have been made in recent times. The complex radiator cowling, bodywork details, and interior make these amongst the most difficult and expensive

Roger Harvey - looking very 1970s Jonathan King – wins the class award in his beautiful Austin Swallow sports, at the North Herts Rally (that year held in Melbourne). Clive Ball follows in 'Samantha.' (Courtsey David Edroff)

Frank Hernandez, in Mouseblau, comes across a spot of bother at the Mallory hairpin. Stanley Mann's immense Bentley never did get by, prompting much muttering when back in the paddock. (Courtesy Frank Hernandez)

projects, but, again, even among the top end of the coach-built luxury Sevens, the Swallows are perhaps the ultimate, and therefore highly desirable.

The Austin Seven engine in two-bearing form will always emit a rumble from its main bearings within 1000 miles (1609km) of a rebuild. This does not then get worse, and has to be accepted as a characteristic – although particular engines may have a 'harsh' period which when driving is to be avoided if possible.

The splash-fed engine might register 15psi or more when cold, dropping to almost zero on idle when thoroughly warmed up. Again, this can be alarming to see for the first time, but zero on idle or 2 or 3psi when running shows that all is well, and that a vital oil jet is not blocked up (and therefore not requiring a judicious poke to clear it, using a piece of wire carried in the tool kit). There is currently a school of thought that advocates boring out the oil jets to ⅛in (3mm) diameter, to give even more volume of oil flow, combined with an oversize bored oil pump to increase delivery.

Part of the value of splash-fed lubrication is that the bearings and undersides of the pistons are cooled by the sheer volume of oil constantly flying about inside the crankcase. It appears to be optimistic to expect much oil to arrive and be collected by the original little troughs in the crankshaft, and therefore delivered to the bearings. A pressure-fed crankshaft, by comparison, may not have much oil actually flowing across the faces of the bearings, which may, if not addressed, sometimes lead to failure of the bearing by heat build-up.

Jack French wisely advocated the careful and thorough warming-up of the engine prior to any competition. He was also not a fan of deep sumps, reasoning that there was sufficient capacity in a standard sump for normal short competitive events, whilst doubling the quantity of oil simply took far too long to reach operating temperature. With the double-capacity 'tropical' radiator four-bladed fan and a sports-type deep sump, the author's 'export'-spec military Austin engine takes a good ten miles (16km) on the road to get thoroughly warm, and the car gets significantly faster and more responsive after driving this distance. Jack French also counselled against revving the engine until warm, and even then never warming it up by 'wumping' it up and down on the accelerator – thereby reversing the directional thrust on the crankshaft, leading to stress cracks and ultimate failure.

The clutch travel on an Austin Seven is famously very short, although a new driver gets used to this quite quickly. Frequently, the cause is wear on the pivots for the clutch toggle levers, with the fix being to drill and tap a short length of steel stud to restore the bearing face, or to carefully build up with weld and then filing flat inside the toggle slot. The original toggle levers may – with extreme care – be slightly bent to bring the clutch plate operation square, and uneven toggle levers can be felt as a tremble on the clutch plate. Modern replacement toggle levers may be prone to snapping if bent cold, and the supplier's advice should be sought. The clutch thrust race, if dry, emits obvious noise that is easily identified by de-clutching with the

TONY SOUTHGATE

Just as Nigel Mansell is the last Formula One World Champion who learnt to drive in an Austin Seven, so Tony Southgate is perhaps the last major player in the army of British automotive design engineers that started their careers racing a 750cc Austin.

Tony took a design apprenticeship at Dowty, and was introduced to the monthly meetings of the 750 Motor Club's Midlands Centre, frequented by Johnnie Moore, Tony Cross, Bill Boult, and others. He was soon designing and building his own super-low 750 Formula car, which he named Elmo. He raced the vehicle for a season, and also took part in sprinting, but – with the performance he required – was continually having to rebuild the engine. A thousand valuable lessons were learnt fast, but with the Austin rebuilds costing more than he was making, he opted instead to design an 1172 Formula Elmo car, by which time his apprenticeship was finished.

Thus fired up, the young Tony knew that he wanted to be involved in motorsport. Taking the drawings of his new 1172F car with him, he went along to Lola to see fellow 750 man, Eric Broadley, where he was warmly welcomed. Tony feels that – back in those days, and with a smaller motorsports industry – most people were in the industry because they loved it, and not for the money, which tended to be patchy.

Nevertheless, Tony's career took off, and he never looked back. After Lola, he moved on to designing world-class race cars for Eagle, BRM, Shadow, Lotus, Arrows, Ford, Jaguar, Toyota, Ferrari, TWR, and Audi – an astonishing record. Memorable for many is the 1988

victory of Tony's beautiful and radical TWR 'Silk Cut' Jaguar XJR-9LM at Le Mans. Upon the Jaguar winning, we – normally phlegmatic – Brits invaded the track.

Today, Tony Southgate is the President of the 750 Motor Club, and frequently presents trophies at The National Austin Seven Rally at Beaulieu. Obviously, after the Jaguar Le Mans win, Tony always gets to hand out the trophy for the William Lyons Swallow class.

19-year-old Tony Southgate, with his radically low 750 Formula car "Elmo" at the start of a glittering race car design career, spanning more than four decades. (Courtesy Tony Southgate)

pedal, and some thrust races seem to make a bit of a whirring noise even when in good order and properly lubricated.

One frequent source of engine noise is from wear in the timing gears, and brand new pairs are available in cast iron – which have to be handled with care to avoid cracking – or, for safety, in steel for high revving or rare engines.

Austin Seven dynamos frequently give trouble in maintaining an adequate charge, especially when you most need it, as, for instance, when running distances with headlights on. The overhaul of dynamos and starter motors is straightforward but not cheap, and there are discrete modern voltage regulators available that seem to work well.

The standard thermosiphon action – self-circulating heated water from the cylinder head to the top of the radiator, and round again – is efficient, but old radiator cores frequently become 'furred up,' particularly in hard water districts. Radiators can be readily re-cored

using the original top and bottom tanks, either in a modern free-flowing core, or in a pattern very close indeed to the original, for the purist or where originality is needed.

Seven brakes come in for a lot of criticism, and it is true that the standard system relies on a good number of levers, and that each of these levers has the potential to wear in its bearings. Apart from the very early and rare 6in (152mm) diameter brakes, Austin Seven brake drums are 7in (177mm) in diameter. These are quite big enough, when hydraulically-operated, to stop a mid-1950s Morris Minor weighing almost as much as two Austin Chummys.

The lever ratio arm of the 7in (177mm) diameter brake drum to the 26in (660mm) tyre outer rolling diameter on a 19in (482mm) diameter wheel was improved with the 17in (431mm) diameter wheel, introduced in 1934 on the Ruby. Later Austin Seven specials, using 15in (381mm) diameter wheels, immediately have improved braking as well as acceleration and cornering. When introduced, the standard

Vince Leek, in Mouse, leads Nick Windley's single-seater out of Shaw's Hairpin at a 1992 750 Motor Club Austin Seven race at Mallory Park. (Courtesy Fred Scatley)

Austin direct cable pull braking system was completed, by the standards of the day, to be good. When tested for MOT purposes in modern times, brakes kept in good order are adequate to pass the Tapley Meter test.

The standard Seven brake, with a single pivot and single actuator, involves one leading shoe and one trailing, so it is never going to give a lot of bite. Standard brakes can be improved with very careful balancing, with the car jacked up and all four wheels off the ground. Several small but effective modifications can show benefits, such as slightly radiusing the effective diameter of the operating cam face where it bears on the brake shoe, or replacing the steel end caps to the ally shoes. Brake drum wear is common, and careful selection of used stock at autojumbles often pays dividends.

Putting on longer brake levers all round may be effective, but that extra lever arm length then has to be related to pedal travel length. Putting longer brake levers only on the front seems initially an attractive idea but usually guarantees that the rear brakes, if still fitted with standard short levers, will be actuated before the fronts, and the fronts will never come on as hard as the rears.

Bowden cable operation, either full front cables or half cables on stops on the front radius arms, do not seem to offer the expected improvement in the author's experience, but others feel that they are a worthwhile improvement. Again, such modifications have to be considered relative to the whole

The angled supercharged engine of the 2017 Pedersen single-seater – 80bhp and 120mph performance. (Author collection)

car rather than in isolation, and the same can be said of variations on the well-known Birkett and French self-compensating brake arrangements.

With coupled or uncoupled brakes, it is often convenient to pull the handbrake on by a few notches when descending steep hills in order to steady the car, particularly if the driver has both hands busy with a steering wheel! It also becomes second nature for a Seven driver to haul back on the long lever standard handbrake at the same instant as stamping on the foot-brake in an emergency stop, and even with coupled brakes the car will still brake better with double help from the cockpit.

The later Ruby range had wider brake shoes and semi-Girling, then more powerful full-Girling, braking systems to cope with the increased all-up weight. The earlier light pressed metal brake drums were replaced by cast items to cope with the increased brake pressures. The cast drums are much more effective if converting to hydraulic brakes, particularly if changing to two leading-shoe arrangement, but will not fit inside the centres of early wheels.

It is essential that king pins are unworn and properly fitted tightly into the axle eyes. Any looseness of the pin in the axle eye can quickly lead to broken king pins, and potential catastrophic loss of a complete wheel and brake unit if the king pin snaps into three pieces. This was experienced by the author after an incorrect over-hard and 'as brittle as glass' king pin suddenly broke up – fortunately when only travelling at 30mph (48km/h).

That great special builder and engineer Harold Perry jacked up his car before each journey and gave it a grease, claiming that he had no metal to metal contact on his car and that it would therefore never wear out.

Wheel hubs are worth careful attention; original, and now 80 years old, wheel studs can stretch if wheel nuts are constantly over-tightened, and can even pull right out of the hub. A depressed dimple in the rear face of the stud at the hub end is a good indicator that all is not well. New high-tensile wheel studs are desirable for distance driving or competitive events.

When the Austin Seven was originally built, most mechanics did not possess socket sets, and the factory Austin Seven tool kit includes only short open-ended spanners. These are a good reminder not to hang on to over-length ring spanners or sockets; apart from engine internals and head studs, the car was not designed for the torque loads of modern tools, which can over-tighten and stretch or break studs and strip threads. For this reason, it is wise to have all the threaded holes in the aluminium crankcase Helicoiled when rebuilding.

The great thing about the Austin Seven is that the mechanical parts are each uncomplicated, and so – with a very few special pullers, a clutch centring plate, and normal hand tools – most jobs can be tackled in a home garage with a small bench vice, as indeed Sir Herbert intended and expected.

Of immense interest to Austin Seven special builders, or enthusiasts who wish to upgrade for other reasons – perhaps long-haul journeys or improved general performance – many later parts are interchangeable with their earlier equivalents. This may send purists or historians reaching for their original specification sheets, but it was accepted contemporary practice to try to improve the performance of the Austin Seven, almost from the moment it was created. This was done both by the factory and by enthusiastic owners, and many later parts were found on newly-purchased but secondhand Sevens going right back to the 1950s.

Mike Martin, with son Giles, swings into the Curborough paddock in 2017 after a fast run in the ex-Cameron Millar wide-IFS Super Accessories special. (Author collection)

The beautifully detailed and quick replica Side-Valve of Francesca Wilton – a regular at VSCC Hillclimbs. (Courtesy F Wilton)

The compact packaging of the front suspension elements of Francesca Wilton's single-seater, including the modern slow threaded revolving tubular axle sleeve joint to reduce wheel lifting when cornering and in roll. (Author collection)

a futile attempt to pass the newly introduced MOT test. The original front axle and date-stamped spring had been kept in the loft, as had the original Army-pattern wheels, but this example is typical of how Sevens are and were found. One must expect the unexpected when buying a 90-year-old motor car.

Many Sevens originally fitted with updraught carburettors had these changed to later sidedraught manifolding and carburettors in the 1940s and 1950s. At this time, many cars were also fitted with Bowdenex brake conversions and different headlights, as well as having their radiators swapped and much else besides. This was a time when, at least with a cheap car like a Seven, it was much more important on a daily basis to keep motoring than to worry about originality. Now however, all that has completely changed. Pride (and plaudits) in originality carry a premium amongst enthusiasts and success in the highly competitive rally field.

If one is building up a car from an assemblage of secondhand parts, one usually chooses the 'best of the worst' when selecting from the pile. However, virtually all of the parts of an Austin Seven that wear out are available from a number of enthusiastic and knowledgeable dealers – some completely full-time and professional, and some, it would seem, simply helping out fellow enthusiasts.

More expensive major or difficult items like cylinder blocks, crankshafts, crankcases, and crown wheel and pinion sets, tend to be re-made in batches. These will be available through word of mouth, and it may take a year or so for one of these items (which, in Austin Seven terms, involve a sizeable financial investment) to be made with your name on it.

For rarer – particularly works sports or racing – engines and parts, a small number of individuals seem to know the traced history of nearly every such priceless acquisition that there is to be found.

Sir Herbert Austin's policy was to incorporate constant small improvements to his product, on a piecemeal basis as need or necessity demanded. As a result, many fundamental elements barely changed (wheel hubs being an example); apart from the very early 6in

When the author had the good fortune to buy a decrepit (but complete and extremely early) 1929 Military Mulliner Scout car in the 1990s, it came with complete 1936 Ruby front suspension (but with better king pins). It had been bolted on by the owner in 1962, in

There have been many more Austin single-seaters built in the past 30 years than during its production period. This is the super quick, beautifully engineered blown example belonging to Ed Mariott. (Courtesy David Edroff)

(152mm) brakes, the brakes and wheels of later cars will fit straight on to earlier axles if required.

Broadly, the magneto-era engines up to 1928 had the same crankcase with rearward starter, with only small differences. The magneto drive was done away with on rearward starter coil ignition engines up to 1932, and front starter pattern crankcases with a forward-facing starter boss cast-in were present up to 1935. Three-bearing crankshaft types were generally used thereafter.

The three-speed gearboxes remained similar up to 1926/27, and lost the gate change to a ball change around 1929. Four-speed gearboxes arrived in the early 1930s, and are less than 1in (25mm) longer than the three-speed versions, and so frequently swapped.

Glamourous events like Goodwood Revival have significantly raised the profile of the old car movement in recent times. The author's 1932 Export Military Mulliner is seen here as a gate guardian to Lord March's own start-line enclosure. (Author collection)

Veteran Sevenist John Barlow campaigns one of the dozen or so superb works replica single-seaters built by Alan Wragg. (Author collection)

Still applying original thought to extract more power from a nonagenarian engine design – just one of the very effective breathing arrangements of Mouseblau. (Courtesy Frank Hernandez)

Improved change/synchromesh was gradually introduced, and when swapping gearboxes it may be simpler to change the propshaft to suit the particular gearbox output spider than try to change the gearbox internals.

The early rear axles tend to be complex in their variations, and carriers may have to be changed if later crown wheel and pinion sets are introduced. The short-lived screw-in torque tube types of the late 1920s – which included military and van types – can wind themselves in or out on the threaded portion, unless a discrete small grub screw to prevent this happening is added.

The catalogue of changes has been very well documented previously, and is outside the scope of this work. Suffice it to say that the intricacies of the small variations in Austin Seven constituent parts and their availability continue to keep a good many people in rapt study, and provide hours of enjoyable browsing at auto-jumbles throughout the land. They have also created a very healthy cottage industry for those enthusiasts gainfully employed in sourcing, making, and marketing parts for Sir Herbert's baby, an astonishing 80 years after the last Austin Seven left Longbridge.

The Austin Seven-based 750 Formula, which came into being years before Formula One was created, came to be regarded as one of the great triumphs of British racing car design philosophy. It was from this that the idea evolved of assembling a car from a selection of available components. This was a fundamental shift from a single manufacturer building the whole car, and owes much to the old traditional Shelsley Specials from earlier decades. It is certainly true that the frenzy of Austin Seven special building in the 1950s spawned a whole generation of enthusiasts at the centre of postwar motorsport. These individuals went on to found the motorsport industry of which Britain is still the centre, now employing perhaps 100,000 people in a great web-like network of multiple sporting activities, from historic events right up to global Formula One.

Frank Hernandez's ultra-quick Mouseblau VSCC racer at Cadwell, displaying original thinking in its up-draught carburation … "If I lift the carburettor piston and open the butterfly, I can see into the combustion chamber." (Courtesy Frank Hernandez)

It is no accident that Britain is a world-class centre of excellence in all motorsport disciplines, over a broad spectrum. At the core of the origins of this is the vast band of enthusiasts born out of the rigours of the Second World War, many of them Austin Seven people, who ensured the immortality of Sir Herbert Austin's little baby in the greater order of things. The United Kingdom has also become the recognised centre for historic motorsport, whether it be Lakeland Trials, Sprints, Hillclimbs at many hallowed venues, race meetings, or simply gatherings at the local pub.

Over the past 20 years, the old car movement has been increasingly taken into the great public consciousness, and nowhere more so than at Goodwood. There, two or three times a year, not only do you get three days of glorious historic hillclimbing or motor racing and aeronautical displays, but the 100,000 plus spectators each get to take part too. Most now embrace the idea of driving up in period costume from the 1930s to the 1960s, and are accompanied with live music from Jazz to Rock, high-end historic car auctions, and all the atmosphere that the Sussex ex-World War Two fighter station can provide.

The Goodwood model, in particular, has a trickle-down effect on the whole of the old car scene, and Austin Sevens are not immune to values steadily rising. However, they remain affordable, for the most part, simply due to the number of survivors.

The Austin Seven is the most versatile prewar car to own, in terms of the sheer number of events in which an owner can participate. On

RETURN TO LE MANS

When Peter Butler was Member of Parliament for South Bedfordshire, he introduced legislation to abolish road tax on pre-1973 cars – encouraging owners not only to use their classic cars on the road, but saving them huge sums of money. Peter is a keen Austin 'Sevenist,' and the privileged owner of not one, but two, 75 Speedys. This includes CZ 6324 which, in 1935, won the prestigious 750cc Class at Le Mans, covering 1913km in the 24 hours, at a speed of 79.7km/h. In 2006, Peter hatched a plan to take the 75 back to Classic Le Mans in 2010 – exactly 75 years after its prewar triumph.

The car was entrusted to Mike New for a full restoration, and Peter assembled 'The Butler Boys' as a Le Mans team – a mixture of 750 Motor Club, VSCC and PWA7C members, under manager Jeremy Batchelor and including David Wilcox, Stuart Ulph, Ian Bancroft, and Graham Beckett, with the author as press officer. Andy Storer was the driving force behind the team, with Longstone Tyre's Chris Hudson as co-driver. Team members covered their own expenses, and the eye-watering entry fee was defrayed a little by sponsorship from the 750 Motor Club and PWA7C.

The Speedy was carefully prepared with fool-proof electrics, and the precious historic running gear set aside. A Girling front axle was fitted with double dampers, less cambered springs all round, an engine with a milder non-Nippy cam profile, and light flywheel. The original Grasshopper remote-control gear level was dispensed with for the event and all items balanced – including the propshaft – and safety wired, with double throttle return springs and catch tank, all to familiar MSA standards.

Christmas 2009, and the envelope accepting the entry landed on the mat; Le Mans was on, and the organisers had even allocated the car's original race number – 62.

The atmosphere at the track was building together with the air temperature, which soared to 40°c (104F). This was a worry, as the Speedy was losing large quantities of water down the radiator overflow under hard braking. With day and night-time practice giving a lap time of nine minutes 30 seconds, the drivers found themselves well away from the back of the grid. The Speedy's two race-experienced drivers found some of the opposition over-cautious on bends where you could not see the apex, and the Speedy overtook many potentially faster cars, only to be gobbled up on the lengthy straights.

It was decided that there was just enough cooling water left in the system at each driver change to safely allow topping up between stints. At the start, Andy ran across the track to the Austin, the

Classic Le Mans 2012 Butler's Boys. From left to right: Ian Bancroft, driver Andy Storer, Graham Beckett, Le Patron Peter Butler, Stuart Ulph, driver Chris Hudson, Chris Garner, missing Team Manager Jeremy Batchelor. (Author collection)

engine fired first time, and – without glancing to this left – he booted the car straight for the opposite side of the track, overtaking half the field on the run up to the Dunlop bridge, and arriving there in 15th place!

The night time run was magically made just as dawn was breaking, and the Austin, running at a strict rev limit, lapped quicker and quicker, even as temperatures soared again.

At the finish, the Austin was in 36th place – the smallest car in the field, ahead of several 3.0- and 4.5-litre Bentleys, Bugattis, Aston Martin Ulsters, Lagondas, and all manner of potentially quicker cars. It was also an amazing and gratifying 16th in the Index of Performance.

Jeremy Batchelor remarked that many other teams were working on their cars more and more frantically as the race wore on, just to keep them going. By contrast, the Butler Boys had less and less to do on the Austin – a tribute to the little car and to Peter's team. The 2010 return had proved just as exciting and successful as the 1935 original.

In 2012, Peter Butler's Speedy team were privileged to run at Classic Le Mans again, with Chris Garner in place of Dave Wilcox, who had sadly recently passed away. The little Austin again covered itself in glory.

Peter Butler's 1935 ex-Le Mans Speedy flew round the track again in 2010 and 2012. Here, Andy Storer leads a Bentley and Bugatti through the final chicane. (Courtesy Iain Mansell)

The 750 Motor Club's Annual National Austin Seven Rally at Beaulieu attracts several hundred examples of Sir Herbert's 'Baby,' and each year previously unseen variations inevitably turn up. (Courtesy Nick Salmon)

every weekend of the year, and three or four evenings in the week, there is something going on. The high point for many is the 750 MC National Austin Seven Rally at Beaulieu, with many entrants making a long weekend of it.

It seems that it has always been in the nature of the Austin Seven to attract rather likeable people. The camaraderie is tremendous, and the multiplicity of clubs now catering for the little car is testimony to both the social aspects of Seven ownership, and the gently competitive nature of the events that continue to be organised in some numbers. Certainly, when driving an Austin Seven today the reaction from other road users and pedestrians is first to smile, and second to engage the driver in conversation. The subject of the well-worn opening line "I used to have one of those" is now often replaced by "my father," or "my grandfather."

There is something about the car – its spindly wheels, upright stance, and tiny scale – that is visually very appealing to all age groups, for differing reasons. Everybody is amazed at the ease with which many a 'Sevenist' uses his or her car for a whole variety of enjoyable events and lengthy excursions.

In a world where even local journeys are undertaken, by many, in thumping great 4x4s, it is ironic that the 'Holy Grail' of every aspiring automotive design engineer remains the lightweight personal micro town car. It represents a type and need that was recognised by Sir Herbert Austin a century ago, and in very different road use circumstances.

At several levels, then, the Austin Seven can therefore truly be said to be immortal. When originally conceived, 'the motor for the millions' changed the common man's perception of how he could live his life.

SEVEN FAMILIES

There are many entire families involved in vintage motoring, and with Austin Sevens in particular, and one of the best known is the Way family from Sussex. The families of brothers John and Edward Way appear to have owned at least a dozen Sevens over almost 50 years, with John's son Thomas currently owning an Ulster replica.

Edward has owned his Nippy for 48 years, and a 1934 Box Saloon only a few years less. He also has the ex-Kay Petre supercharged Side-Valve (which revs to 9500 at 22psi blower pressure), and plans to reunite the car with its original repaired chassis frame.

Edward also owns the fantastic prewar Harker Special – totalling 1500cc from two Austin Seven blocks and crankshafts – and the 1911 Austin Hall-Scott; a giant racer, with propulsion from a 10-litre aero engine.

Edward's sons are also heavily involved. Oliver, built the Seven-based Salamander Special for Amanda Fane de Salis, amongst several Bugattis and other exotica. William is well known for his recent attacks on all the VSCC Class One hill records in the family Ulster, and for rarely using a trailer to and from events. William is the principal development engineer at Cosworth. Jeremy has rebuilt Mrs Jo Jo, recovered from a Suffolk barn, and returned her to an early iteration. He has also trialled an ex-Nigel Orlebar Austin.

All this, and now there are also eight grandchildren who are eagerly following in family Austin Seven ways. The Way family represent well the generational nature of Austin Sevens, enabling young people to get involved, become enthusiastic, and ultimately become hooked for life – a continuum of Herbert Austin's original vision.

John Way in the 'Hornby' Ulster, chasing New Zealand visitor Grant Cowie's Rubber Duck jade works racer, in the Spero and Voiturette race, Cadwell Park, 2005. (Courtesy John Way)

Personal transport was transformed, and opportunities opened up for a newly aspirational man, woman, and their children, to travel and embrace the wider world – a family lifestyle model that still remains with us.

The sporting and endurance achievements of the Seven, which were enthusiastically promoted by the factory for two decades before World War Two, were reborn at the end of hostilities by equally aspirational and hungry amateur young men and women. In using the Seven as a base to making the most of their new circumstances, they ignited the flame of postwar British fledgling motorsport. They acted as eager participants in the development of the world-class historic and current motorsport industry, now providing employment for the 100,000 Britons already mentioned.

Conceived and built during a truly tumultuous period of world history, the Austin Seven may be considered to be one of the most influential motor cars ever devised. In addition to its own place in automotive history under the Austin badge, the Austin Seven has been directly instrumental in the birth of the world-famous marques BMW, Rosengart, Jaguar, Jeep, Lotus, Jensen, Cooper, Holden, Lola, Vanwall and McLaren. There is Austin Seven DNA, too, in the Mini, Austin Healey, and Datsun/Nissan, as well as many specialist mainly-British sporting cars like Marcos, Davrian, Chevron, and others, and even the engine builders Cosworth and Ricardo. The influence of the Austin Seven is still all around us.

The third ingredient in the immortality of the species is self-evident in the astonishing number of surviving Austin Sevens. It is not only the most well-known and best loved of all prewar motor cars, but the most numerous extant at historic sporting and social events of all kinds. In virtually every class of competition for which it is eligible, the Austin Seven is invariably the car that the others still have to try to beat, and thousands of owners still enjoy this versatile little car as an important part of their lives. With many continually being revived or rebuilt, there are more Austin Sevens today than there were ten years ago, and it is very likely therefore that in the next ten years there will be even more than there are today – immortality assured!

Sir Herbert Austin – gone, but with his spirit all around us – must be a most contented man.

APPENDIX
AUSTIN SEVEN CLUBS

UK SEVEN CLUBS

750 Motor Club
www.750mc.co.uk
The Conservatory Suite,
Donnington Park,
Derby DE74 2RP
T: 01332 814548 / F: 01332 811422
E: racing@750mc.co.uk

Austin Seven Owners Club (London)
www.austinsevenownersclub.com
Bob Cross, 303A Sussex Drive,
Walderslade, Kent ME5 0NJ
T: 01634 865598
E: services@bobex.freeserve.co.uk

Austin Seven Section
Keith Dobinson, Pendle,
Beech Crescent, Heighington,
Darlington, Co. Durham DL5 0PT
T: 01325 317146
E: keithatpendle@gmail.com

Beds and Herts Vintage and Classic Car Club
Alan and Lorna Martin, Tamrin,
61 Manor Road, Caddington,
Luton, Beds LU1 4EE
T: 01582 412556
E: lornaalanaustins@btopenworld.com

Bongtree Austin Seven Club
Chris Blower, Willows Cottage,
Fairy Hall Lane, Rayne,
Braintree CM77 6SZ
E: bongtree7@hotmail.com

Bristol Austin Club Seven
www.ba7c.org
Daniel Cole, 11 Cherrington Road,
Westbury-on-Trym,
Bristol BS10 5HB
T: 01179 625712
E: dancole1978@hotmail.co.uk

Cambridge Austin Seven & Vintage Car Club
Paul Lawrence,
3 Housman Avenue,
Royston, Herts SG8 5DN
T: 01763 249210
E: fishylobby@btinternet.co.uk

Cornwall Austin Seven Club
www.austin7.org
Sarah Mason, Trenoweth,
Carlidnack Road, Mawnan Smith,
Cornwall TR11 5HA
T: 01326 250220 / M: 07837 229982
E: ca7c.secretary@gmail.com

Devon Austin Seven Club
Howard Palmer,
19 Sweetbriar Lane, Holcombe,
Dawlish, Devon EX9 0JZ
T: 01626 864212
E: devona7c@talktalk.net

Dorset Austin Seven Club
www.da7c.co.uk
Ian Mason-Smith,
Hollybush Cottage, Barrack Lane,
Crow Hill, Ringwood,
Hants BH24 3ES
E: hollybushcottage1@btinternet.com

Essex Austin Seven Club
www.ea7c.co.uk
Dave Orange, 27 Tufted Close,
Great Notley, Braintree,
Essex CM77 7YE
E: d.orange431@btinternet.com

Hereford A7 Club
Mike Ward, Riverhill,
Goodrich, Ross-on-Wye,
Hereford HR9 6JD
T: 01600 890902
E: m.ward789@btinternet.com

Midlands Austin Seven Club
Bob Prophet,
Soley's Orchard, Rectory Road,
Upton upon Severn,
Worcs WR8 0LX
T: 01684 592509
E: rsprophet@tiscali.co.uk

Norfolk Austin Seven Club
E: paul-liz@maulden21.plus.com

North Hampshire Austin Enthusiasts' Group
Denise Adams, 6 Esher Close,
Basingstoke, Hants RG22 9JP
E: nhaegcommittee@gmail.com

North of England Classic and Prewar Automobiles
Janek Grakewski,
5 Chatsworth Drive,
Haxby, York YO3 3QS
T: 01904 763085
E: grajewski4@aol.com

Online Austin Seven Club
www.oa7c.com
E: john.cox12@sky.com

Prewar Austin Seven Club
www.pwa7c.co.uk
Gerald Mulford, 76 Firs Road,
Edwalton, Nottingham NG12 4BX
T: 01159 143581
E: gerald.mulford@ntlworld.com

Scottish Austin Seven Club
www.scottishaustinsevenclub.co.uk
David Lodge, The Bungalow,
Coalhall, Ayr KA6 6ND
T: 01292 591256 / M: 07999 957344
E: dandjlodge@gmail.com

Solent Austin Seven Club
www.solent-austinclub.co.uk
Graham Smith, 2 Hearne Gardens,
Shirrell Heath, Southampton,
Hants WO32 2NR
T: 01329 834297
E: grahamjsmith@talktalk.net

South Wales Austin Seven Club
John Williams, 24 West Road,
Nottage, Porthcawl CF36 3SN
T: 01656 786591
E: jonniejumble@googlemail.com

Surrey Austin Owners
David Harris, 23 Rustington Walk,
Morden, Surrey SM4 5QR
T: 0208 646 1279
E: harris61@btinternet.com

Ulster Prewar Austin Seven Club (Northern Ireland)
Ella McLoughlin
E: advertising@gazette.ireland.anglican.org

Vintage Austin Register
Alan Martin,
Tamrin, 61 Manor Road,
Caddington, Luton,
Bedfordshire LU1 4EE
T: 01582 412556
E: lornaalanaustins@btopenworld.com

The Vintage Sports Club Ltd
The Old Post Office, West Street,
Chipping Norton, Oxfordshire
OX7 5EL
T: 01608 644777
E: info@vscc.co.uk

The Wanderers
Bob Hewston, 157 Woodrow Lane,
Catshill, Bromsgrove,
Worcs B61 0PL
T: 01214 535022

Worthings
Steve Hodgson, 9 The Crescent,
Manor Road, East Preston,
West Sussex BN16 1QB
T: 01903 779684
E: stevehodgo@hotmail.co.uk

UK SEVEN REGISTERS

Austin Seven Arrow Register
Jim Blacklock,
30 St. Edmunds Road,
Acie, Norwich NR13 3BP
T: 01493 750805
E: a7arrowreg@tesco.net

Austin Seven Coupé Register
Mick Brodribb, 73 Meadow Lane,
Newhall, Swadlincote,
Derby DE11 0UW
T: 01283 219541
E: mickatsteammill@aol.co.uk

Austin Seven Special Register
www.a7special.co.uk
David Charles,
Beighton House,
North Burlington,
Norwich NR13 4EL
T: 01493 752016
E: mail@a7special.co.uk

Austin Ten Drivers Club
www.austintendriversclub.com
Geoff Stovold, 2 Brook Villas,
Blackham, Tunbridge Wells,
Kent TM3 9UL
T: 08446 931104
E: info@austintendriversclub.com

Big Seven Register
Robin Taylor, 101 Derby Road,
Chellaston, Derby DE73 1SB
T: 01332 700629
E: robin.e.taylor@talktalk.net

Boat Tail Two-Seater Register
Chris Chubb, 4 Gibbon Road,
Staplehurst, Kent TN12 0LT
T: 01580 891029
E: chris@gchubb.plus.com

British Austin Society
John Raeburn, 107 Percy Avenue,
Kingsgate, Broadstairs CT10 3LD
T: 01843 866107
E: johnraeburn@hotmail.co.uk

Cornwall Vintage Vehicle Society
Tony Barfield,
The Little Cottage, Breage,
Helston, Cornwall TR13 9PD
T: 01326 564330
E: tonybarfield@talktalk.net

Fabric Register
David Mawby, 41 Normanton Lane,
Keyworth, Nottingham NG12 5HB
T: 01159 377833 / M: 07721 382619
E: djmawby@btinternet.com

Gordon England Register
Ruairdh Dunford, 64 Campsie
Drive, Bearsden,
Glasgow G61 3HX
T: 01419 428037
E: dunford1@aol.com

Hamblin Register
Tom Hamlin, 1 Stonedene,
Sherborne, Dorset DT9 4EJ
T: 01935 812982
E: nhamblin@btinternet.com

Military Register
Ashley Hollebone,
22 Warburton Road,
Twickenham,

Middlesex TW2 6EP
T: 07796 347026
E: wizzyalong@gmail.com

Mulliner Register
Mike Tebbett, Little Wyche,
Walwyn Road, Upper Colwall,
Nr. Malvern, Worcs WR13 6PL
T: 01684 563315
E: m.tebbutt@tiscali.co.uk

Pram Hood Register 1922-26
David Cochrane,
18 Russell Avenue, Dunchurch,
Rugby CV22 6PX
T: 01788 532222
E: david@a7c.co.uk

RN Register
Dave Mann, 19 Flowery Field,
Woodsmoor, Stockport,
Cheshire SK2 7ED
T: 01612 925838
E: sue.mann1@ntworld.com

Sports Register
Chris Dickinson,
Hay Green House,
Hay Green Lane, Birdwell,
Barnsley S70 5XE
T: 01226 743590
E: dickinson901@btinternet.com

Swallow Register
Lorna Mountford, Moyglare Farm,
Stoney Heath, Baughurst,
Tadley RG26 3SN
T: 01256 851185 (leave a message) /
M: 07903 083979 (not during office
hours)
E: lorna@leonardo-cad.co.uk

Tickford Register
Mick Ward, The Old Bakery,
32 Fox Street, Great Gransden,
Beds SG19 3AA
T/F: 01767 176248
E: michaeljrward@btinternet.com

Van Register
Ray Edge, 30 Stapleton Avenue,
Heaton, Bolton BL1 5ET
T: 01204 492063
E: r.f.edge@talk21.com

OTHER SEVEN CLUBS

American Austin Bantam Club
www.austinbantamclub.com
Marilyn Sanson, 7704 Bridgeport,
Kirkville Road, NY 13082, USA
E: marilyn.aabc@yahoo.com

Austin Bantam Society
www.austinbantamsociety.com
Norman T. Booth Jnr,
1589 N. Grand Oaks Avenue,
Passadena, CA 91104, USA
T: (626) 791 2617
E: njbooth@earthlink.net

Austin Club of Jamaica
Dr Ron DuQuesnay,
28 Great House Boulevard,
Kingston 6, Jamaica, West Indies
T: (876) 927 0145 / (876) 909 8818
F: (876) 977 6995

Austin Club of NSW Inc
www.austin7clubnsw.org.au
PO Box 6009, North Ryde,
NSW 2113, Australia
E: info@austin7clubnsw.org.au

Austin Club of South Australia
www.austin7clubsa.com.au
Ron Burchett,
262 Tapleys Hill Road,
Seaton, 5023 South Australia
E: secretary@austin7clubsa.com.au

**Austin Club of
Western Australia**
Robyn Coleman, PO Box 117,
Burswood, Perth 6100,
Western Australia
T: 0061 418 959 595
E: robyn@sterob.com

Austin Seven Club Deutschland
Gerhard Brennelsen,
Hinterer Rindweg 27,
D68526 Ladenburg, Germany
T: +49 6203 180774
M: +49 1712 038232
E: president@austin-seven-club.de

Austin Seven Club France
Ian Wilson, Autograph Racing,
Chez Mautret, 16490 Hiesse,
Confolens, France
T: +33 5 45 85 59 95
M: +33 6 43 76 56 48
E: autographracing@live.com

Austin Seven Club Inc
www.austin7club.org
PO Box 462, Moorabbin,
Victoria 3189, Australia
E: grant@thecampbelis.net.au

Austin Seven Club of India
Manjo Sharma, D315, Sadarpura,
Jodhpur, 342 002, Rajasthan, India

Austin Seven Club of South Africa
Ajetta Boys, PO Box 194,
Sundowner, 2161,
Johannesburg, 2034, RSA
T: 011 795 3534 / F: 086 512 4078
M: 082 453 9283
E: ahboys@telkomsa.net

**Austin Seven Owners
Club Canada**
Roy Wilkins,
644 Bluegrouse Place, Tsawwassen,
BC, Canada V4L 2G8
T: 604 943 3882
E: roywilkins@hotmail.com

Austin Seven Register of Japan
Kazumuto Sasaki,
1-7-10 Nishi Tokorozawa,
Saitama, Japan 359-1144
T: 042 923 1121 / F: 042 923 3909
E: cuya-sasaki-821@tb3.so-net.ne.jp

Austin-Freunde
www.amwf.ch
Austin-Morris-Wolseley Friends
Switzerland, Section Austin Seven,
PO Box 26, CH-8042 Zurich
T: +41 44 367 6787
E: infor@amwf.ch

**Cairde an Seact bhig
(Friends of the Little Seven)**
Ian Clayton, Trawlebane,
Bantry, Co. Cork, Eire
T: 027 52759
E: lanceclayton@iolfree.ie

**Dutch Prewar Austin
Seven Owners**
www.austinseven.nl
Martin van der Zwan,
Margaretha van Oostenriklaan 24,
2353 EN Leiderdrop,
The Netherlands
E: secretary@austinseven.nl

Italia Austin Seven Club
Stefano Marongiu,
Via San Francesco 43,
21020 Inarzo VA
T: +39 0332 964012
F: +39 0332 964029
E: infor@austin7italia.org

Norsk Austin Seven Club
Martin Faella, Meierivelen 10,
N-3032, Drammen, Norway
T: +47 03 821232

Vintage Austin Club of Sri Lanka
www.janashakthi.com
Secretary VCOC,
Lalithe Munasinghe, 637/2,
Kandy Road, Kelanya, Sri Lanka
T: +94 11 2309840 /
+94 11 7309298
E: lalithe@janashakthi.com

BIBLIOGRAPHY

Barker, R & Harding, A. *Automobile Design – Great Designers and Their Work*. David and Charles, 1970.

Boddy, W. *The Austin Seven*. Grenville Publishing, 1972.

Boddy, W. *The History Of Brooklands Motor Course – 1906-1940*. Grenville Publishing, 1957.

Brown, C. *Austin Seven Competition History – The Cars and Those Who Drove Them*. TwinCam Ltd, 2006.

Caunter, CF. *The Light Car: A technical history of cars with engines of less than 1600cc capacity*. HMSO Science Museum, 1970.

Church, R. *Herbert Austin – The British Motor Car Industry to 1941*. Europa Publications, 1979.

Clark, RM. *Austin Seven Cars*. Brooklands Books, 1970.

Coleman, John. *Coleman's Drive*. Faber and Faber, 1964.

Design Museum. *Fifty Cars that Changed the World*. Conran, 2009.

Dun, Major TI. *From Cairo to Siwa – Across the Libyan Desert with Armoured Cars*. E&R Schindler, 1933.

Eyre, M. *Austin Seven – Competition Cars 1922-1982*. 750 Motor Club, 1982.

Hanna, M & Hornby, P. *A Comprehensive History of the A7 Grasshopper*. The Prewar Austin Seven Club, 2014.

Harrison, RC. *Austin Racing History*. Cable Publishing, 1949/1968.

Harvey, C. *Austin Seven*. Oxford Illustrated Press, 1985.

Henry, F. *Austin from the Inside – The Recollections of Freddie Henry on the Austin Motor Company*. 750 Motor Club, 1998.

Henry, F. *Austin 'The Old Man' – The Story of the First Baron Austin of Longbridge (1866-1941)*. 1968.

Lawrence, P. *The Lone Furrow – The Story of Arthur Mallock and His U2 Racing Cars*. TFM Publishing Ltd, 1997.

Mills, R. *Original Austin Seven*. Bay View Books, 1996.

Morgan, D. *Seven Fifty Motor Club – The Birthplace of Modern British Motorsport*. Haynes, 2009.

Purves, B. *The Austin Seven Source Book*. Haynes, 1989.

Ricardo, HR. *The Ricardo Story – The Autobiography of Sir Harry Ricardo, Pioneer of Engine Research*. Society of Automotive Engineers Inc, 1990.

Roe, GE. *Bert Hadley – A Son of Birmingham*. The Prewar Austin Seven Club, 2013.

Russell, T. *Out In Front: The Leslie Ballamy Story*. Motor Racing Publications Ltd, 2004.

Smith, IH. *Lotus – The First Ten Years*. Motor Racing Publications, 1958.

Stephens, PJ. *Building and Racing My '750'*. GT Foulis & Co, 1953.

Stowe, P. *BACkfire*. Laxton Press, 2001.

Ulph, S. *Would Suit Enthusiast – LM Williams and his Austin Seven Specials*. Prewar Austin 7 Club, 2012.

Underwood, J. *Whatever Became of the Baby Austin?* Heritage Press, 1965.

Various. *PWA7C Magazine*. The Prewar Austin Seven Club, 2000 to present.

Various. *750 Motor Club Bulletin*. 750 Motor Club, 1939 to present.

Wheldon, J. *Machine Age Armies*. Abelard-Schuman, 1968.

Williams, LM. *Austin Seven Specials*. Foulis, 1958.

Wood, J. *Alec Issigonis – The Man Who Made the Mini*. Breedon Books Publishing, 2005.

Wyatt, RJ. *The Austin Seven - The Motor for the Million, 1922-1939*. Macdonald & Co, 1968.

GREAT CARS

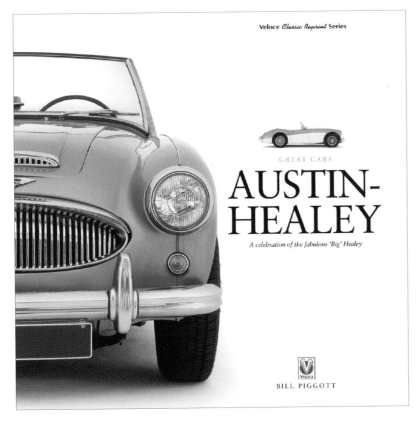

AUSTIN-HEALEY – A CELEBRATION OF THE FABULOUS 'BIG' HEALEY

The Austin-Healey – or 'Big' Healey – is one of the iconic British sports cars. The first Austin-Healey 100 model was unveiled at the 1952 Earls Court Motor Show, and when the last car rolled off the production line in 1967, over 73,000 examples had been built.

ISBN: 978-1-845848-55-2
Hardback • 25x25cm • 160 pages • 270 pictures

For more information and price details, visit our website at www.veloce.co.uk • email: info@veloce.co.uk
• Tel: +44(0)1305 260068

TRIUMPH TR

ISBN: 978-1-845848-54-5
Hardback • 25x25cm • 160 pages
• 295 pictures

JAGUAR MARK 1 & 2

ISBN: 978-1-787110-24-3
Hardback • 24.8x24.8cm • 160 pages
• 269 pictures

JAGUAR E-TYPE

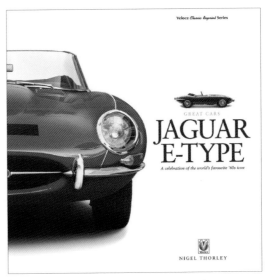

ISBN: 978-1-787110-25-0
Hardback • 25x25cm • 184 pages
• 264 pictures

THOSE WERE THE DAYS ...

THE LAST REAL AUSTINS – 1946 TO 1959

Reprinted after a long absence, this book examines how Austin bounced back after WWII, and how, despite the severe materials shortage, it developed the largest range of vehicles produced by any automaker in postwar Britain. It examines how these vehicles were received and used, and is illustrated with rare archive photography.

ISBN: 978-1-787111-12-7
Paperback • 19x20.5cm • 96 pages
• 89 colour and b&w pictures

For more information and price details, visit our website at www.veloce.co.uk • email: info@veloce.co.uk
• Tel: +44(0)1305 260068

DON HAYTER'S MGB STORY

BRITISH WOODIES FROM THE 1920s TO THE 1950s

AMERICAN WOODIES 1928-1953

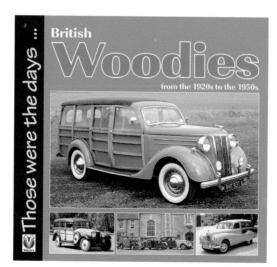

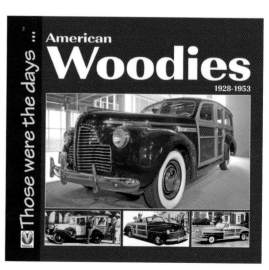

ISBN: 978-1-845844-60-8

ISBN: 978-1-84584-169-0

ISBN: 978-1-845842-69-7

THOSE WERE THE DAYS ...

ENDURANCE RACING AT SILVERSTONE IN THE 1970s & 1980s

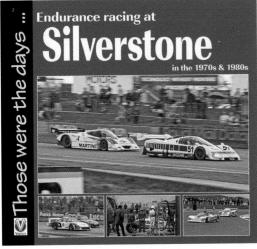

ISBN: 978-1-845842-77-2

SUPERPRIX – THE STORY OF BIRMINGHAM'S MOTOR RACE

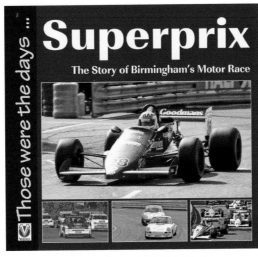

ISBN: 978-1-845842-42-0

AMERICAN 'INDEPENDENT' AUTOMAKERS – AMC TO WILLYS 1945 TO 1960

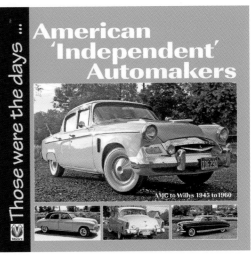

ISBN: 978-1-845842-39-0

MOTOR RACING AT BRANDS HATCH IN THE EIGHTIES

ISBN: 978-1-84584-214-7

MOTOR RACING AT THRUXTON IN THE 1980s

ISBN: 978-1-845843-69-4

ANGLO-AMERICAN CARS FROM THE 1930s TO THE 1970s

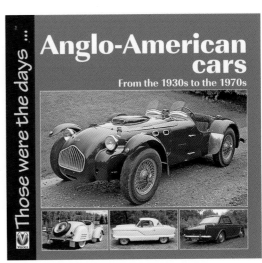

ISBN: 978-1-845842-33-8

THE MORGAN 3 WHEELER

Revealing why Morgan returned to its original 3 Wheeler concept after a century. How the new 3 Wheeler was created, became a best-seller, and was made, this book shows what it's like to drive, strengths, weaknesses, and factory improvements made since the 2011 launch – from modifications, possible developments, and even why it is – or isn't – your kind of vehicle.

ISBN: 978-1-845847-63-0
Hardback • 25x25cm • 144 pages • 101 colour and b&w pictures

For more information and price details, visit our website at www.veloce.co.uk • email: info@veloce.co.uk
• Tel: +44(0)1305 260068

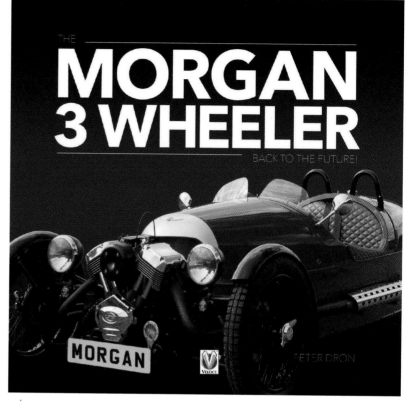

ARMSTRONG SIDDELEY MOTORS

If ever there was a car that exuded style it was the Armstrong Siddeley. From the vast leviathans of the 1920s to the Art Deco inspired cars of the thirties and the restrained post modernism of the 1950s. Somehow for all the design influences it comes out looking very British indeed.

ISBN: 978-1-904788-36-2
Hardback • 25x25cm • 496 pages • 365 b&w pictures

For more information and price details, visit our website at www.veloce.co.uk • email: info@veloce.co.uk
• Tel: +44(0)1305 260068

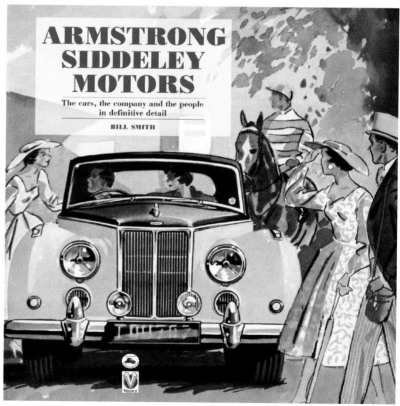